TRANSFER OF LEARNING

Contemporary Research
and Applications

THE EDUCATIONAL TECHNOLOGY SERIES

Edited by

Harold F. O'Neil, Jr.

U.S. Army Research Institute for
the Behavioral and Social Sciences
Alexandria, Virginia

TRANSFER OF LEARNING

Contemporary Research and Applications

Edited by

Stephen M. Cormier
Joseph D. Hagman

Army Research Institute
Alexandria, Virginia

ACADEMIC PRESS, INC.
Harcourt Brace Jovanovich, Publishers

San Diego   New York   Berkeley   Boston
London   Sydney   Tokyo   Toronto

ACADEMIC PRESS, INC.
1250 Sixth Avenue, San Diego, California 92101

United Kingdom Edition published by
ACADEMIC PRESS INC. (LONDON) LTD.
24–28 Oval Road, London NW1 7DX

Library of Congress Cataloging in Publication Data

Transfer of learning.

(The Educational technology series)
Includes index.
1. Transfer of training.   2. Learning, Psychology of.
I. Cormier, Stephen M.   II. Hagman, Joseph D.   III. Series.
LC1059.T73   1987   370.15   87–1218
ISBN 0–12–188950–5 (alk. paper)

PRINTED IN THE UNITED STATES OF AMERICA

87 88 89 90   9 8 7 6 5 4 3 2 1

Contents

Contributors

Numbers in parentheses indicate the pages on which the authors' contributions begin.

E. SCOTT BAUDHUIN (217), Statistica Incorporated, Rockville, Maryland 20850

JOHN A. BOLDOVICI (239), Army Research Institute, Field Unit at Fort Knox, Fort Knox, Kentucky 40121

LARRY W. BROOKS (121), Xerox International Center for Training, Leesburg, Virginia 22075

TERESA CARIGLIA-BULL (81), Department of Psychology, University of Western Ontario, London, Ontario, Canada N6A 5C2

STEPHEN M. CORMIER (1, 151), Army Research Institute, Alexandria, Virginia 22333

DONALD F. DANSEREAU (121), Department of Psychology, Texas Christian University, Fort Worth, Texas 76129

ROBERT EVANS (261), Naval Training and Equipment Center, Orlando, Florida 32813

MARY L. GICK (9), Department of Psychology, Carleton University, Ottawa, Ontario, Canada K1S 5B6

WAYNE D. GRAY[1] (183), Army Research Institute, Alexandria, Virginia 22333

JOSEPH D. HAGMAN (1), Army Research Institute, Alexandria, Virginia 22333

KEITH J. HOLYOAK (9), Department of Psychology, University of California at Los Angeles, Los Angeles, California 90024

JUDITH M. ORASANU (183), Army Research Institute, Alexandria, Virginia 22333

MICHAEL PRESSLEY (81), Department of Psychology, University of Western Ontario, London, Ontario, Canada N6A 5C2

ANDREW ROSE (261), American Institutes for Research, Washington, D. C. 20007

[1]Present address: Department of Psychology, Carnegie–Mellon University, Pittsburgh, Pennsylvania 15213-3890

RICHARD A. SCHMIDT (47), Department of Kinesiology, University of California at Los Angeles, Los Angeles, California 90024

BARBARA L. SNYDER (81), Department of Psychology, University of Western Ontario, London, Ontario, Canada N6A 5C2

GEORGE WHEATON (261), American Institutes for Research, Washington, D. C. 20007

DOUGLAS E. YOUNG (47), Department of Kinesiology, University of California at Los Angeles, Los Angeles, California 90024

Foreword

Transfer of learning (often called transfer of training) is pervasive in everyday life, in the developing child and in the adult. Transfer takes place whenever our existing knowledge, abilities, and skills affect the learning or performance of new tasks. But what are the principles regarding effective transfer of learning? How can we design educational and training programs to facilitate transfer? It is no wonder that the topic of transfer of learning has been of theoretical importance to the behavioral scientist and of practical importance to the educator and trainer. Given the centrality of the topic to so many areas of basic research and application, it is indeed surprising that there has been no comprehensive book on the subject.

The present volume fills this need for a contemporary treatment of the topic. The book is especially welcome since it draws together, in a convenient sourcebook, basic and applied research, theoretical implications, and practical applications and integrates these with recent developments in cognitive psychology.

The book is timely for a number of reasons. First, a new upsurge in interest in transfer of learning has occurred among researchers with a cognitive or information-processing approach to human learning. For many years, cognitive psychologists seemed to reject the topic, and it was difficult to locate references to transfer in the indexes of books on cognitive psychology. The interests of these psychologists seemed not to be in transfer of learning but in the structures and processes involved in the encoding and retrieval of information during initial task acquisition and retention. This is a far cry from the centrality accorded the topic in earlier days. Thus, McGeoch and Irion's classic 1952 book on human learning states that transfer of learning "is one of the most general phenomena of learning and, by means of its influence, almost all learned behavior is interrelated in various complex ways." And Battig, in a 1966 review of the topic, concluded that "the magnitude and generality of the effects produced by previous learning upon performance in new learning tasks require that transfer phenomena be placed at or near the head of the list insofar as overall importance to psychology is concerned.'' Despite the benign neglect by subsequent cognitive psychologists, it is reasonable to assume that the large volume of recent data from information-processing research has relevance to our understanding of transfer of learning, even if this has not been its primary focus. And, as this book demonstrates, interest among cognitive psychologists in issues of transfer has been increasing with the significant enrichment in our conceptualization and applications of research in this area.

Another reason for the timeliness of this integrative volume is the urgent need for principles to apply to the design of educational and training systems for increasingly complex jobs. For example, the increasing level of complexity of the activities and tasks required of military personnel makes it less likely that training can be done on-the-job while still maintaining efficiency and safety. Thus, training settings will increasingly be away from the job environment, making it necessary to design training programs which will have effective transfer to the target jobs. Consequently, we need a better understanding of the factors involved in transfer of learning.

Since the thrust of this book is on contemporary developments, it seems useful to reflect briefly on some historical precedents of this area of research. The study of transfer of learning has a dominant place in the early history of experimental psychology. The pioneering studies of Thorndike and Woodworth, in 1901, advanced the theory of transfer as a function of *identical elements* in common between learning and transfer tasks. In various forms, this theory is still with us, where a major concern is how to conceptualize these elements. This early work showed it was much easier to produce positive than negative transfer, a finding reinforced in later years despite concerted and programmatic attempts to produce such negative effects in the laboratory (e.g., Buxton, Don Lewis, and their associates, in the 1930s and 1940s).

Early research (e.g., by E. S. Robinson, *The "Similarity" Factor in Retroaction*, in 1927, and by R. W. Bruce, *Conditions of Transfer of Training,* in 1933) initiated subsequent research in which the conditions of transfer, such as the amount of initial training or differences in task difficulty, were studied. Osgood's work, in particular his 1949 publication, was significant in dealing with the theoretical analysis of the conditions of transfer and providing a model (the *Osgood Transfer Surface*) for predicting task-to-task transfer in terms of positive, zero, and negative effects. During this period, the 1948 *Psychological Bulletin* paper by Gagné, Foster, and Crowley had considerable impact in providing a basis for the measurement of transfer effects. Issues of stimulus and response generalization, stimulus predifferentiation, and retroactive inhibition were the fashion of this period. Hilgard and Marquis, in 1961, provided a comprehensive summary of the findings on stimulus generalization and, in 1960, Underwood and Postman provided important reviews, which included the role of transfer in remembering and forgetting. These efforts were constrained by the S–R framework within which the investigators worked, and many variables affecting transfer were not taken into account.

The very existence of transfer phenomena appears to have been ignored or denied in most of the Skinnerian operant conditioning work of this period. In fact, much of this work implied that any transfer effects from previous learning are so unimportant that they can be completely obliterated prior to the subsequent introduction of a new learning task. The skills and knowledge brought by the subject to the learning of a new task were regarded as insignificant compared to the efficiency of the practice schedule.

Part of the apparent decline of interest in transfer in the 1960s and 1970s is that the methodology of transfer experiments became widely used in other areas of human learning and so no longer appeared as a distinct area. Thus, survey issues of the *Journal of Experimental Psychology* and of the *Journal of Verbal Learning and Verbal Behavior* showed the term *transfer*, or its synonyms, were not often used in the titles, although the research had been concerned with relations between at least two different learning tasks. Also, in the 1960s (see, e.g., Battig's work during this period), there was a growing concern with a more microscopic analysis of those individual component sources within a single task which produce positive or negative effects of performance on a subsequent task rather than with the gross analysis of overall intertask positive and negative transfer effects. Another reason for the illusion that transfer research had decreased was the substitution of the terms *facilitation* and *interference* and emphasis on the component sources of transfer, as distinguished from overall transfer.

Much of the work on transfer was also recast in terms of part- or whole-task learning and intratask performance-facilitation issues. Thus, Gagné, Foster, Baker, and Wylie were examining the effects of verbal and other kinds of pretraining on whole-task performance. These studies were forerunners of some of the studies carried out in the newer cognitive traditions. Other studies, including those by E. A. Bilodeau, by Ellison, and by me, examined the relations between subtasks and total-task performance. Total performance could, in fact, be improved by the proper arrangements of part-task practice schedules. My own finding suggested that the best predictions of total-task performance were achieved from performance on those components having common ability requirements with the total task.

Another historical development bears on the issue of general versus specific transfer of learning, an issue which has not yet been resolved. Certainly, the S–R view of identical elements initially stressed a specificity view. The most extreme *generalist* view of transfer of learning was represented by the doctrine of formal discipline, which held that the objective of educators was to train the powers of the mind. The teaching of Latin to improve English was a derivative, if misdirected application. Although the type of transfer assumed was too great and too general, the educational objectives which followed from this doctrine are still with us. The implication is that students will acquire skills that will generalize widely and be applied to the solution of novel problems. The objective of teaching students how to think or learn for themselves is very current, although the processes for attaining this objective still need a great deal of research.

Two other historical lines of thinking in the psychology of learning are related to the generality–specificity issue. The Gestalt school held that permanent learning, especially problem solving and creative learning, is achieved by insight rather than rote acquisition. Much of the Gestalt emphasis has been on arranging learning situations so that the student can gain *insight* into the problem to be solved. Insight may be recognized by the sudden improvement which occurs, and this learning is thought to be permanent and to transfer to new situations. Insight seems to occur most readily where the learner can bring previously established skills to bear on the solution of a new problem. Here, one can say, practice is seen as a mechanism for aligning the conditions of stimulus generalization and positive transfer of learning.

Harlow's work in *learning sets*, or *learning to learn* provided a basis for interpreting insightful learning. The operative concepts involve the ability to solve new problems of the same general class more easily after exposure to many different problems in this class. It is assumed that even trial-and-error learning involves more than just learning a specific skill; the assumption is that more general expertise concerning a whole class of problems is being acquired that will allow the student to exercise more initial expertise in solving new problems. As Irion has pointed out, it would be imprudent to assume there will be much generalization between widely different classes of problems. Furthermore, the formation of *learning sets* rests upon the learning of many rudimentary skills, the learning of which may be laborious at early stages. The findings on learning sets did not produce easy solutions to practical problems of training and education.

Our own work on relations among learning measures from different tasks as well as Herbert Woodrow's earlier work on the correlations between *gain* scores indicated that *learning sets*, if they exist, are more limited in scope. The question of which categories of tasks within which transfer are likely to occur remains a central problem, but recent advances in the taxonomies of tasks hold considerable promise. Later work on learning strategies and our own attempts to train more general abilities offer leads for further research. Recent taxonomic research clusters tasks into categories with common ability requirements, and other cognitive approaches to componential analysis (e.g., Sternberg's) offer some encouragement for training skills which are transferable to a number of different tasks. Also relevant are current discussions on the importance of general knowledge representations on schemas versus specific remembered instances as the basis of learning, as is the discussion of general reasoning skills versus domain-specific knowledge as contributors to expertise.

The primary focus in transfer-of-learning research is on the question of how learning in one task affects one's performance capability in another task; a problem, not unique to the study of transfer, is in defining what a task is and how one task is identified as being different from another. Elsewhere, in my 1984 book (with M. Quaintance), *Taxonomies of Human Performance,* we tried to clarify this definitional problem, to identify the dimensions along which tasks differ, and to provide and evaluate alternative task-classification systems. Thus, we can describe tasks in terms of dimensionalized task characteristics which are independent of the human subject, such as stimulus complexity, response precision requirements, goal requirements, and environmental conditions. Or we can describe tasks in terms of the underlying abilities required to perform them (e.g., verbal comprehension, multilimb coordination), or in terms of broader performance functions (e.g., scanning, coding, problem solving), or by more limited task-descriptive categories (manipulating control handles, reading dials, etc.).

The issue of defining *similarity* between tasks is still with us, but some of these more recent formulations may hold the key. It is my own view that such conceptualizations need to include information about the abilities of the learner required by both the training and transfer tasks. The input side (subject abilities) has not been easily integrated into transfer-of-learning paradigms. Examples of attempts to do so have included such earlier investigators as Woodrow, in 1938, and George Ferguson, in 1954, and my own studies on the relations between prior practice on task components and subsequent performance on more complex total tasks. A relevant study by James Parker and me, which can be seen as anticipating later cognitive emphases, involved the analysis of general abilities involved at different stages of acquiring a very difficult tracking skill (over a six-week period). The most effective training method involved focusing the subjects' attention, through instructions, on the ability requirements of the task at the appropriate stage of learning. The key to the success of this effort was the prior identification of the ability components.

While I have chosen to stress earlier laboratory research on transfer in this brief foreword, it is clear that a major impetus to developments in this field has come from practical needs in the world of education and training. World War II found many basic scientists attempting to cope with sophisticated systems, where the consequence of error and poor performance was disastrous. Traditional results from the experimental psychology of learning did not prove useful enough to those concerned with the development of curricula and training simulators for complex systems. Psychologists who worked with such problems had to develop new ideas and concepts. In the transfer-of-learning area, defining the notion of *fidelity of simulation* as a criterion for training simulators raised more questions than it answered. First, it was clear that extreme fidelity was not feasible or possible, or even necessary, but what aspects of the complex task should be represented for effective transfer? And how was this to be measured? The concepts and methods which seemed to have subsequently had impact in the real world of educational curriculum and military training included those of Instructional Systems Design (ISD) and task analysis. Pioneering contributors here included individuals such as Gagné, Robert Miller, and Robert Glaser.

If anything, the complexity of systems for which training needs to be developed continues to increase and has been extended to newer industrial situations (e.g., nuclear power operations) and even outer space. Fortunately, developments from cognitive psychology are providing new concepts to assist. A number of these developments are represented in this book. However, it seems useful to point out, from a historical point of view, that many of these concepts originated in the field of engineering psychology, where the need was to conceptualize the human as an information transmitter and processing device within a system. Human functions, such as signal detection, interpretation of information, and decision making, had to be dealt with. We needed to know more about such matters as human storage capacities and human processing limits. It has been only recently, however, that these concepts have been linked to concerns about transfer of learning.

Two final points: We need more research on possible individual differences in ability to transfer. I have mentioned the potential of considering the abilities of the subjects in transfer-of-learning paradigms. The interactions of abilities and training methods remain a fruitful area (e.g., Cronbach and Snow's work). Most definitions of *intelligence* include the notion of *ability to transfer* or the *ability to make use of one's past experiences.* However, we need to make better use of our current taxonomic knowledge about different cognitive abilities in the design of transfer experiments.

For transfer of learning to be successful, there must be an environment conducive to transfer of learned skills to the transfer setting. I have had at least two firsthand research experiences in which such situational variables have overwhelmed the effects of a carefully designed training program. One was in the evaluation of managerial training in a situation in which the managers had to put into practice newly trained managerial skills. While the training showed effects immediately after training, back in the plant these effects were minimal. The major factor influencing exercise of these skills was the reward system in the plant, which was still reinforcing the old patterns. In another study, turnover among telephone service representatives was high, due to the fact that the training emphasized service components and the company rewarded sales activities. Clearly, the effects of situational or contextual variables on transfer of learning from training to job have not received sufficient attention.

The chapters in this book cover the significant recent developments in transfer of learning in a variety of contexts and areas. I have tried to avoid stealing any thunder from these remarkable contributions. We are indebted to Cormier and Hagman and their colleagues for bringing this material together. The book brings together a widely scattered literature on transfer, yet provides some conceptual structure to the literature under review. It illustrates that there is no firm distinction between basic and applied research in the current transfer literature. One of the most interesting aspects of the new literature is the extent to which real-world tasks are used in both applied and laboratory studies. The book provides valuable insights into the ways in which research on transfer has been conducted and into the potential applicability of this research to the design of real-world training.

Edwin A. Fleishman
University Professor of Psychology
George Mason University
Fairfax, Virginia

Preface

This book is intended to be a compact but comprehensive source for contemporary basic and applied research on transfer of learning, a topic of theoretical interest to the behavioral scientist and practical interest to the educator and trainer. It fills a need created within the scientific and educational communities by the lack of a similar source for post-1970 transfer research. It also appears at a time of renewed interest in transfer among researchers adhering to a cognitive or information-processing approach to the study of human learning and performance.

Perhaps because successful transfer of learning from one task to another is of such practical importance in both educational and organizational settings, researchers have had a long-standing interest in the topic. For years, this research was performed within an associative learning framework and dominated by interference theory.

With the shift to more cognitive-based accounts of learning and performance during the 1960s and 1970s, the visibility of transfer research declined. Despite its decreased prominence over this period, transfer research was kept alive within the context of various issues and paradigms outside the specific purview of interference theory.

Within the last half-dozen years or so, cognitive psychologists have steadily become more and more interested in transfer, to the point where it is once again a principal focus of research. The Army Research Institute for the Behavioral and Social Sciences, for example, has been actively promoting transfer research in response to Army training needs. In addition, interest in transfer issues has spread to the international community as reflected in the Proceedings of the 1985 NATO Symposium "Transfer of Training to Military Operational Systems." We hope that the present book will provide further impetus to future basic and applied transfer research.

We thank the authors for their dedication and hard work, Harry O'Neil for his support and encouragement during the planning stages of this book, and our editors at Academic Press for their help during all phases of the publication process.

CHAPTER 1

Introduction

STEPHEN M. CORMIER[1]
JOSEPH D. HAGMAN

Since the domain of transfer phenomena is so large and varied, all the more need exists for a methodical way of exploring and organizing the research findings. This chapter presents a brief discussion of what we consider to be the important issues of current transfer research which have relevance beyond the confines of any single methodological approach.

In essence, transfer of learning occurs whenever prior-learned knowledges and skills affect the way in which new knowledges and skills are learned and performed. When later acquisition or performance is facilitated, transfer is positive; when later acquisition or performance is impeded, transfer is negative. Transfer can be general (i.e., content independent), affecting a wide range of new knowledges and skills, or specific (i.e., content dependent), affecting only particular knowledges and skills within a circumscribed subject matter (see Mandler, 1962).

In our view, there are four generic issues important to a comprehensive description of transfer, both as a learning phenomenon and as an event with substantial importance to real-life situations. These issues are: (a) how transfer should be measured, (b) how training for transfer differs from training for rapid acquisition, (c) how direction and magnitude of transfer are determined, and (d) whether different principles of transfer apply to motor, cognitive, and metacognitive elements.

I. THE MEASUREMENT OF TRANSFER

The measurement of transfer has long been a contentious issue. Actually, there are several aspects to this problem. First, the degree of transfer is usually defined in relative terms where performance on a transfer task (i.e.,

[1]The views expressed are the authors' and not necessarily those of the Army Research Institute, Department of the Army, or Department of Defense.

Task 2), for example, is compared between an experimental group receiving some prior task training (Task 1) and a control group receiving no such Task 1 training. Under this paradigm, the experimental group generally outperforms the control group if Task 1 transfers positively to Task 2. How much better this performance is, however, depends upon which of a half dozen formulas are used, each of which has its own particular strengths and weaknesses. Thus an understanding and awareness of the particular formula(s) used across different transfer studies is necessary for a correct interpretation of their results.

Second, it is important to be aware of the kind of performance being measured, for example, overall Task 2 learning rate or accuracy, or initial (first-trial) Task 2 performance. Even then, there is really no one "correct" performance measure to use in all cases. As a result, the purpose of the transfer study will many times dictate which transfer criteria are most appropriate. The point we wish to make here is simply that the criteria used will limit conclusions that can be made about transfer and should be kept in mind when comparing the results of different studies. Just because Task 1 learning may enhance first-trial performance on Task 2, for example, does not mean it will necessarily have the same effect on learning rate over trials, or vice versa.

Third, one should be concerned with the reliability and validity of experimental and control-group performance. Degree of Task 1 learning, for example, must be the same for both groups in order to make relative comparisons about Task 2 performance, yet degree of Task 1 learning is often difficult to assess with complete confidence. Ceiling effects, for example, may mask degree of learning once performance has reached 100% on the dependent variable scale, for example, number correct; percentage correct (Underwood, 1964). Besides ceiling effects, other significant sources of measurement error in transfer experiments include small sample sizes, floor effects, insufficient practice, and inadvertent differential treatment of groups, to mention only a few.

Fourth, it needs to be recognized that the applied environment often poses obstacles to the implementation of particular transfer paradigms or methodologies regardless of their accepted validity. The amount or kind of training that can be conducted on simulators, for example, is often constrained by operational training requirements or internal needs of the organization. Industry or military training systems usually cannot suspend or even substantially modify operations in order to permit either the required experimental control over treatment conditions or the measurement of a particularly diagnostic aspect of performance, although many times, suitable compromises can be arranged. Consequently, the results of applied research should undergo careful scrutiny, not because applied researchers are unaware of particular experimental pitfalls, but because they are unable to avoid these pitfalls due to operational constraints.

These and other performance measurement problems are not unique to the study of transfer. They all, however, can affect the interpretability and replicability of results. Fortunately, substantial progress has been made in the area of performance measurement during recent years because of increased sophistication of experimental methodologies and a better understanding of what variables are likely to affect transfer. Even with these advances, the issue of performance measurement will still be a matter for concern for years to come until we achieve our ultimate goal of accurate performance prediction on the basis of sound psychological principles (see chapters 8–10).

II. TRAINING FOR TRANSFER VERSUS RAPID ACQUISITION

Trade-offs between desired goals are a common occurrence in everyday life, and many examples exist in the psychological domain as well. Perhaps the best known is the speed-accuracy trade-off, but another trade-off occurs between training for transfer and training for rapid acquisition. In other words, initial training experiences which tend to increase the amount and kind of observed transfer seem to have negative effects on the rate at which the tasks are learned to some criterion level.

This effect is undoubtedly related to the relationship between the training on the original Task 1 and the target Task 2. By training for rapid acquisition, we are making the implicit assumption that the training tasks are the target tasks. To this end, Task 1 training will involve more time spent on fewer task elements. Conversely, training for transfer involves not only training individuals on the original task, but also preparing them for related but distinct target tasks.

The extent to which acquisition or transfer considerations should predominate in designing Task 1 training will depend on the target tasks to be performed. At the conceptual level, the goal is to specify which training procedures can optimize transfer or acquisition and from that develop functions which permit trade-off estimations to be made for particular situations.

At the practical level, this trade-off must be taken into account in evaluating the success or failure of particular training programs. A training program may take more time and have lower trainee performance than a second program and yet result in higher target task performance. Of course, this result is likely only in a carefully designed training program which has set transfer as its goal. Nevertheless, this illustrates the care which must be taken in choosing appropriate criteria for transfer evaluation in real world settings (see chapters 2, 8, 9, and 11).

III. THE DIRECTION AND EXTENT OF TRANSFER

A. DIRECTION OF TRANSFER

Predicting whether transfer would be positive or negative from one task to another was a dominant preoccupation of human learning researchers for many years (e.g., Osgood, 1949). Explanations of transfer were typically based on the theory of identical elements and couched in the stimulus–response (S–R) language of interference theory.

The body of interference theory research uncovered many important phenomena about transfer (primarily negative interference) and forgetting (primarily retroactive interference). Positive transfer and proactive interference were less thoroughly examined. Despite the methodological brilliance of the investigators, the conceptual understanding of transfer did not seem to advance as fast as the empirical findings accumulated. As one of the foremost researchers in this area put it:

> It is fair to say that the total picture is complex and beset by uncertainties . . . with respect to the general conceptualization of the underlying mechanisms of interference. One cannot help but wonder why after so many years of patient experimental effort interference theory today finds itself entangled in so many empirical inconsistencies and theoretical complications. (Postman, 1976, p. 179)

In effect, we still have difficulty predicting whether transfer will be positive or negative in particular cases because of incomplete knowledge of what was learned originally and how the transfer task is represented. Perhaps part of the problem can be attributed to the narrowness of the methodological approaches employed, such as arbitrary word lists, and the absence of much critical attention to the assumptions embodied in interference theory. An implicit adoption of the investigatory methods of the physical sciences can be seen, in which domain a factor can be manipulated precisely while keeping other factors at least relatively constant. In this situation, the progressive refinement of a methodology designed to measure one factor makes sense. However, in psychology, it is much more difficult to manipulate one factor without affecting other factors as well. In addition, a narrow methodology increases the odds that some critical factors will be omitted from consideration and experimental manipulation.

One of the by-products of an information-processing approach to the study of human learning is the wealth of different methodologies used, thereby creating the opportunity to arrive at solutions to various problems by way of converging operations. As the reader will see, there is a tremendous variety in the methodological procedures used to study transfer and a greater concentration on the conceptual basis of the factors hypothesized to underlie transfer phenomena. Information-processing theories have more explicit descriptions of the processes which are hypothesized to contribute to the encoding, storage and transformation, and retrieval of memories than the S–R-based interference theory offered. Of course, any new theory of transfer must be able to account for the data collected in the classical studies of interference theory as well as the present research summarized in this volume (see chapters 2, 3, and 5–7).

B. EXTENT OF TRANSFER

The extent to which initial task training will transfer to other tasks is as important both theoretically and practically as is knowing the direction of transfer. Intuitively, the extent or generalization of transfer must be profoundly affected by the nature of the intertask relationships and the prior training received.

Gagné (1970) has addressed the issue of intertask relationships by distinguishing between vertical and lateral transfer. Vertical transfer occurs when a skill or knowledge contributes directly to the subsequent acquisition or performance of a superordinate task or skill. Someone who can multiply and subtract numbers, for example, should acquire the skill of long division more rapidly than someone who has not learned multiplication and subtraction. Lateral transfer is defined in less exact terms because it involves positive or negative transfer effects to tasks which share domains or elements without having part–whole relationships. Gagné refers to lateral transfer as "a kind of generalization that spreads over a broad set of situations at roughly the same level of complexity" (p. 231). This is taken to mean the sort of transfer which occurs when children recognize that the fractions they are learning about in school pertain to real-world situations, such as how to divide an apple pie up into equal shares.

Of course, the obvious question, then, is how domains and elements are going to be defined in objective and meaningful fashion. Cognitive behaviors present particular difficulties because often the important relationships between tasks exist in their underlying structure rather than in their surface similarities or dissimilarities. Although the cognitive analysis of task structure is still in its early stages, the methodologies being currently developed have made substantial progress in identifying principles of cognitive organization.

In addition to such task and procedural variables, it is also possible that individual aptitudes are an equally strong determinant of transfer generalization. We call someone intelligent, for example, when they can correctly apply existing knowledge to novel situations and when they are quick to learn a new field of study. The study of transfer processes may illuminate this crucial aspect of human aptitude by identifying the relative contributions of these three factors in transfer generalization (see chapters 2 and 4–7).

IV. MOTOR VERSUS COGNITIVE VERSUS METACOGNITIVE TRANSFER

A major goal of human learning research is to determine the bases of functional differences observed between the three basic classes of behavior, namely, motor, cognitive, and metacognitive. Motor responses involve voluntary movements of the skeletal muscles. Cognitive responses, broadly defined, involve manipulation of verbal or symbolic information such as words and concepts. Metacognition refers to understanding of one's own cognitive behavior involved in the planning and monitoring of performance, and in the use of cognitive strategies (see Pylyshyn, 1978).

Although many similarities exist in the learning and performance requirements of these response classes, systematic differences have been found as well. In general, motor and metacognitive responses are less susceptible to negative transfer and forgetting than most cognitive behaviors (Bilodeau & Bilodeau, 1961). It is not yet clear, however, whether motor and metacognitive responses are learned and retained differently from cognitive behaviors (see Squire & Cohen, 1984). For example, it is not easy to equate the salience of particular motor and verbal responses, which makes it difficult to interpret differences in acquisition or retention rates.

In any event, we believe that distinctions of this sort play an important part in the comprehensive understanding of transfer phenomena. Apparent inconsistencies in the experimental literature will occur if insufficient attention is paid to the class of behavior under investigation in the transfer environment or to other fundamental distinctions touched upon previously (see chapters 3 and 5). Having examined some of the common conceptual problems faced by researchers in this area, we now turn to the organization of the transfer research presented in the chapters of this volume.

V. ORGANIZATION OF THE BOOK

Transfer research has been conducted in a variety of psychological disciplines such as instructional psychology or motor learning. The chapter topics reflect these domain divisions for the most part, for this allows for some systematization of the methodologies and approaches which a community of researchers have established.

Although both basic and applied research on transfer are covered in this book, it was deemed inadvisable to create a formal division of basic and applied research chapters because of their strong interconnection. However, there is a rough progression from chapters mainly examining laboratory studies to those examining transfer experiments and applications in real-world settings. Indeed, one of the aims of the book is to acquaint researchers or trainers whose work has been limited to one of these areas with the nature of the problems and issues encountered in the other area.

As editors, we have striven to minimize the overlap of material between different chapters. Actually, for the most part, the authors themselves have saved us the trouble of doing so. One of the things that has struck us in compiling this book is the tremendous diversity of paradigms which have been employed in analyzing or applying transfer principles. Although this could create an unhealthy diffuseness in certain circumstances, the chapters in this book give evidence of that most elusive of scientific goals, namely, the emergence of certain unifying principles, for example, schema theory, which can provide a consistent interpretation to studies which otherwise might seem unconnected.

The book commences with a chapter by Gick and Holyoak on the cognitive basis of knowledge transfer. In this chapter, they sketch out a framework for understanding transfer based on current conceptions of the content and format of mental representations and then discuss how task structure, encoding conditions, retrieval conditions, and background knowledge of the learner determine transfer effectiveness.

Next Schmidt and Young discuss current research on motor transfer. After covering definitional and experimental design questions surrounding transfer, they discuss fundamental principles of motor behavior and control that have emerged over the past few decades and propose specific, invariant movement characteristics that underlie effective motor transfer.

The next two chapters take us into the area of classroom instruction. Pressley, Snyder, and Cariglia-Bull discuss research on the instruction of cognitive strategies to children and their ability to apply this knowledge to new situations. They analyze several major research programs and discuss their relative effectiveness in producing generalization of such skills to a variety of learning situations. Brooks and Dansereau analyze instructional transfer in terms of the interaction between subject matter content and skills composed of procedural and metaknowledge. These interactions are broken down factorially so that within-domain transfer effects can be compared to the between-domain effects of content-to-skill transfer and skill-to-content transfer.

Cormier's chapter provides evidence for the existence of several fundamental information-processing factors which are critical to the expression of transfer in a wide variety of laboratory and applied paradigms. Particular attention is paid to the distinction between structural processes, whose operation is relatively invariant, and the control strategies employed by individuals on a task-specific basis.

The chapter by Gray and Orasanu applies concepts derived from cognitive theories to the analysis of performance on real-world transfer tasks such as computer text editing. Gray and Orasanu discuss the use of concepts such as the problem space in defining domain relationships and predicting transfer in cognitive tasks. In this context, they take a detailed look at empirical findings on human versus computer simulations of expert performance.

The last three chapters continue this focus on transfer in real-life settings in the context of simulator training. Since fine reviews of simulator training per se appear frequently, these papers explore less discussed aspects of the role of simulation and transfer in military and civilian settings. Baudhuin's chapter describes the engineering context in which most simulator development takes place and analyzes the way in which this influences the design of aviation and industrial simulators and their resulting transfer value. Boldovici describes basic problems encountered in the evaluation of training device effectiveness and proposes procedures for avoiding their negative effects. Finally, Rose, Evans, and Wheaton examine the utility of analytic methodologies for the evaluation of simulator effectiveness. In addition, they present a new application methodology which they have developed to estimate device effectiveness.

REFERENCES

Bilodeau, I. M., & Bilodeau, E. A. (1961). Motor skills learning. *Annual Review of Psychology, 12,* 243–280.

Gagné, R. M. (1970). *The conditions of learning.* New York: Holt.

Mandler, G. (1962). From association to structure. *Psychological Review, 69,* 415–427.

Osgood, C. E. (1949). The similarity paradox in human learning: A resolution. *Psychological Review, 56,* 132–143.

Postman, L. (1976). Interference theory revisited. In J. Brown (Ed.), *Recall and recognition.* New York: Wiley.

Pylyshyn, Z. (1978). When is attribution of beliefs justified? *Behavioral and Brain Sciences, 1,* 592–593.

Squire, L. R., & Cohen, N. J. (1984). Human memory and amnesia. In G. Lynch, J. L. McGaugh and N. M. Weinberger (Eds.), *The neurobiology of learning and memory.* New York: Guilford Press.

Underwood, B. J. (1964). Degree of learning and the measurement of forgetting. *Journal of Verbal Learning and Verbal Behavior, 3,* 112–129.

CHAPTER 2

The Cognitive Basis of Knowledge Transfer

MARY L. GICK
KEITH J. HOLYOAK

I. INTRODUCTION

Our world confronts us with ceaseless variation and perpetual novelty. Yet the routine patterns of our lives quickly grow familiar, as we learn to recognize recurrent types of situations and to apply reliable procedures for achieving our goals. Human learning mechanisms allow us to accumulate knowledge of constancies embedded in variations, so that we often are unaware of much of the variety of experience. We learn, for example, where to shop for food, how to get to the store, and how to pay for the groceries. We are seldom troubled that the available parking spaces have changed each trip, new items are on the shelf, different customers surround us, and an unfamiliar cashier greets us at the check-out counter. The accumulation of knowledge acquired from past shopping experiences is transferred without difficulty to the present one.

Sometimes, however, problems arise that have no simple precedents. We may have to learn a specific new skill, such as computer programming, or adjust to a new social role, such as leaving college to start a career. In such cases we have to actively struggle to assemble whatever pieces of knowledge can be brought to bear on the novel problematic situation. The transfer of knowledge from the past to the present is no longer smooth and may even hinder rather than help us.

How is the transfer of knowledge effected? What are the cognitive mechanisms that allow the results of past experience to impact on present performances? These are the questions that will concern us in this chapter.

TRANSFER OF LEARNING

A. VARIETIES OF KNOWLEDGE TRANSFER

We begin by delimiting our topic. At the most general level, transfer is a phenomenon involving change in the performance of a task as a result of the prior performance of a different task. It is immediately apparent that this definition scarcely distinguishes "transfer" from "learning." The only hint of difference is that in cases of transfer, the two tasks are said to be "different," whereas learning often occurs when the "same" task is repeated. Strictly speaking, however, no two occasions for performance of a task are identical; each repetition occurs in its own time and context. Indeed, the effect of a task performance on the subsequent performance of the same task is sometimes called "self-transfer" (J. Hayes, K. Kotovsky, H. Simon, & S. Smith, personal communication), placing this case as the degenerate extreme on a continuum of task similarity. This same case of simple repetition may also be termed "ordinary learning" (Osgood, 1949). We take the view that no empirical or theoretical chasm separates transfer from the general topic of learning. Rather, the consequences of prior learning can be measured for a continuum of subsequent tasks that range from those that are mere repetitions (self-transfer), to those that are highly similar (near transfer), to those that are very different (far transfer). The range of cases that span near to far transfer will be our primary concern.

A transfer task can be near or far from the initial training task in terms of *time* as well as overall similarity. Indeed, these dimensions are related, in that the passage of time will tend to decrease the similarity of the training and transfer contexts, as well as allowing other mechanisms that produce forgetting to operate. For both practical and theoretical reasons, learning that has an impact on delayed as well as immediate transfer tests is of central interest in understanding transfer. However, studies of delayed transfer have been infrequent in contemporary work, and most of the experimental studies to be discussed examine transfer after relatively brief delays.

In transfer paradigms the second task is typically selected to be novel to the subject (i.e., the case of "forward" transfer). However, it is also possible to observe the effect of performing the second task on subsequent performance of the original task (i.e., Task 1 is followed by interpolated Task 2, followed by Task 1 again). As Osgood (1949) pointed out, this "retroaction" paradigm simply involves transfer to a familiar rather than a novel task and produces no major differences in empirical results. Therefore, we will limit our discussion to transfer tasks of the forward variety.

Transfer can be either *positive,* when initial training benefits performance on the second task relative to a control group; *negative,* when it produces a performance decrement; or nonexistent, when it has no effect on the second task. As we will see, the magnitude and direction of transfer reflects the similarity relationship between the structure of the two tasks.

Another distinction involves the *specificity* of transfer effects (see Mandler, 1962). Performance of some initial task may have a highly selective influence on the performance of a particular transfer task, or it may influence performance on a broad class of transfer tasks. Some general transfer effects can be ascribed to the positive effect of simple warm-up, as when the learner gives greater attention to the transfer task; similarly, fatigue can give rise to negative transfer. We will have nothing to say about such relatively transitory forms of general transfer.

There nonetheless remains an entire continuum of specificity along which can be placed the kinds of knowledge that have been found to influence transfer performance. Indeed, debates about the generality of transfer effects have dominated theoretical discussions from the turn of the century up to the present. In the context of early "faculty psychology," it was argued that entire cognitive systems, such as memory, could be improved by training. The failures of many tests of such hypotheses led to the opposing view that transfer is only obtained between highly similar specific tasks. Echoes of this debate are found in current discussions of the relative importance of general knowledge representations (often termed *schemata*) versus specific remembered instances as the basis of classification learning, and of general reasoning skills versus domain-specific knowledge as contributors to expertise.

As we will see, there is ample evidence that transfer is often quite specific. However, we will review other evidence that implicates more general forms of structural transfer, some of which can be construed as "learning to learn" in the sense of acquiring general strategies for solving a class of problems sharing only abstract commonalities (Harlow, 1949). From the theoretical perspective laid out below, it is inevitable that transfer effects will span a wide range from the specific to the general. Furthermore, we will argue that general skills and specific knowledge should be viewed as complementary rather than competing processes.

Finally, transfer phenomena can be differentiated by the nature of the tasks being learned. In general, the commonalities that hold across content domains appear to be at least as compelling as the differences. However, we will defer discussion of motor skills to the chapter by Schmidt and Young, of classroom instruction to that by Brooks and Dansereau, and of developmental research to that by Pressley, Snyder, and Cariglia-Bull. The focus of our review will be on studies of adult learning and problem solving.

B. Transfer Paradigms

The essential feature of a transfer paradigm is that performance on a transfer task is compared with and without performance on some related prior task. Woodworth and Schlosberg (1954, p. 735) describe some of the particular experimental designs that allow such comparisons. The dependent measures used to assess transfer include all of those that can be used to assess the success or qualitative nature of performances, for example, error rate, reaction time, and classification of strategies. Transfer can be measured either on a single trial or by rate of learning over a succession of trials.

Table 1 illustrates a generic transfer paradigm as exemplified in traditional verbal-learning tasks (e.g., learning lists of paired associates). Task A is related in some way to Task A ', whereas Task B is unrelated to Task A ' (or nonexistent). Transfer effects are obtained if the rate of learning Task A ' items differs between the experimental and control groups. If learning Task A items enhances Task A ' learning, positive transfer is found; whereas negative transfer is obtained if learning Task A hinders the learning of Task A '. No transfer is obtained if Task A does not influence the learning of Task A '.

Table 2 illustrates a generic paradigm for most contemporary work in transfer. As in verbal-learning studies, the experimental group learns material relevant to the subsequent transfer task, whereas the control group learns irrelevant material or does nothing. Many contemporary studies of transfer do not involve the intentional *learning* of a transfer Task A '. Instead, transfer is reflected in the *performance* of Task A ' on the basis of knowledge acquired by performing Task A. For example, in category-learning research, the effect of learning about a category of items is measured on a subsequent transfer task requiring classification of novel category items. In problem-solving research, the capability of producing a specific solution to a novel transfer problem is assessed as a function of prior problems solved. In memory paradigms, subjects' knowledge of previously learned words may be determined by means of an incidental retrieval task involving, for example, fragment completion (Tulving, Schacter, & Stark, 1982) or perceptual indentification (Jacoby, 1983), rather than by subsequent intentional recall. The basic assumption is that transfer results when the original encoding of Task A can be applied to guide performance of Task A '.

We have now sketched the scope of transfer phenomena that will figure in our discussion. Before proceeding to a review of relevant work, we will present a theoretical framework within which empirical findings can be interpreted.

Table 1

Transfer Paradigm in Verbal Learning

Experimental group	Learn A	→	Learn A '
Control group	Learn B	→	Learn A '

Table 2
Contemporary Transfer Paradigm

Experimental group	Learn A ------>	Perform A '
	↓	↓
	(Encode A)	(Retrieve and apply A)
Control group	Learn B ----->	Perform A '

II. A THEORETICAL FRAMEWORK FOR UNDERSTANDING TRANSFER

A theory of transfer is of necessity a theory of learning and inference. What is learned from prior experience, and what inferences can be generated from the knowledge? These are the key questions that must be answered to predict transfer. The difficulty of predicting transfer effects in particular cases typically lies largely in our incomplete knowledge of what was initially learned and how the transfer task is itself first represented. In this section we will outline a framework for learning and inference based on relatively recent work in cognitive science. As we will see, this framework can be used to extend and clarify some classic analyses of transfer.

A. KNOWLEDGE AND ITS REPRESENTATION

We will begin with a sketch of current conceptions of mental representations and their modification by learning mechanisms. We will first consider the *content* of mental representations—what knowledge is about—and the *format* of its representation in memory—the kinds of structures used to represent knowledge of various sorts.

At the most general level, the contents of mental representation include *concepts* and *procedures*. Concepts are representations of general categories, such as "dog," "number," and "multiplication problems," and of more specific categories and instances, such as "Rover," "5," and "5 × 8 = ?." Procedures are operations that are adapted to achieve particular goals. Examples include dog training and multiplication. Concepts and procedures are closely interrelated. Thus arithmetic operations and procedures are defined in part by the concepts to which they apply, such as "number." Concepts and procedures are often learned together; new concepts allow new procedures to be constructed that apply to them (Riley, Greeno, & Heller, 1982).

The second issue concerns the format in which knowledge is represented. Knowledge about concepts and procedures can be encoded in *condition-*

action rules: "if-then" rules of the form, "IF Condition 1, Condition 2, . . . , Condition *n*, THEN Action 1, Action 2, . . . , Action *n*" Anderson, 1983; Newell, 1973). Examples of condition-action rules (also called *production rules*) are "If something is an animal that wags its tail and barks, then it is a dog" (a rule classifying instances of a general concept) and "If something is a dog, then it can be trained to fetch newspapers" (a rule indicating a procedure for which instances of a general concept can be used).

Rules can be used to place instances in categories and to make predictions about how category members will change over time in response to actions. A pragmatically important concept will typically play a role in a number of procedures, just as an important procedure will apply to a range of different concepts. Both concepts and procedures will therefore often be represented not by some single rule but by interrelated clusters of rules with overlapping conditions or actions (Holland, Holyoak, Nisbett, & Thagard, 1986). Such rule clusters can represent the kind of organized knowledge often referred to as a *schema* for a concept or procedure.

Rules are not always general or abstract. A rule can be used to recognize a particular instance (e.g., "If an object is small, has four legs, wags its tail, barks, and wears a tag with the name 'Rover' on it, then it is Rover"). Similarly, a rule might be used to classify a particular category member (e.g., "If an object is Rover, then it is a dog"). Thus condition-action rules can be used to represent knowledge at the level of both general categories and specific instances.

We do not assume, however, that all knowledge is stored in the form of rules. Factual knowledge may also be stored in the format of a list of features (i.e., as a set of properties, much like the condition side of a rule, but without the explicit implicational structure of a rule). A feature representation allows storage of a representation of an event or specific instance without a firm assignment of category membership. The information can be stored in a relatively neutral fashion; at some later time it may be recoded in terms of rules.

An example of such recoding is provided by a story (told by a colleague of Gick's) about his encounter with a "monster" at Lake Michigan. He was windsurfing in Green Bay, and a brown organism that appeared as large as a man, but was not a fish, came straight up out of the water for a few seconds and then disappeared. The object was too far away to permit identification. Terrified, the man left the scene, carrying in his memory, we might assume, a representation of the creature as a list of features. He related this incident to his mother 3 months later. After listening to his description of the behavior of the monster, she informed him that many years ago seals commonly inhabited that particular part of the lake and that perhaps he had seen one. In light of this new information, the man might have formed a rule such as "If you encounter a large, brown, upright organism that emerges from Lake Michigan, it is probably a seal (so don't panic!)." Of course, if the "monster" had never been identified, a feature-list representation might have remained the only format in which the man's encounter was encoded in memory.

Although our discussion of transfer will emphasize the role of rules, feature-list representation also play an important role, especially in processes (such as analogical reasoning) that depend upon retrieving representations of specific instances.

Rule-based models of knowledge representation make it possible to see how what is learned will influence transfer. For example, suppose a young girl forms a rule such as "If something is small and has a tail, then it is called 'doggie.'" The condition of this rule would be satisfied if a cat were subsequently observed, leading to overgeneralization of the term "doggie" (a kind of negative transfer). Furthermore, the rule would *not* be matched by a Great Dane, leading to undergeneralization (absence of transfer). On the other hand, the rule would allow correct labeling of a spaniel (a case of positive transfer). Thus the relationship between the rules formed during training and the initial representation of the transfer situation affects the kind of transfer observed. The appropriate correction in cases of transfer failure is to form a more general rule (one with a less restrictive condition), whereas in the case of negative transfer, the correction requires forming a more specific rule (one with a more restrictive condition that will not be matched by erroneous cases).

In rule-based systems such as those described by Anderson (1983) and Holland *et al.* (1986), rules have attached to them *strength* values that are revised to reflect the degree to which individual rules have proven useful in the past. In any problem situation multiple rules with conflicting actions may compete for the "right" to suggest possible solutions, and the strongest rules will be most likely to prevail. The stronger a rule is, the more likely it will determine the response when its condition is satisfied in the future. Rules can complement each other as well as compete; novel situations may evoke multiple rules that each provide a partial description of the situation and which may collectively suggest responses. It follows that transfer of knowledge can vary by degrees as a function of the appropriateness of the applicable rules established and strengthened during prior training. We will now consider how our theoretical framework can be extended to provide an analysis of the relationship between similarity and transfer.

B. Types of Similarity

The most fundamental ideal required to understand transfer is that two tasks may differ yet share some common components, which provide the basis for intertask transfer. This notion, sometimes call the "theory of identical elements," was first articulated by Thorndike (1903). For example, certain facts about addition (e.g., that $5 + 7 = 12$) are involved in the procedure usually used to perform multiplication of two-digit numbers; accordingly, prior knowledge of addition facts may prove beneficial to learning to multiply. More general procedures, such as carrying, are also used in multiplication as well as in addition, and hence also provide a possible basis for transfer. As this example indicates, "common components" must be construed in a general way to include not only simple perceptual features but also (again following Thorndike) shared categories (e.g., "digit"), elements of procedures, principles, and even emotional attitudes. Note that this liberal interpretation of the nature of components is consistent with the possibility of both highly specific and highly general transfer effects. Shared components might consist of rules with conditions sufficiently general to apply in both the training and transfer situations, or of feature lists with overlapping properties.

In order to predict transfer on the basis of components shared by the training and transfer tasks, it is necessary to analyze the central concept of *similarity*. As theorists such as Hesse (1966) and Tversky (1977) have pointed out, the continuous notion of similarity can be reduced to a function of discrete components: Two situation are similar to the extent they share many common components and have few distinctive components. To a first approximation, more common components will constitute greater similarity and lead to greater transfer.

A more refined analysis of types of similarity is required, however, to predict both the overall *magnitude* of transfer and its *direction* (positive or negative). These separable aspects of transfer can be related to the impact of different types of similarity on the retrieval versus application of previously acquired knowledge. Specifically, we propose that any salient similarity of two situations will influence their overall *perceived* similarity, which will in turn affect retrieval of the representation of the training situation during the transfer task—the greater the perceived similarity of the two situations, the more likely it is that transfer will be attempted. If transfer is in fact attempted, then the direction of transfer will be determined by the similarity of the two situations with respect to features causally relevant to the goal or required response in the transfer task.

Components of a situation that are causally or functionally related in outcomes or goal attainment will be termed *structural*, and those not so related will be termed *surface* (Holyoak, 1985; Holyoak & Koh, in press). As these authors argue in the context of discussing the use of analogies in problem solving, salient common components of either a surface or a structural nature will increase the likelihood that a problem solver will relate the two situations to each other. That is, salient surface or structural components will affect perceived similarity. Conditional on transfer being attempted at all, shared structural components will tend to yield positive transfer, as the solution of the initial problem is transferred in an appropriate way to the transfer task. Conversely, distinctive structural components will tend to yield negative transfer.

A simple example may help clarify the surface–structural distinction. Suppose that the weather one summer is unusually dry in both Oklahoma and southern California, and we know that crops were severely damaged in Oklahoma. What outcome might be predicted for California? Clearly, lack of rain is a salient common component of the two situations that might lead to a prediction of crop damage. On the other hand, farms in southern California have better irrigation systems than do those in Oklahoma, so we might predict a more favorable harvest in the former case. The factors of rainfall and irrigation are structural components of the two situations. California and Oklahoma are stucturally similar with respect to rainfall but structurally dissimilar with respect to irrigation. In addition to structural components, the two situations will have surface features that may be the same or different. For example, the varying accents of persons living in the two states constitute surface differences, functionally unrelated to the outcome of crop damage (Collins, Warnock, Aiello, & Miller, 1975).

It is important to note that the salience of features of two situations, and hence perceived similarity, cannot be determined by simply referring to the objective properties of the two situations. Perceived similarity will be influenced by many psychological factors, such as the knowledge or expertise of the person performing the transfer task. For example, if we did not know that California is better irrigated than Oklahoma (or did not know that irrigation affects crops), we might predict identical outcomes for both states. Chi, Feltovich, and Glaser (1981) have shown that novice problem solvers in the domain of physics are often unaware of the structural features of problems and hence treat problems sharing only surface features (e.g., problems involving inclined planes) as if they were structurally similar (i.e., as if they required the same solution method). Perceived similarity based on surface features, in the absence of structural similarity, sets the stage for negative transfer.

The context of two situations can also affect perceived similarity. For example, Tversky and Gati (1978) found that when subjects were asked to rate pairs of American cities, they gave higher similarity ratings if half of the total set were European as opposed to all being American. The feature "American" differentiated instances in the former case, but not in the latter, in which it was shared by all members of the set. The importance of context has also been noted in work on classification learning (Fried & Holyoak, 1984; Medin & Schaffer, 1978). Specifically, the probability of classifying an item as a category member increases as a function of not only its similarity to other members of its category but also of its dissimilarity to examples of other alternative categories.

What defines the context in a transfer situation? The context of a transfer situation will be determined by events that occur close to it in time or that are retrieved from memory during performance of the transfer task. If different prior situations or examples are retrieved, and hence become part of the transfer context, there will be competition among the candidates for the best match to the transfer task.

In summary, perceived similarity, which is influenced by context, will determine whether transfer between two situations is attempted. Any salient shared component, whether surface or structural, will increase the probability that two situations will be viewed as similar by a learner. Whether the salient similarities that are noticed are in fact surface or structural will depend on factors such as the learner's expertise in the area. If transfer is attempted, objective structural similarity will determine whether transfer is positive or negative.

C. SIMILARITY AND TRANSFER

The above analysis of similarity can be used to account for the most pervasive phenomena concerning similarity and transfer. Two empirical generalizations, termed the "Bruce-Wylie laws" after their originators (Bruce, 1933; Wylie, 1919; see Thyne, 1963, pp. 218–221), summarize these phenomena. Consider any two situations, whether they be as simple as the stimulus terms of two paired associates or as complex as the initial states of realistic problems; and the responses appropriate to each situation, whether these are the response terms in the paired associates or the procedures for solving the problems. The first law states that the amount of transfer depends on the degree of similarity between the two situations; the second states that the direction of the transfer depends on the similarity of the two responses. The laws can be restated in terms of our analysis of similarity: perceived similarity, based on both surface and structural components, affects the amount of transfer obtained; objective structural similarity of the two situations determines the direction of transfer.

To take a simple example, suppose a child has learned to write the words "night," "tight," and "flight" when she hears them. If now asked to write the word "sight," the sound of the new word (the transfer situation) will be perceived as highly similar to the earlier training situations, so transfer will likely be attempted. Because the required response is structurally similar, transfer will be positive. In contrast, if the child is asked to write "height," transfer will also likely be attempted, because perceived similarity is high (i.e., the words sound the same), but the result will be interference with the appropriate response, because the required responses are structurally

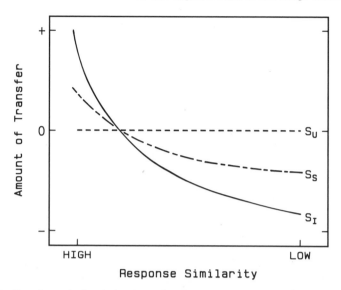

Figure 1. Transfer typically obtained as a function of response similarity when the transfer situation is perceived as identical (S_I), similar (S_S), or unrelated (S_U) to the initial situation. (Adapted from Osgood, 1949.)

dissimilar. The classic phenomenon of *Einstellung* (Luchins, 1942)—negative transfer produced by the inappropriate application of previously learned problem-solving strategies to superficially similar problems—illustrates the same point. In such cases a strong rule (or set of rules) is activated and applied in the new situation, because it is perceived as similar to previous situations, but the action evoked is inappropriate.

Figure 1 presents a schematized picture of these empirical generalizations as they were elaborated by Osgood (1949). When two situations are perceived as unrelated, no transfer occurs regardless of response similarity, defining a baseline for transfer performance. When the situations are perceived as similar or identical, transfer occurs; the greater the similarity of the situations, the greater the absolute magnitude of transfer. If transfer occurs, it becomes increasingly negative as the appropriate responses become objectively more dissimilar. If the required transfer response is highly similar to the training response (many shared structural components and few distinctive ones), transfer is positive. But as the response appropriate to the transfer task becomes less similar (few shared components and many distinctive ones), overall transfer shifts to the negative side. The structural dissimilarities cause the training response, evoked by strong perceived similarity, to interfere with the new response that must be acquired for the transfer task. As we review recent investigations of transfer, we will see that many empirical findings can be interpreted in terms of the general framework we have presented.

III. DETERMINANTS OF TRANSFER: FOUR TYPES OF FACTORS

Because transfer depends on the application of previously acquired knowledge, it is inherently dependent on memory. We will organize our review in terms of four classes of factors that determine transfer performance, adapted from the four-factor model of memory performance developed by Jenkins (1979). As we will see, the impact of these factors on memory, and hence transfer, is largely the result of their influence on the perceived similarity of situations.

First, it is important to consider the structure of the task to be initially learned and its relationship to the transfer task. The learner's representation of the task is necessarily dependent on the structure of the task itself. For example, is there a simple rule that characterizes the response to be learned? Second, it is necessary to assess whether the conditions at encoding foster learning of the material and are appropriate for the subsequent transfer task (Bransford & Franks, 1976). For instance, what range of examples is provided? The encoding conditions will constrain the operation of learning mechanisms, such as generalization and discrimination, and hence influence the representation of the training task that is achieved by the learner. The representation of the training task in turn may affect its perceived similarity to the transfer task.

The third class of factors concerns conditions at retrieval (i.e., the performance of the transfer task) that influence access to and application of appropriate knowledge. Prior knowledge, often encoded as rules, will need to be activated in memory. Knowledge may be retrieved incidentally, with retrieval being "driven" by the environment and context of the transfer task (Craik, 1985), or intentionally, as the learner consciously strives to retrieve and apply appropriate prior knowledge. In either case, the transfer task cues the retrieval of the prior knowledge. If the context of the transfer task is substantially different from that of the training task, then potentially relevant knowledge may not be accessed, as perceived similarity will be low. The similarity of *processing* performed in training and transfer tasks will be particularly important (Bransford & Franks, 1976; Tulving & Thomson, 1973), for both retrieval and application of prior knowledge. If different processes are required for the transfer task, the procedures learned for the training task may yield no transfer or even negative transfer.

Finally, the fourth important factor to be considered is the background knowledge of the subject. For example, expertise in an area may result in successful application of knowledge, despite apparent dissimilarities between the contexts of initial encoding and eventual retrieval.

A. STRUCTURE OF THE TRAINING AND TRANSFER TASKS

What is learned from training, and hence the knowledge potentially available for transfer, is constrained by the structure of the task itself. Our framework suggests that transfer will often depend on the acquisition of rules that characterize a category of tasks. Often it will be possible to develop a set of rules that classifies the items of the training and transfer tasks as members of a common category. If so, then the learning of these rules would be an efficient means of ensuring positive transfer. For example, in a category-learning task, classification during transfer could proceed on the basis of whether the instance satisfied the relevant rules. Similarly, solving a novel problem of a known type would involve classifying the new problem as belonging to a previously learned problem category, followed by implementation of appropriate solution procedures.

For complex tasks, of course, it may not be easy to learn a rule cluster or schema for a category. Rule induction is influenced by the complexity of the possible rules, as well as by the availability of other successful strategies not requiring rule acquisition. Thus, for example, it will be difficult to demonstrate transfer between instances of a category of problems defined by a complex rule if the problems can be solved more easily by trial and error than by learning the rule (Sweller, 1980).

The complexity of the rules defining a category has been shown to influence the relative efficacy of alternative learning strategies. If a category can be described by a simple rule, then a stategy of explicit hypothesis testing is likely to succeed in identifying the appropriate rule. To take an extreme example, suppose you were presented with a series of letter strings: ABC, AABBCC, and AAABBBCCC. You would surely notice that the strings can be described by a rule such as "If the string consists of some number of *A*s followed by the same number of *B*s followed by the same number of *C*s, then it is a legal string." This simple rule would allow you to then decide that AAAABBBBCCCC is a legal string.

Suppose, however, that the example strings were GLVL, MPB, GLLLSPB, and MPRL. In this case no simple rule is likely to suggest itself—indeed, none exists. These strings were generated by the finite-state network depicted in Figure 2. A "grammatical" string in this artificial grammar is any string that can be generated by traversing the arcs connecting the nodes from the start to the end nodes, producing the indicated letter as each arc is followed. Thus MSLLLVL would also be a grammatical string, whereas MPLVL would not. Reber and his colleagues (Reber, 1967, 1976; Reber & Allen, 1978; Reber, Kassin, Lewis & Cantor, 1980) have

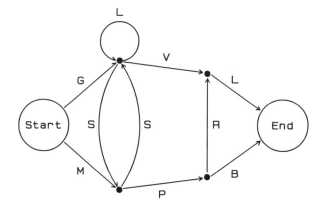

Figure 2. Finite-state network for generating an artificial "language" consisting of letter strings.

found that subjects are able to learn to make grammaticality judgments on the basis of observing examples of strings generated in this manner. Furthermore, when the underlying grammer is relatively complex, better transfer performance is obtained when subjects are asked simply to observe or memorize the training strings, rather than to try to learn a rule.

For strings with a complex underlying structure, for which no single deterministic rule can be found, subjects who use an explicit hypothesis-testing strategy may try out a series of candidate "monolithic" rules without success. In contrast, subjects using more implicit learning strategies may learn a number of partial regularities (e.g., "if the first letter is a G or an M, then the string may be grammatical"; "If there is an S followed by some number of Ls, then the string may be grammatical"). A broader set of imperfect rules of this sort will allow substantial accuracy during the transfer phase. Thus the structure of the task itself determines the optimal learning strategy for subsequent transfer.

The influence of task structure, of course, merges with the general topic of task encoding, to which we now turn.

B. ENCODING OF THE TRAINING TASK

In this section we examine a number of variables that affect the amount and type of knowledge acquired during training. One factor is the degree of learning attained during acquisition. Another major factor concerns the types of examples or instances of the to-be-learned category presented during training. In particular, we consider the number and variability of examples, their order of presentation, and the explicit inclusion of abstract rule or schema training along with examples. Finally, we will consider the effects of different types of strategic instructions given to learners.

1. Degree of Learning

Effective transfer of knowledge depends on its prior acquisition. As long as structurally similar responses are required in the training and transfer tasks, positive transfer increases with degree of initial learning (Ellis, 1965). Despite the importance of this basic fact, studies of transfer have not always demonstrated the requisite degree of initial learning. For example, in one experiment Reed, Dempster, and Ettinger (1985) provided subjects with brief experience solving a single example of an algebra problem and subsequently found no transfer to a similar problem. In this experiment it was unclear whether the degree of initial learning was able to support transfer. With a more elaborative training procedure, some transfer was in fact obtained. In some studies a criterion of learning is established and followed, and transfer performance is examined only for subjects who meet the criterion. However, amount of learning per se has generally not been manipulated in recent work. A few studies of complex problem solving, however, have shown that subjects' performance improves with experience and familiarization with the rules defining the task (e.g., Anzai & Simon, 1979, and Kotovsky, Hayes, & Simon, 1985, for the Tower of Hanoi problem).

The effect of degree of original learning has been extensively studied in paradigms in which different responses are required in the training and transfer tasks. As was illustrated in Figure 1 (section II.C), structurally dissimilar responses typically give rise to negative transfer. However, this generalization must be qualified when degree of learning is considered. Mandler (1962) reviewed an extensive series of studies of transfer in animal learning and human verbal-learning tasks and identified a consistent pattern, illustrated in Figure 3. As degree of original learning increases, transfer is at first increasingly negative. However, as practice is extended, the direction of transfer reverses, and at high levels of initial learning, positive transfer is obtained. On the surface, this pattern seems inconsistent with our rule-based framework. Learning strong rules that elicit a response differing structurally from that required to perform the transfer task would be expected to impair transfer, because the rules acquired during training would compete and interfere with the response to be learned during transfer. How, then, can extended practice on a different response actually produce facilitation at transfer?

In fact, the contradiction seems to be only apparent. Mandler (1962) argues that the negative factor of response competition indeed increases monotonically to some asymptote as training is extended. However, extended training also produces some more general learning that is structurally consistent with the response to be learned for the transfer task; these positive effects eventually outweigh the negative effect of response competition. Some positive general transfer is attributable to "learning to

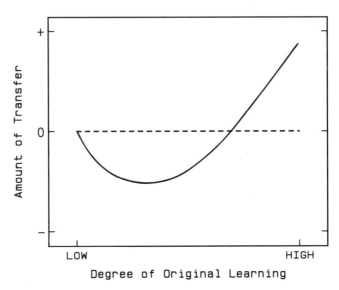

Figure 3. Typical relationship between degree of original learning and transfer of training.

learn'': acquiring general problem-solving strategies appropriate to both training and transfer tasks, such as a "win-stay, lose-shift" strategy for discrimination learning. In some cases more specific knowledge may yield positive transfer. For example, if the rewarded response in a discrimination task is reversed (e.g., selecting white rather than black stimuli), the higher order similarity between the training and transfer responses (e.g., attention to the color of the stimuli, rather than to shape or some other dimension of variation) will create a structural overlap between the original and transfer responses. The nonmonotonic impact of degree of original learning on transfer is thus best interpreted as evidence that rules at multiple levels of abstraction are acquired as training is extended.

2. Number and Variability of Examples

Many recent transfer studies have exposed the learner to instances or examples during category acquisition in order to facilitate subsequent transfer. The results of several studies from different domains indicate that positive transfer increases with the number of instances provided during training (e.g., Gick & Holyoak, 1983; Homa & Cultice, 1984). Opportunity to learn appropriate rules, based on features that are structurally related to category membership, will increase with the number of examples provided. As Gick and Holyoak (1983) argued in the context of problem solving by analogy, the provision of more than a single example may be especially crucial. Once two or more examples are available, it is possible to induce more general rules by abstracting the components that are shared by the examples. To take a simple example, if we observe that a small dog barks and a large dog barks, we may generalize that dogs bark regardless of size. Generalization by intersection (finding common components) is a technique frequently used in artificial intelligence programs that learn (Hayes-Roth & McDermott, 1978; Winston, 1975). Once a more general rule has been acquired, transfer will result simply from applying the rule to new cases that satisfy the rule's condition.

Optimal generalization will depend not only on the sheer number of examples provided, but also on their representativeness with respect to the category. Natural categories typically cannot be summarized by a single deterministic rule; rather, a set of partially predictive rules will be required to capture the inherent variability of the category instances (Rosch, 1978). In experimental studies of the acquisition of inherently variable categories, people are shown a series of instances of categories of visual forms, such as dot patterns (Posner & Keele, 1968). Each category is based on a standard form, from which instances are generated by applying a statistical distortion rule. As illustrated in Figure 4, the variability of the instances can be manipulated by varying the degree of distortion used to construct instances. Several studies have found that exposure to relatively variable training instances facilitates subsequent classification of novel instances at high distortion levels (Fried & Holyoak, 1984; Homa & Vosburgh, 1976; Posner & Keele, 1968). Within the rule-based framework, the positive effect of training variability is attributable to the opportunity it affords to learn partially predictive rules describing the diverse set of category instances (Anderson, Kline & Beasley, 1979). Learners who have not seen highly distorted instances during training enter the transfer task without rules for classifying such examples and hence tend to assign them to none of the learned categories (Fried & Holyoak, 1984).

Although high variability of examples generally aids transfer, it may hinder initial learning, especially if the number of examples is small. Using random-dot patterns in a classification task, Peterson, Meagher, Chait, and Gillie (1973) found that high variability of instances, as defined by degree of distortion from a standard form, was detrimental to transfer performance. In this study, however, only three training patterns per category were used in the learning phase. The poor transfer obtained was most likely due to poor initial learning, since it will be difficult to form veridical general rules characterizing a category from a very small set of diverse examples.

The variability of examples also has a major impact on the transfer of problem-solving procedures. Bassok and Holyoak (1987) investigated transfer between two classes of problems taught in high school algebra and physics courses. The algebra problems involved arithmetic progressions

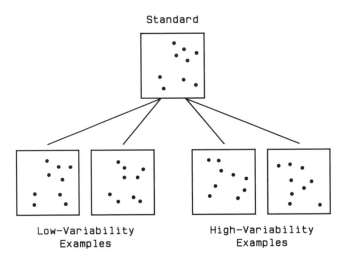

Figure 4. A standard dot pattern and instances generated by a mild distortion (low variability) or a severe distortion (high variability).

(e.g., "If a number series starts at 3 and is incremented by 8 a total of 5 times, what is the final term in the series?"), and the physics problems involved constant acceleration (e.g., "If a car starts at a speed of 10 mph and accelerates 5 mph each second for 6 s, what is its final speed?"). The equations for solving these two classes of problems are isomorphic (i.e., the terms can be placed in one-to-one correspondence). Bassok and Holyoak were interested in whether students who had learned one of these topics, from a combination of abstract training in equations plus a variety of word problems, would transfer what they had learned to the other class of problems. A strong asymmetry was observed: High school students exhibited much greater transfer from arithmetic-progression problems to constant-acceleration problems in physics, than vice versa.

Bassok and Holyoak suggest that this asymmetry in transfer may be due to the different ranges of examples used to teach the two topics. In the case of the algebra problems, subjects had learned the solution method for many problems in a wide variety of surface contexts (e.g., growth of savings accounts, lengths of a series of boards). By abstracting the commonalities among these diverse examples, the students induced abstract rules for categorizing progression problems. Thus the physics transfer problems were seen simply as further examples of the problem type in a new context. In contrast, even though the physics students had been exposed to many constant-acceleration problems, the variety of contexts was more restricted (e.g., problems involving the motion of cars versus balls). These students therefore learned rules that applied only to motion problems and hence did not readily transfer this knowledge to the broader class of arithmetic-progression problems.

In the above examples, the varied examples were created by altering surface features that did not affect category membership or, in the case of problems, the appropriate solution method. Exposure to instances that vary in surface features will allow people to form generalized rules that are not restricted to overly specialized contexts, thus facilitating transfer (e.g., Bassok & Holyoak, 1987). Variability of instances will not facilitate transfer, however, if the variation involves changes in structural features—those relevant to category membership or to the applicability of a solution method. For example, training in two contexts did not produce better transfer than training in one context in a task involving the learning of mental-arithmetic procedures (Elio, 1986). The variation in the two contexts involved changing certain "component" equations that later fed into "integrative" equations that combined various calculations from the component parts. Elio suggested that changing the component parts resulted in changes in how the subject completed the procedure (e.g., the exact ordering of steps to be completed), even though the integrative part of the procedure remained unchanged across the two contexts. In this case the variability introduced structural differences in the appropriate responses.

3. Order of Examples

When highly variable instances are presented during training, their order of presentation may influence acquisition. In a concept-learning task involving the acquisition of novel words, Nitsch (1977) found that highly variable instances (e.g., uses of the words in different contexts, such as sentences about cowboys and restaurants) facilitated transfer. Many subjects in the high-variability group, however, committed more errors in acquisition and failed to reach criterion in learning. This result is consistent with other work, reviewed above, which indicates that high variability impairs initial learning although it aids transfer if learning is successful.

A simple order manipulation made Nitsch's (1977) task easier for the high-variability group. A "hybrid" group, in which low-variability instantiations of the concept (e.g., all "cowboy" examples) were followed by instantiations drawn from a wider range of contexts, transferred the concepts just as well as did the high-variability group but reported less confusion during acquisition.

The optimal order of examples may vary with subjects' approach to the learning task. In a classification task involving hypothetical club members described by verbal attributes (e.g., "plays jazz," "college educated," "single"), Elio and Anderson (1984) found that transfer was optimized when low-variability instances (the most frequently occurring examples) were introduced first, but only when the subjects were led to take an implicit approach to the task (i.e., they were not instructed to find a deterministic rule for category membership). These investigators found that high-variability instances, more representative of features occurring in all items of the category, were best introduced first for subjects led to take an explicit hypothesis-testing approach (i.e., those who were instructed to look for a rule defining category membership).

These results can be interpreted in light of our earlier characterization of explicit versus implicit learning strategies (section III.A). When learners operate in an explicit mode, they may use only a subset of the information contained in the examples. Accordingly, as Elio and Anderson (1984) suggest, it will be important that the examples provide exposure to representative variation from the start of learning. Otherwise, learners may attempt to abstract a rule based on a limited set of stimulus dimensions and ignore others deemed unimportant. If the variation in early exemplars is not representative, then subjects may discard information about important relevant attributes that they will be unable to recover later.

When subjects operate in an implicit learning mode, on the other hand, they may rely on a generalization process that develops multiple rules based on similarities among instances. Initial exposure to relatively similar items may help establish generalized rules; more variable instances can be used to elaborate the rule set once the initial rules have been established and strengthened. Some research supports this interpretation. Elio and Anderson (1981), using the same type of classification task as in the 1984 study by the same investigators, found that blocked presentation of similar study items facilitated generalization. In addition, Reber *et al.* (1980) found that blocking items in ways that highlight invariant patterns (e.g., grouping by grammatical subrules) facilitated transfer in an artificial-grammer learning study of the sort described in Section III.A. In general, early blocking of similar examples, followed by subsequent exposure to a more varied set, may often optimize learning and transfer.

4. Roles of Abstract Training and Examples

The transfer studies described thus far primarily have involved learning by examples, without the experimenter or instructor supplying the learner with a definition of the category. When a schema or rule sufficient to perform the task is directly supplied to the learner, an important question is whether such abstract training is sufficient for transfer, or whether inclusion of examples is necessary. Research indicates that examples aid transfer. Nitsch (1977) found that subjects who learned only the abstract definitions of novel words performed less well on transfer tasks than did subjects who received examples along with the definition. Similarly, Gick and Holyoak (1983) found that a verbal or spatial summary of a solution schema did not facilitate transfer to a target problem unless it was accompanied by two examples. Finally, studies of logic training have revealed that subjects trained on an abstract description of conditional reasoning do not adequately transfer this knowledge to test problems unless illustrative examples are included during training (Cheng, Holyoak, Nisbett, & Oliver, 1986). Examples appear to be important in showing how an abstract concept can be instantiated, even when rules are directly presented during training, especially if the concept is not part of the intuitive repertoire of the learner.

Other work has shown, however, that people can sometimes derive considerable benefit from abstract training even when only minimal examples are provided. Fong, Krantz, and Nisbett (1986) found that subjects were able to benefit from abstract training in a statistical principle. Cheng *et al.* (1986) demonstrated that direct training on an abstract pragmatic schema for reasoning (involving the intuitive concept of obligation) facilitated transfer to instances that could be interpreted via obligation schemas (also see section III.D below). In general, an abstract rule or schema included with the acquisition instances may facilitate transfer to novel examples, especially when the acquisition and transfer items are superficially dissimilar (Gick & Holyoak, 1983) or when the rule is difficult to induce from examples alone (Cheng *et al.*, 1986; Fong *et al.*, 1986).

5. Strategic Variations in Learning

In section III.A as well as in section III.B.3, we discussed differences in learning and transfer performance associated with implicit versus explicit learning strategies. Other studies of categorization have also involved manipulations of the learning strategies employed during training (Brooks, 1978; McAndrews & Moscovitch, 1985; Medin & Smith, 1981). Instructions can affect processing strategies employed during acquisition, which in turn can influence both learning and transfer.

Instructional variations that effect strategies have also been employed in studies of problem solving. For example, Sweller, Mawer, and Howe (1982) found that use of a "means–ends" strategy (a general method for decomposing problems and solving them by working backward from the stated goal) facilitated initial problem solving; however, use of the means–ends strategy hindered the acquisition of a rule (involving alternation) that described the structure of the problems. It is possible to influence the use of means–ends strategies and consequent learning and transfer performance by suitable instructional manipulations. In several studies, Sweller and his colleagues (Mawer & Sweller, 1982; Owen & Sweller, 1985; Sweller & Levine, 1982; Sweller, Mawer, & Ward 1983) have demonstrated that reducing the goal specificity in the problem statement can result in a decrease in working-backward and means–ends strategies and in an increase in a working-forward strategy. In one study, for example, a specific question that required calculation of the final velocity in a physics problem was compared with a question with reduced goal specificity, which required calculation of all of the unknown variables (Sweller *et al.*, 1983). Subjects in both instruction groups had access to the identical equations, and in fact the same equations were required to solve both versions of the problem. However, for subjects given the specific version, the specific goal controlled the sequence of moves; in contrast, for subjects given the less specific version, control of moves was shifted to the given information in the problem, or to a combination of the given information and previously executed moves. If the problem solver is forced to pay attention to the given information and associated moves, rules connecting givens and moves may be formed. Such rules will produce increased transfer to similar problems, as Sweller *et al.* demonstrated.

Several basic ideas emerge from our review of research on the relationship between encoding of the training task and subsequent transfer. Manipulations that foster the acquistion of generalized rules, sufficiently abstract as to characterize both the training task and the subsequent transfer task, will increase positive transfer. The rules acquired must be well learned and based on an overall set of examples diverse enough to allow generalization mechanisms to abstract the common structural components from surface differences. Direct abstract training in rules embodying appropriate solution procedures is likely to be useful, but rules for classifying novel instances into the category must also be acquired to ensure successful transfer. Unless such rules for classification have been acquired earlier, it will be necessary to augment training in abstract rules with exposure to concrete examples. In general, the conditions at encoding influence whether or not the training task is encoded in terms of structural components that are shared with the transfer task.

C. RETRIEVAL FACTORS

Transfer of knowledge depends upon its appropriate access and application, in addition to its initial acquisition. In this section we consider factors operating at retrieval that influence transfer performance.

1. Similarity of Goals and Processing

As we emphasized in section II, a fundamental determinant of transfer is the similarity of the learner's mental representations of the training and transfer tasks. The likelihood that transfer will be obtained increases with the components common to the final representation of the training task and the initial representation of the transfer task.

An important aspect of subjective similarity involves the *processing* associated with the training and transfer tasks. In most of the transfer paradigms described so far, the learner's goals were highly similar during training and transfer (e.g., first learning to classify examples of a category, and then attempting to transfer the resulting knowledge to the task of classifying additional instances). In such cases the overt similarity of the tasks and the goals to be achieved will increase perceived similarity and encourage transfer. Sometimes, however, the training and transfer tasks will be associated with substantially different processing and goals. Indeed, some of the most spectacular and widely decried failures of transfer—failures to apply knowledge learned in school to practical problems encountered in everyday life—may largely reflect the fact that material taught in school is often disconnected from *any* clear goal and hence lacks a primary cue for retrieval in potentially relevant problem contexts.

Some experimental studies that have failed to find transfer seem to illustrate the effect of lack of similar goals and processing. Weisberg, Di Camillo, and Phillips (1978) gave subjects an initial task of learning paired associates. They then were asked to solve Duncker's (1945) candle problem, which requires finding a method of affixing a candle to a wall, given certain materials. One of the pairs memorized in the prior paired-associates task, "box-candle," was intended to suggest a possible solution to the subsequent transfer problem. (One solution is to empty a box of tacks, attach it to the wall, and then place the candle in it.) However, few subjects noticed the relevance of the crucial cue. This lack of transfer, in the face of objective identity of the memorized words and key elements of the problem, may reflect the absence of similar goals or processing across the training and transfer tasks. As Weisberg *et al.* (1978) point out, a problem solver uses a goal (e.g., "Find a way to attach this candle to the wall") as a cue to search memory. It is the goal itself, and not the separate problem elements (e.g., the box or candle), that cues past experience. The previously acquired association between "box" and "candle" is not accessed because the subject is not searching for ways to connect these problem elements together.

As Bransford and Franks (1976) have emphasized, transfer is much more likely to be obtained when the learner processes the training and transfer tasks in a similar manner, producing compatible responses in both tasks. For example, Lund and Dominowski (1985) found that a training task involving the strategy of extending and intersecting lines, which is necessary for the solution of the gestalt "nine-dot problem," facilitated transfer to it.

Research by Lockhart, Lamon, and Gick (1987) also supports the importance of processing similarity to transfer. Their transfer task required subjects to solve riddles (e.g., "How can a man marry several women each week and yet remain single?"). Some subjects, those in the "aha" group, first read a puzzling statement that presented the misconception usually perceived by subjects on the transfer riddle. For example, the puzzling statement corresponding to the above riddle might be "A man marries several women each week because it makes him happy." The subjects were then

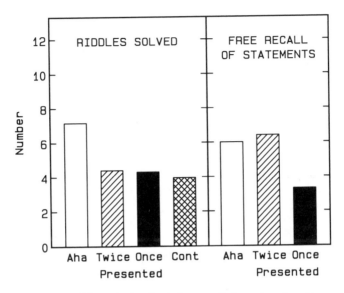

Figure 5. Number of riddles solved and solutions recalled as a function of presentation condition (R. S. Lockhart, M. Lamon, & M. L. Gick, 1987).

given a phrase that effectively solved the puzzle (e.g., "clergyman"). Subjects in two "sentence-elaboration" groups were simply presented with corresponding straightforward statements, such as "A clergyman marries several women each week because it makes him happy," either once or twice. [The latter condition was intended to control for superior memory for the information presented in the "aha" condition, as demonstrated by Auble and Franks, (1978).] Subjects in the "aha" group who received the solution phrase in the context of the puzzling statement were more likely to apply it spontaneously to the subsequent riddle than were subjects who received the identical clue beforehand without the initially puzzling statement. Subjects in the sentence conditions were no more likely to generate the solution to the riddles than were control subjects who were not presented with any sentences prior to the riddles.

Subjects in the various conditions were subsequently asked to free-recall the statements presented earlier. As illustrated in Figure 5, memory did not guarantee transfer. Those subjects who were presented with the solution twice, and who had equally good memory for it (as evidenced by the free-recall test), still were not as successful in transfer as those subjects in the "aha" group who had been presented with the solution in the context of the misconception.

Why should prior exposure to the puzzling statement facilitate transfer of the solution to the riddle? Presumably, when subjects later attempted the riddle and were led to focus on the misconception again (i.e., "How can a man

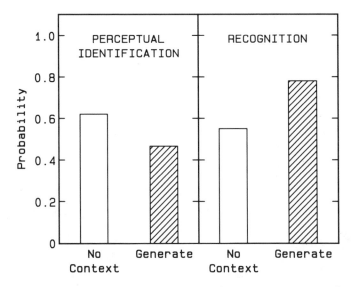

Figure 6. Probability of perceptual identification and recognition memory as a function of the previous treatment of words. (Adapted from Jacoby, 1983. Copyright 1983 by the American Psychological Association. Adapted by permission of the author.)

marry yet remain single?''), they were reminded (Schank, 1982) of the earlier puzzling statement, which served as a strong retrieval cue for the appropriate answer (''a clergyman marries others but need not be married''). Training and transfer tasks both involved the common goal of resolving the misconception.

Recent research in incidental memory has also demonstrated the importance of similarity of processing between encoding and retrieval. As illustrated in Figure 6, Jacoby (1983) found that if subjects simply read a word in the absence of any context (e.g., ''cold''), performance on a later task involving perceptual identification (i.e., tachistoscopic identification) was better than if the prior task involved generating an antonym (e.g., ''What is the opposite of ''hot?''). However, if the transfer task was a test of recognition memory, then the antonym-generation task facilitated performance relative to reading the word in the absence of context.

Jacoby (1983) argued that if the training task involves word generation, semantic processing is required. However, if the initial task involved reading words without any context, perceptual processing is emphasized to a greater degree than is semantic processing. The task of perceptual identification involves more perceptual than semantic processing, whereas recognition memory requires greater semantic analysis. Hence, according to this explanation, performance will be facilitated on an incidental task of perceptual identification if the initial task requires only reading a word in the absence of context, whereas generation will facilitate performance on a recognition test.

In what might at first appear to be an exception to the generalization that similarity of processing increases transfer, Horton (1985) found no advantage to reading inverted text in exactly the same orientation (e.g., inverted or reversed) on the training and transfer tasks. As long as the text had been somehow transformed in training, performance was faster in transfer than if it had been in a normal orientation. This result, however, may actually reflect the importance of similar processing of the two tasks. Horton argued that reading inverted text of any kind requires semantic processing (e.g., predicting the next word on the basis of the preceding words) to an even greater degree than in normal reading. This extra processing performed during training on an inverted text will transfer to a similar as well as an identical transformed text. This explanation suggests that if the task were proofreading, which presumably depends heavily on graphemic processing, an advantage might be obtained for having the same orientation of text at training and transfer. Levy (1983) in fact found an advantage for proofreading text for the second time only if the text was in the same type font on both occasions.

In summary, a wide range of evidence indicates that similarity of goals and processing between training and transfer tasks is extremely important in enabling facile transfer. Similar goals and processing increase perceived similarity, which facilitates retrieval of appropriate situations to apply to the transfer task.

2. Informed versus Uninformed Transfer

A goal of some transfer research is to determine the conditions under which knowledge will be transferred sponteneously, without a hint from the experimenter to inform the subject of its relevance. Studies of uninformed transfer typically use some incidental orienting task to ensure that knowledge will be acquired. The transfer task is then presented without mention of the relevance of the knowledge acquired previously. Many studies indicate that informing subjects facilitates transfer. An important issue, both for theory and for educational practice, is to determine the conditions under which uninformed transfer is possible.

Research on problem solving suggested initially that uninformed transfer was invariably poor. Results supporting this dismal generalization were obtained in studies in which a single training problem was presented, either as a problem to be solved by the subject or in the guise of a story, followed by a superficially different but analogous transfer problem (Gick & Holyoak, 1980, 1983; Reed, Ernst, & Banerji, 1974; also Weisberg *et al.*, 1978, in a paired-associate paradigm). In these experiments, subjects often failed to apply appropriate knowledge in the absence of a hint by the experimenter to do so (although positive transfer was sometimes found; Hayes & Simon, 1977). For example, in the studies performed by Gick and Holyoak, the transfer problem used as the target was the "radiation problem" first studied by Duncker (1945). The problem is as follows:

Suppose you are a doctor faced with a patient who has a malignant tumor in his stomach. It is impossible to operate on the patient, but unless the tumor is destroyed, the patient will die. There is a kind of ray that at a sufficiently high intensity can destroy the tumor. Unfortunately, at this intensity the healthy tissue that the rays pass through on the way to the tumor will also be destroyed. At lower intensities the rays are harmless to healthy tissue but will not affect the tumor either. How can the rays be used to destroy the tumor without injuring the healthy tissue?

To provide subjects with a potential source analogue, the experimenters first had subjects read a story about a general who wished to capture a fortress located in the center of a country. Many roads radiated outward from the fortress. These were mined in such a manner that, although small groups could pass over them safely, any large group would detonate the mines. Yet the general needed to get his entire large army to the fortress in order to launch a successful attack. He solved his problem by dividing his men into small groups and dispatching them simultaneously down multiple roads to converge on the fortress.

As long as they were prompted to use the story to help solve the radiation problem, subjects who received this story analogue were especially likely to suggest an analogous "convergence" solution—directing multiple weak rays at the tumor from different directions. Across many comparable experiments, Gick and Holyoak found that about 75% of college students tested generated the covergence solution after receiving the corresponding military story and a hint to apply it. In contrast, only about 30% of students generated this solution in the absence of a hint that the source analogue was relevant. Uninformed transfer was thus much less frequent than informed transfer, although even the uninformed subjects produced significantly more convergence solutions than control subjects who did not receive a source analogue, only 10% of whom generated the critical solution.

Other research, however, has demonstrated that relatively high levels of spontaneous transfer can be obtained in some situations. These situations appear to be of two general types. The first, discussed extensively in section III.B, involves training conditions that establish generalized rules directly applicable to the transfer task. For example, Gick and Holyoak (1983) had subjects read and compare *two* source analogues, such as the fortress story and a story about fire fighting in which multiple hoses were used to extinguish a blaze. This manipulation, which should foster abstraction of a generalized schema for convergence problems, produced a substantially greater frequency of spontaneous transfer to the radiation problem (see also Bassok & Holyoak, 1987).

The second type of situation conducive to transfer is more dependent on retrieval processes. Even if only a single prior example is available, it is likely to be retrieved and applied if subjects perceive it to be highly similar to the transfer problem, as discussed in sections II.B and III.C.1. For example, Gick (1985) included an identical diagram with both the story analogue and the subsequent radiation problem and obtained substantial uninformed transfer. Holyoak and Koh (in press) illustrated the convergence solution using a story analogue in which multiple converging lasers were used to repair the filament of a light bulb. Various salient common components (e.g., the fact that both lasers and x rays are rays) contributed to a very high rate of transfer to the radiation problem (over 80% spontaneous transfer after an interval of several days between presentation of the story and the transfer problem).

In the above examples the linking components often seem to be more surface than structural in nature (see section II.B). Other studies that have obtained uninformed transfer also provided salient surface cues. For example, Weisberg and Alba (1981) demonstrated that training in dot problems with solutions that had a similar shape to the nine-dot problem facilitated transfer to it. Ross (1984; Ross & Sofka, 1987) found that subjects solving probability problems were often reminded of earlier problems with similar surface components (e.g., story contexts).

There is also evidence, however, that more structural similarities can also facilitate uninformed transfer. Holyoak and Koh (in press) constructed variations of the "laser and light bulb story" that differed in the reason given for invoking converging forces rather than using a single large force. In one version the reason was to prevent damage to the glass surrounding the filament (analogous to protecting the healthy tissue surrounding the tumor), whereas in another version the reason was simply that no single laser source of sufficient strength was available. The latter version, which removed a structural parallel with the radiation problem, significantly reduced uninformed transfer. Indeed, this structural dissimilarity (unlike a more surface difference that was also manipulated) continued to impair transfer even after a hint to use the prior story was provided. The latter result is consistent with other studies discussed earlier in which structural dissimilarity produced negative transfer.

Ross (in press) showed that the facilitating effect of superficial similarity (in the form of a similar story context) is attenuated if the principles learned in training are all distinctive (i.e., not confusable). Ross suggested that *relative* similarity—the similarity of transfer problems to training problems based on the same principle, relative to their similarity to other training problems based on different principles—is an important determinant of transfer performance, as research on categorization has demonstrated (e.g., Fried & Holyoak, 1984; Medin & Schaffer, 1978). Ross found that when the principles used in different problems were highly distinctive, superficially dissimilar problems were accessed appropriately by problem solvers with only minimal knowledge of the domain, indicating that even novices are sensitive to structural similarities under conditions of minimum confusability. As discussed in section II.B, context can influence perceived similarity, and hence transfer.

One important constraint on informed transfer is that the benefit of a hint may be reduced if the problem solver first attempts the transfer task in the absence of a hint and does not spontaneously apply the knowledge acquired during training. Perfetto, Bransford, and Franks (1983) performed a study using a variant of the riddle paradigm discussed above (section III.C.1) in connection with the study by Lockhart et al. (1987). Perfetto et al. found that informing subjects that sentences supplied during acquisition could be used to solve riddles did not always result in their successful solution. In particular, if subjects had already attempted one unsuccessful solution to the riddle, informing subjects of the prior sentences' relevance was ineffective. In contrast, if subjects were attempting to solve the riddles for the first time, the informing manipulation was beneficial. Perfetto et al. argued that an incorrect solution on the first encoding of a riddle makes it a less effective retrieval cue for the earlier sentence than if no solution had been attempted. The availability of the initial unrelated solution attempt will reduce the similarity of the representations of the riddle and of the earlier sentence.

In summary, the acquisition of generalized rules, as discussed in the previous section on encoding variables, is not the only basis for transfer. Sufficient similarity of goals and processing may increase perceived similarity between the training and transfer tasks and trigger reminding and transfer, even in the absence of an externally provided hint to apply the relevant prior knowledge. As these forms of similarity are reduced, the likelihood of exploiting opportunities for transfer will correspondingly decrease.

D. ROLE OF BACKGROUND KNOWLEDGE

Only recently has the learner's background knowledge been considered in relationship to transfer of knowledge. Perhaps this neglect is due to researchers' excessive use of artificial materials, for which little prior knowledge was relevant, in both category-learning and problem-solving tasks. More recent work has made use of more naturalistic materials; accordingly, the role of prior knowledge has become a more central concern.

Some studies have explored how knowledge acquired outside the experimental context can be transferred to novel tasks. Bransford and Franks (1976) investigated the impact of prior knowledge on learning to classify

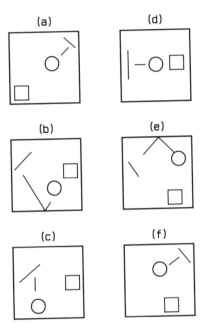

Figure 7. Visual patterns used in classification study. (From Bransford & Franks, 1976. Copyright © 1976 by Academic Press, Inc. Reprinted by permission.)

visual patterns (illustrated in Figure 7) into two categories. One group of subjects was told simply to classify the items into two categories. The other group was told that the patterns were related to baseball. In particular, they were informed that the circle was a ball, the square a glove, the long line a bat, and the short one (or the angle) the path of the ball. Subjects informed that the stimuli were related to baseball were better able to discern the difference between the two patterns of stimuli than were subjects who were not given information about the stimuli. Bransford and Franks argued that the baseball framework helped subjects focus on relevant features that would discriminate between the categories and to determine that in Category A items, the "ball" could be caught by the "glove," but in Category B items, the "ball" missed the "glove." (In Figure 7, a, b, and d are Category A items, while c, e, and f are Category B items.)

Providing a framework based on prior knowledge can have both positive and negative effects on transfer. For example, in Mayer and Greeno's (1972) work on binomial probability, subjects in a "concept" group were taught concepts about probability (e.g., "trial") in the context of familiar concepts (e.g., batting averages and rain forecasts). In contrast, subjects in a "formula" group only learned the components of the binomial theorem and were given practice at solving problems. The concept group performed better on far transfer tasks dissimilar from those at training (e.g., they were able to tell when a problem had no solution); however, the formula group outperformed the concept group on straightforward problems to which the formula was easily applied. As this experiment illustrates, there may be a cost associated both with narrow, specific rules, such as those learned by the formula group, and with general rules of the sort learned by the concept group. Presumably, optimal training would provide both a framework that can be used to increase understanding of concepts, and formulas that allow efficient application of the acquired knowledge. (See Mayer, 1975, 1985, for related research on learning computer programming.)

A framework based on prior knowledge will only yield positive transfer, of course, if it is structurally similar to the transfer topic. Gentner and Gentner (1983) demonstrated that alternative models of electricity ("water flow" or "traffic") improved performance only on types of problems with corresponding structure. For example, a traffic-flow model, but not a water-flow model, improved performance on problems involving resistors. Similarly, Burstein (1986) has observed the mixed impact of teaching the concept of a "variable" to novice programmers in relation to a "box" model (e.g., to *put* a number in a variable, as in "$X = 5$," is like putting an object in a box). Although this analogy provides a first approximation to the notion of a variable, it also leads to systematic errors. For example, the statement "$X = Y$" might be misinterpreted as indicating that the "box" Y is to be somehow placed inside the "box" X, or that the value of Y is to be moved into X leaving Y "empty."

Finally, an important question related to the role of prior knowledge concerns the effect of expertise in a topic area on transfer. Research on the development of expertise in technical fields such as physics indicates that experts shift their basis for categorizing problems from relatively surface attributes of problems to more abstract structural attributes that cue principles relevant to the solution (Chi *et al.*, 1981; Larkin, McDermott, Simon & Simon, 1980). The altered categories developed by experts will presumably change the perceived similarity of problems and hence affect various types of transfer (Novick, 1986). Gick (1986) noted that most research on expertise in problem solving compares experts with novices using problems that are fairly simple and familiar to novices. Research is needed to determine the conditions under which experts are able to transfer strategies to more difficult problems, including problems in areas outside, but related to, their domain of expertise.

IV. SUMMARY AND FUTURE DIRECTIONS

The research we have reviewed provides a detailed picture of the interrelationships between task structure, encoding and retrieval processes, and the prior knowledge of the learner, as these factors relate to transfer. Several broad principles emerged, which deserve brief reiteration. We drew a distinction between perceived similarity of the training and transfer situations, based on salient common features of their representations, and objective structural similarity, based on the actual nature of the task components determining appropriate responses. We argued that transfer is affected by both types of similarity. Perceived similarity determines whether transfer will be attempted, whereas objective structural similarity determines whether transfer will be positive or negative.

Several factors that influence perceived similarity were discussed. The structure of the tasks to be mastered places constraints on the representation that the learner can achieve (e.g., the complexity of an adequate set of rules for performing the task), which in turn influences the optimal learning strategy. The encoding of the training task will foster subsequent transfer to the extent that the learner acquires rules that will be applicable to a range of superficially different tasks with structural commonalities. If the transfer task evokes similar goals and processing mechanisms, or has salient surface resemblances to the training task, these common components then serve as the basis for retrieval of the acquired knowledge in the transfer context.

Several factors that influence learning and retention merit more extensive investigation in relation to transfer. One such factor is the role of context and contrast in determining the learner's representation of the training task. As noted in section III.D, novice problem solvers typically have difficulty attending to the structural components of problems, which determine the appropriate solution principles, and instead focus on surface features (Chi et al., 1981). An effective contrasting category might prove useful in focusing the learner's attention on the important features of the solution method that might distinguish it from other problems that use a different solution method, increasing the potential for later transfer to superficially different problems.

Another important influence on encoding of the training task is direct feedback about performance levels, often termed "knowledge of results." Feedback supplied during the acquisition phase increases the rate of learning. Feedback is not essential to learning in classification tasks if the categories are relatively discriminable, but it is nonetheless helpful, especially when the categories are based on highly variable instances (Fried & Holyoak, 1984; Homa & Cultice, 1984). Feedback concerning the correct move to be made facilitates learning for the Missionaries and Cannibals problem (Greeno, 1974; Thomas, 1974), and feedback supplied in the form of subgoals to be attained during problem solving facilitates transfer in visual maze-learning and Tower of Hanoi problems (Sweller, 1983). Delayed feedback results in slower learning of the functions of operators or moves in a game-learning situation (Lewis & Anderson, 1985). Delayed feedback can, however, be beneficial. Subjects in Lewis and Anderson's (1985) game-learning task who received delayed feedback learned to "back up" by recognizing "dead ends" (search paths that should be abandoned) because they had encountered them in training. In contrast, subjects who received immediate feedback had never encountered dead ends and therefore could not recognize them as easily. In addition, delayed feedback in a testing situation can increase retention (e.g., Kulhavey & Anderson, 1972) by reducing interference from incorrect responses. Work on delayed feedback has important educational implications and deserves to be explored more thoroughly.

Indeed, the robustness of transfer over long delays after learning is a general topic that requires greater attention. Given that a training task has been mastered, for how long will transfer persist? Will more general knowledge be available over longer intervals than specific knowledge? In at least one study of the use of analogy in problem solving, high levels of transfer were obtained after a delay of a few days (Holyoak & Koh, in press). Homa and Vosburgh (1976), extending work by Posner and Keele (1970), found evidence of selective retention of knowledge in a classification task: a delay reduced classification accuracy for highly distorted instances, but not for mildly distorted instances or the standard form. In memory tasks, delay sometimes actually facilitates transfer performance, perhaps by reducing interference (Thorndyke & Hayes-Roth, 1979). Further work is needed to distinguish transfer effects that are short-lived from those that are more permanent.

In addition, transfer should be more often examined over an extended series of transfer tasks. It is possible, for example, that transfer will not be apparent on the first attempt at a transfer task but will be triggered at some later time if the same or additional transfer tasks are repeated. Most contemporary research on transfer employs one transfer test, so that transfer is measured on a single occasion (but see Ross, 1984, in press, for exceptions). More sensitive indexes of transfer might be obtained if the impact of the training task were assessed as a function of the number and type of transfer tasks (Ferguson, 1956; Gagné, Foster, & Crowley, 1948). It is important to remember that a complex task may have numerous response components to be mastered; if prior learning affects some of these components, but others must be acquired independently, it is possible that no overt transfer will be observed in the early stages of learning the transfer task.

Future research on transfer is likely to have a major impact on our understanding of human cognition. Understanding the mechanisms of transfer is inextricably linked to our knowledge of human memory, learning, categorization, reasoning, and problem solving. Transfer phenomena, as they manifest themselves in these allied research domains, may reveal some of the most basic aspects of cognition. In addition, of course, fostering successful transfer of training remains a key goal of education. There is reason to hope that continued investigation of transfer will improve the ability of educators to grapple with this eminently practical concern.

ACKNOWLEDGMENTS

Preparation of this chapter was supported by Grant A1212 from the Natural Sciences and Engineering Research Council of Canada to M. Gick and Grant BNS-8216068 from the National Science Foundation to K. Holyoak. The chapter was written while K. Holyoak was supported by a National Institute of Mental Health Research Scientist Development Award. 1-K02-MH00342-05, and was a Visiting Scholar at the Learning Research and Development Center, University of Pittsburgh. Miriam Bassok, Joe Hagman, and Lise Paquet provided useful comments on an earlier draft.

REFERENCES

Anderson, J. R. (1983). *The architecture of cognition*. Cambridge, MA: Harvard University Press.

Anderson, J. R., Kline, P. J., & Beasley, C. M. (1979). A general learning theory and its application to schema abstraction. In G. H. Bower (Ed.), *The psychology of learning and motivation* (Vol. 13). New York: Academic Press.

Anzai, Y., & Simon, H. A. (1979). The theory of learning by doing. *Psychological Review, 86*, 124–140.

Auble, P. M., & Franks, J. J. (1978). The effects of effort toward comprehension on recall. *Memory and Cognition, 6*, 20–25.

Bassok, M., & Holyoak, K. J. (1987). *Schema-based interdomain transfer between isomorphic algebra and physics problems*. Manuscript in preparation. University of Pittsburgh, Learning Research and Development Center, Pittsburgh, PA.

Bransford, J. D., & Franks, J. J. (1976). Toward a framework for understanding learning. In G. H. Bower (Ed.), *The psychology of learning and motivation* (Vol. 10). New York: Academic Press.

Brooks, L. (1978). Nonanalytic concept formation and memory for instances. In E. Rosch & B. Lloyd (Eds.), *Cognition and categorization*. Hillsdale, NJ: Erlbaum.

Bruce, R. W. (1933). Conditions of transfer of training. *Journal of Experimental Psychology, 16*, 343–361.

Burstein, M. K. (1986). Concept formation by incremental analogical reasoning and debugging. In R. S. Michalski, J. G. Carbonell, & T. M. Mitchell (Eds.), *Machine learning: An artificial intelligence approach* (Vol. 2). Los Altos, CA: Kaufmann.

Cheng, P. W., Holyoak, K. J., Nisbett, R. E., & Oliver, L. M. (1986). Pragmatic versus syntactic approches to training deductive reasoning. *Cognitive Psychology, 18*, 293–328.

Chi, M., Feltovich, P., & Glaser, R. (1981). Categorization and representation of physics problems by experts and novices. *Cognitive Science, 5*, 121–152.

Collins, A. M., Warnock, E. H., Aiello, N., & Miller, M. L. (1975). Reasoning from incomplete knowledge. In D. G. Bobrow & A. M. Collins (Eds.), *Representation and understanding*. New York: Academic Press.

Craik, F. I. M. (1985). Paradigms in human memory research. In L. G. Nilsson & T. Archer (Eds.), *Perspectives in learning and memory*. Hillsdale, NJ: Erlbaum.

Duncker, K. (1945). On problem solving. *Psychological Monographs, 58*(No. 270).

Elio, R. (1986). Representation of similar well-learned cognitive procedures. *Cognitive Science, 10*, 41–73.

Elio, R., & Anderson, J. R. (1981). The effects of category generalizations and instance similarity on schema abstraction. *Journal of Experimental Psychology: Human Learning and Memory, 7*, 397–417.

Elio, R., & Anderson, J. R. (1984). The effects of information order and learning mode on schema abstraction. *Memory and Cognition, 12*, 20–30.

Ellis, H. C. (1965). *The transfer of learning*. New York: Macmillan.

Ferguson, G. (1956). On transfer and the abilities of man. *Canadian Journal of Psychology, 10*, 121–131.

Fong, G. T., Krantz, D. H., & Nisbett, R. E. (1986). The effects of statistical training on thinking about everyday problems. *Cognitive Psychology, 18*, 253–292.

Fried, L. S., & Holyoak, K. J. (1984). Induction of category distributions: A framework for classification learning. *Journal of Experimental Psychology: Learning, Memory and Cognition, 10*, 234–257.

Gagné, R. M., Foster, H., & Crowley, M. E. (1948). The measurement of transfer of training. *Psychological Bulletin, 45*, 97–130.

Gentner, D., & Gentner, D. R. (1983). Flowing waters or teeming crowds: Mental models of electricity. In D. Gentner & A. Stevens (Eds.), *Mental models*. Hillsdale, NJ: Erlbaum.

Gick, M. L. (1985). The effect of a diagram retrieval cue on spontaneous analogical transfer. *Canadian Journal of Psychology, 39*, 460–466.

Gick, M. L. (1986). Problem solving strategies. *Educational Psychologist, 21* (1 and 2), 99–120.

Gick, M. L., & Holyoak, K. J. (1980). Analogical problem solving. *Cognitive Psychology, 12*, 306–355.

Gick, M. L., & Holyoak, K. J. (1983). Schema induction and analogical transfer. *Cognitive Psychology, 15*, 1–38.

Greeno, J. G. (1974). Hobbits and orcs: Acquisition of a sequential concept. *Cognitive Psychology, 6*, 270–292.

Harlow, H. F. (1949). The formation of learning sets. *Psychological Review, 56*, 51–65.

Hayes, J. R., & Simon, H. A. (1977). Psychological differences among problem isomorphs. In N. J. Castellan, Jr., D. B. Pisoni, & G. Potts (Eds.), *Cognitive theory*. Hillsdale, NJ: Lawrence Erlbaum.

Hayes-Roth, R., & McDermott, J. (1978). An interference matching technique for inducing abstractions. *Communications of the ACM, 21*, 401–410.

Hesse, M. B. (1966). *Models and analogies in science*. Notre Dame, IN: University of Notre Dame Press.

Holland, J. H., Holyoak, K. J., Nisbett, R. E., & Thagard, P. R. (1986). *Induction: Processes of inference, learning, and discovery*. Cambridge, MA: MIT Press.

Holyoak, K. J. (1985). The pragmatics of analogical transfer. In G. H. Bower (Ed.), *The psychology of learning and motivation* (Vol. 19). New York: Academic Press.

Holyoak, K. J. & Koh, K. (in press). *Surface and structural similarity in analogical transfer. Memory and Cognition.*

Homa, D., & Cultice, J. (1984). Role of feedback, category size, and stimulus distortion on the acquisition and utilization of ill-defined categories. *Journal of Experimental Psychology: Learning, Memory and Cognition, 10*, 83–94.

Homa, D., & Vosburgh, R. (1976). Category breadth and the abstraction of prototypical information. *Journal of Experimental Psychology: Human Learning and Memory, 2*, 322–330.

Horton, K. (1985). The role of semantic information in reading spatially transformed text. *Cognitive Psychology, 17*, 66–88.

Jacoby, L. L. (1983). Remembering the data: Analyzing interactive processes in reading. *Journal of Verbal Learning and Verbal Behavior, 22*, 485–508.

Jenkins, J. J. (1979). Four points to remember: A tetrahedral model of memory experiments. In L. S. Cermak & F. I. M. Craik (Eds.), *Levels of processing and human memory.* Hillsdale, NJ: Erlbaum.

Kotovsky, K., Hayes, J. R., & Simon, H. A. (1985). Why are some problems hard? Evidence from Tower of Hanoi. *Cognitive Psychology, 17*, 248–294.

Kulhavey, R. W., & Anderson, R. C. (1972). Delay-retention effect with multiple choice tests. *Journal of Educational Psychology, 63*, 505–512.

Larkin, J., McDermott, J., Simon, D., & Simon, H. A. (1980). Expert and novice performance in solving physics problems. *Science, 208*, 1335–1342.

Levy, B. A. (1983). Proofreading familiar text: Constraints on visual processing. *Memory and Cognition, 11*, 1–12.

Lewis, M., & Anderson, J. R. (1985). Discrimination of operator schemata in problem solving: Learning from examples. *Cognitive Psychology, 17*, 26–65.

Lockhart, R. S., Lamon, M., & Gick, M. L. (1987). *Conceptual transfer in simple insight problems.* Manuscript submitted for publication.

Luchins, A. (1942). Mechanization in problem solving. *Psychological Monographs, 54*(No. 248).

Lung, C. T., & Dominowski, R. (1985). Effects of strategy instructions and practice on nine-dot problem solving. *Journal of Experimental Psychology: Learning, Memory and Cognition, 11*, 804–811.

Mandler, G. (1962). From association to structure. *Psychological Review, 69*, 415–427.

Mawer, R. F., & Sweller, J. (1982). Effects of subgoal density and location on learning during problem solving. *Journal of Experimental Psychology: Learning, Memory, and Cognition, 8*, 252–259.

Mayer, R. E. (1975). Different problem-solving competencies established in learning computer programming with and without meaningful models. *Journal of Educational Psychology, 67*, 725–734.

Mayer, R. E. (1985). Learning in complex domains: A cognitive analysis of computer programming. In G. H. Bower (Ed.)., *The psychology of learning and motivation* (Vol. 19). New York: Academic Press.

Mayer, R. E., & Greeno, J. G. (1972). Structural differences between learning outcomes produced by different instructional methods. *Journal of Educational Psychology, 63*, 165–173.

McAndrews, M. P., & Moscovitch, M. (1985). Rule-based and exemplar-based classification in artificial grammar learning. *Memory and Cognition, 13*, 469–475.

Medin, D. L., & Schaffer, M. M. (1978). Context theory of classification learning. *Psychological Review, 85*, 207–238.

Medin, D. L., & Smith, E. E. (1981). Strategies and classification learning. *Journal of Experimental Psychology: Human Learning and Memory, 7*, 241–253.

Newell, A. (1973). Production systems: Models of control structures. In W. G. Chase (Ed.), *Visual information processing.* New York: Academic Press.

Nitsch, K. (1977). *Structuring decontextualized forms of knowledge.* Unpublished doctoral dissertation. Vanderbilt University, Nashville, TN.

Novick, L. (1986). *Analogical transfer in expert and novice problem solvers.* Unpublished doctoral dissertation, Stanford University, Stanford, CA.

Osgood, C. E. (1949). The similarity paradox in human learning: A resolution. *Psychological Review, 56*, 132–143.

Owen, E., & Sweller, J. (1985). What do students learn while solving mathematics problems? *Journal of Educational Psychology, 77*, 272-284.

Perfetto, G., Bransford, J., & Franks, J. (1983). Constraints on access in a problem solving context. *Memory and Cognition, 11*, 24-31.

Peterson, M. J., Meagher, R. B., Jr., Chait, H., & Gillie, S. (1973). The abstraction and generalization of dot patterns. *Cognitive Psychology, 4*, 378-398.

Posner, M., & Keele, S. (1968). On the genesis of abstract ideas. *Journal of Experimental Psychology, 77*, 353-363.

Posner, M., & Keele, S. (1970). Retention of abstract ideas. *Journal of Experimental Psychology, 83*, 304-308.

Reber, A. S. (1967). Implicit learning of artificial grammars. *Journal of Verbal Learning and Verbal Behavior, 5*, 855-863.

Reber, A. S. (1976). Implicit learning of synthetic languages: The role of instructional set. *Journal of Experimental Psychology: Human Learning and Memory, 2*, 88-94.

Reber, A. S., & Allen, R. (1978). Analogic and abstraction strategies in synthetic grammar learning: A functionalist approach. *Cognition, 6*, 189-221.

Reber, A. S., Kassin, S. M., Lewis S., & Cantor, G. W. (1980). On the relationship between implicit and explicit modes in the learning of a complex rule structure. *Journal of Experimental Psychology: Human Learning and Memory, 6*, 492-502.

Reed, S., Dempster, A., & Ettinger, M. (1985). Usefulness of analogous solutions for solving algebra word problems. *Journal of Experimental Psychology: Learning, Memory, and Cognition, 11*, 106-125.

Reed, S., Ernst, G., & Banerji, R. (1974). The role of analogy in transfer between similar problem states. *Cognitive Psychology, 6*, 436-456.

Riley, M. S., Greeno, J. G., & Heller, J. I. (1982). Development of children's problem-solving ability in arithmetic. In H. P. Ginsburg (Ed.), *The development of mathematical thinking*. New York: Academic Press.

Rosch, E. (1978). Principles of categorization. In E. Rosch & B. B. Lloyd (Eds.), *Cognition and categorization*. Hillsdale, NJ: Erlbaum.

Ross, B. H. (1984). Remindings and their effects in learning a cognitive skill. *Cognitive Psychology, 16*, 371-416.

Ross, B. H. (in press). *The use of earlier problems and the separation of similarity effects. Journal of Experimental Psychology: Learning, Memory and Cognition.*

Ross, B. H., & Sofka, M. D. (1987). *Remindings: Noticing, remembering, and using specific knowledge of earlier problems.* Manuscript submitted for publication.

Schank, R. C. (1982). *Dynamic memory.* London and New York: Cambridge University Press.

Sweller, J. (1980). Hypothesis salience, task difficulty and sequential effects on problem solving. *American Journal of Psychology, 93*, 135-145.

Sweller, J. (1983). Control strategies in problem solving. *Memory and Cognition, 11*, 32-40.

Sweller, J., & Levine, M. (1982). Effects of goal specificity on means-ends-analysis and learning. *Journal of Experimental Psychology: Learning, Memory, and Cognition, 8*, 463-474.

Sweller, J., Mawer, R., & Howe, W. (1982). Consequences of history-cued and means–ends strategies in problem solving. *American Journal of Psychology, 95*, 455-483.

Sweller, J., Mawer, R., & Ward, M. (1983). Development of expertise in mathematical problem solving. *Journal of Experimental Psychology: General, 112*, 639-661.

Thomas, J. L., Jr. (1974). An analysis of behavior in the hobbits-orcs problem. *Cognitive Psychology, 6*, 257-269.

Thorndike, E. L. (1903). *Educational psychology.* New York: Lemcke & Buechner.

Thorndyke, P., & Hayes-Roth, B. (1979). The use of schemata in the acquisition and transfer of knowledge. *Cognitive Psychology, 11*, 82-106.

Thyne, J. M. (1963). *The psychology of learning and techniques of teaching.* London: University of London Press.

Tulving, E., Schacter, D., & Stark, H. A. (1982). Priming effects in word-fragment completion are independent of recognition memory. *Journal of Experimental Psychology: Learning, Memory, and Cognition, 8*, 336–342.

Tulving, E., & Thomson, D. M. (1973). Encoding specificity and retrieval processes in episodic memory. *Psychological Review, 80*, 352–373.

Tversky, A. (1977). Features of similarity. *Psychological Review, 84*, 327–352.

Tversky, A., & Gati, I. (1978). Studies in similarity. In E. Rosch & B. B. Lloyd (Eds.), *Cognition and categorization*. Hillsdale, NJ: Erlbaum.

Weisberg, R., & Alba, J. (1981). An examination of the alleged role of "fixation" in the solution of several "insight" problems. *Journal of Experimental Psychology: General, 110*, 169–192.

Weisberg, R., Di Camillo, M., & Phillips, D. (1978). Transferring old associations to new situations: A non-automatic process. *Journal of Verbal Learning and Verbal Behavior, 17*, 219–228.

Winston, P. H. (1975). Learning structural descriptions from examples. In P. H. Winston (Ed.), *The psychology of computer vision*. New York: McGraw Hill.

Woodworth, R. S., & Schlosberg, H. (1954). *Experimental psychology*. New York: Holt.

Wylie, H. H. (1919). An experimental study of transfer of response in the white rat. *Behavioral Monographs, 3*(No. 16).

CHAPTER 3

Transfer of Movement Control in Motor Skill Learning

RICHARD A. SCHMIDT
DOUGLAS E. YOUNG

One important concern for any examination of human learning—and of the aspects of learning concerned with transfer discussed in this book—is the area of skilled *motor* behavior and its acquisition. It is difficult to provide a simple distinction between those aspects of human functioning that we wish to term "motor" and "nonmotor," and yet these divisions of human responding are generally understood. The difficulty is that, on the one hand, every "motor" response (except perhaps simple reflexes) has a perceptual-cognitive component and requires at least minimal decision making. On the other hand, even the most "cognitive" of tasks involves a movement of some sort in order that the subject convey a response to the experimenter (a button press, or verbal report).

Nevertheless, it makes sense to consider a motor/nonmotor dichotomy, if by it we mean that "motor" tasks are those for which the primary problem for the responder is to determine *how to produce a given action* which is clearly specified by instructions and/or stimulus materials, rather than to determine *which of a number of previously learned actions* to produce when a particular stimulus situation is encountered. This focus on "motor" behavior emphasizes how the performer controls his or her limbs in ways that we term skilled (piano playing, pole vaulting, etc.), where the precise patterning and timing of muscle forces are the primary determinants of success, and where decisions and the choice *among* movement patterns of activity are minimized. Thus, motor behavior involves situations in which the learner's problem is "how to do it" rather than "what to do" (Schmidt, 1982).

47

This chapter is concerned with transfer of learning in situations involving the kinds of responses that we have defined here as primarily motor behaviors. Specifically, we have focused on research where *movement control* is learned in one situation and transferred to another, where findings often provide insight into the nature of the representations that are learned and transferred. We have deliberately de-emphasized research examining the transfer of perceptual, cognitive, or information-processing capabilities, because these are addressed in the chapter by Cormier. Thus, our two chapters here can be seen as providing complimentary treatments of the motor and cognitive bases of transfer (see also Lintern, 1985).

I. TRANSFER: DEFINITIONAL ISSUES

Transfer of learning is usually defined as the gain (or loss) in the capability for responding on a transfer or criterion task as a function of practice or experience on a training task. Transfer is involved when we want to understand how (nonsimultaneous) tasks contribute to, or interact with, each other in training situations, and it forms the basis for understanding training efforts involving the use of simulators for learning complex criterion tasks (e.g., piloting a 747), the use of various instructional strategies (e.g., lead-up activities), and the intelligent design of effective environments for maximizing learning. Here, the focus is on how learning one *task* affects the performance capability of another *task*.

A. PROBLEMS IN DEFINING A "TASK"

The field of transfer has a problem in precisely defining what a task is and how one task is identified as being different from another. Consider pairs of activities such as (a) throwing a ball 20 m versus 25 m or (b) skiing in sunlight versus moonlight. Do the activities within each pair represent different tasks, or merely variations of the "same" task? We often arbitrarily define two "tasks" by altering minor goal requirements (distance thrown) or performance conditions (lighting conditions). It is clear, however, that one can progressively change these conditions along various continua so that, beyond some point, we would all agree that two "tasks" have been formed by such alterations (e.g., throwing 2 m versus throwing 100 m).

We can carry this extension somewhat further. If it can be argued that minor variations in an activity (e.g., distance thrown) produce two different tasks, then the same can be said for variations which occur "naturally" in the course of learning to throw an object, say, exactly 30 m. Because of the inherent variability in such actions, some of the throws will be too long, others too short, and we must according to this argument consider each of these throws as examples of "different" tasks. It is also well known that the structure of the underlying abilities required for effective task performance shifts with practice (e.g., Fleishman & Hempel, 1955; Schmidt, 1982). Thus, it could be argued that a task is "different" (in terms of its factorial structure) in early practice than it is in late practice. If so, then performance on Trial n of any motor task is dependent on the transfer from Trial $n - 1$ and all previous trials.

B. Implications for Understanding Learning

This realization has important implications for the study of learning and transfer. If this analysis is correct, then many earlier approaches in which the transfer of learning was considered as a particular *category* of learning, with its own laws, experimental designs, and spaces allotted in textbooks, are not defensible. Rather, our view implies that transfer and learning are indistinguishable and that care should be taken when searching for the principles of transfer as if they were in some way distinct from those of learning.

II. FUNDAMENTAL PRINCIPLES OF MOTOR BEHAVIOR AND CONTROL

Consistent with the notion that the goal of transfer research is to understand the nature of what is learned and transferred, we have found it useful to bring some of the recent findings and concepts in the area of movement control and learning—which recently have focused on the underlying representations for actions—to bear on the problems of movement transfer. In the next few sections, we discuss some of the concepts of movement control, and then we turn to a discussion of how they contribute to a better understanding of movement transfer.

A. Motor Programs

One of the most important ideas in motor control is that (at least some) movements are controlled by an open-loop process, with a centrally "stored" structure (motor program) responsible for the grading, timing, and coordination of muscular activities necessary for skilled movement behavior. The motor program idea has had many forms, and it is difficult to characterize the various notions under this banner. There are, however, a few features which serve to define these kinds of ideas reasonably well. Three lines of evidence support the existence of motor programs.

First, the results of early (Lashley, 1917) and more recent (Taub & Berman, 1968) deafferentation research have shown that movements are possible without sensory feedback from the responding limb. Some movements, such as those involved in climbing, swinging, and grooming in monkeys, are controlled well without feedback, whereas others such as fine finger movements show serious disruptions. The major point, however, is not how much they are disrupted under these conditions but that movement can occur at all. These findings support the notion that some central representation not absolutely dependent on response-produced feedback is responsible for movement control. At the same time, these data weaken a large class of models emphasizing chaining of responses to feedback produced from a prior part of the chain (e.g., James, 1890) or closed-loop models based strictly on error nulling (Adams, 1971).

A second line of evidence suggests that sensory information processing is too slow for effective moment-to-moment control in rapid movements. Systems that use response-produced feedback are very sensitive to feedback delays and will oscillate uncontrollably if feedback is delayed too much (particularly so if the gain of the feedback loop is large). Although response-produced sensory feedback undoubtedly plays a role in slower, ongoing movements (e.g., steering a car), it is unlikely that quick responses can be controlled in this way. Considerable evidence shows us that subjects who are suddenly and unexpectedly asked to change a movement in progress (Henry & Harrison, 1961), or to abort it completely (Logan, 1982; Slater-Hammel, 1960), cannot change the movement response before approximately 200 ms has elapsed. Presumably, the movement is being controlled by some motor program in the mean time.

The existence of motor programs is further strengthened by the findings from research on the control of rapid limb movements (Magill, Schmidt, Shapiro, & Young, 1987; Shapiro & Walter, 1984; Wadman, Denier van der Gon, Geuze, & Mol, 1979). These experiments record electrical activity from contracting muscles (via electromyograph—EMG) to show that muscular patterns are structured in advance (by a motor program). In Figure 1 are EMG records from one of Wadman et al.'s (1979) experiments in which the subject made a quick elbow-shoulder extension movement to a new position 15 cm away. The trace labeled "normal" shows the patterning of EMGs during the normal execution of this movement. It reveals a distinct temporal structure in which the agonist is active for about 100 ms, followed by the antagonist activity, with the agonist acting again near the end of the movement. A feedback-based view of movement control would argue that the observed patterning is determined by sensory information from the responding limb switching the muscles on and off.[1] Wadman et al. (1979), however, also used a condition in which the limb was unexpectedly blocked mechanically to prevent movement from occurring. The EMG patterns for

[1]Other models, also using sensory information from the responding musculature as a critical feature, are possible also. See Fel'dman (1974, 1986) for one such example, and Schmidt (1986) for a critique of it.

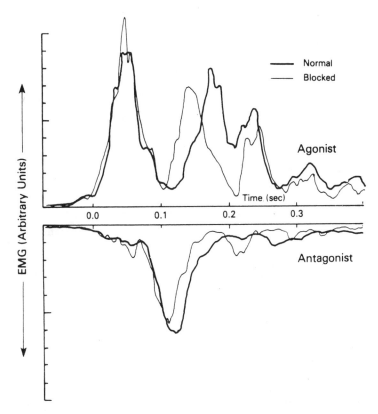

Figure 1. Rectified EMG patterns from a rapid arm movement (Normal), and for trials (Blocked) on which the movement was unexpectedly blocked mechanically; many features of the EMG patterns occurred even though the limb was prevented from moving. (After Wadman *et al.*, 1979.)

the "blocked" movement are almost identical to those for the "normal" movements for the first 100 ms or so and then are modified (presumably reflexively) during the later portion of the movement. The important point is that the antagonist muscle is switched on at the proper time, even though the feedback from the "responding" limb was disrupted. This suggests that the patterning of the EMGs was structured before the movement and was carried out in an open-loop process, at least until the reflexive activities could exert an influence.

A third line of evidence comes from an analysis of movement reaction time (RT) conducted by Henry and Rogers (1960). Here, movement RT depended on the "complexity" of the response. Because RT measurement begins when the stimulus appears and ends when the movement begins, it is difficult to understand how RT, which occurs *before* the movement, could be affected by something that occurred later (i.e., movement complexity). Presumably, the motor system is organized, during a response-programming substage of RT, to produce the required movement and that more "complex" movements require additional time for such processes to occur.

1. Feedback Involvement

Original statements of the program view (e.g., Lashley, 1917), and even more recent ones (e.g., Keele, 1968), have been too strong in insisting that the movement control be strictly open loop, with essentially *no* involvement from peripheral feedback. Evidence has always favored feedback control of slower movements, and more recent evidence suggests considerable feedback involvement in movement control even for quicker actions. For example, there is now strong evidence of spindle contributions to the fine details of an ongoing response and that these spindle activities may be responsible for compensations in unexpected loads (Dewhurst, 1967) or the maintenance of important mechanical (springlike) properties of muscles (Crago, Houk, & Hasan, 1976). Recent work suggests that vision can also operate far more quickly than we had earlier believed (Zelaznik, Hawkins, & Kisselburgh, 1983). In addition, Forssberg, Grillner, and Rossignol (1975) have found that a specific stimulus presented during locomotion (e.g., a tap on the top of a cat's foot) leads to a completely different response depending on the phase of the step cycle in which the stimulus is delivered. Analogous findings have been reported in speech motor control by Abbs, Gracco, and Cole (1984) and Kelso, Tuller, Vatikoitis-Bateson, and Fowler (1984). These so-called reflex reversals can be interpreted to mean that motor programs, in addition to controlling commands to musculature, are also involved in the "choice" of reflex pathways. Presumably, this ensures that particular subgoals of an action are carried out faithfully during that phase if the limb is perturbed.

These results do not detract at all from the idea that movements are centrally represented and that feedback can interact with this central structure. Under consistent movement conditions, where peripheral influences are predictable or absent, the central representation could assume the dominant role in movement production.

2. Summary

The main idea is that at least quick movements are organized in advance, with some central representation defining the muscular activities that are to occur. Movement is then initiated and carried out, with minimal involvement from response-produced feedback. Current thinking is that some oscillator-like neural network (motor program, coordinative structure, central pattern generator, etc.) is activated and that the rhythmic properties of this structure are responsible for the control of movement timing, with this control lasting for 1 s, or longer (Shapiro, 1978).

B. GENERALIZED MOTOR PROGRAMS

Researchers have been concerned that the notion of motor programming seems to require that *each* movement have a separate program to control it. This has led to logical problems about where so many programs could be stored and how novel movements could be produced (Schmidt, 1975, 1976, 1982). Various attempts to save the attractive features of movement programs discussed above, while addressing these storage and novelty problems, have resulted in various ways of considering how motor programs could be generalized across a class of movements.

1. Rate Parameters

The first suggestion of a generalized motor program came from Armstrong's (1970) experiment in which subjects learned a complex arm movement pattern defined in both space and time. In Figure 2, the criterion pattern is shown as the solid line, and a movement that happened to end too early is shown as the dotted trace. Armstrong observed that when the movement was performed too quickly, the whole movement sped up as a unit. Notice that the dotted trace leads the solid one by only 90 ms at the first peak, by 230 ms at the trough (downward "peak"), and by 620 ms at the third peak. Thus, the entire movement was sped up more or less proportionally. This suggested that the movement might be represented as an abstract temporal structure that could be produced on any trial by selecting a *rate parameter* to define the particular movement time, while maintaining an invariant temporal structure.

2. Relative Timing

Important to this idea was the identification of an invariant feature of the movement, one that remained essentially constant while others (e.g., overall movement time) changed (Schmidt, 1985a). One such feature is *relative timing*, which measures the overall temporal structure of the action. Invariant relative timing means that the proportion of time devoted to movement segments (e.g., the time from the first peak until the second) remains constant while the total movement time changes. This invariance seems to be present because the value for the solid trace ($2.94 - 0.75/3.59 = 0.61$), and that for the dotted trace ($2.28 - .066/2.90 = .056$) are approximately the same. Although the invariance is not perfect in this example, it does suggest that some underlying timing structure is operating.

These and later findings in rapid limb movements (Shapiro, 1978; Summers, 1977), typing (Terzuolo & Viviani, 1979), and locomotion

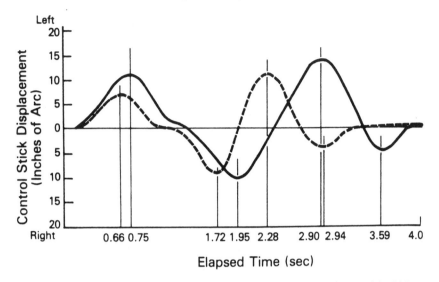

Figure 2. Position-time trace of a criterion movement pattern (solid) and of a trial which was performed too rapidly (dotted); the dotted trace appears to be roughly "compressed" in time. (After Armstrong, 1970.)

(Shapiro, Zernicke, Gregor, & Diestel 1981) show general support for the notion of invariant timing and thereby provide one solution to the storage and novelty problems associated with earlier motor program concepts. Further, they suggest that an abstract motor program structure is one product of motor learning and that each program might have a particular relative timing "signature," allowing us to recognize when one program or another has been produced (e.g., Schmidt, 1982, 1985b). These "signatures" could also provide evidence of *what* is transferred if it were shown that a particular timing structure learned in the training task is also present in the criterion task after transfer.

3. Other Movement Parameters

The research supporting an invariance in relative timing has also revealed other ways that movements can be varied while retaining their original relative timing structure. One common example is the parameter of movement size, revealed particularly well in handwriting. Consider one's signature, written on a check versus on a blackboard, where there is approximately a 10-fold difference between them. The two patterns, reduced photographically to the same size, are nearly identical (Merton, 1972), suggesting that the same pattern was produced in both instances, but with a variable amplitude parameter. This example is interesting from another perspective when one realizes that the muscles and joints involved in the two actions are different. Check-sized writing involves mainly the fingers, with the "heel" of the hand fixed on the writing surface; blackboard writing involves essentially fixing the fingers, and moving the elbow and shoulder joints. The similarity between these patterns implies that the movement representation was more abstract than the level of specific muscles and joints. In addition, other parameters, such as direction (Shapiro & Schmidt, 1983), loading (Denier van der Gon & Thuring, 1965; Sherwood, Schmidt, & Walter, 1987), and the slant in writing (Hollerbach, 1981), have been identified. This work suggests that movements learned in one condition can be *easily* transferred to another condition requiring the same underlying temporal structure.

4. Current Status of the Generalized Motor Program Concept

In reviewing this research over the past decade, some general conclusions can now be stated. First, there is clear evidence that the patterns of activity in skilled and innate actions "expand" and "contract" with changes in movement time, with the various segments in the action being nearly proportional to movement time. A careful analysis of this problem by Gentner (1985), however, reveals that a *proportional* expansion model is too simple to account for the data. And various nonlinear expansions have been shown both in limb movement studies (Schmidt, Sherwood, Zelaznik, & Leikind, 1985; Zelaznik, Schmidt, & Gielen, 1986) and in speech motor control (Kelso *et al.*, 1984; Ostry & Cooke, in press). Although these data detract from the idea of a simple, abstract, temporally organized movement program, they do not deny the involvement of *some* abstract structure. In addition, they do not detract substantially from the idea that these abstract structures, however defined, are a major basis for the learning and transfer of movement control.

C. MOVEMENT SPECIFICITY

We turn now to a completely different set of findings from the work on individual differences in skills. These investigations, using entirely separate methodology, tasks, and analyses, have consistently shown that movement skills are *specific*. That is, even skills that appear to be quite similar to each other show very low intercorrelations. Evidence supporting this phenomenon originates from two different but related lines of research.

1. Intercorrelations

The formation of the *specificity* concept for motor behavior appeared against a backdrop of thinking about the generality of motor (and cognitive) abilities that had emerged from the factor analytic work of the 1930s, in which a "general motor ability" was thought to underlie much of human motor responding. Although it was never precisely spelled out, the overall idea was that motor behavior was based on a relatively small number of movement capabilities, such as "balance," "eye-hand coordination," "agility," and the like. It was not until the 1960s that the underlying structure of movement skills was studied in earnest, with Fleishman's (e.g., 1965) work leading the way.

Back in the 1950s and 1960s, Henry (e.g., 1968) noticed that the correlations among a wide variety of movement skills were never very large. Even tasks which required almost identical skills, and thus were based on the same ability structures, showed low intercorrelations. One example from this series is Bachman's (1961) study of two balancing tasks (i.e., the stabilometer balance platform and the Bachman ladder-climb task). The correlation between these two tasks, for subjects of different ages and sexes, ranged from +.25 to −.15, with an average correlation close to 0. This was surprising to many who expected an important "balancing ability" to account for much more of the variance between these two tasks.

An impressive volume of work on various motor skills shows that the correlations among tasks are generally very low. For example, Parker and Fleishman (1960) studied 50 widely varied tasks and evaluated the intercorrelations among them as a basis for later factor analysis. Of the 1,225 separate correlations, most were on the order of .40 or lower, and only rarely was there a correlation greater than .50. Thus, motor skills tend to be poorly correlated with one another unless they are essentially identical.

The usual interpretation of these findings is that the underlying abilities for movement skills tend to be very *specific* to the task. Henry's (1958/1968) and Fleishman's (e.g., 1957) views are that the number of abilities underlying all motor behavior is very large, perhaps 100 or so. Each skill, therefore, has a large number of these abilities supporting it, and these abilities are "selected" differently depending on the exact nature of the task. Even a slight modification in task requirements, such as a shift in the control-display relationship, the overall force requirement, or the role of sensory information, would be expected to require a substantial number of different abilities. Because these abilities are presumably independent, subtle shifts in task requirements cause the correlations to drop sharply. Even though we might agree subjectively that two tasks were the same and assign them the same name (e.g., a test of "anticipation"), they might not correlate to any appreciable degree.

2. Shifting Ability Structure with Practice

Another principle emerging from the work on motor skills, with important implications for understanding transfer, is that the pattern of abilities underlying a skill appears to shift with practice. For example, Fleishman and Rich (1963) had subjects learn a two-hand coordination task, in which

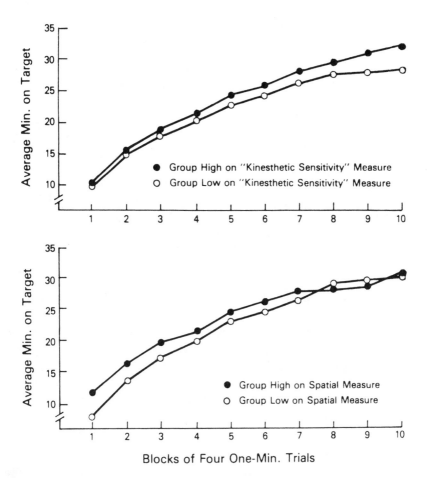

Figure 3. Performance on the two-hand coordination test over trials. Top: groups classified as high and low on kinesthetic sensitivity; bottom: groups classified as high and low on spatial relations. (After Fleishman & Rich, 1963.)

movements of two handwheels had to be coordinated to cause a pointer to follow a target. Subjects were tested separately on two other tasks—a kinesthetic sensitivity task involving judging the differences among lifted weights and a spatial relations test involving awareness of spatial orientation. They were then divided into two groups based on how they performed on these two tests. Performance on the two-hand coordination test was then plotted separately for each group, although both were treated *identically*.

Figure 3 (top) shows the two-hand coordination test scores for subjects grouped as high and low on kinesthetic sensitivity. Although no performance difference was found between groups early in practice, a difference favoring the high-sensitivity group did emerge as practice continued. Thus, kinesthetic sensitivity became increasingly important with continued practice on the task. The bottom panel shows the two-hand coordination performances for the groups classified as high and low on the spatial relations test. Here, "high" subjects performed more effectively than "low" subjects during early stages of practice, but this difference disappeared during later stages of practice. Generally, the interpretation of this work has been that the pattern of abilities underlying a given skill shifts with practice, with some abilities (e.g., kinesthetic sensitivity) becoming more important with practice, others (e.g., spatial relations) becoming less important. One is tempted to say that the cognitive abilities seem to drop out, while motor abilities come more into play. But it is clearly more complicated than this, as Adams (1953) has shown that verbal abilities can become more important, and motor abilities can become less important, with practice.

III. PRINCIPLES OF MOTOR TRANSFER

In this section, we consider some of the more common "kinds" of transfer, or at least situations or experimental designs in which transfer is seen. After describing some generalizations from the empirical work, updated with the relatively few new findings in this area from the past decade, we provide an analysis in terms of the principles of movement control discussed in the previous sections.

A. MEASUREMENT OF MOTOR TRANSFER

We will first describe the "amount of transfer" found in motor task situations, where a rough estimate of this "amount" can be obtained through *percentage transfer*. Consider a simple two-group design, in which both groups transfer to the criterion Task B, but where Group I practices some Task A beforehand and Group B does not. Some hypothetical results (shown in Figure 4, left) show that Group II performs more effectively than Group I on the first Task B trial(s) to provide evidence for positive transfer from Task A to B. Considering the improvement on Task B by Group II (i.e., $X - C$ in the figure) as a kind of total, the gain in initial performance of Group I over Group II (i.e., $X - Y$) can be expressed as a percentage of this total [i.e., $(X - Y)/(X - C) \times 100$]. Negative transfer is shown on the right. Although these and similar measures (Murdock, 1957) have limitations (see the chapter by Boldovici), they do provide some insight into the magnitude of motor transfer.

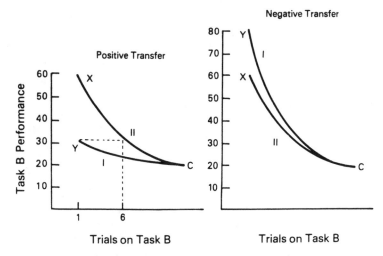

Figure 4. Hypothetical performance curves on Task B for Group I (prior practice on Task A) and Group II (no prior practice on Task A); percentage transfer is $[(X - Y)/(X - C) \times 100]$ both for positive transfer (left) and negative transfer (right) situations. (From Schmidt, 1982.)

B. Transfer among Different Motor Tasks

When such measures are applied to experiments on motor transfer, the outcomes are relatively consistent: Motor transfer is generally very small. Consider a case in which the various "tasks" were formed by varying the speeds of pursuit-rotor rotation (e.g., Lordahl & Archer, 1958; Namikas & Archer, 1960), with groups practicing at either 40 or 80 rpm before being transferred to a 60-rpm criterion task. From our computations of percentage transfer to the 60-rpm task, transfer never exceeded 64%, and the average percentage transfer computed across these various experiments was only 37%. This low transfer is remarkable, considering that the tasks were essentially the same, with only minor variations in speed. When the pursuit rotor is varied by changing the radius of rotation on the rotor, transfer in the Lordahl-Archer (1958) study was somewhat higher (54% by our computations) than for changes in speed, which lends support to our previous notion that changes in the temporal structure are more detrimental to transfer than changes in size.

These findings of low transfer are consistent with some of the principles from the motor control literature discussed earlier. First, when task requirements are shifted slightly (e.g., different speeds for the pursuit rotor) to produce two "different" tasks, the literature on specificy suggests that the two variations would not correlate well with each other, implying considerable differences in the underlying ability structures of the tasks. If so, then it is understandable how even slight shifts in the response requirements, which subjectively only alter the task in a minor way, may actually provide massive changes in the skills and in the underlying motor control requirements of the task. Thus an important point from this literature, as viewed from a motor control perspective, is how "fragile" the structure of tasks is to variations in response requirements.

These results on low transfer among skills seem surprising in view of the work on generalized motor programs. One idea was that a given program could be used at different speeds, maintaining the relative timing structure, simply by using a different speed parameter. One could ask, therefore, why variations in the pursuit-rotor speed did not show large positive transfer, because each variant would presumably be controlled by the same structure, but with a different overall rate parameter. We have no particularly satisfying answers. One possibility, however, is that the "span" of variations over which a generalized motor program can operate is much narrower than the motor control literature suggests. Thus, variations in rotor speed might not have resulted in simply parametric changes, but could have produced a shift from one program to another. If so, there should be little reason to expect much positive transfer among speeds because there is good reason to suspect that these programs are distinct and generally nonoverlapping. Determining the "span" of movement programs is a difficult empirical question because of problems in distinguishing (a) two different variations of a given program from (b) two different programs (Schmidt, 1985b), and good answers are not available at present.

Another possibility is that shifting the speed requirements of these tasks disrupts not only the motor control requirement but also the cognitive plans (e.g., information processing, strategies) of the learner. For example, a shift in speed could change the percived subgoals of the task (e.g., being quick versus being accurate), the attentional focus of the subject (attending to what has happened versus what will happen), the strategies (Fumoto, 1981) brought by the learner, or any combination of these plans. All are possible in tasks like rotary pursuit, where ample time is available during a 30-s trial to process sensory information, modify strategies, and the like, because not all the performance is determined by the effectiveness of some motor program as it would be in a more rapid movement. If so, then these changes in the fundamental information-processing activities when the movement requirements are changed even slightly may explain the relatively small transfer found.

C. BILATERAL TRANSFER

Bilateral transfer is one of the oldest subdivisions of the transfer problem (e.g., Davis, 1898) and was studied extensively early in this century using tasks like handwriting, drawing and figure production, and maze learning

(Cook, 1934; Weig, 1932; see Ammons, 1958, for a review). Although all of this work required manual responding, the "motorness" of these tasks was not particularly high. In most cases, the transfer produced could be attributed largely to the subject's symbolic learning of the maze structure, the figure, and so on, and applying this largely cognitive representation to the production of the same response with the other hand. This literature and similar recent additions (e.g., Dunham, 1977; Puretz, 1983; Tsuji & Ide, 1974) represent additional support and some limitations (e.g., Hicks, Frank, & Kinsbourne, 1982) for bilateral effects but unfortunately do not provide much insight into the nature of *motor* transfer.

Tasks which require more complex motor skills do provide insight into this problem. One example comes from Shapiro (1977), who had subjects learn a complex wrist-rotation task similar to that used by Armstrong (1970; see Figure 1). The learner had to move to seven target positions in the correct order and in the proper time (i.e., 1,600 ms). Subjects practiced this task for 5 days with the right hand, receiving feedback of their spatiotemporal patterns after each trial from a computer screen. The average movement patterns produced on the 5th day are shown in Figure 5 (open circles). These patterns are expressed in terms of *relative timing*, where the proportion of the total movement time for each segment provides a description of the temporal structure. This patterning changed considerably over the 5 days, and that shown here is the result of considerable practice.

On the 5th day, Shapiro unexpectedly asked her subjects to perform the task again but this time with the *left* hand. The solid circles in Figure 5 represent the proportions for these left-handed trials. It is immediately apparent that the left-hand patterning was almost identical to that produced with the right hand, demonstrating very high transfer from the right to left sides. This was true even though the left- and right-hand movements were not anatomically opposite to each other; the same *directions* of the handle were required for each limb, thus requiring opposite movement directions and muscle groupings (defined anatomically). Thus, something abstract was being transferred, which was not related to the specific muscles and joints involved.

These results, at first glance, might not be seen as involving *motor* transfer, because the abstract basis for transfer could be some cognitive representation of "what to do." Other evidence, however, converges to suggest a more "motoric" interpretation. Other aspects of Shapiro's work (right-handed performances only) showed that when subjects were asked to speed up this movement pattern, they did so with only minor shifts in the temporal patterning; and, when they were asked to speed up these patterns, and to ignore the timing they learned in previous practice, they again maintained the relative timing. This evidence, plus other work cited earlier, strongly suggests that the representation for action was a kind of generalized motor program that was

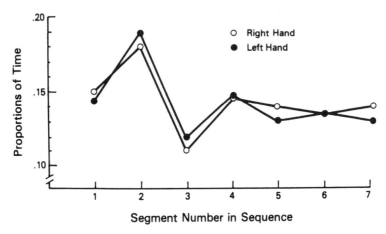

Figure 5. Proportions of time for the seven segments in a wrist-twist task for right-hand practice and after transfer to the left hand. (After Shapiro, 1977.)

run off at various speeds depending on instructions. Our interpretation of the bilateral transfer effects, consistent with this programming view, suggests a relatively abstract program structure that can employ various limb systems in producing a response.

Previous findings also support this interpretation. Bray (1928) showed transfer of mirror-tracing performance from the hand to the foot. Raibert (1977) produced similarities in the movement patterning when he recorded his own writing with the dominant hand, with the dominant arm (hand fixed), with the nondominant hand, with the pen gripped in his teeth, and with the pen taped to his foot. The example cited earlier, by Merton (1972), in which a check-sized and blackboard-sized signature were structured similarly, makes an additional point; the muscles and joints used in the two movements are entirely different, involving primarily the fingers in small writing and the elbow and shoulder in larger writing.

All of this work is consistent with the notion that movement control is based on a central movement program, with a rigid temporal structure defined in terms of relative time. When the same structure is used to produce a movement in another way, perhaps at another speed, with another magnitude, with another limb, or with two limbs simultaneously, the motor system has relatively little difficulty in doing so. This is not to say that all of the learning that occurs is muscle independent, because that view would require perfect bilateral transfer, which is usually not the case. It does force the view that a sizable part of what is learned, and what is then transferred, is some motor program representation. The work showing similar kinematic patterning of the left- and right-hand movements supports this viewpoint and provides strong direction for future work in which similar bases might be sought.

D. PART-WHOLE TRANSFER

Research examining the effects of part-task practice on subsequent whole-task performance (i.e., "part–whole transfer") is not extensive in the area of motor skills, but a number of results support a motor programming explanation of transfer. Part–whole transfer effects are relevant for training situations, where instructors are tempted to "break down" a task into its parts for individual practice before transferring to the whole task.

If we define a "task" as a series of serially organized subactions, with a relatively long task duration (e.g., > 10 s), then there is clear evidence that practicing the subtasks in isolation can transfer substantially to the whole task (e.g., Seymour, 1954). This is not surprising, because subtasks with long movement times are treated as essentially independent activities, and there is little difference in performing them alone versus in the "context" of other subtasks. If the task is continuous, with segments that are less defined sequentially, then the effectiveness of part practice decreases markedly. If, however, the "parts" are defined as two simultaneous dimensions (e.g., X and Y in tracking), the practice on these parts can transfer to the whole task, with transfer increasing as the task "complexity"[2] increases (e.g., Naylor & Briggs, 1963; Stammers, 1980).

If the task is discrete, the effectiveness of part practice changes markedly. Lersten (1968) examined a rapid (< 1 s) sequentially organized discrete movement. Grasping a knob attached to a lever, the subject made a circular movement to contact a stop, then released the knob and made a linear movement to a target, attempting to minimize the movement time for the whole (circular plus linear) response. Different groups practiced various parts of this task (circular, linear, etc.) in isolation before transferring to the whole task. Unlike slower sequential tasks, part–whole transfer was low (less than 7%) or zero. Surprisingly, for the group that practiced the linear component alone, transfer to the whole task was *negative*, measured as − 8%, but it is uncertain whether or not this effect was significantly different from zero. In any case, no part–whole transfer was shown.

One interpretation of this interaction between part–whole transfer and task type is based on the notions discussed earlier about movement programming. In long-duration sequential tasks, parts can be controlled by movement programs organized sequentially, where the learner's task is to initiate each of the programs when its predecessor has run its course. In rapid movements, however, there is insufficient time during the whole task to initiate each of the subparts sequentially, and thus, it can be argued that the whole task is organized as a separate unit. Even though, at one level, the

---

[2]Complexity is defined as any response which requires the coordination of two or more parts for proper execution.

part in isolation and the part in the whole-task context are formally identical, on closer examination there may be considerable differences between them. In Lersten's (1968) case, for example, performance of the linear part in isolation required the subject to accelerate from a stop located at the end of the circular phase. In contrast, this part performed within the context of the whole task already had the limb moving at a high velocity when it began. Thus, marked differences existed between these two linear phases, especially when viewed in terms of the movement kinematics or in the EMG structures.

If the kinematic or neuromuscular (i.e., EMG) structure of the "same" part is fundamentally different depending on whether it is performed alone or within context of the whole movement sequence, then it is reasonable to think of these otherwise identical parts as being *different* movements, with different temporal structures, and different motor programs. Thus, part practice in this situation involves performing a motor program which is not involved in the whole task and should provide no transfer benefits. This interpretation holds that the programs for the part and for the whole are distinct and that the part program cannot be "merged" or transferred into the whole program.

When can practice of parts be beneficial for whole-task performance? From the motor programming perspective, the answer could be based on an analysis of the whole-task structure. If the whole task consists of two separate motor programs run sequentially, then practice on the first part in isolation should transfer to that part in context. An example might be a tennis serve, where (apparently) the movement is made up of a ball toss and backswing as the first program, followed by a second program that produces the hit at the proper time and place. Between programs, the performer analyzes the result of the first program (where the toss sent the ball) and decides where and when to produce the hitting motion. Presumably, effective decisions about whether or not to divide a task into its component parts for practice in isolation could be based on estimations of the structure of the actions involved. According to this view, parts should be formed only on natural boundaries, and tasks that are programmed as a single unit (e.g., volleying a tennis ball) should probably not be divided at all.

Although such analyses of motor skills have not, to our knowledge, been conducted, adequate bases for separating a task into parts already exist. For example, the temporal structure *within* each of the programmed parts should vary little across trials, whereas the temporal structure *between* two different programmed parts should show more variability across trials. Thus, points at which variability increases could be taken as boundaries between two movement programs. Such analyses could provide a link between movement control and predictions concerning part–whole transfer.

E. NEGATIVE TRANSFER

In spite of its importance for understanding motor learning and transfer, negative transfer has not received much investigation since the examination of these problems by Lewis and colleagues (Lewis, McAllister, & Adams, 1951; Lewis, Smith, & McAllister, 1952; McAllister, 1952; McAllister & Lewis, 1951). Lewis *et al.* (1951) used the "complex coordination task," in which subjects had to move a two-dimensional joystick and a foot control to match each of three stimulus positions, where a "standard" version of the task had the display respond in the same direction as the controls. They studied the effect of practicing this task with a *reversed* control-display relationship on transfer to the standard task, by varying the number of original (standard-task) trials and the number of reversed-task trials. They showed considerable negative transfer, which increased as the number of reversed-task trials increased, as shown in Figure 6.

Although little new evidence of negative transfer has been reported since the early 1950s, current speculation is that negative transfer will not be such a large problem after all. First, most of the transfer experiments examined in a previous section showed essentially zero or low positive transfer and never showed negative transfer, leaving the Lewis *et al.* experiments as the only ones that provide clear evidence of negative transfer. Second, in order to achieve negative transfer, Lewis *et al.* completely *reversed* the control-display relationships—a drastic change that probably exceeded the task-to-

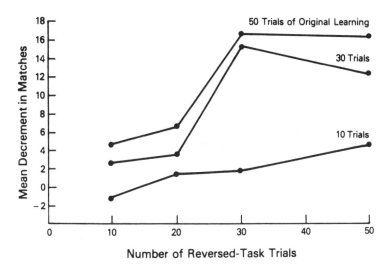

Figure 6. Mean decrement in number of correct matches on the Mashburn task as a function of number of original learning trials and the number of reversed-task interpolated trials; clear negative transfer is shown. (After Lewis *et al.*, 1951.)

task interference found in most everyday learning situations. And third, it is likely that the negative transfer was mediated in large part by cognitive processes (confusions about "what to do") rather than by any negative transfer of motor control; see also Holding (1976) for similar considerations.

These ideas are supported by one of the few recent studies directed at negative transfer. Ross (1974) examined a common idea that two tasks having many early features of a motor pattern in common, but with some critical difference later on (e.g., a tennis versus a badminton stroke), provides a sufficient condition for negative transfer to occur. In a laboratory analogue of this situation, where the force requirements of the final segment of an otherwise identical three-segment, limb movement task was manipulated, only minimal negative transfer between the two versions was demonstrated; and what negative transfer did occur was eliminated with just 10 trials of criterion task practice. Again, negative transfer did not seem to be a serious problem in these movement situations. Rather, when the tasks are changed from being opposite to being merely different, transfer quickly switches from negative to zero, or perhaps to low positive if similarities outweigh the differences.

Various divergent findings, however, make us uneasy about our conclusions concerning the general lack of negative transfer. As mentioned earlier, Shapiro (1978) had subjects learn a nine-segment movement with a particular spatial and temporal pattern. When asked to speed up the movement and to *ignore* the temporal pattern learned earlier, subjects had great difficulty in doing so. Rather, they sped up the same pattern practiced earlier, thus failing to produce a different pattern that might have been faster. This effect can be regarded as negative transfer, where doing the task at maximal speed was interfered with by prior learning of the particular temporal structure experienced earlier. Such effects have important implications for practice situations in which the learner attempts to modify only *part* of an action, and they suggest that such patterns could be resistant to modification.

Another example showing the presence of negative transfer involves second-language learners. Speech *production* (not grammar or vocabulary) can be thought of as an example of a complex motor skill involving many muscles and articulators. We all know that difficulties in producing particular speech sounds in, say, English are related to the speaker's first language; for example, the "same" acoustic goals is produced *systematically* differently by speakers whose first language is French versus German. If negative transfer were *not* occurring, we would not expect these pronunciation difficulties to be common for a particular group of first-language speakers, and we would not expect to be able to recognize someone with a French accent. As such, "foreign accents" might be our best evidence for negative transfer.

1. Specificity

Even with the two examples just given from limb patterning and speech production, the evidence still points to a general lack of negative transfer for motor skills. This conclusion fits well with the evidence discussed earlier about movement specificity. Slight changes to a task presumably alter the processes and abilities involved in its execution, with only minor alterations being needed before intertask correlations approach zero. If so, then perhaps the reason we find so little negative transfer is that the task variations used in the literature are related so poorly to each other that there is no common basis for negative transfer to occur. We argued earlier that changing a movement task *slightly* involves the same generalized motor program, but parameterized differently. However, changing it more than slightly, perhaps beyond the narrow limits of the program's capabilities, demands use of a completely different movement program. If the practice of one program does not alter the "strength" of others, then neither negative nor positive transfer would be expected between apparently similar tasks that use *different* movement programs.

2. Forgetting

The evidence on lack of negative transfer also agrees well with the common findings of nearly perfect long-term retention of at least some movement skills. Bicycling is the common example, and continuous tasks like pursuit tracking and stabilometer balancing provide the empirical justification (Fleishman & Parker, 1962; Ryan, 1962; see Adams, 1986, for a review). If, as the interference theory suggests, forgetting is mainly caused by negative transfer from other tasks learned either prior to or after the original learning of some motor task, and negative transfer does not appear unless the tasks are essentially opposite to each other, then long-term retention might be so complete because at least some motor tasks do not have any other motor tasks to interfere with them.

Short-term retention, however, is influenced by various interfering tasks. Evidence from retroactive interference paradigms (Laabs, 1980; Laabs & Simmons, 1981) show that discrete movement responses (e.g., unidimensional movements to a specific distance or location) assimilate (i.e., are biased) toward the interpolated activity, as measured by spatial errors (e.g., Hagman, 1978, 1983). Proactive interference is also found (e.g., Ascoli & Schmidt, 1969; Stelmach, 1969). On the surface, this evidence seems to contradict our previous notions regarding forgetting. But, these effects are based on discrete tasks where the amount of original learning is slight, and perhaps they can be viewed as short-term perceptual biasing effects which can be removed with a few practice trials (Adams & Dijkstra, 1966). They may not have much to do with the long-term retention of skills discussed earlier.

IV. TRANSFER AMONG VARIOUS CONDITIONS OF PRACTICE

At this point, we change directions to deal with a somewhat different, but related area of transfer research—that dealing with transfer among different conditions of practice. At first glance, this area does not seem to fall within the bounds of transfer research, which is concerned with transfer from one task variation to another. However, remember that changing the conditions under which a task is to be performed, such as eliminating illumination, changing the mass of the control lever, or even performing under massed versus distributed conditions, can be thought of as altering the task.

Using this approach, a number of lines of research have been conducted which provide insight into *what* is learned (and, hence, transferred) in practice situations. Two recent areas of research which can provide such information include variability in practice and contextual interference effects.

A. VARIABILITY OF PRACTICE

The motivation for much of this work was Schmidt's (1975) schema theory, which holds that practice generates abstract rules that govern *classes* of responses, with each class being represented by a generalized motor program. For example, throwing motions are presumably produced by a generalized throwing program, and invididual instances (e.g., throwing a particular object a particular distance at a particular speed) are generated by specifying *parameters* for the generalized motor program. Parameter selection is based on rules (or *schemata*), formed on the basis of past experience with the program, which define the relationship between the environmental outcomes of the movements and the values of the parameters chosen. Thus, when the performer wants to throw a particular distance, the schema defines the parameter for the generalized throwing program, and the program is run off with this parameter value. In this way, each separate throwing movement does not have to be represented, and the person can generate novel movements which he or she has not produced previously (see Schmidt, 1975, 1982, for more details).

One major prediction of this theory is that increased variability in practice along the task dimensions relevant to the generalized motor program should result in greater performance on a novel variant of that task. Numerous recent experiments have examined this prediction in a variety of tasks (e.g., Husak & Reeve, 1979; Johnson & McCabe, 1982; Kerr & Booth, 1977, 1978; McCracken & Stelmach, 1977; Pease & Rupnow, 1983; Pigott & Shapiro, 1984; Siegel & Davis, 1980; Wrisberg & Mead, 1981; see Shapiro & Schmidt, 1982, for a review of earlier work). One study which shows the

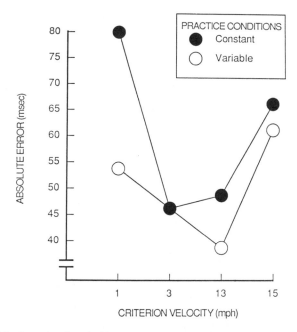

Figure 7. Absolute error in coincidence anticipation after transfer to four stimulus velocities outside the range of previous experience; practice under varied conditions in acquisition produced less error in transfer than practice under constant conditions. (After Catalano & Kleiner, 1984.)

effectiveness of variable practice for learning novel task variants particularly well was reported by Catalano and Kleiner (1984). Two groups performed a coincidence anticipation task, in which a series of lights "moved" toward the subject, who responded with a button press when they "arrived." A constant group received practice at the same speed of light travel on each trial, which was either 5, 6, 7, or 8 mph for each of four subgroups. The variable group received practice at each of these speeds in a variable order, with the number of total trials held constant across groups. After a rest, all subjects then transferred to four novel light speeds, two slower (1 and 3 mph) and two faster (13 and 15 mph) than in previous experience.

Absolute errors on the transfer tests for these two groups are shown in Figure 7. Errors increased as the speed of light travel deviated more from the speeds practiced previously, and there was a clear advantage for the variable-practice groups on the novel transfer tests. Such findings are reminiscent of generalization gradients, in which errors become smaller as the test situation is made more similar to that involved in earlier learning. If so, then one can say that variable practice flattened the generalization gradient, providing improved capability to generalize earlier skill learning to novel situations. Such results are reasonably well established (but are occasionally absent) for adults (Shapiro & Schmidt, 1982) and are very strong for children (but see Wrisberg & Mead, 1981).

These variable-practice effects have been important for theory in various ways. Their major impact has been in terms of support for schema theory, especially because the prediction of variable practice leading to improved performance on some *novel* variant of the task could not be made by earlier viewpoints (e.g., Adams, 1971). Consequently, such results have been interpreted to mean that variable practice produces "stronger" rules for parameter selection, a view strengthened by the converging evidence from motor control on generalized motor programs. Although there have been other lines of support, results that show variable practice produces more effective transfer to novel variants of the task have been the single strongest line of evidence for the concept that motor learning is based on schemata.

B. CONTEXTUAL IINTERFERENCE EFFECTS

Recent findings, however, concerned with so-called context effects have detracted from the schema viewpoint. Shea and Morgan (1979) examined the acquisiton of three similar motor tasks which involved knocking over a series of barriers in a prescribed order, with minimum movement time as the goal. Each of the tasks (referred to here as A, B, and C) was defined by a separate pattern of barrier contacts, indicated by a diagram available to the subject for each trial. Subjects practiced these tasks in two different ways, for a total of 54 trials. Blocked practice involved doing 18 trials of Task A, then 18 trials of Task B, and then 18 trials of Task C, whereas random practice involved a random ordering of Tasks A, B, and C across the 54 trials. Subjects were then transfered to either blocked or random conditions after 10 min or 10 days.

Figure 8 shows the results during acquisition and transfer. Consider first the blocked test (squares). Subjects who practiced under the random conditions during acquisition (solid squares) performed more effectively than those who practiced under the blocked condition in acquisition (open squares), suggesting that the random practice was more effective for learning. Next, for the random test (circles), subjects practicing under random conditions during acquisiton (open circles) were again more effective than those who practiced under blocked conditions in acquisition (solid circles), but the differences here were very much larger than in the blocked test. Thus, even though the random-practice groups produced less effective performances during the acquisition phase, they learned more as measured by their performance on a transfer test; this was true regardless of the nature of the test (random versus blocked) or the length of the retention interval. Other studies have shown much the same thing (e.g., Lee, in press; Lee &

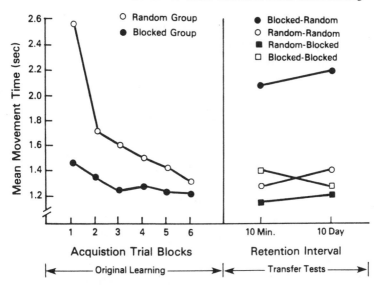

Figure 8. Movement time on a discrete arm movement task as a function of the practice conditions in acquisition and of the practice conditions in transfer; practice under random conditions in acquisition produced faster performance in transfer than practice under blocked conditions. (After Shea & Morgan, 1979.)

Magill, 1983; Lee, Magill, & Weeks, 1985; Shea & Zimny, 1983), although the effects to not appear to be present in children (Wrisberg & Mead, 1983) or in "inexperienced" subjects (Del Rey, Wughalter & Whitehurst, 1982).

The leading explanations of these effects come in essentially two forms. On the one hand, Shea and Morgan (1979; Shea & Zimny, 1983) have argued convincingly that the interference produced by random practice results in "deeper" processing of task-related information, the formation of more extraexperimental relationships, and increased distinctiveness among the various tasks to be learned. This "deeper" processing then results in more effective transfer. Lee and Magill (1983; Lee, in press), on the other hand, argue that random practice in acquisition causes forgetting of the *solution* to the movement problem, so when the subject faces that problem again, a solution must be regenerated, with this being an important process in learning. Subjects with blocked practice can presumably use the solution generated on the previous trial (perhaps with slight modification), leading to fewer generations, and to less learning as seen on the transfer tests. Converging evidence from repeated-testing paradigms (e.g., Hagman, 1983) also supports this viewpoint, as mere presentations to the goal are not as effective as actual movement generations.

Whatever the explanation, these findings produce considerable difficulty for the schema theory. First, if random practice is viewed as a kind of variable practice, then across the whole acquisition phase both the random and blocked conditions receive essentially the same degree of variability; the difference is merely in the ordering of trials. Thus, contrary to what was found, the schema theory would predict that transfer would be equivalent, because the variability between groups is equal. Second, the versions of the tasks studied in the context effect experiments cannot easily be thought of as "parametric variations" of each other; there is no simple way that one movement task can be transformed into another and hence no way that a single generalized motor program (at least as conceptualized by schema theory) could control all of them with only a parameter change.

But most importantly, the variability of practice experiments supporting schema theory can be considered as studies of blocked and random practice. Along with promoting more response variability, variable-practice conditions also force the subject to do something different on successive trials, whereas the constant-practice conditions do not. Thus, it is likely that the basis of the variable-practice effect is mainly related to the prevention of similiar responses produced sequentially, rather than more varied practice per se across the range of movements. If so, then there is no compelling reason to continue to believe that variability of practice effects—the most solid evidence for schema theory—indicate the learning of schemata and the use of generalized motor programs.

In terms of the major goals of this chapter, a discussion of the evidence about the nature of motor control transfer, these contextual interference effects detract from the credibility of our earlier arguments. Earlier, we argued that motor learning involved acquiring generalized motor programs and schemata to parameterize them. In addition, we argued that these motor program representations were primary "ingredients" in transfer, perhaps even to the point that *what* is or is not transferred could be recognized by the kinematic structures produced. Such optimism was based on the belief that the concepts of the generalized motor program and schemata were secure and well protected by the compelling evidence about variability of practice. Now, however, with the plausible suggestion that variability in practice effects may actually be nothing more than random practice effects, much of the strength of the argument for schema learning and generalized motor programs has been withdrawn.

Two kinds of findings, however, make us wonder whether *all* of the effects of variable practice are capable of being explained in terms of blocked/random practice effects. First, for children, variable practice is consistently more effective than constant practice (Shapiro & Schmidt, 1982), and yet random practice is *not* more effective than blocked practive (e.g., Wrisberg & Mead, 1983). Second, variable practice conditions in which practice on a given variant of the task is presented in small blocks seem to be more effective for learning than completely randomized practice with children (Pigott & Shapiro, 1984; Wrisberg & Mead, 1983) not less effective as might be expected if random practice dominated. Also, there is the question of how novel behaviors are produced, which does not seem predictable from the notions of how blocked and random practice operate. The issues are complex, and future research concerned with issues about the amount of functional variability produced by "switching" between tasks, to name one example, need to be addressed. Therefore, it is probably premature to reject the concept of generalized motor programs and schemata, as a number of lines of evidence do support them relatively well.

V. GENERALIZATIONS AND FUTURE DIRECTIONS

We have described a number of important ideas from the literature on movement control and have attempted to show how such concepts might be merged with various phenomena involved in transfer of motor learning. The outcome provides mixed messages, with some interesting suggestions about the basis of motor control transfer, but at the same time with some definite shortcomings.

On the positive side, we appear to be close to identifying some important invariant features that are a part of the representations of at least programmed acts, the most important of which is the idea that relative timing is reasonably well preserved across changes in a number of "surface" features such as movement time and movement amplitude. If so, then an exciting possibility is that this relative timing structure can be used as a kind of "fingerprint" to identify whether, or under what conditions, a particular movement program has become a part of, or has been transferred to, some other movement task. As we indicated, these ideas have a number of weaknesses, and they do not account for the precise details in the data very well (e.g., Gentner, 1985). Perhaps future models along similar lines will be able to account for the phenomena more effectively. If this can be done, then a number of important hypotheses can be evaluated with respect to what is learned and what is transferred.

Even if these ideas about the nature of generalized motor programs do not provide the kinds of explanations we need, the fundamental data about the specificity of skills, the sensitivity of these correlations to apparently small changes in task situations, and the underlying motor program structure of at least quick actions seems to help considerably in understanding the important findings in transfer of motor learning. The overall amount of transfer found is apparently low because of the lack of commonality among even similar-appearing movement tasks. The lack of negative transfer, and the nearly perfect long-term retention of many skills, may arise because there are almost no tasks similar enough to interfere with a particular learned action. In addition, understanding some of the fundamental ideas of motor programming may provide a way to explain why part practice is effective for slow, sequential actions and is essentially ineffective for quick movements. The answers are incomplete about movement programming, and as a result there are many gaps in our capability to apply these findings to transfer phenomena. With the additional emphasis on kinematic and kinetic analyses of movement skills, progress in this area is occurring quickly, and these newer insights should be relevant to problems of transfer of movement control in ways we have suggested here.

A final problem is that movement transfer issues have not been studied very extensively in the past few decades. In reviewing the recent literature on transfer in preparation for writing this chapter, we were shocked to find so little interest in problems of transfer of movement control capabilities. We find this curious, because transfer is certainly important in practical issues related to simulator design and many training methods. We also see transfer as being more fundamentally related to, and perhaps inseparable from larger problems of motor learning, which has also been relatively neglected lately. We do detect a renewed interest in motor learning (Schmidt, 1986) fueled by the interesting new findings in contextual interference discussed briefly here, as well as new insights into the ways that feedback processes operate to maximize learning (Salmoni, Schmidt, & Walter, 1984). A rekindled interest in learning, together with the presently strong emphasis on kinematic and kinetic analyses that inform us about motor programming processes, should contribute significantly to the related area of motor transfer, hopefully generating a more systematic approach to transfer problems that have been awaiting a solution for so long.

ACKNOWLEDGMENTS

This work supported in part by Contract No. MDA903-85-K-0225 from the U.S. Army Research Institute for the Behavioral and Social Sciences to R. A. Schmidt and D. C. Shapiro, UCLA. The opinions expressed hereing are those of the authors and do not necessarily reflect the views of the Army Research Institute, the U.S. Army, or the Department of Defense.

REFERENCES

Abbs, J. H., Gracco, V. L, & Cole, K. J. (1984). Control of multimovement coordination: Sensorimotor mechanisms in speech and motor programming. *Journal of Motor Behavior, 16*, 195–231.

Adams, J. A. (1953). *The prediction of performance at advanced stages of training on a complex psychomotor task* (Research Bulletin No. 53–49). Lackland Air Force Base, TX: Perceptual and Motor Skills Research Laboratory, Human Resources Research Center.

Adams, J. A. (1971). A closed-loop theory of motor learning. *Journal of Motor Behavior, 3,* 111-150.

Adams, J. A. (1987). Historical review and appraisal of research on the learning, retention, and transfer of human motor skills. *Psychological Bulletin 101,* 41-74.

Adams, J. A., & Dijkstra, S. (1966). Short term memory for motor responses. *Journal of Experimental Psychology, 71,* 313-318.

Ammons, R. B., Ammons, C. H., & Morgan, R. L. (1956). Transfer of skill and decremental factors along the speed dimensions in rotary pursuit. *Perceptual and Motor Skills, 6,* 43.

Armstrong, T. R. (1970). *Training for the production of memorized movement patterns* (Tech. Rep. No. 26). Ann Arbor: University of Michigan, Human Performance Center.

Ascoli, K. M., & Schmidt, R. A. (1969). Proactive interference in short-term motor retention. *Journal of Motor Behavior, 1,* 29-36.

Bachman, J. C. (1961). Specificity vs. generality in learning and performing two large muscle motor tasks. *Research Quarterly, 32,* 3-11.

Bray, C. W. (1928). Transfer of learning. *Journal of Experimental Psychology, 11,* 443-467.

Catalano, J. R., & Kleiner, B. M. (1984). Distant transfer and practice variability. *Perceptual and Motor Skills, 58,* 851-856.

Cook, T. W. (1934). Studies in cross education: III. Kinesthetic learning of an irregular pattern. *Journal of Experimental Psychology, 17,* 749-762.

Crago, P. E., Houk, J. C., & Hasan, Z. (1976). Regulatory actions of the human stretch reflex. *Journal of Neurophysiology, 39,* 925-935.

Davis, W. W. (1898). Researches in cross education. *Studies from the Yale Psychological Laboratory, 6,* 6-50.

Del Rey, P., Wughalter, E. H., & Whitehurst, M. (1982). The effects of contextual interference on females with varied experience in open sport skills. *Research Quarterly for Exercise and Sport, 53,* 108-115.

Denier van der Gon, J. J., & Thuring, J. P. H. (1965). The guiding of human writing movements. *Kybernetik, 2,* 145-148.

Dewhurst, D. J. (1967). Neuromuscular control system. *IEEE Transactions on Biomedical Engineering, BME-14,* 167-171.

Dunham, P. (1977). Effect of bilateral transfer on coincidence/anticipation performance. *Research Quarterly, 48,* 51-55.

Fel'dman, A. G. (1974). Change of muscle length due to shift of the equilibrium point of the muscle-load system. *Biophysics, 19,* 544-548.

Fel'dman, A. G. (1986). Once more on the equilibrium point hypothesis (model) for motor control. *Journal of Motor Behavior, 18,* 17-54.

Fleishman, E. A. (1957). A comparative study of aptitude patterns in unskilled and skilled psychomotor performances. *Journal of Applied Psychology, 41,* 263-272.

Fleishman, E. A. (1965). The description and prediction of perceptual-motor skills learning. In R. Glaser (Ed.), *Training research and education.* New York: Wiley.

Fleishman, E. A., & Hempel, W. E. (1955). The relation between abilities and improvement with practice in a visual discrimination task. *Journal of Experimental Psychology, 49,* 301-312.

Fleishman, E. A., & Parker, J. R. (1962). Factors in the retention and relearning of perceptual-motor skill. *Journal of Experimental Psychology, 64,* 215-226.

Fleishman, E. A., & Rich, S. (1963). Role of kinesthetic and spatial-visual abilities in perceptual motor skill learning. *Journal of Experimental Psychology, 66,* 6-11.

Forssberg, H., Grillner, S., & Rossignol, S. (1975). Phase dependent reflex reversal during walking in chronic spinal cats. *Brain Research, 85,* 103-107.

Fumoto, N. (1981). Asymmetric transfer in a pursuit tracking task related to a change of strategy. *Journal of Motor Behavior, 13,* 197-206.

Gentner, D. R. (1985). *Skilled motor performance at variable rates: A composite view of motor control* (Tech. Rep. No. CHIP 124). San Diego: University of California, Center for Human Information Processing.

Hagman, J. D. (1978). Specific-cue effects of interpolated movements on distance and location in short term memory. *Memory and Cognition, 6*, 432-437.

Hagman, J. D. (1983). Presentation- and test-trial effects on acquisition and retention of distance and location. *Journal of Experimental Psychology: Learning, Memory, and Cognition, 9*, 334-344.

Henry, F. M. (1968). Specificity vs. generality in learning motor skill. In R. C. Brown & G. S. Kenyon (Eds.), *Classical studies on physical activity*. Englewood Cliffs, NJ: Prentice-Hall. (Original work published 1958)

Henry, F. M., & Harrison, J. S. (1961). Refractoriness of a fast movement. *Perceptual and Motor Skills, 13*, 351-354.

Henry, F. M., & Rogers, D. E. (1960). Increased response latency for complicated movements and a "memory drum" theory of neuromotor reaction. *Research Quarterly, 31*, 448-458.

Hicks, R. E., Frank, J. M., & Kinsbourne, M. (1982). The locus of bimanual skill transfer. *Journal of General Psychology, 107*, 277-281.

Holding, D. H. (1976). An approximate transfer surface. *Journal of Motor Behavior, 8*, 1-9.

Hollerbach, J. M. (1981). An oscillation theory of handwriting. *Biological Cybernetics, 39*, 139-156.

Husak, W. S., & Reeve, T. G. (1979). Novel response production as a function of variability and amount of practice. *Research Quarterly, 50*, 215-221.

James, W. (1890). *The principles of psychology* (Vol. 1). New York: Holt.

Johnson, R., & McCabe, J. (1982). Schema theory: A test of the hypothesis, variation in practice. *Perceptual and Motor Skills, 55*, 231-234.

Keele, S. W. (1968). Movement control in skilled motor performance. *Psychological Bulletin, 70*, 387-403.

Kelso, J. A. S., Tuller, B., Vatikoitis-Bateson, E., & Fowler, C. A. (1984). Functionally specific articulatory cooperation following jaw perturbations during speech: Evidence for coordinative structures. *Journal of Experimental Psychology: Human Perception and Performance, 10*, 812-832.

Kerr, R., & Booth, B. (1977). Skill acquisition in elementary school children and schema theory. In D. M. Landers & R. W. Christina (Eds.), *Psychology of motor behavior and sport* (Vol. 2). Champaign, IL: Human Kinetics Publishers.

Kerr, R., & Booth, B. (1978). Specific and varied practice of motor skill. *Perceptual and Motor Skills, 46*, 395-401.

Laabs, J. G. (1980). On perceptual processing in motor memory. In C. H. Nadeau, W. R. Halliwell, K. M. Newell, & G. C. Roberts (Eds.), *Psychology of motor behavior and sport, 1979*, Champaign, IL: Human Kinetics Publishers.

Laabs, J. G., & Simmons, R. W. (1981). Motor memory. In D. Holding (Ed.), *Human skills*, New York: Wiley.

Lashley, K. S. (1917). The accuracy of movement in the absence of excitation from the moving organ. *American Journal of Physiology, 43*, 169-194.

Lee, T. D. (in press). Testing for motor learning: A focus on transfer appropriate practice. In O. Meijer & K. Roth (Eds.), *Complex movement behavior: The motor-action controversy.* Amsterdam: Elsevier.

Lee, T. D., & Magill, R. A. (1983). The locus of contextual interference in motor-skill acquisition. *Journal of Experimental Psychology: Learning, Memory, and Cognition, 9*, 730-746.

Lee, T. D., Magill, R. A., & Weeks, D. J. (1985). Influence of practice schedule on testing schema theory predictions in adults. *Journal of Motor Behavior, 17*, 283-299.

Lersten, K. C. (1968). Transfer of movement components in a motor learning task. *Research Quarterly, 39*, 575-581.

Lewis, D., McAllister, D. E., & Adams, J. A. (1951). Facilitation and interference in performance on the modified Mashburn apparatus: I. The effects of varying the amount of original learning. *Journal of Experimental Psychology, 41*, 247-260.

Lewis, D., Smith, P. N., & McAllister, D. E. (1952). Retroactive facilitation and interference in performance on the modified two-hand coordination task. *Journal of Experimental Psychology, 44*, 44-50.

Lintern, G. (1985). *A perceptual learning approach to skill transfer for manual control.* Paper presented at the meeting of the NATO Defense Research Group Panel VIII, Brussels, Belgium.

Logan, G. D. (1982). On the ability to inhibit complex movements: A stop-signal analysis of typewriting. *Journal of Experimental Psychology: Human Perception and Performance, 8*, 778-793.

Lordahl, D. S., & Archer, J. E. (1958). Transfer effects on a rotary pursuit task as a function of first task difficulty. *Journal of Experimental Psychology, 56*, 421-426.

Magill, R. A., Schmidt, R. A., Shapiro, D. C., & Young, D. E. (1987). Manuscript in preparation. UCLA.

McAllister, D. E. (1952). Retroactive facilitation and interference as a function of level of learning. *American Journal of Psychology, 65*, 218-232.

McAllister, D. E., & Lewis, D. (1951). Facilitation and interference in performance on the modified Mashburn apparatus: II. The effects of varying the amount of interpolated learning. *Journal of Experimental Psychology, 41*, 356-363.

McCracken, H. D., & Stelmach, G. E. (1977). A test of the schema theory of discrete motor learning. *Journal of Motor Behvior, 9*, 193-201.

Merton, P. A. (1972). How we control the contraction of our muscles. *Scientific American, 226*, 30-37.

Murdock, B. B. (1957). Transfer designs and formulas. *Psychological Bulletin, 54*, 313-326.

Namikas, G., & Archer, J. E. (1960). Motor skill transfer as a function of intertask interval and pre-transfer task difficulty. *Journal of Experimental Psychology, 59*, 109-112.

Naylor, J. C., & Briggs, G. E. (1963). Effects of task complexity and task organization on the relative efficiency of part and whole training methods. *Journal of Experimental Psychology, 65*, 217-224.

Ostry, D. J., & Cooke, J. D. (in press). Kinematic patterns in speech and limb movements. In E. Keller & M. Gopnick (Eds.), *Symposium on motor and sensory language processes.* Hillsdale, NJ: Erlbaum.

Parker, J. F., & Fleishman, E. A. (1960). Ability factors and component performance measures as predictors of complex tracking behavior. *Psychological Monographs, 74* (Whole No. 503).

Pease, D. G., & Rupnow, A. A. (1983). Effects of varying force production in practice schedules of children learning a discrete motor task. *Perceptual and Motor Skills, 57*, 275-282.

Pigott, R. E., & Shapiro, D. C. (1984). Motor schema: The structure of the variability session. *Research Quarterly for Exercise and Sport, 55*, 41-45.

Puretz, S. L. (1983). Bilateral transfer: The effects of practice on the transfer of complex dance movement patterns. *Research Quarterly for Exercise and Sport, 54*, 48-54.

Raibert, M. H. (1977). *Motor control and learning by the state-space model* (Tech. Rep. No. AI-TR-439). Cambridge, MA: MIT, Artificial Intelligence Laboratory.

Ross, I. D. (1974). *Interference in discrete motor tasks: A test of the theory.* Doctoral dissertation, University of Michigan, Ann Arbor.

Ryan, E. D. (1962). Retention of stabilometer and pursuit rotor skills. *Research Quarterly, 33*, 593-598.

Salmoni, A. W., Schmidt, R. A., & Walter, C. B. (1984). Knowledge of results and motor learning: A review and critical reappraisal. *Psychological Bulletin, 95*, 355-386.

Schmidt, R. A. (1975). A schema theory of discrete motor skill learning. *Psychological Review, 82,* 225-260.

Schmidt, R. A. (1976). Control processes in motor skills. *Exercise and Sport Sciences Reviews, 4,* 229-261.

Schmidt, R. A. (1982). *Motor control and learning: A behavioral emphasis.* Champaign, IL: Human Kinetics Publishers.

Schmidt, R. A. (1985a). The search for invariance in skilled movement behavior. *Research Quarterly for Exercise and Sport, 56,* 188-200.

Schmidt, R. A. (1985b). Identifying units of motor behavior. *Behavioral and Brain Sciences, 8,* 163-164.

Schmidt, R. A. (in press). Toward a better understanding of the acquisition of skill: Theoretical and practical contributions of the task approach. In J. S. Skinner (Ed.), *Future directions in exercise and sport research.* Champaign, IL: Human Kinetics Publishers.

Schmidt, R. A. (1986). Controlling the temporal structure of limb movements. *Behavioral and Brain Sciences, 9,* 623-624.

Schmidt, R. A., Sherwood, D. E., Zelaznik, H. N., & Leikind, B. J. (1985). Speed-accuracy trade-offs in motor behavior: Theories of impulse variability. In H. Heuer, U. Kleinbeck, & K. -H. Schmidt (Eds.), *Motor behavior: Programming, control, and acquisition.* Berlin & New York: Springer-Verlag.

Seymour, W. D. (1954). Experiments on the acquisition of industrial skills. *Occupational Psychology, 28,* 77-89.

Shapiro, D. C. (1977). *Bilateral transfer of a motor program.* Paper presented at the AAHPER annual meeting, March, 1977.

Shapiro, D. C. (1978). *The learning of generalized motor programs.* Doctoral dissertation, University of Southern California, Los Angeles.

Shapiro, D. C., & Schmidt, R. A. (1982). The schema theory: Recent evidence and developmental implications. In J. A. S. Kelso & J. E. Clark (Eds.), *The development of movement control and coordination.* New York: Wiley.

Shapiro, D. C., & Schmidt, R. A. (1983). The control of direction in rapid aiming movements. *Societey for Neuroscience Abstracts, 9*(2), 1031.

Shapiro, D. C., & Walter, C. B. (1984). *The control of rapid positioning movements with spatiotemporal constraints.* Unpublished manuscript. UCLA.

Shapiro, D. C., Zernicke, R. F., Gregor, R. J., & Diestel, J. D. (1981). Evidence for generalized motor programs using gait-pattern analysis. *Journal of Motor Behavior, 13,* 33-47.

Shea, J. B., & Morgan, R. L. (1979). Contextual interference effects on the acquisition, retention, and transfer of a motor skill. *Journal of Experimental Psychology: Human Learning and Memory, 5,* 179-187.

Shea, J. B., & Zimny, S. T. (1983). Context effects in memory and learning movement information. In R. A. Magill (Ed.), *Memory and control of action.* Amsterdam: North-Holland.

Sherwood, D. E., Schmidt, R. A., & Walter, C. B. (1987). *Rapid movements with reversals in direction: II. Control of movement amplitude and inertial load.* Manuscript in preparation. UCLA.

Slater-Hammel, A. T. (1960). Reliability, accuracy, and refractoriness of a transit reaction. *Research Quarterly, 31,* 217-228.

Stammers, R. B. (1980). Part and whole practice for a tracking task: Effects of task variables and amount of practice. *Perceptual and Motor Skills, 50,* 203-310.

Stelmach, G. E. (1969). Prior positioning responses as a factor in short term retention of a simple motor task. *Journal of Experimental Psychology, 81,* 523-526.

Summers, J. J. (1977). The relationship between the sequencing and timing components of a skill. *Journal of Motor Behavior, 9,* 49-59.

Taub, E., & Berman, A. J. (1968). Movement and learning in the absence of sensory feedback. In S. J. Freedman (Ed.), *The neuropsychology of spatially oriented bahavior.* Homewood, IL: Dorsey Press.

Terzuolo, C. A., & Viviani, P. (1979). The central representation of learning motor programs. In R. E. Talbot & D. R. Humphrey (Eds.), *Posture and movement.* New York: Raven Press.

Tsuji, K., & Ide, Y. (1974). Development of bilateral transfer skills in the mirror tracing. *Japanese Psychological Research, 16,* 171-178.

Wadman, W. J., Denier van der Gon, J. J., Geuze, R. H., & Mol, C. R. (1979). Control of fast goal directed arm movements. *Journal of Human Movement Studies, 5,* 3-17.

Weig, E. (1932). Bilateral transfer in the motor learning of young children and adults. *Child Development, 3,* 247-267.

Wrisberg, C. A., & Mead, B. J. (1981). Anticipation of coincidence in children: A test of schema theory. *Perceptual and Motor Skills, 52,* 599-606.

Wrisberg, C. A., & Mead, B. J. (1983). Developimg coincident timing skill in children: A comparison of training methods. *Research Quarterly for Exercise and Sport, 54,* 67-74.

Zelaznik, H. N., Hawkins, B., & Kisselburgh, L. (1983). Rapid visual feedback processing in single-aiming movements. *Journal of Motor Behavior, 15,* 217-236.

Zelaznik, H. N., Schmidt, R. A., & Gielen, C. C. A. M. (1986). Kinematic properties of rapid aimed hand movements. *Journal of Motor Behavior, 18,* 353-372.

CHAPTER 4

How Can Good Strategy Use Be Taught to Children? Evaluation of Six Alternative Approaches

MICHAEL PRESSLEY
BARBARA L. SNYDER
TERESA CARIGLIA-BULL

How can children be taught to be good strategy users, that is, people who know a lot of strategies and transfer them readily and appropriately to new settings? Unfortunately, there is no simple answer at this time. Strategy use and acquisition of sophisticated strategic competence are very complicated matters, and many difficulties must be overcome in order to elicit good strategy use in children. In this chapter we review and assess six alternative approaches to strategy instruction, with specific attention paid to whether these approaches can promote general strategy application. It is necessary first to clarify the components of good strategy use, since the alternative instructional models will be evaluated as to how well they promote the many aspects of competent strategic behavior.

I. THE GOOD STRATEGY USER

Pressley, Borkowski, and Schneider (1987) have presented a detailed description of good strategy use along with extensive commentary on the substantial body of data supporting their good strategy user model of cognitive competence. Here we distill the most important features of that model, ones that are relevant to children's performance. This model has evolved from previous

81

conceptions of intelligent performance (e.g., Pressley, Borkowski, & O'Sullivan, 1984, 1985) and shares features with other frameworks that include strategic, metacognitive, and knowledge-based components as important contributors to intellectual functioning (e.g., A. L. Brown, Bransford, Ferrara, & Campione, 1983; Flavell, 1985, Chaper 7; Sternberg, 1985a, 1985b).

A. Strategies

First and foremost, good strategy users possess strategies, including (a) goal-specific procedures that achieve particular memory, comprehension, and problem-solving goals; (b) monitoring strategies that keep track of cognition and performance, instigating processing shifts when cognition is not going smoothly; and (c) higher order sequencing strategies that chain goal-specific and monitoring strategies into larger, articulated sequences to accomplish complex goals.

A good strategy user has hundreds of strategies, many of them specific to domains in which the individual is an expert. Indeed, although expertise involves acquiring a lot of declarative knowledge about a subject area, it also requires mastery of the domain-particular strategies. One case in point is the good reader who possesses a host of comprehension strategies. (Proficient readers selectively take notes, underline, summarize, elaborate text, and answer questions that occur to them about material they are reading (Cook & Mayer, 1983; Forrest-Pressley & Gillies, 1983). Goal-specific strategies for comprehension are often combined into higher order strategies that can be summarized with catchy acronyms. One of these is REAP (Eanet & Manzo, 1976), which involves four strategies executed in a fixed order: reading, encoding, annotating, and pondering.

The preponderance of work relevant to the good strategy user model has involved investigation of particular goal-specific, monitoring, and higher order strategies. There have been many studies to determine who can produce what strategies when. Entire programs of research have been devoted to particular memorization strategies (e.g., categorization, Moely, 1977; elaboration, Pressley, 1982; rehearsal, Flavell, 1970), to certain self-control procedures (e.g., self-verbalization, Pressley, Reynolds, Stark & Gettinger, 1983), and to specific problem-solving regimens (e.g., analogical identification, Gick & Holyoak, 1980, 1983). Monitoring procedures have also been examined in detail. One line of research focused on factors that determine whether and when young children can compare the effects produced by different strategies (e.g., Ghatala, Levin, Pressley, & Goodwin, 1986; Ghatala, Levin, Pressley, & Lodico, 1985; Lodico, Ghatala, Levin, Pressley, & Bell, 1983; Pressley, Ross, Levin, & Ghatala, 1984). The integration of goal-specific and monitoring strategies into higher order procedures has been a concern in several literatures, including child clinical psychology (e.g., Kendall & Braswell, 1982, 1985), reading (e.g., Palincsar & Brown, 1984), and problem solving (e.g., Charles & Lester, 1984; Riley, Greeno, & Heller, 1982). What most of these research programs have in common has been an exclusive focus on strategic procedures insulated from other factors. This has resulted in age-graded catalogs of procedures that benefit various aspects of performance (e.g., Pressley, Forrest-Pressley, Elliott-Faust, & Miller, 1985; Pressley, Heisel, McCormick, & Nakamura, 1982). But there is more to proficient strategy use than just knowing procedures.

B. Specific Strategy Knowledge

Good strategy users not only know strategic procedures; they also know when and where to apply them. Excellent adult learners abstract what we refer to as specific strategy knowledge when they use strategies. That is, they figure out the general features of a situation that define when the strategy in question can be used profitably (e.g., O'Sullivan & Pressley, 1984; Pressley, Levin, & Ghatala, 1984).

As an illustration, consider the keyword strategy for associative learning. When taught as an aid to vocabulary learning, learners are instructed to recode unfamiliar, to-be-learned vocabulary words (e.g., *carlin*, which means "old woman") to acoustically similar words (i.e., keywords). The learner then creates interactive relationships between the keywords and definitions (e.g., for *carlin*, an image of an old woman [definition] driving a car [keyword], or the sentence, "The old woman drove the car"). While using the strategy, good strategy users might also discover or infer that the method and variations of it work (a) whenever associative learning is required, (b) when there is enough time to execute the strategy, and (c) if one invests the effort necessary to carry out the strategy. Once in possession of these three pieces of specific strategy knowledge, good strategy users are far more likely to maintain and generalize the strategy.

Readers familiar with artificial intelligence might infer that the construct of strategy and associated specific strategy knowledge resemble production systems that are common in models of artificial intelligence (i.e., the if-then devices that specify an action that is executed if and only if certain conditions hold). Such conditional information is only part of specific strategy knowledge, however. Good strategy users encode motivational information (i.e., which strategies are fun and which ones are not) as well as a great deal of episodic information, such as when and where the strategy was acquired and who taught it to them. The role played by this episodic information is unspecified at this time, but we suspect that it probably has some functional significance. For instance, when a strategy like the keyword method is acquired in the context of a language class, students might be more likely to transfer the strategy to novel language problems than to other equally appropriate applications, such as learning science or social studies material (Pressley & Levin, 1986).

A particularly important piece of specific strategy knowledge is under-standing that the strategy benefits a particular aspect of performance. In sup-port of this claim, there are many demonstrations of increased strategy use when strategy utility is made obvious, such as when the teaching agent in-cludes utility information as part of strategy instruction (e.g., Black & Rollins, 1982; Borkowski, Levers, & Gruenenfelder, 1976; Cavanaugh & Borkowski, 1979; Kennedy & Miller, 1976; Lawson & Fuelop, 1980; Ringel & Springer, 1980). In addition, both adults and children can derive strategy utility information from strategically mediated performances, and this abstracted utility information can be used to regulate subsequent strategy use. However, such abstraction and exploitation of specific strategy knowledge is more certain in adults than in children (Lewis & Anderson, 1985; Pressley, Levin, & Ghatala, 1984; Pressley, Ross, Levin, & Ghatala, 1984; Sternberg & Ketron, 1982). In short, it seems important for learners to recognize that their performance is better when they use a strategy versus when they do not and for them to attribute the improvement in performance to the use of the strategy. Possession of such beliefs should do much to motivate use of the strategies to which they are attached (Clifford, 1984).

C. GENERAL BELIEFS AND GENERAL STRATEGIC TENDENCIES

In addition to strategies that accomplish specific goals and subgoals and specific strategy knowledge about those procedures, good strategy users possess certain general tendencies that set the stage for and facilitate the ex-ecution of specific strategies. For instance, good strategy users understand that effort is often important to achieve goals, particularly effort channeled through strategy use. They realize that particular skills often can be modified a bit to fit slightly different circumstances. Thus, good strategy users confront new problems with a general set to expend effort and to reshape strategies to fit new problems.

One of the most important general attributes of the good strategy user is the tendency to shield cognitive procedures from other behaviors, potential distrac-tions, and debilitating emotions. This is important because uncontrolled emo-tion, attention to non-task-relevant stimulation, and execution of competing behaviors could undermine successful performance. The good strategy user engages in what Kuhl (e.g., 1985) has identified as action control. Neither the joy of strategically mediated victory over cognitive challenges, nor the agony of failure due to use of inappropriate procedures, is overwhelming.

D. KNOWLEDGE BASE

Strategic knowledge is not the only knowledge that good strategy users possess. They also know a lot about the world in general. They have an extensive declarative knowledge base. This knowledge includes schemata; ones possessed by most well-educated adults include what to expect and how to behave at a symphony, when checking into a hotel, when pumping gas at the self-serve station, and when attending a major league baseball game (Mandler, 1983). Individuals also have schemata specialized to their areas of expertise. For instance, professorial types possess detailed schemata about course structures, departmental organization, and university governance. In addition, people have complex associative networks (e.g., Anderson, 1983), parts of which are arranged hierarchically (e.g., Mandler, 1979). They also possess imaginal (e.g., Finke, 1985; Kosslyn, 1983) and nonverbal representations, for instance, memories of specific tastes and odors (e.g., Paivio, 1986). In short, there is an extensive knowledge base encoded in a number of different modes.

The knowledge base affects strategic behaviors in a number of ways:

It often contains information that makes use of a strategy unnecessary. For instance, when the first author recently encountered the word *lapillus* in an article about a Columbian volcanic eruption, he did not need to execute any strategy to figure out the word's meaning. Years of Latin instruction resulted in the entry *lapillus* (the Latin diminutive of stone) being in his long-term memory. Someone who lacked a comparable knowledge base would do well to exploit all the context clues that were available to infer the word's meaning and, if that failed, to use the strategy of consulting a dictionary.

Sometimes material that is learned by relying on the knowledge base stimulates strategy use for material that is not so congruent with the learner's prior knowledge. That is, sometimes strategy use is data driven, rather than exclusively goal driven as emphasized to this point in the chapter (e.g., Lindsay & Norman, 1977). For instance, when children process highly related items in a categorical fashion, it may occur to them that categorization is a good learning technique, in turn, prompting use of categorization strategies even with materials that are not so highly related. In fact, this carry-over hypothesis enjoys considerable empirical support for the specific case of categorization-organizational strategies (Best & Ornstein, manuscript submitted for publication; Bjorklund, 1985; Bjorklund & Jacobs, 1985; Bjorklund & Zeman, 1982).

Many strategies can only be executed by people who possess a lot of knowledge, for the knowledge base enables strategy execution. For instance, a common reading comprehension strategy is to activate what one knows about a topic before reading material about it (e.g., Levin & Pressley, 1981). Readers can do this, however, only if they possess knowledge about the topic. Given a well-developed knowledge base, the knowledge activation strategy results in many appropriate and comprehension-facilitating inferences; of course, no such inferences are possible if there is nothing stored away that can be activated (e.g., Hasselhorn & Körkel, 1986). Additional examples include categorization strategies that can only be executed for easily accessed categories (e.g., Ornstein & Corsale, 1979). There are also verbal rehearsal techniques that are facilitated if the to-be-rehearsed materials are personally meaningful to the learner (Tarkin, Myers, & Ornstein, in preparation).

E. An Example of Good Strategy Users:
   The Hardy Boys

Up until this point, the discussion has been rather abstract. When concrete illustrations have been offered, they have been derived from a variety of domains. To provide a more vivid description of good strategy use, we consider in this section two adolescents who are undoubtedly familiar to much of the readership of this volume and who are decidedly good strategy users: Frank and Joe Hardy (e.g., Dixon, 1972).

The Hardy Boys possessed a lot of strategies for investigating crimes. These ranged from such general strategies as trying to put themselves in the criminal's place both mentally and physically to very specific procedures for lifting fingerprints from difficult places. The Hardy Boys employed a lot of strategies that were specifically cognitive in nature, such as using rehearsal and mental imagery to remember critical information. In retrieving descriptive information about people, they used their own version of a top-down strategy, beginning with the top of the person's head and proceeding down the body in constructing the description. They were also aware of constructive memory errors and thus made habits of photographing the scene of a crime; of making drawings rather than relying only on their own memories; and of always carrying a notebook to record clues.

Most impressive, the Hardy Boys knew how to articulate these strategies and used them appropriately. The boys had encoded a lot of specific strategy knowledge. They always seemed to call up the correct strategy and automatically sequenced strategies together. For instance, when they arrived at a crime scene, they first secured the sight so that evidence would not be destroyed, and then they executed a series of search-and-record exercises. In short, the boys possessed higher order sequencing strategies. Another notable aspect of the Hardy Boys' behavior was their calm collectedness, even in the face of peril. These boys knew about and practiced action control. The many strategies that the boys possessed were used in combination with an extensive knowledge base about the law, criminals' behaviors, criminals' language, the nature of fingerprints and other types of physical evidence, hard and soft drugs, as well as knowledge of virtually every other aspect of modern life. These pieces of information were used while the boys executed surveillance strategies, search strategies, and undercover procedures.

There are several points that emerge from an analysis of the Hardy Boys that are relevant to the concerns of this chapter. First, the boys were competent because they possessed *all* of the elements of good strategy use. Second, the lengthy education of a good strategy user is apparent from reading the novels, with the boys building up their expertise over the course of many years (and more than 60 volumes!). Third, reading the Hardy Boys is informative about the complexity of instruction required to inculcate good strategy use. The prime mover in the boys' education was their father, Fenton Hardy, a famous detective. He provided years of strategy instruction to his offspring, using a variety of teaching procedures, including some of the ones that are assessed in this chapter.

F. SUMMARY OF THE GOOD STRATEGY USER MODEL

In short, good strategy users know a lot of strategies; they know a lot about those strategies; and they know a lot more. These strategic, metastrategic, and knowledge-base components are well articulated in good strategy users. When good strategy users confront a new learning, comprehension, or problem-solving task, they often identify elements of the new situation that are similar or identical to previous academic encounters. These similar elements can frequently be used to guide selection of an appropriate strategy for this new situation, since the specific strategy knowledge that a child possesses for a strategy includes the attributes of tasks where the procedure can be employed. On occasions when a strategy is not apparent initially, it may become obvious as learning/comprehension/problem solving proceeds, sometimes because there are matches between to-be-processed materials and the knowledge base that in turn suggest ways to process other materials. Thus, a problem solver may suddenly realize that the physics problem that she is working on is analogous to another problem that she knows how to solve. The student might then try to find analogies between subsequent tasks and previously worked problems. Strategic, metastrategic, and knowledge components are continually interacting. Although there are occasions when cognition more resembles purely strategic processing and occasions when processing more resembles knowledge-based mediation (Glaser, 1984, 1985), there are also many times when processing is a mixture of all three elements specified here (Sternberg, 1985a, 1985b).

How can the mind juggle so many balls at one time, given limited capacity? There are two important factors. First, good strategy use is largely sequential. It proceeds one subcomponent at a time, from initial examination of the task, to the formation of a strategic plan, to the execution of that plan. Second, good strategy users have most aspects of strategy use automatized. With time and experience, the critical aspects of a task that map onto specific strategy knowledge are perceived effortlessly, with especially important elements being perceptually salient. Once accessed, strategies are executed efficiently with relevant aspects of the knowledge base used as necessary. Good strategy users know to switch strategies when all is not going well; they also know to turn off strategy use and rely on the knowledge base exclusively if they already "know" the material.

II. ALTERNATIVE APPROACHES TO STRATEGY INSTRUCTION

Having outlined the characteristics of the ideal good strategy user, the question of how to instruct children to reach this ideal remains. In this section, we review six general methods of strategy instruction. Although there is some overlap in components that compose the six general methods, each approach is more than the sum of its parts. Thus, the emphasis is on the six methods and not on the specific components that make them up. On the other hand, we do point out what seems to be missing from each of the approaches that are reviewed. These missing components flag important shortcomings that, more often than not, reduce the likelihood of strategy transfer. The discussion generally proceeds from simpler instructional procedures to more complex ones.

A. DISCOVERY AND GUIDED-DISCOVERY LEARNING OF STRATEGIES

The first method considered, discovery learning, is notable for its deemphasis on teaching! Discovery is often recommended as an optimal approach to the development of good thinking skills, despite generally negative evaluations of the method (e.g., Ausuble, 1961; R. M. Gagné, 1965; Rohwer, 1970; Wittrock, 1966). A teacher following this approach permits students to discover on their own the strategies that are important in a domain. Students would do this either by simple practice at the tasks that compose the domain or through practice combined with opportunities to generate questions that are answered by the teacher (e.g., Suchman, 1960). The general advantages of discovery are hypothesized to be higher motivation, better learning and retention of strategies, and more complete understanding of the strategies that facilitate transfer (Wittrock, 1966).

Although the Piagetians did not originate the doctrine that discovery learning is superior to more explicit instruction (Brainerd, 1978, pins the blame on Rousseau), they certainly promoted self-discovery over virtually all approaches where external agents teach cognitive skills to children. In fact, Piaget frequently claimed that nondiscovery approaches were harmful to the child: "Remember also that each time one prematurely teaches a child something he could have discovered for himself, that child is kept from inventing it and consequently from understanding it completely" (Piaget, 1970, p. 715).

The Genevan and Genevan-inspired experiments that supported this point of view were severely flawed, however. In addition, many North American investigators were able to produce better learning of Piagetian conceptual rules (e.g., conservation) than occurred when children were left to their own devices to discover relationships. The successful training methods included ones that resemble what we later refer to as direct explanation, guided participation, and modeling (Brainerd, 1978).

Non-Piagetian research consistent with the discovery hypothesis also gets a lot of attention. For example, Groen and Resnick (1977) demonstrated that children as young as 4 and 5 years of age invent a particular addition strategy, given only practice in addition: They come to understand that they should start with the larger of two addends and count up by the number specified by the smaller addend. Children also invent an efficient subtraction heuristic, either counting down from the minuend or up from the subtrahend, whichever requires less counting (Svenson & Hedonborg, 1979; Woods, Resnick, & Groen, 1975).

Certainly these are impressive demonstrations of children's mathematical inventiveness. Nevertheless, there are questions. First of all, was the acquisition of these rules by invention as efficient as acquisition would have been with more explicit instruction? Even though children may invent rules successfully, the procedures they discover sometimes contain flaws or "bugs" (J. S. Brown & Burton, 1978). Also, how much can be discovered? Although some cognitive rules and procedures become evident with simple practice, there are many strategies that are not so apparent. Readers need only consider the many strategies that humans can be taught (e.g., Pressley & Levin, 1983a, 1983b) versus the ones that most adults spontaneously employ (e.g., Bransford, Stein, Arbitman-Smith, & Vye, 1985; Dansereau, Long, Evans, & Actkinson, 1975; Lochhead, 1985).

These problems with simple discovery learning suggested that a more structured environment might guarantee more certainly that discovery would occur. Hence, an approach that we call guided discovery gained in popularity. Guided discovery is more explicit, involving an external agent posing questions to students. This questioning presumably leads the student to discover the correct strategy. Direct comparisons between simple-discovery and guided-discovery learning, in fact, supported the hypothesis (e.g., R. M. Gagné & Brown, 1961; Kersh, 1958) that guided discovery produces more certain cognitive gains.

A recent, prominent instantiation of guided discovery is Collins and Stevens's (1982) method of inquiry teaching. Their approach to teaching a strategy (or any other concept) is to present a series of questions. These questions include examples of the strategy being applied successfully as well as examples of the strategy proving not to be helpful. In constructing questions that will get the student to zero in on a particular strategy, the teacher poses inquiries that focus attention on both factors that are relevant and those that are irrelevant to the strategy. "Trick" questions are included to demonstrate misconceptions to students. Once students have figured out some aspects of the strategy, the teacher asks for explicit formulation of a cognitive rule with clear specification of the necessary and sufficient conditions that must hold in order for the strategy to apply. The teacher provides additional probes until the strategy is completely formulated. Questioning continues with comparison and evaluation of the present strategy with respect to other procedures and with predictions about how the cognitive rule could be transferred to novel situations.

Collins and Stevens's (1982) arguments in favor of this approach are similar to arguments for discovery learning in general. They believe that inquiry teaching models scientific thinking and, thus, believe that students might internalize the approach used by the teacher and apply it to the real world. The students are involved and presumably experience the exhilaration of discovery that motivates additional discovery. This approach is supposed to lead to deep understanding because of the presentation of a variety of cases, some of which just meet the sufficient conditions for use of the strategy and others of which just lack the sufficient conditions. The transfer component is also built in, since the teacher tries to get the student to deal with novel cases.

The problems are at least as telling as the presumed advantages, however. Collins and Stevens (1982) admit that it is faster to get information across by lectures or reading. The method requires a sophisticated teacher who can think quickly and who is good at constructing questions and examples. Most telling on the negative side, though, is the lack of evidence that the method is effective!

In closing this subsection, we note that there is a clear bias among many developmentalists to favor discovery approaches (e.g., Glaser, 1984), presumably because they are more natural (Brainerd, 1978) and more consistent with theoretical prescriptions as to how development naturally occurs (e.g., Gibson, 1969; Piaget, 1970). This is not a bias that we endorse or wish to encourage, however. One of the real hallmarks of human intelligence is that tools can be passed from generation to generation, eliminating needless, slow, and uncertain reinventions.

B. INSTRUCTION THAT IS LARGELY OBSERVATIONAL LEARNING: WATCHING STRATEGY USE AND READING ABOUT OTHERS USING STRATEGIES

Inspired by demonstrations of children acquiring many different types of behaviors by watching models, observational learning of cognitive behavior has been studied in detail in recent years. In general, social learning interventions apply in the conceptual arena, with many demonstrations of observational learning of a variety of simple concepts (Rosenthal & Zimmerman, 1978). These successes partially motivated studies of vicarious learning of strategies. Observational learning research has also been stimulated by the fact that so many strategy instructional packages include modeling as one of the components. In fact, the modeling components may be one of the more potent parts of the intervention (e.g., Elliott-Faust, Pressley, & Dalecki, 1986).

McGivern, Levin, Ghatala, and Pressley (1986) illustrate the potential gains and pitfalls provided by modeling of cognitive strategies. Their study involved grade 5 children who watched a peer execute two associative-learning strategies that were differentially effective—one very powerful, one very weak. On the positive side, the children picked up enough from simply watching the model to execute both of the strategies, and they knew which strategy worked better. On the negative side, they failed to make use of this observationally gained information when later given an opportunity to choose between the two strategies that had been modeled. McGivern *et al.* (1986) concluded that the complicated articulations that are required to execute strategies do not always follow from brief observational learning.

Perhaps strategy acquisition is more certain when observational learning experiences are more extensive than occurred in McGivern *et al.* (1986). We present discussion of two interventions in which modeling is the predominant component of instruction in order to illustrate some of the creative ways that modeling can occur during strategy instruction and the results that might be expected.

1. Pair Problem Solving

Lochhead and his associates (e.g., Whimbey & Lochhead, 1980) have developed a type of instruction called "pair problem solving". Two students work on problems together. While one student (the model) vocalizes what she or he is doing to solve the problem, the other student (the observer) continually monitors the model for accuracy and keeps the model on task by demanding constant vocalization. There are three ways that observational learning can occur in this setup: (a) Each model demonstrates a number of strategies in the course of working the problem. (b) Watching the partner-model struggle with a problem makes the observer aware of human frailty and the difficulty of problem solving, as well as of the alternative approaches to solving problems and their associated advantages and disadvantages (i.e., specific strategy knowledge is presumed to be abstracted from these observations). (c) The partner who verbalizes his own strategies makes more obvious to himself what strategies he is using and how these strategies can be managed.

2. Symbolic Modeling

Symbolic models (Bandura, 1969, 1977), in the form of fictional characters, are being used to teach strategies that are appropriate for children. One of the best known examples is provided by Lipman (1985) in his philosophy for children program. Participants read a series of novels about fictional children. These characters exist in a classroom community, but unlike normal children, they do a lot of thinking out loud about important philosophical problems like truth, friendship, identity, fairness, goodness, and freedom. Their conversations and thought processes made transparent provide models of good, strategic thinking. Over the course of the novels, the readers are exposed to children using many strategic processes such as formulating concepts precisely, making generalizations, inferring cause-and-effect relationships, monitoring the consistency of arguments, avoiding ambiguities and vague thinking, and means–ends reasoning.

These novels are used in conjunction with classroom discussions and exercises. Such interactions permit elaboration of the thinking principles that are modeled through practice, using the demonstrated strategies and opportunities to watch peers exhibit the skills. These interactions encourage children to reflect on thinking skills, to consider others' points of view, and to apply critical analysis to the thinking of self and others.

3. Advantages and Disadvantages

Evaluations of modeling are far from complete (Bransford *et al.*, 1985; Lochhead, 1985), and this approach to strategy teaching has not been studied in great detail with children. The data that do exist suggest that observation of strategy use does not inevitably lead to deployment of a strategy (e.g., McGivern *et al.*, 1986).

There are several good reasons to be particularly skeptical about the potency of peer modeling, such as that used in Lochhead's (1985) pair problem-solving approach: First, the strategies that the model comes up with may not be the most efficient ones possible, with this possibility being more likely the younger the model. Second, the observer might not realize this, with such lack of realization being ever more likely the younger the observer. However, it has been recognized for a long time that children experience real difficulty reflecting on their own thought processes and those of others (e.g., Flavell, 1985, Chaper 4). Thus, observing one's own strategies as self-verbalization proceeds and evaluating the strategies used by peers is probably not straightforward for children.

A strength of the symbolic modeling approach using texts is that well-written novels could be extremely interesting. The main hypothesis is that this type of presentation, when integrated with class discussion that it motivates, would be both exciting to children and effective in altering thinking processes. Unfortunately, there are very few evaluative studies that have been conducted (see Lipman, 1985, for a review), and those that do exist are more product than process oriented. The most striking finding to date is that exposure to the novels improves reading comprehension (Shipman, 1982). Nonetheless, much more work is needed before there is a data-based reason for great enthusiasm about learning from models as a method for promoting strategy acquisition. This work will be important because there are many opportunities to provide television and in-the-text models of strategic processing to children. Students can be exposed to strategies used by farmers, scientists, and writers (to mention but a few of the possibilities). If nothing else, such exposure should result in a deeply entrenched general understanding that strategic processing occurs all the time and in virtually every sector of society, even those places that can only be experienced vicariously by children.

C. GUIDED PARTICIPATION IN FREQUENTLY ENCOUNTERED, NORMAL SCHOOL TASKS

Sometimes teachers lead students through strategic sequences with the expected processing specified very explicitly every step of the way, but with little or no information provided about when or where to use the strategy. There is usually no overview of the strategy. The assumption is that the student will acquire the strategy simply as a function of experiencing it. If the child is taken through the exercise enough times, the strategic processing becomes habitual.

One of the better recent examples of guided participation was provided by Hansen and Pearson (1983). They led fourth-grade children through a complex reading strategy with guided participation continuing for 10 weeks, 2 days a week. The intervention could be broken down into prereading and postreading activities. Before a text was read, there was a discussion of the virtues of comparing your own life with situations represented in a text. This is a specific instantiation of the prereading process, schema activation (Levin & Pressley, 1981). The discussion included information about the utility of schema activation, that its execution would in fact increase learning from text. Prereading discussion continued with presentation of six questions based on three important ideas about the to-be-read selection.

Questions alternately required relating personal knowledge to text content and making predictions about what would occur later in the text. This exercise was intended to model the inferential process of understanding new information by relating it to old information. Discussion of these questions occurred in a reading group. Then, children read the selection on their own and answered interpretive postquestions presented by the teacher. These questions were meant to promote children's understanding that text can be something to interpret. An example illustrates the type of interaction that went on:

> In a discussion of a basal version of "Charlotte's Web," the following question was asked: "What kind of person do you think Templeton (the rat) would be if he were human?"
> The discussion among the students transpired as follows: "Mean." "Nasty." "Cruel." "Greedy." "No, if Templeton were human he would be different than he was as a rat because he would have money and could buy food." "Yes, I think so, too; then he wouldn't have to be so mean." (p.824)

The most striking findings involved reading measures taken at the conclusion of training. Poor readers were able to remember more literal details from passages that they read, as well as answer more inferential questions. The benefits for good readers were not as consistent. Hansen and Pearson (1983) assumed that they had modified text processing in the poor readers. There were no direct measures of process on the pretests and posttests, however, so there was no converging evidence of a processing shift as a function of instruction. For the sake of the current argument, we will accept the inference from the performance measures that children's processing shifted to conform to the strategies that had been presented repeatedly over the course of 10 weeks.

One of the greatest strengths of guided participation is that it can be incorporated into school content so easily. For instance, see Herber (1970, 1985) for an illustration of how students in class can be guided to use reading comprehension strategies similar to those studied by Hansen and Pearson (1983). In addition, see Jones, Amiran, and Katims (1985) for a review of one of the most ambitious attempts to embed cognitive skills training in the regular curriculum. As part of the regular reading program, their participants were exposed to a vast array of strategies (including organizational, imagery, context, and monitoring procedures), with these skills introduced in a guided participation fashion.

The opportunity for repeated exposure to instruction is a real virtue of 5-days-a-week, 36-weeks-a-year schooling. Given that a strategy sequence can be repeated many times in the school setting, guided instruction may not be a bad instructional tool, although careful study of it is required before any definitive, positive conclusion would be warranted. Multiple guided participation episodes should permit the correct strategy sequence to be learned, overlearned, and automatized (Schneider, Dumais, & Shiffrin, 1984) as well as provide many opportunities to be exposed to the subtleties of strategy execution.

More negatively, there is very little explicit information provided during guided participation about when to use the strategy or how to modify it to fit novel situations. This is left for the learner to abstract. Such abstraction should be more likely with extended practice of the strategic sequence, and hence, a few trials of guided participation seems like an especially bad idea. A lot of work needs to be done to determine the conditions that surround the abstraction of specific strategy knowledge during guided participation.

One other potential difficulty with guided participation is that students may simply get in the habit of executing a strategic routine without trying to generate their own strategies (Kail, 1984, p. 31; Weinstein & Underwood, 1985). On the other hand, for tasks that children perform a lot and for which powerful strategies exist, such habitual strategy application could be very helpful. Certainly, potent strategic habits that facilitate important educational goals are more "intelligent" than the impoverished processing of poor comprehenders, poor memorizers, and poor problem solvers.

D. STRATEGY INSTRUCTION THROUGH BOOKS AND COURSES

The alternative to teaching strategies in the context of regular school content is to provide strategic instruction independent of any particular content. For instance, volumes dedicated to memory instruction have been available for almost two centuries (Fenaigle, 1813).

Higbee (1977), for example, presents both learning techniques and information about when the various methods are useful and how they work. Thus, interactive imagery mnemonics are discussed with respect to the vividness, bizarreness, and concreteness of mental images. Higbee covers the time required to execute the mnemonics, how the methods can be adapted to abstract materials, the role of mnemonics in learning versus retention, whether there are imagery ability by strategy instruction interactions, the greater appropriateness of imagery for memory of gist versus verbatim memory, and problems of interference when using mnemonics. In short, there is a fair amount of specific strategy knowledge in the Higbee book, although it is certainly not the case that the presentation of this type of information is exhaustive.

There are also entire learning skills courses that are widely disseminated. One is de Bono's (1983a, 1983b) 2-year course for teaching thinking skills. CoRT (Cognitive Research Trust) is intended to be a simple and practical program for people of various ages and abilities. De Bono claims the program contains skills needed in real life that can be learned without much prior knowledge. He sees transfer as an important goal of his training, which is based largely on the role of perception in thinking (de Bono, 1985). The most fundamental principle is that good teaching consists of getting people to direct attention to important attributes of a problem, with attention direction inculcated through instruction in particular principles of thinking. The actual teaching occurs through a series of 60 lessons, with one basic process (attention strategy) the focus of each lesson. The teacher first explains the purpose of a lesson and illustrates the principle. This is then followed by practice. Each lesson has eight practice problems from various domains. The items are intended to mirror the array of situations that people might encounter in life. Students work on these problems in groups, with feedback and discussion aimed at clarifying the process that is the object of the lesson. Visual devices are used to aid students in understanding and remembering the principles.

Covington's (e.g., 1985) *Productive Thinking Program* is also aimed at developing effective thinking and problem-solving skills, specifically in the upper elementary grades. The skills are taught in 15 lessons with each lesson involving an illustrated story presenting a problem the student is to solve. Sixteen basic rules of thinking are covered in the 15 lessons. These rules are dealt with in several problem sets that the student solves. For instance, Lesson 9 ("Plans and Inventions") begins with an illustrated story about a boy visiting a house with a ghost in it. The objectives of the lesson are to provide practice in identifying and explaining puzzling events. To that end, two new basic rules of thinking are introduced. One is to try to reconcile puzzling facts with a single explanation, and the other is to explore things around one for ideas about how to solve puzzling events. Along the way, students are advised to think of all the ways they can to explain how the protagonist of the story could have seen something in the old house that looked like a ghost. Students are reminded several times to let their minds explore freely, searching the environment for cues that would suggest a solution. As the story proceeds, the main characters zero in on a solution, always on the lookout for puzzling facts about the problem and ways to unite all the givens in the story into a single explanation. Metaphorical thinking is introduced, as is searching for analogies. In particular, students are advised to think of the separate clues as pieces of a puzzle that could be put together to form a full picture.

There are some advantages to these courses and books. They teach many related strategies and tend to be systematic in their coverage of classes of strategies. For the most part, they have a good face validity. The main problem is that we know very little about whether these programs work or how they work. To be sure, global evaluations of the courses have been conducted, and, in general, these studies have been positive (e.g., Covington, 1985; de Bono, 1976). Nevertheless, all the studies have methodological difficulties that make it impossible to accept the evidence uncritically (e.g.,

Polson & Jeffries, 1985). There are also plenty of reasons to suspect that these books and courses may not be as effective as their proponents hope. Particularly lacking in all these programs is extensive instruction about where and when to apply the various strategies that are taught (Bransford *et al.*, 1985). When opportunities for practice are provided at all, students are usually left to their own devices to abstract much of the specific strategy knowledge that they need in order to direct deployment of a strategy. As we have argued throughout this chapter, it simply cannot be assumed that children will abstract such information from practice with strategies, or use the information profitably if they do abstract it (e.g., O'Sullivan & Pressley, 1984; Pressley, Ross *et al.*, 1984).

E. DIRECT EXPLANATION: STRATEGY INSTRUCTION THAT IS LARGELY TEACHER DIRECTED

There have been thousands of studies in which adults tell children how to execute a strategy and then ask them to do it (Pressley, Heisel *et al.*, 1982). Studies of such unembellished instruction have been very informative, for it was important to establish that there are many memory, comprehension, problem-solving, writing, athletic, self-control, and general attentional strategies that children can execute given a simple explanation. Such teaching, however, does not produce durable strategy use (i.e., maintenance or transfer; e.g., A. L. Brown *et al.*, 1983). In contrast to research on simple explanation of strategies, there are investigations of much more complete instruction, which Roehler and Duffy (1984) refer to as *direct explanations*. The best direct explanations provide very explicit and detailed information about how to carry out all the components that make up a strategy as well as relevant specific strategy knowledge or information about the strategy.

One piece of *specific strategy knowledge* that an adult can provide to a child is information about the utility of the strategy that is being taught. The adult can make clear that the strategy will enhance performance. Teaching that contains such utility information has been termed "informed instruction" (A. L. Brown *et al.*, 1983), and the effects produced by informed instruction have been investigated extensively in true experiments. The addition of utility information to strategic teaching increases the likelihood that the strategy will continue to be produced after training concludes, when the subsequent tasks are very similar to the training tasks (e.g., Black & Rollins, 1982; Borkowski *et al.*, 1976; Cavanaugh & Borkowski, 1979; Kennedy & Miller, 1976; Lawson & Fuelop, 1980; Ringel & Springer, 1980).

Why does this maintenance occur? Continued strategy use is contingent on learners attributing their successes and failures to the execution of appropriate and inappropriate strategies respectively (Clifford, 1984). Such attributions are likely, given the cooccurrence of strategy execution, the provision of utility information, and the improved performance due to strategy execution (e.g., Paris, Newman, & McVey, 1982). One recent study with hyperactive children is particularly telling with respect to the position that consistent strategy use follows from directly explaining to children that they should attribute strategically mediated success to strategy execution.

Reid and Borkowski (1985) included three conditions. One was a package of strategies designed to improve memorization. A second included the same cognitive strategies, with the addition of attribution retraining. The children were taught that their improved performance during training was due to the cognitive strategies that were part of the package. Control subjects were provided neither the strategy nor attribution training. The most relevant result was that long-term maintenance and near transfer of the strategies occurred only in the condition that included both the strategic and the attributional training. Knowing that good performance is a result of strategy execution is an important piece of information. It is specific strategy knowledge of the form "If I carry out procedure X, benefits Y and Z will follow."

Additional specific strategy knowledge is necessary if broad generalization of a procedure is to occur, consistent with the metacognitive theoretical point that generalization requires knowledge of how, when, and where to use a strategy (e.g., A. L. Brown et al., 1983; Pressley, Borkowski, & O'Sullivan, 1984, 1985). Unfortunately, experimental investigation of this theoretical position is much less complete than is investigation of effects produced by providing simple utility information. O'Sullivan and Pressley (1984) illustrated how this work can be done, demonstrating greater generalization of a strategy by adding when-and-where information to instruction. Children in Grades 5 and 6 were presented two memory tasks during the study, first learning city-product pairings and then the meanings of Latin words. Control subjects learned both sets of materials without strategy instruction. Subjects in four other conditions were taught to use the keyword method, with the four conditions varying in the amount of when-and-where information that was covered during training. In general, the more specific strategy knowledge that was included in keyword training with the cities task, the greater the transfer of the strategy to the learning of Latin. That the addition of such specific strategy knowledge seems to have striking effects on generalization (see Heisel & Ritter, 1981, for additional relevant data) is more than enough motivation to justify additional experiments on specific strategy knowledge.

Thus far, we have made the case that teachers can present a variety of strategies, ranging from very simple to quite complex ones. They can also provide metacognitive information in the form of specific strategy knowledge. How does the teacher go about doing this? Certainly there is a lot of verbal exhortation to use the strategic process. Children are told to make mental images in their heads that represent stories that they hear, they are told to say word lists over and over, they are instructed to sort materials into sensible categories, and they are encouraged to activate world knowledge.

In addition, direct explanation almost always includes *concrete examples, modeling*, and *practice*. Strategy instructors using direct explantion try to make teaching as comprehensible as possible. For instance, O'Sullivan and Pressley (1984) modeled the construction of keyword mediators for subjects and provided examples of keyword strategy execution in the form of pictures (e.g., for the city-product task, referents of the keywords and products interacting). As a second illustration that strategy instructions can be concretized and embellished in ways that are sensitive and responsive to children, consider the recent study by Elliott-Faust *et al.* (1986). Children in Grades 3 and 4 were taught a three-component goal-specific strategy. The child's task was to generate a one-word clue so that a listener would know which of two words she was referring to (e.g., *baby* or *child*). The most compelling theoretical analyses of this task (Higgins, Fondacaro, & Mc-Cann, 1981; Rosenberg & Cogen, 1966) suggest that efficient performance is dependent on the communicator generating an associate to the referent; then comparing the candidate clue to the referent and the nonreferent to determine the extent of association to both referent and nonreferent; and finally, evaluating whether a candidate clue has greater association to the referent than the nonreferent. The most complete condition in Elliott-Faust *et al.* (1986) involved an adult teaching children all three components. Consistent with the theoretical analysis cited above, this three-component training package resulted in better clue production than occurred in a no-training control condition.

Much of the instruction in Elliott-Faust *et al.* (1986) consisted of the experimenter-teacher explaining and modeling the strategy. However, the child was also given practice generating clues, and as part of this practice, the experimenter provided feedback as to clue adequacy. When the child generated an inadequate clue, the experimenter explained why the clue was not a good one. This instruction was customized to each child, depending on the types of errors produced by the young communicator.

Although it must be admitted that direct explanations have not always been as complete as they could have been, in virtually every study of instruction involving children that has been conducted by Pressley and his associates, the experimenter used some form of direct explanation. For instance, in Pressley (1976) 8-year-olds were given extensive guided practice in generating mental images that represented the content of text they were reading. Subjects described their imaging activity, and the experimenter-teacher corrected it as required in order to bring the children's processing in line with the representational imaginal processing that was the concern in that investigation. The children carried out the imagery strategy on their own only after extended practice that was adjusted to each child's errors. Similar adjustments have been made in Pressley's research on keyword–elaborative mnemonics, comprehension monitoring, strategic monitoring, listening comprehension, and pictorial facilitation of prose learning. What is more, although there has been little formal study of these adjustments, there is no doubt that rewordings of directions and reworkings of examples have been both more numerous and more explicit with younger than with older children. (So obvious because of exhaustion experienced by the experimenters when running very young children versus somewhat older participants!)

The best direct explanations include carefully planned explanations or demonstrations by external agents. These are followed by some form of experimenter- or teacher-guided practice with adjustments for individual children made as necessary. Moreover, the laboratory examples of good direct explanation mirror well the structure of direct explanations in actual classrooms. There are many well-known strategic procedures that can be presented to children in class using only verbal explanations and modeling, followed by any required adjustments and rewordings (e.g., Tierney, Readence, & Dishner, 1985).

Some of the most intriguing documentations of this type of direct explanation have been provided by Duffy and Roehler and their associates at Michigan State. Here is a description of a direct explanation provided by a particular teacher:

> Consider a main idea lesson taught by Teacher B. The content of Teacher B's talk patterns reflected an explanation of what one needs to do to find the main idea of a paragraph. Information was initially presented about (1) what the mental process was, (2) how to use salient features of the skill, and (3) why the mental process is useful in connected text. After this direct explanation of what was to be learned, why it was important, and how to do it, Teacher B moved to a turn-taking model where he checked the students' restructuring of skill and modified or reinforced that restructuring. Finally, when the students demonstrated that they understood, practice was provided. (Roehler & Duffy, 1984, pp. 268–269)

Roehler and Duffy (1984) make the case that direct explanation of strategic processing often includes the teacher presenting a lot of specific strategy knowledge. Direct explanation is usually followed by the teacher sampling the children's understanding, with additional explanation as required. Then there is practice.

In an extremely ambitious, well-conducted, and important experiment, Roehler et al. (1986) obtained convincing experimental data documenting that direct explanations in the classroom have general effects on grade school students' cognitions and performances. Their study included 10 Grade 3 teachers who were taught to make direct explanations during the instruction of reading processes and strategies, as well as 10 teachers who were taught general classroom management skills. The teachers and their students were monitored over the course of the school year. The teachers who were trained to use direct explanation did in fact do so, and the effects on their students were dramatic. At the end of the year, students taught by direct explanation teachers were more aware of lesson content and of the strategic nature of reading than were students taught by teachers in the management-training control condition, replicating an earlier finding by Duffy *et al.* (1984). Most telling, students in the direct explanation classrooms outperformed control children on a variety of reading tasks, including standardized reading achievement tests. Correlational data consistent with the experimental outcomes were also reported. There was striking evidence in favor of the direct explanation approach in the Roehler *et al.* (1986) study.

The positive effects of direct explanations in classrooms probably can be extended beyond simply reading, however. A demonstration of this was provided by Herrmann (1986). She taught four graduate students to use direct explanations when teaching mathematics to children who were experiencing difficulty solving mathematical story problems. The four graduate student teachers differed, however, in the quality and extent of direct explanations that they provided to their pupils. The better the teacher's direct explanations, the more aware students were of when and how to use strategic processing during problem solving. Most importantly, the quality of students' actual problem-solving behaviors covaried with the quality of their teacher's direct explanations, with better problem solving associated with better direct explanations. Although experimental work is needed to determine unambiguously whether direct explanations can improve children's mathematical competence, the correlations provided by Herrmann (1986) are consistent with this interpretation and provide great motivation for such research.

The hallmark of the direct explanation approach is the initial presentation of explicit, well-structured descriptions and demonstrations of the strategic processing that is the object of the lesson. Implicit in this method is the belief that children are very capable of acquiring strategies quickly. In fact, there is an overwhelming volume of data supporting the conclusion that children can execute many strategies, provided they are given explanations of how to sequence and carry out all of the components included in the strategy. However, even though children can execute strategies on demand, it is not necessarily the case that they will generalize them. Students also need to know when and where to deploy the procedures. An important role for the direct explanation teacher is to be a conveyer of this specific strategy information. If the teacher's direct explanation includes all of the relevant cognitive and metacognitive information, generally competent use of the strategy is more likely than when instruction is less complete.

Although direct explanation includes teacher–student interaction, the main thrust of the direct explanation approach is the instruction that is provided to learners. Much greater emphasis on the social aspects of teaching characterizes the approach that we take up next, although one should see Turnure (1985, 1986) for a stimulating social-communicative analysis of direct explanation.

F. Dyadic Instruction

According to theorists like Vygotsky (1978) and Feuerstein (1980), mature thought develops in social contexts. Children first experience sophisticated processing in interpersonal situations, with more mature thinkers modeling good thinking and guiding young children's problem solving, often by providing cues to assist the children when they cannot manage on their own. These adults provide what has been referred to as proleptic instruction (i.e., instruction that anticipates the child's needs). Adults direct children's attention appropriately; they provide strategies to children; in general, they serve a supervisory role, making their own good processing as visible as possible. They also try to guide the child to process in the same efficient fashion (e.g., A. L. Brown & Ferrara, 1985; Childs & Greenfield, 1980; Day, 1983; Greenfield, 1984; Palincsar & Brown, 1984; Vygotsky, 1978; Wertsch, 1985; Wood, Bruner, & Ross, 1976). Eventually children adopt as their own the thought processes that adults have externalized for them and encouraged them to use. They *internalize* the mature processing they have witnessed and participated in, although the internalized version is not an exact copy of the external processing. The explicit, heavily verbal processing that characterizes the adult–child interactions becomes abbreviated and highly efficient as it becomes intrapsychological functioning (Vygotsky, 1962).

There is a growing body of data suggesting that adults often interact with children in the fashion described by Vygotsky (Greenfield, 1984). Most relevant to this chapter, Rogoff and her colleagues (Ellis & Rogoff, 1982; Rogoff & Gardner, 1984) have shown that parents prepare their children to generalize cognitive skills in a proleptic fashion. Ellis and Rogoff (1982) presented mothers with the task of teaching their children to use classification both in a home setting (i.e., placing items on appropriate kitchen shelves) and when schoollike constraints held (i.e., placing photos of kitchen utensils into appropriate colored boxes). In both cases the teaching involved 18 items that could be classified into six categories. Mothers provided a lot of guidance to their children as they taught them the classification strategy. Once items were appropriately categorized, the mothers prompted their children to rehearse within categories in order to prepare for an upcoming memory task. The children asked for clarifications at appropriate points. Throughout the instruction the mothers explicitly pointed out similarities between the schoollike task and the kitchen task; they provided glances of encouragement and nonverbal prompts as required by their charges. Parental directives decreased as children's competence increased, but parents were usually ready to step in to help when the child experienced difficulties.

The Vygotskian/Feuerstein theoretical analyses and the supporting correlational data suggest that one way to promote good strategy use in children is to provide them with regular opportunities to interact with adults who provide instruction sensitive to the level of each individual child. There are three hallmarks to the reciprocal teaching approach: (a) Teachers and students take turns executing the various strategic components, with these strategies being executed in a true dialogue. (b) The strategic processes are made quite overt, and students are given a lot of exposure to them over a number of lessons. (c) Teachers assume more responsibility for direction of activities at the beginning of the intervention; self-regulation being gradually transferred to the students.

One way to understand proleptic instruction is to compare it with direct explanation. One striking difference is that direct explanations flow more from the teacher to the student, whereas reciprocal instructions are the result of continuous, mutually responsive interactions between teachers and students. Direct explanation assumes that a child can internalize a strategy quickly, while proleptic instruction is more piecemeal, with the child internalizing the strategy gradually and only after exposure to many examples of good processing. More is left for the child to infer during reciprocal teaching, although the teacher does everything possible to lead the child to inferences that he or she would fail to make unassisted. When using direct explanation, on the other hand, the teacher tells the student exactly what processing is expected. Adjustments are made during direct explanation when and if the child falters, but these adjustments are much less prominent than with reciprocal instruction.

Proleptic instruction seems to be a very effective method for teaching strategies. The most prominent work on this topic has been carried out by Palincsar and Brown (A. L. Brown & Palincsar, in press; Palincsar & Brown, 1984; Palincsar, 1986). Palincsar's subjects have usually been children in their early teen years who can decode text adequately but who fail to comprehend it. Palincsar and Brown's (1984) diagnosis is that these readers do not engage in the same strategic processes that good comprehenders do; thus, appropriate strategy instruction should remedy their deficit. Palincsar and Brown specifically prescribe that these deficient readers be taught to *summarize* and self-review what they are reading; to formulate potential test questions and in turn to *question* themselves about the material; to *clarify* occasions when there is ambiguity, and to *predict* what is coming in the text. This is a complex strategic intervention in that summarization, questioning, clarification, and prediction are each higher order strategic sequences, and each of these strategic components serves to enhance both encoding of information and comprehension monitoring. For instance, summarizing involves retrieving what one has read, searching through both internal encodings of the text content and the external text itself, and sifting through the material for the most important information. As part of the process, learners monitor the adequacy of their comprehension. If there are large discrepancies between what is encoded internally and what is on the written page, that is a high sign that comprehension is not going well.

A lesson begins with an assigned text, with either the adult teacher or a student leading the group. The participants in the exercise then read the segment, followed by a summary of the content from the leader. The leader then takes a stab at posing a question that might occur on a test. Discussion of the question then follows with clarification provided as needed. Finally, the leader makes a prediction about future content. Whenever a student falters, the adult teacher lends a hand. Of course, this is a demanding role for the adult, requiring a great deal of cognitive diagnosis (Flavell, 1972). Yet the teacher must make such diagnoses in order to know when to introduce even more demanding tasks and to know when to turn over cognitive self-regulation to the student. Throughout instruction, every effort is made to emphasize to the students the benefits that strategies provide to them and to provide other specific strategy knowledge, such as when and where to use the strategies and some information about why the techniques are effective.

Palincsar and Brown (1984) observed striking improvements in the comprehension of students who were taught using the reciprocal instruction approach. Not only were there pretest to posttest improvements within learners, there were improvements relative to both no-strategy and alternative intervention control subjects. Perhaps most striking of all, Palincsar and Brown (1984) reported improvements in in-the-classroom comprehension, with trained subjects showing better understanding of both science and social studies material that they encountered in class (i.e., they transferred their use of the trained strategies from the instructional setting to actual school tasks). Since the Palincsar and Brown (1984) report, Palincsar and her associates have replicated the reciprocal training effect several times (Palincsar, 1986). They have also compared reciprocal instruction to a variety of less complete treatments, including ones that contained some but not all of the components of the reciprocal training approach (Palincsar & Brown, 1984). Palincsar (1986) has also succeeded in adapting the strategy to younger children, producing improvements in the listening comprehension of Grade 1 children.

All of the tailoring that occurs during dyadic instruction is expensive in terms of teacher's time and effort. Fortunately, many children's worlds are filled with potential teachers in the form of relatives and friends who do not mind giving the child a lot of attention. For schools however, the great personnel expense associated with the dyadic method is a serious disadvantage.

Given that there are parents, aunts, uncles, and grandparents who can provide proleptic instruction, it is puzzling that many 20- to 30-year-old adults are not as strategic as they could be, with enormous individual differences evident in strategic propensity (e.g., Rohwer & Thomas, 1986; Thomas & Rohwer, 1986). For instance, despite the fact that adults have learned thousands of vocabulary items in their lives, both naturalistically and in school, only a minority of grownups have discovered the potent mnemonic approaches to vocabulary learning that are collectively known as the keyword method (e.g., Pressley, Levin, & Delaney, 1982; Pressley, Levin, Kuiper, Bryant, & Michener, 1982). It may be that although adults do a lot of proleptic instruction, the focus is usually on the acquisition of particular content rather than teaching of powerful strategic procedures. This point of view enjoys some support as far as classroom teachers are concerned (e.g., Durkin, 1979; Moely et al., 1986). Another factor is that one cannot teach what one does not know. To rephrase the claim that opened this paragraph, most adults have less than complete knowledge of potential strategies. This ignorance probably undermines methods like dyadic teaching in a number of ways. One of the more insidious was discussed by Rohwer (1980), who made the case that teachers probably often teach ineffective strategies when they teach them at all. In short, proleptic instruction may require competencies that some teachers do not possess.

III. DISCUSSION: IS THERE A BEST APPROACH TO STRATEGY INSTRUCTION?

There is no convincing evidence that any of the six approaches to strategy instruction outlined here produce generally competent strategy users, although some are certainly more promising than others. There are many strategies, much metacognition, and a massive declarative knowledge base that must be mastered. The development of good strategy use takes years, and the optimal approach to instruction is probably an amalgamation of the six approaches. We organize this discussion around the elements of good strategy use.

A. STRATEGIES

Children often experience difficulties executing strategies if the processing is not detailed extensively and explicitly (e.g., Elliott-Faust & Pressley, 1986; Elliott-Faust *et al.*, 1986; Ghatala *et al.*, 1986; Miller, 1985; Pressley & Levin, 1980; Pressley & MacFadyen, 1983). For this reason, we gravitate toward more complete instruction, like that provided with direct explanation. An added advantage of this approach is that it seems suited to classroom-size groups compared to the resource-demanding alternative of reciprocal teaching, which otherwise seems to be a very good method. With direct explanation the teacher presents a detailed summary of processing and carefully regulated practice of complete processing. The child is exposed to (a) the complete strategic sequence, (b) specific strategy knowledge, and (c) practice that includes feedback and encouragement.

While arguing in favor of direct explanation, we hasten to add that there are very few within-experiment comparisons of alternative approaches to training strategies. A recent study by Bereiter and Bird (1985) is illustrative of the type of inquiry that is needed. In the present context, their results support our enthusiasm for direct explanation. Bereiter and Bird (1985) were concerned with how to teach reading comprehension strategies. They studied direct explanation, modeling, and guided participation approaches. In three of the four experimental conditions, Grade 7 and 8 subjects were instructed in the use of four strategies. These had been identified as procedures used by good adult readers in a preliminary study conducted by Bereiter and Bird (1985). These were (a) attempting to restate difficult-to-understand text, (b) backtracking in text when failing to comprehend or make connections with previous sections of the reading, (c) posing self-questions that alert oneself to watch out for particular types of information, and (d) formulating problems and trying to dispose of them by inference, closer examination of the text, and rejection of information.

The most complete of these three strategy instructional conditions was a specific instantiation of direct explanation. The instructor defined and modeled each strategy, explaining when and where it could be applied as part of the strategy demonstrations that were carried out over a wide variety of sample passages. These initial explanations were followed by additional teacher modeling, with students required to identify strategies as the teacher used them. Students also evaluated whether use of the particular strategy was advisable in the situation where it was employed and were asked to indicate places where the teacher could have used a strategy but did not. Students then practiced using the strategies themselves, marking the practice texts at each point as they used the instructed strategies. During this final portion of instruction, students also did some overt demonstrations of strategy use.

In the second strategy instructional condition, techniques were modeled by the instructor, followed by opportunities for the students to practice the strategies they had watched the model carry out. Notably, strategies were neither defined nor named by the model in this condition.

The third instructional treatment resembled guided participation. Students were lead through exercises that demanded the four strategic processes instructed and modeled in the other two instructional conditions. The students practiced these processes in response to specific questions posed by the teacher and in text. For instance, to mirror the processing associated with the strategy of problem formation and solving, students were asked (a) to determine if there were errors in particular text segments, and to correct them if present; (b) to determine if information was missing from particular text segments, and if so to mark the place and make a guess at what should be present; and (c) to answer questions about confusing passages.

A fourth condition was a no-strategy control condition. Subjects in this condition took the same reading pretests and posttests as subjects in the three instructional groups.

There were no pretraining differences in reading comprehension between the four groups of subjects. After strategy training, however, the direct explanation group outperformed the other three groups, none of which differed significantly. Think-aloud protocols were collected and analyzed in the direct explanation, modeling, and control conditions. In general, direct explanation subjects used the trained strategies more than did subjects in the other two conditions.

Direct explanation induced more strategy use than did the two less complete approaches to instruction, guided participation, and modeling. Nonetheless, many more comparative experiments are required to establish definitively the relative efficacy of the various strategy instructional tactics. In our view, this type of work should be a high priority for instructional researchers. Regardless of what the research reveals, however, we expect that all of the approaches covered in this chapter can contribute to an overall program of strategy instruction. Let us consider the alternative methods one by one.

Discovery of strategies will occur some of the time regardless of the type of instruction that is presented to children. For instance, Ornstein, Bjorklund, and their associates have documented that processing of materials that suggest mediators stored in the knowledge base can increase strategic processing of subsequently presented material. Sometimes children reflect on their stimulus-driven strategiclike behaviors (e.g., categorical reorganization of categorizable lists), realize the significance of the strategiclike behaviors (i.e., memory of this list is easier because of the categorical reorganization), and consequently "discover" a strategy (e.g., categorical reorganization, or category invention if one is not immediately apparent). This is a process similar to what Piaget (e.g., 1970) referred to as reflective abstraction (Bjorklund, 1985; Bjorklund & Jacobs, 1985; Bjorklund & Zeman, 1982; Ornstein, Baker-Ward, & Naus, in press; Ornstein & Naus, 1985). A real challenge is to figure out how to engineer academic encounters so that discovery of strategies occurs. We know almost nothing about such engineering, although research on guided discovery such as that being conducted by Collins and Stevens (1982), seems like a good start. Even though there will always be opportunities for strategic discoveries, however, we are lukewarm about leaving much of strategy instruction to discovery.

One of the most obvious reservations about guided participation is that repeating a sequence over and over is often boring. Such repetition without explanation of its significance may seem meaningless to children. On the other hand, such repetitive, guided practice should increase efficiency in strategy execution, perhaps to the point where the strategy is automatized (Schneider et al., 1984). When that occurs, fewer intellectual resources are required to carry it out, and thus, there are fewer motivational barriers to students electing the strategy (i.e., it will not seem so hard). Thus, for tasks that could be performed habitually (e.g., some types of reading), there probably is a productive role for guided participation.

The success of modeling depends on the observer attending to the appropriate dimensions of the modeled sequence (e.g., Bandura, 1977; Yussen, 1974) and requires abstraction of components and their integration. Such outcomes are less than certain with children (e.g., McGivern et al., 1986; Pressley, Levin & Ghatala, 1984). Nonetheless, consistently viewing people being strategic should create general strategic tendencies. For intellectual tasks that recur in the child's world (e.g., reading, addition), there are potentially many of these observational learning opportunities. Abstraction and integration are more likely with such repetition. There are also many things that a model can do to make the processing very clear. Models can exaggerate subtle components and explicitly point out difficulties. They can articulate relationships between various components, making cause and effect more obvious. And, of course, modeled actions can be repeated—especially when the model is on videotape or the fictional hero of a text.

In contrast to the ambiguities of modeling, whole courses on strategies make processing very explicit, with lots of strategy demonstrations. Because many strategies can be presented quickly in these courses, they should be considered as one component of strategy education. On the other hand, because strategies are germane to so many school subjects, strategy instruction should not be confined to specific isolated courses. There are opportunities during reading, mathematics, and social studies instruction to introduce sound approaches to processing. The relevance of strategic thinking should be much clearer if presented in such an integrated fashion.

Finally, proleptic instruction has one great disadvantage. It is very expensive since it is one-to-one or one-to-a-few at best. There are many educational settings where such tutoring is simply not feasible given staffing constraints. Thus, deployment of this approach will probably be limited. With slow learners, however, this type of training may be the best bet reviewed here. Certainly the great improvement in the functioning of poor readers following this type of individualized instruction (Palincsar & Brown, 1984) provides motivation for additional investigation of this approach as an important tool in special education. It seems to us that of all the alternative teaching techniques, proleptic instruction is the one most likely to take any given nonstrategic child and turn her or him into a competent strategy user. For most children, however, the same might be accomplished with direct explanation in class-size groups, and thus, it is not clear at this point that the costs of reciprocal instruction are usually necessary. Before any firm conclusions are possible, however, within-experiment comparisons of direct explanation and reciprocal instruction should be made in order to determine the relative costs and benefits of the two approaches.

B. SPECIFIC STRATEGY KNOWLEDGE

There are three basic ways that children can acquire specific strategy knowledge (Pressley, Borkowski, & O'Sullivan, 1984, 1985). The first, and probably the approach most certain to produce children who know a lot about strategies, is for an external agent to provide information about where and when to use strategies, as well as commentary on how to adapt strategies to new situations. Such information can be fit into direct explanations, reciprocal instruction, courses on strategies, and modeling of strategic processing. We believe that it should be and that it can be added to instruction rather easily. See, for instance, Simon's (1980) analysis of how to construct worked-out examples that include what we refer to as specific strategy knowledge.

The second approach to development of specific strategy knowledge is to let people discover it on their own as they use strategies, with two main suggestions for enhancing the likelihood that students will figure out when to use a strategy. One is to vary practice materials across the entire range of strategy applications; the second is to provide opportunities to experience situations where the strategy cannot be applied profitably (e.g., Deshler, Alley, Warner, & Schumaker, 1981; E. D. Gagné, 1985, Chapter 5). The problem with this approach, as with all forms of discovery, is that the learners may never figure out the critical specific strategy knowledge.

That there are many occasions when students could discover pertinent information about strategies makes it unsatisfactory to dismiss discovery learning of specific strategy knowledge completely, however. Thus, the third approach to promoting acquisition of specific strategy knowledge in children is to teach them procedures for discovering metacognitive knowledge, to teach what Pressley, Borkowski, and O'Sullivan (1984, 1985) referred to as *metacognitive acquisition procedures*. The one such procedure that has been examined in detail is comparison of two strategies to determine which one is more potent (Ghatala *et al.*, 1985, 1986; Lodico *et al.*, 1983). What emerges from these studies is a portrait of young children who do not spontaneously use the metacognitive acquisition procedure of strategy comparison but who can be taught to execute the procedure profitably. Specifically, children as young as 6 years of age are able to acquire knowledge about strategy utility by comparing the potency of one strategy to that of another. This utility knowledge can then be used to guide subsequent strategy selections.

A lot of metacognitive acquisition procedures need to be studied in detail before any definitive, general conclusions can be drawn about their effectiveness. Candidate procedures include trying out strategies with diverse materials, comparing performance when a strategy is used versus when it is not, comparing and contrasting strategies with similar components, and comparing strategies given different states (e.g., tired versus wide awake) and/or time requirements (e.g., very little time to learn versus unlimited study opportunity). Metacognitive acquisition procedures boil down to reflecting on strategies and their potential applications and associated utilities. Such reflection is viewed by many strategy theorists as critical to understanding strategies and to using them broadly (e.g., Lipman, 1985; Lochhead, 1985). These metacognitive acquisition procedures can probably be taught with any of the approaches except discovery. As is true for all strategic procedures, their effective acquisition seems more certain with more explicit training, like that provided by direct explanation and reciprocal instruction. In short, we believe that strategy instructors should provide a lot of specific strategy knowledge and information directly.

We conclude this subsection with points about the nature of strategic practice. Strategy practice should involve the full range of relevant tasks. Whether the critical attributes of the task are being pointed out or children have to discover them on their own, acquisition of relevant specific strategy knowledge depends on exposure to tasks that call for the strategy. Some of the strategy courses that are now available fall particularly short on this dimension, although the problem is present whenever training materials do not mirror tasks in the real world of children. Knowledge of when to apply a strategy is most certain following exposure to tasks that have much in common with the criterion. These opportunities can be incorporated easily into direct explanation, reciprocal instruction, guided participation, and modeling.

One real problem with the theoretical position that humans have a large number of strategies, each of which is relatively specific in application, and each of which has associated specific strategy knowledge, is the problem of what Newell (1980) calls *the big switch*. How do humans quickly sort through all that specific strategy knowledge in order to elect the strategy in their repertoire that best fits the current situation? One possibility is that specific strategy knowledge operates consciously in the early stages of strategy acquisition and generalization, but that after a few opportunities to apply a strategy in a situation, there is a direct association between the strategy and the setting. A person just knows to apply strategy Y in context B (Flavell, 1984). Practice using a strategy, however, makes conscious use of specific strategy knowledge less necessary. Thus, such practice should become normal operating procedure in strategy instruction. This type of drill would fit easily into direct explanations, proleptic teaching, and guided participation.

C. GENERAL BELIEFS AND GENERAL STRATEGIC TENDENCIES

General strategy knowledge (e.g., effort is important to successful strategy execution; cognitive skills can often be bent a bit to fit new situations) can be conveyed as part of direct explanations, reciprocal instruction, guided participation, and strategy courses and by models. All that is required is to modify the input provided to students, for instance, by including direct comments about effort and strategy flexibility. In contrast, discovery learning falls short with respect to general strategy information. Such information can only be abstracted over the course of discovering a variety of strategies. It seems possible for three types of errors to follow from discovery. One is that the general tendency may be overextended (e.g., coming to believe that effort is all that is required to do well); the second is that the general tendency may not be discovered at all; and the third is that it may only be partially discovered.

As far as the general action-control tendency is concerned, again all of the approaches except discovery seem to be suited to the task of controlling children's emotions and attention. Nonetheless, approaches that include a lot of personal attention from the teacher (most notably, dyadic instruction) seem to have an edge. An attentive, sensitive teacher is in a good position to detect problems of action control and to try and remedy them. Such a good teacher would try to alter debilitating attributions (e.g., point out the error of thinking, "I can't do this because I am dumb," and replace it with the cognition that "I could do this if I used the right strategy"), eliminate distractions, inform the child of the importance of ignoring distractions, perhaps teach the child some strategies for doing so (e.g., self-instruction to ignore intrusions; Pressley *et al.*, 1983), respond to a child's task-related anxieties with reassurances, and perhaps teach the child relaxation techniques to deal with anxiety. This advantage of proleptic instruction again highlights its applicability with special students.

D. Nonstrategic Knowledge

None of the approaches to strategy instruction deal extensively with the knowledge base. Such inattention is no longer defensible in light of analyses, like the good strategy user model as well as others (e.g., Sternberg, 1985b), that prominently feature strategy by knowledge base interactions. Although some strategies do not require a well-developed knowledge base, there seem to be many more that do (Polson & Jeffries, 1985).

An instructional implication that follows is that strategies and domain-relevant knowledge should probably be taught simultaneously. This is another argument for teaching strategies in the contexts in which they will be used rather than in separate courses. Beyond that, however, is the educational mandate not to sacrifice the declarative knowledge base in favor of teaching strategies. Every effort should be made to increase the world knowledge of students. Knowing facts is important! Efficient processing often does not occur without them, no matter how strategic the learner is.

We reiterate that there is nothing inimical about learning declarative knowledge and forms of strategy instruction, such as direct explanation, dyadic instruction, guided participation, and modeling. In fact, if students are using content-related materials to practice efficient strategies, it would be expected that learning of the declarative content would be better in these instructional situations than when children are left to their own less efficient devices to acquire factual knowledge. There is potential for a real snowball effect as students are armed with more strategies as well as mastery of domain-relevant curricular knowledge.

E. Summary

To return to our fictional example, Fenton Hardy spent years teaching strategies and domain-specific declarative knowledge to Frank and Joe. Like most forms of expertise (e.g., Lesgold, 1984), competent strategy use takes a long time to develop. Thus, we believe that strategy instruction should occur across the school curriculum and in diverse aspects of the child's world. Both direct explanation and reciprocal instruction seem especially well suited to conveying strategies and knowledge about strategies. Direct explanation seems most appropriate for regular classrooms. Given the amount of attention required from the person who is teaching the child, reciprocal instruction seems especially suited to family settings. When small teacher-to-student ratios are possible in school, however, it can be employed there as well. It seems to be powerful with students who experience difficulty learning strategies in the regular classroom setting.

Despite our preference for direct explanation and reciprocal instruction, we realize that the alternative methods have roles in the program of pervasive, long-term teaching that we believe is necessary to develop good strategy users who are broadly knowledgeable both about cognitive processing and the world in general. In making the summary recommendation for extended and pervasive strategy instruction, we recognize that it is more an article of faith than one based on conclusive experimental data. Definitive judgments about long-term strategy instruction must be deferred until there are evaluations of extensive strategy instructional interventions that extend over several years. What if children were given 3 to 5 years of strategy teaching distributed across reading, math, social studies, science, and sports? How would their thinking differ from that of children who experienced the normal curriculum? Such an experiment is possible, and it seems that we are near a point when such an extensive study might be conducted profitably. Many strategies have been identified for many different tasks in many different domains (although most require additional validation), and the six approaches to instruction identified here are available (athough again, each requires additional study). If the graduates of a strategy-rich program really did look better on a variety of cognitive measures compared to children in the regular curriculum, the finding would do much to fuel additional study and implementation of the strategy instructional approach to education. We think it is time to dream big about this approach and to try to translate those big dreams into informative tests about the use of long-term strategy instruction to create generally better thinkers.

ACKNOWLEDGMENTS

Writing of this chapter was supported by a grant to the first author from the Natural Sciences and Engineering Research Council of Canada.

REFERENCES

Anderson, J. R. (1983). *The architecture of cognition*. Cambridge, MA: Harvard University Press.

Ausubel, D. P. (1961). Learning by discovery: Rationale and mystique. *Bulletin of the National Association of Secondary School Principals, 45*, 18–58.

Bandura, A. (1969). *Principles of behavior modification*. New York: Holt.

Bandura, A. (1977). *Social learning theory*. Englewood Cliffs, NJ: Prentice-Hall.

Bereiter, C., & Bird, M. (1985). Use of thinking aloud in identification and teaching of reading comprehension strategies. *Cognition and Instruction, 2*, 91–130.

Best, D. L., & Ornstein, P.A. (manuscript submitted for publication) *Children's generation and communication of mnemonic organizational strategies*. Chapel Hill: University of North Carolina, Department of Psychology.

Bjorklund, D. F. (1985). The role of conceptual knowledge in the development of organization in children's memory. In C. J. Brainerd and M. Pressley (Eds.), *Basic processes in memory development: Progress in cognitive developmental research* (pp. 103–142). Berlin & New York: Springer-Verlag.

Bjorklund, D. F., & Jacobs, J. W., III. (1985). Associative and categorical processes in children's memory: The role of automaticity in the development of organization in free recall. *Journal of Experimental Child Psychology, 39,* 599–617.

Bjorklund, D. F., & Zeman, B. R. (1982). Children's organization and metamemory awareness in their recall of familiar information. *Child Development, 53,* 799–810.

Black, M. M., & Rollins, H. A. (1982). The effects of instructional variables on young children's organization and free recall. *Journal of Experimental Child Psychology, 31,* 1–19.

Borkowski, J. G., Levers, S. R., & Gruenenfelder, T. M. (1976). Transfer of mediational strategies in children: The role of activity and awareness during strategy acquisition. *Child Development, 47,* 779–786.

Brainerd, C. J. (1978). Learning research and Piagetian theory. In L. S. Siegel & C. J. Brainerd (Eds.), *Alternatives to Piaget: Critical essays on the theory* (pp. 69–109). New York: Academic Press.

Bransford, J. D., Stein, B. S., Arbitman-Smith, R., & Vye, N.J. (1985). Improving thinking and learning skills: An analysis of three approaches. In J. W. Segal, S. F. Chipman, & R. Glaser (Eds.), *Thinking and learning skills: Vol. 1. Relating instruction to research* (pp. 133–206). Hillsdale, NJ: Erlbaum.

Brown, A. L., Bransford, J. D., Ferrara, R. A., & Campione, J. C. (1983). Learning, remembering, and understanding. In J. H. Flavell & E. M. Markman (Eds.), *Handbook of child psychology: Vol. 3. Cognitive development* (pp. 77–166). New York: Wiley.

Brown, A. L., & Ferrara, R. A. (1985). Diagnosing zones of proximal development. In J. V. Wertsch (Ed.), *Culture, communication, and cognition: Vygotskian perspectives* (pp. 273–305). London & New York: Cambridge University Press.

Brown, A. L., & Palincsar, A. S. (in press). Reciprocal teaching of comprehension strategies: A natural history of one program for enhancing learning. In J. Borkowski & J. D. Day (Eds.), *Intelligence and cognition in special children: Comparative studies of giftedness, mental retardation, and learning disabilities.* New York: Ablex.

Brown, J. S., & Burton, R. R. (1978). Diagnostic models for procedural bugs in basic mathematical skills. *Cognitive Science, 2,* 155–192.

Cavanaugh, J. C., & Borkowski, J. G. (1979). The metamemory-memory "connection": Effects of strategy training and maintenance. *Journal of General Psychology, 101,* 161–174.

Charles, R. I., & Lester, F. L., Jr. (1984). An evaluation of a process-oriented instructional program in mathematical problem solving in Grades 5 and 7. *Journal for Research in Mathematics Education, 15,* 15–34.

Childs, C. P., & Greenfield, P. M. (1980). Informal modes of learning and teaching: The case of Zinacanteco weaving. In N. Warren (Ed.), *Studies in cross-cultural psychology* (Vol. 2, pp. 169–216). London: Academic Press.

Clifford, M. M. (1984). Thoughts on a theory of constructive failure. *Educational Psychologist, 19,* 108–120.

Collins, A., & Stevens, A. L. (1982). Goals and strategies of inquiry teachers. In R. Glaser (Ed.), *Advances in instructional psychology* (Vol. 2, pp. 65–119). Hillsdale, NJ: Erlbaum.

Cook, L. K., & Mayer, R. E. (1983). Reading strategies training for meaningful learning from prose. In M. Pressley & J. R. Levin (Eds.), *Cognitive strategy research: Educational applications* (pp. 87–131). New York: Springer-Verlag.

Covington, M. V. (1985). Strategic thinking and the fear of failure. In J. W. Segal, S. F. Chipman, & R. Glaser (Eds.), *Thinking and learning skills: Vol. 1. Relating instruction to research* (pp. 389–416). Hillsdale, NJ: Erlbaum.

Dansereau, D. F., Long, G. L., Evans, S. H., & Actkinson, T. R. (1975). *Learning strategy inventory development and assessment* (AFHRL-TR-75-40, Contract F41609-74-C-0013). Brooks Air Force Base, TX: Air Force Systems Command.

Day, J. D. (1983). The zone of proximal development. In M. Pressley & J.R. Levin (Eds.), *Cognitive strategy research: Psychological foundations* (pp. 155-175). Berlin & New York: Springer-Verlag.

de Bono, E. (1976). *Teaching thinking*. London: Temple Smith.

de Bono, E. (1983a). *CoRT thinking, CoRT I, II, III, IV, V: Teacher's notes*. Oxford: Pergamon Press.

de Bono, E. (1983b). *CoRT thinking: Notes*. Oxford: Pergamon Press.

de Bono, E. (1985). The CoRT thinking program. In J. W. Segal, S. F. Chipman, & R. Glaser (Eds.), *Thinking and learning skills: Vol. 1. Relating instruction to research* (pp. 363-388). Hillsdale, NJ: Erlbaum.

Deshler, D. D., Alley, G. R., Warner, M. M., & Schumaker, J. B. (1981). Instructional practices for promoting skill acquisition and generalization in severely learning disabled adolescents. *Learning Disability Quarterly, 4*, 415-421.

Dixon, F. W. (1972). *The Hardy Boys detective handbook*. New York: Grosset & Dunlap.

Duffy, G. G., Roehler, L. R., Vavrus, L. G., Book, C. L., Meloth, M. S., Putnam, J., & Wesselman, R. (1984, April). *A study of the relationship between direct teacher explanation of reading strategies and student awareness and achievement outcomes.* Presented at the annual meeting of the American Educational Research Association, New Orleans, LA.

Durkin, D. (1979). What classroom observations reveal about reading comprehension instruction. *Reading Research Quarterly, 14*, 481-538.

Eanet, M., & Manzo, A. V. (1976). REAP-A strategy for improving reading/writing/study skills. *Journal of Reading, 19*, 647-652.

Elliott-Faust, D. J., & Pressley, M. (1986). How to teach comparison processing to increase children's short- and long-term listening comprehension monitoring. *Journal of Educational Psychology, 78*, 27-33.

Elliott-Faust, D. J., Pressley, M., & Dalecki, L. B. (1986). Process training to improve children's referential communication: Asher and Wigfield revisited. *Journal of Educational Psychology, 78*, 22-26.

Ellis, S., & Rogoff, B. (1982). The strategies and efficacy of child versus adult teachers. *Child Development, 53*, 730-735.

Fenaigle, G. von (1813). *The new art of memory*. London: Sherwood, Neely, & Jones.

Feuerstein, R. (1980). *Instrumental enrichment: An intervention program for cognitive modifiability*. Baltimore, MD: University Park Press.

Finke, R. A. (1985). Theories relating mental imagery to perception. *Psychological Bulletin, 98*, 236-259.

Flavell, J. H. (1970). Developmental studies of mediated memory. In H. W. Reese & L. P. Lipsett (Eds), *Advances in child development and behavior* (Vol. 5, pp. 182-211). New York: Academic Press.

Flavell, J. H. (1972). An analysis of cognitive-developmental sequences. *Genetic Psychology Monographs, 86*, 279-350.

Flavell, J. (1984). Cognitive development during the postinfancy years. In H. W. Stevenson & J. Qicheng (Eds.), *Issues in cognition: Proceedings of a joint conference in psychology* (pp. 1-17). Washington, DC: National Academy of Science, American Psychological Association.

Flavell, J. H. (1985). *Cognitive development*. Englewood Cliffs, NJ: Prentice-Hall.

Forrest-Pressley, D. L., & Gillies, L. A. (1983). Children's flexible use of strategies during reading. In M. Pressley & J. R. Levine (Eds.), *Cognitive strategy research: Educational applications* (pp. 133-156). Berlin & New York: Springer-Verlag.

Gagné, E. D. (1985). *The cognitive psychology of school learning.* Boston, MA: Little, Brown.

Gagné, R. M. (1965). *The conditions of learning.* New York: Holt.

Gagné, R. M., & Brown, L. T. (1961). Some factors in the programming of conceptual learning. *Journal of Experimental Psychology, 62,* 313–321.

Ghatala, E. S., Levin, J. R., Pressley, M., & Goodwin, D. (1986). A componential analysis of the effects of derived and supplied strategy-utility information on children's strategy selection. *Journal of Experimental Child Psychology, 41,* 76–92.

Ghatala, E. S., Levin, J. R., Pressley, M., & Lodico, M. G. (1985). Training cognitive strategy monitoring in children. *American Educational Research Association, 22,* 199–216.

Gibson, E. J. (1969). *Principles of perceptual learning and development.* New York: Appleton.

Gick, M. L., & Holyoak, K. J. (1980). Analogical problem solving. *Cognitive Psychology, 12* 306–355.

Gick, M. L., & Holyoak, K. J. (1983). Schema induction and analogical transfer. *Cognitive Psychology, 15,* 1–38.

Glaser, R. (1984). Education and thinking: The role of knowledge. *American Psychologist, 39,* 93–104.

Glaser, R. (1985). All's well that begins and ends with both knowledge and process: A reply to Sternberg. *American Psychologist, 40,* 573–574.

Greenfield, P. M. (1984). A theory of the teacher in the learning activities of everyday life. In B. Rogoff & J. Lave (Eds.), *Everyday cognition: Its devlopment in social context* (pp. 117–138). Cambridge, MA. Harvard University Press.

Groen, G., & Resnick, L. B. (1977). Can preschool children invent addition algorithms? *Journal of Educational Psychology, 69,* 645–652.

Hansen, J., & Pearson, P. D. (1983). An instructional study: Improving the referential comprehension of good and poor fourth grade readers. *Journal of Educational Psychology, 75,* 821–829.

Hasselhorn, M., & Körkel, J. (1986). Metacognitive versus traditional reading instructions: The mediating role of domain-specific knowledge on children's text processing. *Human Learning, 5,* 75–90.

Heisel, B. E., & Ritter, K. (1981). Young children's storage behavior in a memory-for-location task. *Journal of Experimental Child Psychology, 31,* 350–364.

Herber, H. L. (1970). *Teaching reading in content areas.* Englewood Cliffs, NJ: Prentice-Hall.

Herber, H. L. (1985). Developing reading and thinking skills in content areas. In J.W. Segal, S. F. Chipman, & R. Glaser (Eds.), *Thinking and learning skills: Vol. 1. Relating instruction to research* (pp. 297–316). Hillsdale, NJ: Erlbaum.

Herrmann, B. A. (1986, April). *Strategic problem-solving of mathematical story problems: A descriptive study of the effects and characteristics of direct teacher explanation.* Presented at the annual meeting of the American Educational Research Association, San Francisco, CA.

Higbee, K. L. (1977). *Your memory: How it works and how to improve it.* Englewood Cliffs, NJ: Prentice-Hall.

Higgins, E. T., Fondacaro, R., & McCann, D. (1981). Rules and roles: The "communication game" and speaker-listener processes. In W. P. Dickson (Ed.), *Children's oral communication skills* (pp. 289–312). New York: Academic Press.

Jones, B. F., Amiran, M., & Katims, M. (1985). Teaching cognitive strategies and text structures within language arts programs. In J. W. Segal, S. F. Chipman, & R. Glaser (Eds.), *Thinking and learning skills: Vol. 1. Relating instruction to research* (pp. 259–295). Hillsdale, NJ: Erlbaum.

Kail, R. V. (1984). *The development of memory in children* (2nd ed.). San Francisco, CA: Freeman.

Kendall, P. C., & Braswell, L. (1982). Cognitive-behavioral self-control therapy for children: A component analysis. *Journal of Consulting and Clinical Psychology, 50,* 672–689

Kendall, P. C., & Braswell, L. (1985). *Cognitive-behavioral therapy for impulsive children.* New York: Guilford Press.

Kennedy, B. A., & Miller, D. J. (1976). Persistent use of verbal rehearsal as a function of information about its value. *Child Development, 47,* 566–569.

Kersh, B. Y. (1958). The adequacy of "meaning" as an explanation for superiority of learning by independent discovery. *Journal of Educational Psychology, 49,* 282–292.

Kosslyn, S. M. (1983). *Ghosts in the mind's machine: Creating and using images in the brain.* New York: Norton.

Kuhl, J. (1985). Volitional mediators of cognition-behavior consistency: Self-regulatory processes and action control versus state orientation. In J. Kuhl & J. Beckmann (Eds.), *Action control: From cognition to behavior* (pp. 101–128). Berlin & New York: Springer Verlag.

Lawson, M. J., & Fuelop, S. (1980). Understanding the purpose of strategy training. *British Journal of Educational Psychology, 50,* 175–180.

Lesgold, A. M. (1984). Acquiring expertise. In J. R. Anderson & S. M. Kosslyn (Eds.), *Tutorials in learning and memory: Essays in honor of Gordon Bower* (pp. 31–60). San Francisco, CA: Freeman.

Levin, J. R., & Pressley, M. (1981). Improving children's prose comprehension: Selected strategies that seem to succeed. In C. M. Santa & B. L. Hayes (Eds.), *Children's prose comprehension: Research and practice* (pp. 44–71). Newark, DE: International Reading Association.

Lewis, M. W., & Anderson, J. R. (1985). Discrimination of operator schemata in problem solving: Learning from examples: *Cognitive Psychology, 17,* 26–65.

Lindsay, P. H., & Norman, D. A. (1977). *Human information processing* (2nd ed.). New York: Academic Press.

Lipman, M. (1985). Thinking skills fostered by philosophy for children. In J. W. Segal, S. F. Chipman, & R. Glaser (Eds.), *Thinking and learning skills: Vol. 1. Relating instruction to research* (pp. 83–108). Hillsdale, NJ: Erlbaum.

Lochhead, J. (1985). Teaching analytic reasoning skills through pair problem solving. In J. W. Segal, S. F. Chipman, & R. Glaser (Eds.), *Thinking and learning skills: Vol. 1. Relating instruction to research* (pp. 109–132). Hillsdale, NJ: Erlbaum.

Lodico, M. G., Ghatala, E. S., Levin, J. R., Pressley, M., & Bell, J. A. (1983). Effects of metamemory training on children's use of effective learning strategies. *Journal of Experimental Child Psychology, 35,* 263–277.

Mandler, J. M. (1979). Categorical and schematic organization in memory. In C. R. Puff (Ed.), *Memory organization and structure* (pp. 259–299). New York: Academic Press.

Mandler, J. M. (1983). Representation. In J. H. Flavell & E.M. Markman (Eds.), *Handbook of child psychology: Vol. 3. Cognitive development* (pp. 420–494). New York: Wiley.

McGivern, J. E., Levin, J. R., Ghatala, E. S., & Pressley, M. (1986). Can selection of an effective memory strategy be induced vicariously? *Contemporary Educational Psychology, 11,* 170–186.

Miller, G. E. (1985). The effects of general and specific self-instructional training on children's comprehension monitoring performances during reading. *Reading Research Quarterly, 20,* 616–628.

Moely, B. E. (1977). Organizational factors in the development of memory. In R.V. Kail & J. W. Hagen (Eds.), *Perspectives on the development of memory and cognition* (pp. 203–236). Hillsdale, NJ: Erlbaum.

Moely, B. E., Hart, S. S., Santulli, K., Leal, L., Johnson-Baron, T., Rao, N., & Burney, L. (1986). How do teachers teach memory skills? *Educational Psychologist, 21,* 55–72.

Newell, A. (1980). One final word. In D. T. Tuma & F. Reif (Eds.), *Problem solving and education* (pp. 175–189). Hillsdale, NJ: Erlbaum.

Ornstein, P. A., Baker-Ward, L., & Naus, M. J. (in press). The development of children's mnemonic skills. In F. Weinert & M. Perlmutter (Eds.), *Memory development: Universal changes and individual development.* Hillsdale, NJ: Erlbaum.

Ornstein, P. A., & Corsale, K. (1979). Organizational factors in children's memory. In C. R. Puff (Ed.), *Memory organization and structure* (pp. 219–258). New York: Academic Press.

Ornstein, P. A., & Naus, M. J. (1985). Effects of the knowledge base on children's memory knowledge. In H. W. Reese (Ed.), *Advances in child development and behavior* (Vol. 19, pp. 113–148). San Diego, CA: Academic Press.

O'Sullivan, J. T., & Pressley, M. (1984). Completeness of instruction and strategy transfer. *Journal of Experimental Child Psychology, 38,* 275–288.

Paivio, A. U. (1986). *Mental representations: A dual-coding approach.* London & New York: Oxford University Press.

Palinscar, A. S., & Brown, A. L. (1984). Reciprocal teaching of comprehension-fostering and monitoring activities. *Cognition and Instruction 1,* 117–175.

Palincsar, A. S. (1986). The role of dialogue in providing scaffolded instruction. *Educational Psychologist, 21,* 73–98.

Paris, S. G., Newman, R. S., & McVey, K. A. (1982). Learning the functional significance of mnemonic actions: A microgenetic study of strategy acquisition. *Journal of Experimental Child Psychology, 34,* 490–509.

Piaget, J. (1970). Piaget's theory. In P. H. Mussen (Ed.), Carmichael's *Manual of child psychology* (3rd ed., Vol. 1, pp. 703–732). New York: Wiley.

Polson, P. G., & Jeffries, R. (1985). Instruction in general problem-solving skills: An analysis of four approaches. In J. W. Segal, S. F. Chipman, & R. Glaser (Eds.), *Thinking and learning skills: Vol. 1. Relating instruction to research* (pp. 417–455). Hillsdale, NJ: Erlbaum.

Pressley, G. M. (1976). Mental imagery helps 8-year-olds remember what they read. *Journal of Educational Psychology, 68,* 355–359.

Pressley, M. (1982). Elaboration and memory development. *Child Development, 53,* 296–309.

Pressley, M., Borkowski, J. G., & O'Sullivan, J. T. (1984). Memory strategy instruction is made of this: Metamemory and durable strategy use. *Educational Psychologist, 19,* 94–107.

Pressley, M., Borkowski, J. G., & O'Sullivan, J. T. (1985). Children's metamemory and the teaching of memory strategies. In D. L. Forrest-Pressley, G. E. MacKinnon, & T. G. Waller (Eds.), *Metacognition, cognition, and human performance* (pp. 111–153). New York: Academic Press.

Pressley, M., Borkowski, J. G., & Schneider, W. (1987). Cognitive strategies: Good strategy users coordinate metacognition and knowledge. In R. Vasta & G. Whitehurst (Eds.), *Annals of child development* (Vol. 4). Greenwich, CT: JAI Press.

Pressley, M., Forrest-Pressley, D. L., Elliott-Faust, D., & Miller, G. E. (1985). Children's use of cognitive strategies, how to teach strategies, and what to do if they can't be taught. In M. Pressley & C. J. Brainerd (Eds.), *Cognitive processes in memory development* (pp. 1–47). Berlin & New York: Springer-Verlag.

Pressley, M., Heisel, B. E., McCormick, C. G., & Nakamura, G. V. (1982). Memory strategy instruction with children. In C. J. Brainerd & M. Pressley (Eds.), *Progress in cognitive development research: Vol. 2. Verbal processes in children* (pp. 125–159). Berlin & New York: Springer-Verlag.

Pressley, M., & Levin, J. R. (1980). The development of mental imagery retrieval. *Child Development, 51,* 558–560.

Pressley, M., & Levin, J. R. (Eds.). (1983a). *Cognitive strategy research: Educational applications.* New York: Springer-Verlag.

Pressley, M., & Levin, J. R. (Eds.). (1983b). *Cognitive strategy research: Psychological foundations.* New York: Springer-Verlag.

Pressley, M., & Levin, J. R. (1986). Elaboration learning strategies for the inefficient learner. In S. J. Ceci (Ed.), *Handbook of cognitive, social, and neuropsychological aspects of learning disabilities* (pp. 175–212. Hillsdale, NJ: Erlbaum.

Pressley, M., Levin, J. R., & Delaney, H. D. (1982). The mnemonic keyword method. *Review of Educational Research, 52,* 61-92.

Pressley, M., Levin, J. R., & Ghatala, E. S. (1984). Memory strategy monitoring in adults and children. *Journal of Verbal Learning and Verbal Behavior, 23,* 270-288.

Pressley, M., Levin, J. R., Kuiper, N. A., Bryant, S. L., & Michener, S. (1982). Mnemonic versus nonmnemonic vocabulary-learning strategies: Additional comparisons. *Journal of Educational Psychology, 74,* 693-707.

Pressley, M., & MacFadyen, J. (1983). The development of mnemonic mediator usage at testing. *Child Development, 54* 474-479.

Pressley, M., Reynolds, W., Stark, K. D., & Gettinger, M. (1983). Cognitive strategy training and children's self-control. In M. Pressley & J. R. Levin (Eds.), *Cognitive strategy research: Psychological foundations* (pp. 267-300). New York: Springer-Verlag.

Pressley, M., Ross, K. A., Levin, J. R., & Ghatala, E. S. (1984). The role of strategy utility knowledge in children's strategy decision making. *Journal of Experimental Child Psychology, 38,* 491-504.

Reid, M. K., & Borkowski, J. G. (1985). *The influence of attribution training on strategic behaviors, self-management, and beliefs about control in hyperactive children.* Unpublished manuscript. University of Notre Dame, Department of Psychology, South Bend, IN.

Riley, M. S., Greeno, J. G., & Heller, J. I. (1982). Development of children's problem-solving ability in arithmetic. In H. P. Ginsburg (Ed.), *The development of mathematical thinking* (pp. 153-196). New York: Academic Press.

Ringel, B. A., & Springer, C. J. (1980). On knowing how well one is remembering: The persistence of strategy use during transfer. *Journal of Experimental Child Psychology, 29,* 322-333.

Roehler, L. R., & Duffy, G. G. (1984). Direct explanation of comprehension processes. In G. G. Duffy, L. R. Roehler, & J. Mason (Eds.), *Comprehension instruction: Perspectives and suggestions* (pp. 265-280). New York: Longmans, Green.

Roehler, L. R., Duffy, G. G., Putnam, J., Wesselman, R., Sivan, E., Rockliffe, G., Book, C., Meloth, M., & Vavrus, L. (1986, March). *The effect of direct explanation of reading strategies on low group third graders' awareness and achievement: A technical report of the 1984-85 study* (Tech. Rep.). East Lansing: Michigan State University, Institute for Research on Teaching.

Rogoff, B., & Gardner, W. (1984). Adult guidance of cognitive development. In B. Rogoff & J. Lave (Eds.), *Everyday cognition: Its development in social context* (pp. 95-116). Cambridge, MA: Harvard University Press.

Rohwer, W. D., Jr. (1970). Implications of cognitive development for education. In P. H. Mussen (Ed.), *Carmichael's Manual of child psychology,* (3rd ed., Vol. 1, pp. 1379-1454). New York: Wiley.

Rohwer, W. D., Jr. (1980). How the smart get smarter. *Educational Psychologist, 15,* 34-43.

Rohwer, W. D., Jr., & Thomas, J. W. (1986). The role of mnemonic strategies in study effectiveness. In M. A. McDaniel & M. Pressley (Eds.), *Imagery and related mnemonic processes: Theories and applications.* New York: Springer-Verlag.

Rosenberg, S., & Cohen, B. D. (1966). Referential processes of speakers and listeners. *Psychological Review, 73,* 208-231.

Rosenthal, T. L., & Zimmerman, B. J. (1978). *Social learning and cognition.* New York: Academic Press.

Schneider, W., Dumais, S. T., & Shiffrin, R. M. (1984). Automatic and control processing and attention. In R. Parasuraman & D. R. Davies (Eds.), *Varieties of attention* (pp. 1-27). Orlando, FL: Academic Press.

Shipman, V. C. (1982). Evaluation of the Philosophy for Children program in Bethlehem, Pennsylvania. *Thinking, 4,* 37-40.

Simon, H. A. (1980). Problem solving and education. In D. T. Tuma & F. Reif (Eds.), *Problem solving and education* (pp. 81–96). Hillsdale, NJ: Erlbaum.

Sternberg, R. J. (1985a). All's well that ends well, but it's a sad tale that begins at the end: A reply to Glaser. *American Psychologist, 40*, 571–573.

Sternberg, R. J. (1985b). *Beyond IQ: A triarchic theory of human intelligence.* London & New York: Cambridge University Press.

Sternberg, R. J., & Ketron, J. L. (1982). Selection and implementation of strategies in reasoning by analogy. *Journal of Educational Psychology, 74*, 399–413.

Suchman, J. R. (1960). Inquiry training in the elementary school. *Science Teacher, 27*, 42–47.

Svenson, O., & Hedonborg, M-L. (1979). Strategies used by children when solving simple subtractions. *Acta Psychologica, 43*, 477–489.

Tarkin, B., Myers, N. A., & Ornstein, P. A. (in preparation). *The effects of stimulus meaningfulness on children's spontaneous rehearsal strategies*: Chapel Hill: University of North Carolina, Department of Psychology.

Thomas, J. W., & Rohwer, W. D., Jr. (1986). Academic studying: The role of learning strategies. *Educational Psychologist, 21*, 19–41.

Tierney, R. J., Readence, J. E., & Dishner, E. K. (1985). *Reading strategies and practices: Guide for improving instruction* (2nd ed.). Boston, MA: Allyn & Bacon.

Turnure, J. E. (1985). Communication and cues in the functional cognition of the mentally retarded. In N. R. Ellis & N. W. Bray (Eds.), *International review of research in mental retardation*, (Vol. 13, pp. 43–77). New York: Academic Press.

Turnure, J. E. (1986). Social influences on cognitive strategies and cognitive development: The role of communication and instruction. *Exceptional Children, 53*, 109–116.

Vygotsky, L. S. (1962). *Thought and language.* Cambridge, MA: MIT Press.

Vygotsky, L. S. (1978). *Mind in society: The development of higher psychological processes.* Cambridge, MA: Harvard University Press.

Weinstein, C. E., & Underwood, V. L. (1985). Learning strategies: The how of learning. In J. W. Segal, S. F. Chipman, & R. Glaser (Eds.), *Thinking and learning skills: Vol. 1. Relating instruction to research* (pp. 241–258). Hillsdale, NJ: Erlbaum.

Wertsch, J. V. (1985). *Vygotsky and the social formation of mind.* Cambridge, MA: Harvard University Press.

Whimbey, A., & Lochhead, J. (1980). *Problem solving and comprehension: A short course in analytical thinking* (2nd ed.). Philadelphia, PA: Franklin Institute Press.

Wittrock, M. C. (1966). The learning by discovery hypothesis. In L. S. Shulman & E. R. Keislar (Eds.), *Learning by discovery: A critical appraisal* (pp. 33–75). Chicago, IL: Rand McNally.

Wood, D. J., Bruner, J. S., & Ross, G. (1976). The role of tutoring in problem solving. *Journal of Child Psychology and Psychiatry, 17*, 89–100.

Woods, S. S., Resnick, L. B., & Groen, G. J. (1975). Experimental test of five process models for subtraction. *Journal of Educational Psychology, 67*, 17–21.

Yussen, S. R. (1974). Determinants of visual attention and recall in observational learning by preschoolers and second graders. *Developmental Psychology, 10*, 93–100.

CHAPTER 5

Transfer of Information: An Instructional Perspective

LARRY W. BROOKS
DONALD F. DANSEREAU[1]

One of the major aims of education, whether stated explicitly or implicitly, is to increase students' ability to competently interact with a varied and changing world. To meet this goal, the student must be able to appropriately transfer knowledge and skills acquired in one setting to another (e.g., from one course to another, from courses to a job situation). Given the central importance of transfer in our educational system, it is surprising that relatively little attention has been paid to this issue by educational and psychological researchers (see Voss, 1978).

As a step toward remedying this neglect, the major purpose of this chapter will be to identify teaching and learning principles that facilitate the transfer of knowledge and skills. To achieve this purpose we will first develop an overall framework for examining the factors that influence the efficacy of transfer. Educationally relevant transfer research will then be examined within this framework, and potentially effective transfer principles will be delineated.

I. TRANSFER FRAMEWORK

In developing an overall framework for the transfer of learning in instructional settings, we have borrowed from the work of a number of

---

[1]The names of the authors are in alphabetical order. Each author contributed equally to the completion of this chapter.

TRANSFER OF LEARNING

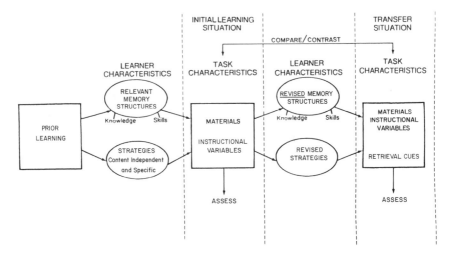

Figure 1. Framework for instructional transfer.

cognitively oriented authors, in particular, Gagné and White (1978). The basis of this framework (see Figure 1) is that learning and transfer involve complex interactions between the learner, the original task, and the transfer task. We will initially outline Gagné and White's model for transfer to provide a general context for the remainder of the chapter. Then, to make the task of overviewing instructional transfer manageable in a single chapter, we will focus our discussion on studies relevant to a subset of that model.

In exploring the interactions suggested by Gagné and White (1978), it is useful to examine the nature of learner and task characteristics separately. In Figure 1, learner characteristics have been divided into two major categories: knowledge and skills that are specifically related to the content of the task at hand, and knowledge and skills that are used to learn and perform in a variety of tasks regardless of content. For example, in learning how to operate a printing press, the student would bring to the situation content-specific knowledge and skills, such as the typical placement and manipulation of control levers, based on experience with printing presses or similar machines. The same student would also bring to the task relatively content-independent learning and problem-solving strategies, such as means–ends analysis, that have been acquired from experiences with many types of tasks and/or from direct "strategy" instruction.

The extent to which the student can use both these content-dependent and content-independent experiences in facilitating performance with the task at hand depends largely on what has been stored in the student's memory, how it has been stored, and the availability of cues for retrieval of the appropriate information. In general, the content and structure of the student's memory is the major mediator between original learning and subsequent performance on a transfer task.

From this perspective, the job of understanding transfer and the learning and teaching principles that facilitate it becomes largely one of determining what types of memory structures are necessary and sufficient for effective performance on a particular class of transfer tasks. Once the nature of these memory structures is determined, the next step is to delineate the teaching and learning strategies that would promote the development of these structures.

Gagné and White (1978) have identified four types of organized memory structures relevant to retention and transfer: (a) networks of propositions, (b) intellectual skills, (c) images, and (d) episodes. In Gagné and White's scheme, propositional memory contains factual or declarative knowledge (see also J. R. Anderson, 1983). Propositions are typically conceived of as subject–predicate constructions put together according to syntactic rules (such as those relating actors and actions, objects and attributes, actions and recipients). A simple example of a verbal proposition would be "For every action there is an equal and opposite reaction." Various types of propositional memory structures have been advocated by a number of cognitive theorists (e.g., J. R. Anderson, 1983; J. R. Anderson & Bower, 1973; Rumelhart, Lindsay, & Norman, 1972).

The term "intellectual skills" has been used to designate the learned memory structures that underlie the identification of concepts and the application of rules (e.g., Gagné, 1976) and can be assumed to be procedural in nature (cf. J. R. Anderson, 1983). One example of an intellectual skill might involve knowing how to make use of the proposition "For every action there is an equal and opposite reaction" in playing a game of billiards.

Image memory structures are perceptually based representations of objects or events and may consist of visual, auditory, and haptic components. Additionally, image memory structures can be formed intentionally by a learner as an alternative way of representing propositional knowledge. In this regard, it is generally agreed that visual imagery is a pervasive and useful encoding strategy (cf. Levin & Pressley, 1985; Paivio, 1971). An example of an image structure would be a mental picture of two billiard balls colliding as an illustration of the Newtonian principle of action–reaction.

The final memory structures identified by Gagné and White are episodes. Tulving (1972) conceived of the episode as a memory representation containing information about temporally dated events and also about temporal-spatial relations among these events. A most important property of episodic memory is its contextual or "autobiographical" nature. Episodes represent events directly experienced by the learner and stored in such a way that the learner can recall that "I did such and such, in such and such a place, at such and such a time" (Tulving, 1972, p. 389). Remembering

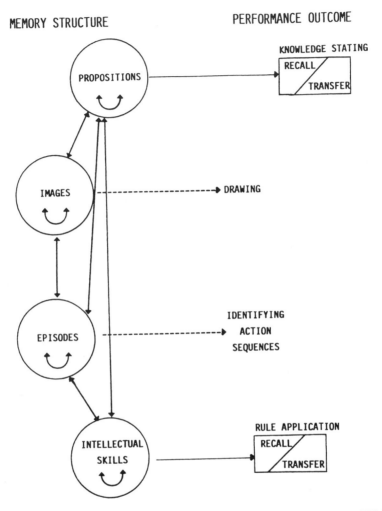

MEMORY STRUCTURE   PERFORMANCE OUTCOME

Figure 2. Outline of Gagné and White model for transfer. (From Gagné, R. M., and White, R. T., "Memory structures and learning outcome." *Review of Educational Research,* 1978, pp. 187–222. Copyright 1978, American Educational Research Association, Washington, D.C.)

the details of a particular game of billiards that one played would be an example of retrieval from episodic memory.

As a result of their review of the relevant literature, Gagné and White concluded that teaching and learning manipulations that lead to the formation of highly integrated, multiple-memory structures (sets of related propositions, intellectual skills, images, and episodes) are most likely to lead to effective retention and subsequent transfer (see Figure 2). Although the present authors agree with this conclusion, it is suggested that the existence of integrated memory structures in some cases is a necessary but *not* sufficient condition for effective transfer. For transfer from one task to another to take place, the individual must be able to determine which aspects (knowledge and skills) of an initial task can be appropriately applied to a second, target task. These skills may be substantially content independent and, thus, may be a part of the individual's repertoire of general learning and problem-solving strategies. Consequently, if these skills are not available, and if compensatory guidance through the transfer task is not provided by an instructor, supervisor, or someone in a similar capacity, then effective transfer will not occur.

The remainder of the chapter will discuss research relevant to different types of transfer situations. To simplify both the presentation and the scope of material, we will organize our overview of instructional transfer around Gagné and White's first two memory structures: proposition networks and intellectual skills. Also, for the purposes of this chapter, we will refer to propositional memory as content knowledge, which can be considered to include relevant facts, concepts, and terms associated with particular topic areas. In other words, this type of knowledge can be described as *what* an individual knows. On the other hand, intellectual skills will simply be referred to as skills knowledge and will be considered to consist of the procedures, algorithms, and activities an individual is able to perform (e.g., solving math problems and playing tennis). Skills knowledge can be thought of as those things an individual knows *how* to do.

Using this basic scheme of content and skills knowledge, four general categories of transfer can be identified: content to content, skills to skills, content to skills, and skills to content (these four types of transfer and associated examples are presented in Figure 3). Within each of these categories the difficulty of transfer will be strongly influenced by the compatibility of the individual's knowledge structure with the characteristics of the transfer task. A high degree of compatibility or similarity will imply "near" transfer, while a low degree will imply "far" transfer (see Royer, 1979, for further discussion concerning the dimensions of transfer).

II. CONTENT-TO-CONTENT TRANSFER

In most educational settings, content-to-content knowledge transfer would consist of transferring knowledge acquired in one course to a second course. For example, in taking a first course in chemistry, a college student may bring with her a repertoire of knowledge concerning biology and physics that could be appropriately applied to learning the new subject. The importance that educators attach to this type of transfer is demonstrated by

CONTENT TO CONTENT

(GENERAL PSYCH TO ABNORMAL PSYCH)

SKILLS TO SKILLS

(RIDING BICYCLE TO DRIVING CAR)

CONTENT TO SKILLS

(LEARNING ABOUT COMPUTERS TO LEARNING TO PROGRAM)

SKILLS TO CONTENT

(CONSTRUCTION OF ELECTRONIC CIRCUITS TO ELECTRONIC THEORY)

Figure 3. General categories of transfer.

the presence of predetermined course sequences in most of the nation's schools. There are at least three ways in which prior knowledge gained in one course may facilitate learning in a second course: (a) The "old" declarative knowledge may provide a general framework for embedding the more detailed "new" knowledge; (b) the "old" knowledge may help in the elaboration of a newly acquired knowledge framework; and (c) the "old" knowledge may provide a convenient analogy which can guide the acquisition of the "new" information.

These three aspects of content-to-content transfer seem to fit well within the context of schema theory. A substantial amount of recent research under the rubric of schema theory has suggested that the amount and form of the relevant background knowledge an individual brings to the instructional situation strongly influences what and how much is learned. Schemata can be viewed as abstract knowledge structures whose elements are other schemata and slots, placeholders, or variables which can take on a restricted range of values (Minsky, 1975; Rumelhart & Ortony, 1977; Schank & Abelson, 1977). A schema is structured in the sense that it indicates typical relationships among component elements. A person will have the subjective sense that a passage has been comprehended when there is a good match between the information presented and the slots in the schema.

It can be assumed that the learner uses two general kinds of schemata in interpreting text. The first embodies knowledge of discourse conventions that signal organization. These are probably specialized conventions characteristic of distinct text forms as well as conventions common to most forms; thus, it is possible to speak of a story schema, a personal letter schema, a news article schema, a scientific report schema, and so on. As a class, knowledge of the discourse-level conventions of text may be called textual schema. Although there has been some research to illustrate the importance of this type of schemata (e.g., Thorndyke, 1977), the vast majority of prior research has been concerned with a second general type, namely, content schema, embodying the learner's existing knowledge of real and imaginary worlds. What the learner already knows and believes about a topic helps to structure the interpretation of new messages about this topic. A large number of research efforts have demonstrated the importance of this second type of schema to the comprehension process (e.g., Schallert, 1982).

If text information is interpreted, organized, and retrieved in terms of high-level schemata or systems of placeholders, it follows that the student who does not possess relevant schemata is going to have trouble learning and remembering the information encountered in stories and textbooks. Educators can do a number of things to alleviate this problem. One possible educational intervention is to present new material in a top-down manner. This would give the student a global perspective of both the structural and factual information on a topic. In later presentations of the material, the student could be given more specific and detailed information (cf. Norman, 1973; Thorndyke, 1977).

Work on the processing of text summaries by Reder and Anderson (1980, 1982) and Brooks (1986) indicates that acquisition of higher order knowledge may in fact be impeded by the presence of details and elaboration. It would follow that educators should clearly separate the presentation of different levels of information. Multilevel textbooks that are processed by students in multiple passes (Dansereau, 1986) may provide a more effective way of communicating complex subject matter.

In addition to assisting the student in establishing relevant schemata, the instructor can facilitate the activation of already existing schemata by providing appropriate cues and bridging materials. In line with this perspective, Ausubel (1963, 1978) proposed that advance organizers can serve as such bridging material, relating a student's prior knowledge to the new material to be learned. Specifically, it has been noted by a number of researchers (cf. Schallert, 1982) that the concept of advance organizers can be thought of as a subset of a schema theory.

Of particular importance for transfer is the work of Mayer (1976, 1978, 1980). He found that subjects given an advance organizer in the form of pretraining with a concrete model of a computer before learning performed better on novel (far) transfer and about the same on near transfer relative to no-pretraining subjects, including subjects who were given posttraining with the same model after learning. He suggests that the concrete model served as an advance organizer which provided subjects with a meaningful learning set to which new information could be assimilated. Those subjects who did not receive the model were apparently encouraged to build more restrictive memory structures by adding the new technical information to their memories in the form presented. Mayer's study indicates that advance organizer material may be effective in promoting delayed retention and far transfer and consequently should be used in settings where these effects are desirable.

In general, two clear findings have emerged from research on advance organizers and text schemata. First, learners make inferences consistent with their schemata. Second, they recall more text information important to their schemata. Although this research has been useful in demonstrating the importance of the interaction of an individual's memory structure with the text to be learned, the focus of this research has been almost exclusively on narrative discourse (i.e., stories). This is unfortunate in that the type of schema that are useful in understanding and recalling narrative prose may not be directly generalizable to many types of academic material where the individual does not have a stored set of directly relevant experiences. In these situations it would appear that more abstract or structural schemata would be of greater importance. In particular, the processing of academic material should be facilitated by form schemata which specify the set of categories of information a well-informed learner should know about a particular topic (cf. Brooks and Dansereau, 1983).

Adjunct questions are another way in which instruction can be modified to potentially facilitate transfer of information. Typically, one or two adjunct questions are inserted either before (prequestions) or after (postquestions) a segment of text. After reading the passage, examination is then made of the amount of questioned (intentional) and nonquestioned (incidental) passage material retained by the learners. The typical finding in studies of this sort (for reviews, see R. C. Anderson & Biddle, 1975; Rickards, 1979) is that the prequestion group retains roughly the same amount of material directly questioned as the postquestion group but that the postquestion group recalls more of the material not actually questioned than the prequestion group or a reading-only control group. It is this so-called indirect effect (R. C. Anderson & Biddle, 1975) which has received the greater degree of empirical attention (for reviews, see Hartley & Davies, 1976; Rickards and Denner, 1978).

Of particular importance in this domain is the research on the use of different types of adjunct questions. Andre (1979), in an extensive review of this literature, concludes that higher level questions (those questions that require the reader to summarize, apply, or make inferences, for example) as opposed to factual questions (those questions that only require the reader to supply or recognize material, primarily verbatim in nature) have facilitative effects on both reproductive and productive knowledge but that the conditions under which such facilitation occurs are not well understood.

With regard to transfer, a number of studies suggest that when students are given adjunct application questions (questions that require the reader to apply a concept or principle to a situation besides the one in which it was presented), as compared to adjunct factual questions, their ability to transfer their knowledge so as to recognize new examples or solve related problems is enhanced (Dapra & Felker, 1974; Watts & Anderson, 1971). The effects of the questions appear to be specific to the concepts and principles asked about in the adjunct questions; the acquisition of other concepts and principles discussed is not facilitated (McConkie, Rayner, & Wilson, 1973; Shavelson, Berliner, Ravitch, & Lodeing, 1974).

Another aspect of instruction related to schema theory and transfer is the organization and structure of instructional material. Any instruction must be presented in some sequence, and indeed this is usually one of the first problems instructors encounter when planning a course of instruction. The problem the instructor faces is that most bodies of information are not clearly organized into a simple sequence. Rather, there are interlocking relationships such that any concept must be considered in relation to several others. Yet language permits the statement of such relationships only one at a time; consequently, a decision must be made as to which relationship is stated first, second, and so on. For example, in describing the operation of a camera, one would ideally present information regarding the operation and interactions of such things as lenses, f-stops, and light meters. However, due to the sequential nature of text, a decision must be made as to what objects and relations are presented first, second, and third.

Although there is some evidence that a "top-down" or "web" teaching sequence is generally preferable (Thorndyke, 1977), the ordering of concepts within a level of the information hierarchy needs to be specified. After an extensive review of the literature, Dansereau, Evans, Wright, Long, and Actkinson (1974) reached three conclusions regarding the sequencing of material. First, although the results are mixed, there is apparently an effect of sequencing on comprehension and retention of academiclike material. Second, except for very specific types of material, there have been very few techniques developed which would provide optimal or near-optimal sequences. Third, the lack of attention to individual differences in academic aptitude has undoubtedly led to the masking of sequencing effects.

On the basis of these conclusions, it is clear that effort should be directed toward the development of technologies for generating sequences and subsequent assessments of the effectiveness of these generated sequences with different bodies of material and with students differing in academic aptitude. As a step in this direction, Dansereau, Long, Evans, and Actkinson (1980) used multidimensional scaling (MDS) as a methodology for creating a composite organizational structure of a set of concepts using the similarity judgments of a number of experts. Systematic algorithms were then employed for sequencing the concepts. The results of this study were promising in that MDS-generated instructional sequences led to higher levels of performance in the learning of technical information than existing sequences.

Additionally, there have been a number of attempts to develop procedures for specifying the structure of texts (Meyer, 1975; van Dijk & Kintsch, 1977). Results of experiments by Kintsch, Kosminsky, Streby, McKoon, and Keenan (1975) and Meyer (1975) using text grammars to specify propositional relationships have indicated that superordinate propositions (those appearing at high levels in the text hierarchy) are better retained, especially at longer retention intervals, than are subordinate propositions (these are defined as propositions appearing at lower level in a text hierarchy). In other words, when reading a newspaper account of an airplane hijacking, one is more likely to remember the name of the country or city in which the hijacking took place, as opposed to the name of the airport, since the former information is superordinate to the later information. Also, Thorndyke (1977) has shown that presenting two successive text passages with the same structure and different content leads to improved learning of the second passage. Apparently the structure acquired by the student from the first passage facilitates the learning of the new information in the second passage.

One educational implication arising from the research on organization and structure is that MDS, as well as other forms of specifying relationships between concepts, may be potentially useful in developing optimal instructional sequences. A second implication, based on the work of Thorndyke (1977), is that the structures of text material should be standardized as much as possible and, where practical, the nature of such structures should be brought to the attention of the students. The latter point will be expanded in a subsequent section on learner variables.

A. Educational Implications

An examination of the research described in this section has led to the following suggestions for improving educational practices designed to foster content-to-content transfer:

Top-down and web-structured instructional material can potentially be used to help students acquire appropriate facts, concepts, and the structural relationships. In turn, the possession of well-structured knowledge may facilitate the transfer of old knowledge to new domains.

Within levels of an information hierarchy, MDS techniques and text grammar formulations should be used to provide a basis for organizing and sequencing instructional materials.

Individuals should have appropriate prerequisite information and create concrete advance organizers to bridge the gaps between their existing cognitive structures and the target learning material.

High-level adjunct postquestions (particularly application questions) should be used to facilitate transfer. These provide "forward" bridges to new materials. They also allow the instructor to assess the present state of the learner's knowledge as a basis for remediation. As illustrated in Figure 1, the learner's cognitive state is of critical importance as a prerequisite to subsequent transfer.

III. SKILLS-TO-SKILLS TRANSFER

In this section the focus will be on the transfer of cognitive skills from one situation to another. The term *cognitive skills* is used here to refer to intellectual skills, such as problem solving and metacognitive monitoring, which depend minimally on motor movement. In a later section concerning skills-to-content transfer, we will discuss the transfer of learning skills that facilitate the acquisition, retention, recall, and transfer of information.

As noted by Frederiksen (1984), problem solving is one of the most important skills an individual can possess, especially in a rapidly changing and increasingly technological world (cf. Rubinstein, 1980; Simon, 1980). Typically, problems are divided into two major categories: well-structured or closed-system problems, and ill-structured or open-ended problems. Bartlett (1958) has suggested that closed-system problems are formed in such a way that all the elements for solution are available, including the appropriate declarative and procedural knowledge necessary for finding a solution. Examples of well-structured problems include anagrams, chess, logic and math problems, and troubleshooting.

On the other hand, Simon (1978) has characterized open-system or ill-structured problems as not providing all the necessary information for arriving at a solution. These types of problems generally do not have specific criteria for determining if a solution is appropriate and frequently have no specified permissible steps for moving from one state to another in attempting to solve the problem. Examples of ill-structured problems include determining unusual uses for common objects, creating titles for movies, solving political disputes, and inventing new devices or products, to name a few. As Simon (1978) has noted, many "real-world" problems are open ended and ill-structured in nature.

A number of researchers (Larkin, 1980; Polya, 1957; Simon, 1980) have attempted to identify processes that are or can be used by humans to solve closed- and open-system problems. These processes, usually labeled heuristics, are rules of thumb for decreasing the extent of an individual's search through his internal problem space. Many of these processes (e.g., means–ends analysis, planning) have recently been incorporated into problem-solving training programs (Segal, Chipman & Glaser, 1986). In particular, Rubinstein (1980) has been conducting a course on problem solving with reasonable success for a decade.

To give the reader a flavor of the possible content for a course on problem solving, we will briefly go into some detail on how a student can be encouraged to advantageously make use of available information in a problem-solving situation. The material reported here is a summarization of a section of Rubinstein's book *Patterns of Problem Solving* (1975) that has been used as the basic material for his problem-solving course. Initially, Rubinstein identifies the difficulty in achieving a solution to a problem: failure to use available information. He then discusses and demonstrates the limitations of human memory in regard to handling large amounts of information. Next Rubinstein points out that by organizing information into chunks, humans can effectively process larger amounts of it. Again, a demonstration is used to actively show the student the advantages of chunking. Finally, a variety of methods for organizing and chunking information are given to the student, along with a specific example of how to use these techniques to solve a typical problem that may be encountered in a classroom setting.

Rubinstein (1980) and others (see Frederiksen, 1984) have generally reported positive results for problem-solving training of this type. However, the effectiveness of these programs appears to be limited to near transfer situations where the test problems are similar to those encountered during training. Evidence for far transfer is generally lacking.

Frederiksen (1984) has extensively reviewed many of these training programs. Based on this review, and work by Rubinstein (1975) and Wickelgren (1973), the following generic steps for solving problems typically taught in these courses can be abstracted:

1. Acquire all available information concerning the problem; this may be both declarative and procedural in nature.
2. Identify the most important and relevant information available for solving the problem.
3. Generate analogies and simplified versions of the problem.
4. Manipulate the information; look for different ways in which parts of the problem may be interrelated, brainstorm.
5. Generate various hypotheses and solutions for solving the problem.
6. Execute, to some degree, the most promising solutions.
7. Compare the outcome of the solution procedure with available criteria.

An interesting aspect of ill-structured problem solving that is receiving increasing attention is the use of analogies and inductive reasoning to facilitate transfer of problem-solving skills from one setting to a second, similar setting. Analogies can be thought of as mental representations that allow one to relate the relevant and essential similarities between two different systems, objects, or knowledge domains. One common example of an analogy is the use of the solar system as a model for an atom and its electrons. Another is the analogy between the flow of electricity in circuits and the flow of water in pipes. Inductive reasoning is based to a large extent on finding appropriate analogies for a problem and then applying the relevant knowledge or rules from the source of the analogy to the target problem.

Recent reviews of this area of research by Holyoak (1985) and Pellegrino (1985) indicate that the use of analogies by students can potentially facilitate the transfer of problem-solving skills. For example, Gick and Holyoak (1980) demonstrated that students originally given a problem and solution concerning the capture of a military installation by dividing an army into smaller, more effective units. were highly likely to transfer the general problem-solving strategy (division and convergence of forces) to a second problem concerning the treatment of a medical illness. Based on this and other research (e.g., Gentner & Gentner, 1983), it seems that students are able, under some conditions, to transfer their knowledge of problem-solving skills to problems that have dissimilar surface features but are isomorphic in relation to their solutions. However, other researchers have had difficulty in obtaining evidence for transfer of problem-solving strategies for isomorphic problems (e.g., Hayes & Simon, 1974).

Closely related to open-system problem solving is creativity training. Generally, program developers have provided instruction on four stages of creativity (open-system problem solving): preparation, incubation, insight, and verification. Evaluations of these creativity programs (e.g., Covington, Crutchfield, Davies, & Oltan, 1974) have also reported positive findings with near transfer tasks, but much less success with far transfer (Mansfield, Busse, & Kroepelka, 1978). Although the prognosis for far transfer of general problem-solving and creativity skills does not appear to be very promising, it is possible that, if training on these skills were embedded in a particular content area, educationally relevant transfer could be facilitated.

A. EDUCATIONAL IMPLICATIONS

By way of summarizing, the following instructional implications have been gleaned from the research on skills-to-skills transfer:

Problem-solving training courses should be developed and administered in close conjunction with a specific technical or academic domain. Since general training on problem-solving skills has not proven successful in the past, the developers of problem-solving courses should tailor the training to those skills required in a particular academic or technical area.

Both closed- and open-system problem-solving techniques should be taught to students. In particular, instruction on the use of open-system problem solving and creativity should be included as part of any problem-solving course.

The use of analogies and inductive reasoning should be explicitly taught in problem-solving and other more traditional courses (e.g., general science).

IV. CONTENT-TO-SKILLS TRANSFER

This type of transfer occurs when an individual's prior knowledge influences the acquisition of a new skill. While content-to-skills transfer is probably involved in all skill-learning situations, it has been the subject of a surprisingly small amount of research. That content knowledge plays an essential role in the development of cognitive skills has been emphasized by J. R. Anderson (1982, 1983) in his formalization of proceduralization. According to Anderson, new skills are originally represented as declarative knowledge, and it is the process of proceduralization that translates declarative, propositional descriptions into a procedural representation. From this perspective, it can be seen that most cognitive skills are based on one or more initial content or declarative representation of the same knowledge and that it is through practice of these skills that the underlying propositional knowledge becomes less important to the execution of these skills as proceduralization takes place.

Related research in the area of problem solving has shown that skill execution is greatly dependent upon content knowledge under at least some conditions. In other words, it appears that in many cases skill knowledge alone is not sufficient for effective skill performance and that in these cases both content and skill knowledge are required to perform a task at the level of an expert. For example, de Groot (1966) and Chase and Simon (1973a, 1973b) have shown that master chess players apparently have a much larger store of content knowledge of specific chess situations compared to less able players. This larger store of information seems to allow the experts to chunk or combine information in ways that are qualitatively different than that of less able players. In turn, this store of chunked or schematized information facilitates the experts' use of chess-playing strategies and skills. The importance of the experts' store of content knowledge is emphasized by the finding that less expert players use the same strategies when playing chess but do not possess the content knowledge of the master players.

Several researchers have attempted to manipulate a learner's prerequisite knowledge relevant to acquiring a skill. Miyake and Norman (1979) have demonstrated that a person's knowledge of a specific content area greatly affects his or her use of a comprehension strategy such as questioning. Matching students, either trained or untrained, in operating a computer terminal with either easy or hard-to-comprehend programming manuals, they found that untrained programmers tended to use a questioning strategy more often when instructed with the easy manual. Conversely, trained programmers tended to ask more questions when instructed with the hard manual. A general conclusion based on this study is that, in order to generate questions, a student needs to have some minimal amount of knowledge relevant to a topic available to him or her at the time of learning.

A number of studies by Mayer (1975; Mayer, Stiehl, & Greeno, 1975) have indicated that, in general, meaningful and interpretative applications of problem-solving skills are enhanced by instruction in content knowledge relevant to the transfer task. Specifically, Mayer *et al.* (1975) found that preinstructional experience directly related to arithmetic problems and varied in content (general knowledge and formula computation) facilitated skill learning under a meaningful-instruction condition. In another study, Mayer (1975) had nonprogrammers learn a computer-programming language either through the use of a diagram model of the computer expressed in familiar terms or without the use of a model. In general, subjects in the model condition excelled on learning and transfer problems requiring interpretation, while nonmodel subjects did better on near transfer tasks requiring only generation of programs similar to those given in the instructions.

Along a similar line, Trollip (1979) used computer-assisted instruction (CAI) to train pilots in the skill of flying holding patterns. This training required the student to artificially "fly" a series of holding patterns at different levels of complexity. Students were given detailed pictorial and verbal feedback about their performance. Consequently, the student should be acquiring both knowledge and experience relevant to performing the required task. Students trained under this condition, when compared with traditionally trained students, demonstrated better performance in an evaluation flight. This suggests that the CAI-trained students could use their prior knowledge gained from feedback on their performance to facilitate their learning of actual flight skills. A final study in this area was conducted by Berg and Stone (1978). Testing whether modeling or verbal instructions were better for enhancing problem-solving skills, they found that both methods of instruction and a combination of the two methods resulted in superior performance on a problem-solving task compared to a control group. These results support the notion that the prior content knowledge that a person has which is relevant to performing a skill will lead to more effective learning and use of that skill.

To briefly summarize, it appears that the prior content knowledge of a learner, if it is meaningful knowledge, functions similarly to Ausubel's (1963) advance organizer. Further, studies by Mayer and Greeno (Egan & Greeno, 1973; Mayer, 1975; Mayer *et al.*, 1975) have given us some information on how different instructional methods interact with the prior knowledge of an individual in skill learning. In general, the basic conclusion of these studies is that those instructional techniques which emphasize meaningful learning are more effective for those students who already possess some degree of content knowledge about the skill to be learned (typically an arithmetic problem). On the other hand, those students who lack prior knowledge about a skill tend to do better under more rote learning conditions. This type of interaction is typically obtained whether the learner's prior knowledge is acquired within the experimental manipulation (preinstruction) or is taken as a preexperimental given.

A. EDUCATIONAL IMPLICATIONS

The research reviewed in this section indicates that the following suggestions for improving educational practices should be considered:

In teaching a new skill, instructions should include relevant content knowledge concerning the acquisition and use of a new skill.

An attempt should be made to present new skills in a meaningful context if broad transfer effects are desired, while a more rote or algorithmic approach should be used if near transfer is the goal of instruction.

Knowledge relevant to acquiring a new skill should be presented without an excess of distracting stimuli. In other words, present a simple example of the skill and the context in which it is used before attempting to instruct the learner in more complicated aspects of the skill.

V. SKILLS-TO-CONTENT TRANSFER

This type of transfer involves the learning of skills that subsequently facilitate the acquisition, retention, retrieval, and transfer of knowledge. These types of skills or strategies are typically taught in separate study skills or learning strategies classes or workshops. In this section the prior research relevant to learning strategy instruction and training will be briefly reviewed. First, research exploring specific, isolated strategies will be discussed, followed by a review of studies of the effectiveness of larger strategy stystems. The research in this general domain examines the type of content-independent knowledge discussed in conjunction with Figure 1.

A. SPECIFIC LEARNING-RELATED STRATEGIES

Most of the prior research on learning strategies has focused on assessing the effects on performance that result from isolated manipulations of component strategies. These experiments have examined cognitive strategies (e.g., identification, comprehension, retention, and retrieval); affective strategies (e.g., concentration); and metacognitive strategies (e.g., monitoring comprehension). A brief overview of prior attempts to study each of these components follows.

Accurate identification of important, difficult, and unfamiliar material is necessary for appropriate allocation of students' time and energy. If such allocations are not accurate, then the resulting learning will be inefficient. In the past, the general approach to research in this area has been to manipulate the identification and selection of stimulus material by varying anticipated recall requirements (Butterfield, Belmont, & Peltzman, 1971; Cermak, 1972; Jacoby, 1973) or monetary payoff conditions (McConkie *et al.*, 1973). These studies do show that students can be flexible in their processing of incoming information, but the manipulations are so task specific that they appear to have little applicability to strategy enhancement in general.

In the area of comprehension and retention, most of the attempts at improving students' skills have been indirect and have entailed stimulating the students to change their comprehension and retention activities with experimenter-generated pre-, post-, and interspersed questions as discussed in the section on content-to-content transfer.

More direct manipulations of comprehension and retention strategies have involved instructing the student on the use of a particular technique. Positive effects on performance have been reported in studies where students have been instructed to form mental images of verbal materials (Schallert, 1980), to state instructional material in their own words (DelGiorno, Jenkins, & Bausell, 1974), and to reorganize instructional materials (DiVesta, Schultz, & Dangel, 1973; Frase, 1973). These instructional manipulations, although somewhat effective as they were first tried, could probably be enhanced by actual training and by integration with training on other aspects of the learning process.

Recent reviews by Bellezza (1981) and Levin and Pressley (1985) reflect an upsurge of interest in mnemonic elaboration as a specific means for enhancing retention. Generally, mnemonic techniques involve embellishing the incoming material by creatively interrelating the items to be learned or by associating the items to a previous[y] learned set of peg words or images (mental pictures). These studies generally support the use of mnemonic strategies as aids in recalling prose. Additionally, there have been a few studies concerned with the transfer of mnemonic devices across situations (see Pressley & Levin, 1983). It appears that transfer of mnemonic strategies does occur under certain circumstances. Minimal criteria for transfer to occur include: (a) an awareness of the need to transfer this strategy to other situations, (b) recognition of appropriate transfer situations, (c) expectation of improved performance, and (d) practice in using mnemonics in different situations.

Direct approaches for improving recall involve the use of retrieval plans for accessing stored materials that are not immediately available. These plans would most likely take the form of coherent search strategies similar to those used in solving problems that have well-defined solutions (e.g., chess problems often require the search for an optimal next move). The problem-solving strategies explored by Newell, Simon, and Shaw (1958) provide a good starting place for the development of such techniques. Additionally, Ritter, Kaprove, Fitch, and Flavell (1973) attempted to improve children's recall performance by instructing them in the use of "planful retrievals" (e.g., systematic search strategies). The results of this study indicated that the retrieval instructions helped, but the stimuli employed (unrelated word pairs) were so artificial that it is difficult to generalize the results to more meaningful tasks.

Research on metacognitive strategies has become a major area of interest within instructional psychology in the last decade (see Baker & Brown, in press). These strategies, which can be thought of as executive processing strategies, are potentially very important mechanisms for enhancing transfer. Previous studies in this area have given researchers a better understanding of the manner in which individuals, especially children, relate their previous knowledge to new learning situations. As summarized by Brown (1980) this area of research has demonstrated that learners frequently have difficulty (a) in recognizing varying tasks and adjusting their cognitive processing to meet task demands (Brown, 1980), (b) knowing when they do or do not understand instructions or other information (Markman 1977), (c) planning and manipulating their study time to the best advantage (Brown & Smiley, 1978), and (d) discriminating between relatively important and unimportant information (Brown & Smiley, 1977, 1978).

To date, relatively little research has been conducted on training students to become more effective monitors of their own cognitive activity. However, recent work by Brown and her associates suggests that one-on-one reciprocal teaching approaches may have considerable promise in this regard. In addition, a number of studies have shown positive results for teaching students to summarize text as one technique for improving comprehension monitoring skills (e.g., Brown & Day, 1983). In particular, Brooks and Given (1986) have demonstrated that students trained (via summarization) to use a comprehension monitoring technique are able to make correct inferences and recall a greater amount of relevant material on a transfer task than students who receive training on cognitive strategies only.

With regard to affective strategies, the primary focus of prior research has been on concentration. Generally, attempts to improve concentration have been oriented toward teaching students to talk to themselves in a constructive, positive fashion as a means of coping with distractions and anxiety (Meichenbaum & Goodman, 1971; Patterson & Mischel, 1975), or they have been oriented directly toward manipulating the student's attention through behavior modification techniques (Alabiso, 1975). Both of these approaches have successfully increased the quantity of task-related behavior, but unfortunately, they have not been coupled with strategies designed to increase the quality of such behavior (e.g., students may be trained to spend more time looking at a textbook, but additional training is probably needed to increase the quality of what they are doing while reading). Clearly this combination should be the ultimate target for a program designed to enhance learning skills.

In summary, the studies that have been reviewed to this point have suffered from at least two problems. First, the materials and tasks used to examine the manipulations have generally been highly artificial (e.g., serial and paired-associate lists of unrelated information). This artificiality limits the generality of these findings to educationally relevant situations. Second, specific components have been studied in isolation (i.e., they have not been integrated with training on other components of the learning process). This lack of integration is extremely troublesome in light of the obvious interrelationships between some of the components (e.g., enhancing comprehension retention skills will clearly have an impact on retrieval, and vice versa). These interrelationships should enable a well-conceived, integrated program to have an impact greater than the sum of its individual parts.

B. Strategy Systems

Many of the reported learning strategies programs have nonempirical foundations, provide relatively superficial strategy training (usually only a subset of the essential learning concepts), are evaluated against nonspecific criteria (such as grade-point average), and consequently, lack specific evidence on which to base modifications. The majority of these learning skills programs are based on the SQ3R (survey, question, read, recall, review) approach proposed by Robinson (1946) or some slight modification of this approach. Generally, SQ3R training is nonspecific; very little detailed information is provided on how to carry out the operations. It is assumed that the individual student is able to arrive at these more specific procedures without guidance. In light of the results with a learning strategy inventory (Dansereau, Long, McDonald, & Actkinson, 1975a), this assumption is probably unwarranted; students appear to have little knowledge of alternative learning procedures, especially at a detailed level.

In any case, a number of programs of this type have been developed and shown to lead to improvement on measures of grade-point average (Briggs, Tosi, & Morley, 1971; Whitehill, 1972) and on self-report study habit surveys (Bodden, Osterhouse, & Gelso, 1972). Although these programs probably benefit the student in a general way, the locus of the effects has not been determined. In addition to general measures of academic success, specific evaluations of learning performance should be made. Furthermore, these evaluations should be related to specific components of the programs to provide a basis for modification. However, even if the previously cited programs are successful, they could probably be improved by incorporating some of the more detailed strategies discussed in the previous section and by adding other strategies derived from the basic cognitive research literature on memory, comprehension, problem solving, and so on. The learning strategy program to be discussed next serves as an example of an approach that overcomes some of these criticisms.

A detailed description of the learning strategy training program developed at Texas Christian University is beyond the scope of this chapter; the various portions of the system have been presented in a number of other publications (see Dansereau, 1978, 1985). The general approach to the development of this strategy system has been strongly influenced by the fact that effective interaction with academic material requires that the student actively engage in a complex system of interrelated activities. To assist the student in this endeavor, a set of mutually supportive strategies has been created. This set can be divided into "primary" strategies used to operate on the material directly and "support" strategies used to help the learner maintain a suitable cognitive climate. The primary set includes strategies for acquiring and storing the information and strategies for subsequently outputting and using the stored information. Networking forms the basis for these primary strategies. During acquisition the student identifies important concepts or ideas in the material and represents their interrelationships in the form of a network map. To assist the student in this endeavor she or he is taught a set of named links that can be used to code the relationships between ideas. The networking processes emphasize the identification and representation of (a) hierarchies (type/part), (b) chains (lines of reasoning/temporal orderings/causal sequences), and (c) clusters (characteristics/definitions/analogies). Assessments of networking (Dansereau *et al.*, 1975b, 1979; Holley & Dansereau, 1984; Holley, Dansereau, McDonald, Garland, & Collins, 1979) have shown that students using this strategy perform significantly better on text-processing tasks than do students using their own methods.

A second major aspect of the primary strategies is the use of knowledge schemata for organizing and retrieving information. These schemata specify the set of categories of information a well-informed learner should know about a particular topic. As an example, six categories of information about a scientific theory were gleaned from questionnaires administered to students at a variety of educational levels. In an independent evaluation of the effects of structured schema training, Brooks and Dansereau (1983) found that this type of training significantly improved performance on a delayed essay test over a 2,500-word passage on the theory of plate tectonics.

The major component of the support strategies is concentration management. This component, which is designed to help the student set and maintain constructive moods for studying and task performance, consists of a combination of elements from systematic desensitization (Wolpe, 1969), rational behavior therapy (Ellis, 1963), and therapies based on positive self-talk (Meichenbaum & Goodman, 1971). The students are first given experiences and strategies designed to assist them in becoming aware of the negative and positive emotions, self-talk, and images they generate in facing a learning task. They are then instructed to evaluate the constructiveness of their internal dialogue and are given heuristics for making appropriate modifications.

In preparing for studying or testing sessions, students report that they usually spend little or no conscious effort establishing constructive moods. To remedy this situation the student is trained on a technique that forms the basis of systematic desensitization: imagination of the target situation during relaxation. More specifically, the students are instructed to spend 2–3 min relaxing and then imagining their actions as they proceed through a productive study or test session. To help them maintain the resulting mood, they are given experiences and techniques to assist them in determining when, how, and why they get distracted, the duration of their distraction periods, and their typical reactions to distraction. They are then trained to cope with distractions by using relaxation and positive self-talk and imagery to reestablish an appropriate learning state.

This particular combination of concentration management strategies has been shown to lead to significantly better performance on text-processing tasks in comparison to students using their own method (Collins, Dansereau, Garland, Holley, & McDonald, 1981). These strategies have been supplemented by training on goal setting, scheduling, and monitoring (see Dansereau, 1978) to form the support strategy component of the program.

Recently, parts of the learning strategy system have been modified to be used by cooperating pairs of students (dyads). In this research both participant-generated and experimenter-imposed study scripts have been examined. These scripts require both members of a dyad to read a section of text and then for one member (the recaller) to recall and summarize from memory the section of text. The second member (the listener) of the pair serves as a metacognitive coach, correcting recall errors and facilitating the use of elaborative and organizational study activities. The partners in the dyad alternate the roles of recaller and listener for succeeding sections of the passage.

Using variants of this study script, a series of experiments have been conducted to determine the impact of various experimental manipulations on content-dependent and content-independent recall and content-independent transfer. Generally, in these experiments the performance of study dyads operating under experimenter-imposed and learner-generated study scripts have been compared with each other and with individual "control" conditions. A brief summary of the results of these experiments will be grouped into three categories for clarity of presentation.

1. Script × Goal Interactions

McDonald, Larson, Dansereau, and Spurlin (1985) found that, in comparison to participant-generated dyadic scripts and individual scripts, an imposed dyadic script, similar to the one described previously, facilitated initial acquisition of scientific text (content-dependent transfer) and led to positive content-independent transfer from dyadic to individual learning. Participant-generated dyadic scripts also facilitated initial acquisition but did not lead to positive content-independent transfer. Participant-generated scripts that capitalized on task-relevant expertise may be relatively useful for content-dependent outcomes. However, since these scripts typically place people in familiar and comfortable information-processing roles, they do not provide significant opportunities for acquiring content-independent strategies. On the other hand, a well-conceived, imposed script that places the participants in roles they might not normally perform can lead to both content-dependent and content-independent transfer.

Spurlin, Dansereau, Larson, and Brooks (1984) have shown that if the goal is to maximize the outcomes for both participants, alternation of recaller and listener roles is more effective than the maintenance of fixed roles and that an active listener role is more effective than a passive listener role. In addition, script x goal interactions have been found in comparing dyads using scripts that amplify metacognitive activities with those scripts that emphasize cognitive activities. Use of metacognitive scripts facilitates content-dependent outcomes compared to the use of cognitive scripts that facilitate content-independent transfer (Larson et al., 1985). Further analysis has suggested that study scripts that require "cognitive" activity (i.e., effort toward memorization) to be distributed evenly across the task are more effective than scripts that required massed "cognitive" activity at the end of a task (O'Donnell et al., 1985).

2. Script × Task Interactions

In the experiments described in the previous section, the tasks consisted of learning and recalling excerpts from college-level science textbooks. To determine the generality and limitations of the basic scripts, experiments employing other types of tasks have been conducted. In one set of experiments, the relationships between study scripts and the learning of technical material was examined. This material typically consists of information on the structure and function of a piece of equipment (declarative knowledge) and a set of procedures for operating or troubleshooting the equipment (procedural knowledge). It has been found that the basic dyadic script is sufficient for improving the learning of structural and functional information (Lambiotte *et al.*, 1986; Larson *et al.*, 1985). However, the learning of procedures requires a slight script modification. If the role of the recaller is expanded to include performance tasks so that the recaller/performer either simulates or goes through the actual task operations with the equipment, then content-dependent and content-independent outcomes are enhanced (Hythecker *et al.*, 1985; O'Donnell *et al.*, 1986). Also in contrast to results obtained with academic material, results of experiments with technical material indicate that learner-generated scripts are not as effective in any situation as are imposed learning scripts.

3. General Boundary Conditions of Imposed Scripts

Although there has been substantial success at improving content-dependent and content-independent outcomes with imposed scripts, there have also been some notable failures. These failures have occurred when the script has led to a high degree of passivity on the part of one or both members of the cooperative pair (Spurlin *et al.*, 1984) or when the script has been too detailed and explicit about prescribed group acitivities (Hythecker *et al.*, 1985; O'Donnell *et al.*, in press). In the first case, social loafing (Latane, Williams, & Harkins, 1979) may lead to poor performance, and in the second case, task overload (Hythecker *et al.*, 1985) and a high degree of incongruence of the script with personal aptitudes and styles (Dansereau, in press) may create problems. It appears that the most effective script is one that encourages active (and, in some cases, nonhabitual) processing among participants and yet is flexible enough to permit the participants to tailor their roles to exploit their own processing strengths.

C. EDUCATIONAL IMPLICATIONS

Many teaching and testing methods implicitly encourage rote memorization by specifying exactly what must be learned, rewarding verbatim answers on tests and putting little emphasis on the development of relationships between incoming and stored information. Rote memorization usually involves multiple readings of the material with little or no effort devoted to assimilating the information. Therefore, the material learned through this method usually is not meaningfully related to other stored information, which limits the facility with which such information can be retrieved and used at a later date. Such a strategy, although perhaps useful in our present educational environments, is very maladaptive in many job situations, where understanding is far more important than mere storage. Although the limitations of rote memorization have been emphasized, the same arguments probably apply to a large number of other strategies developed by students to cope with a teaching-oriented education.

Recommendations to educators to improve current practices in this area are:

Educators should be redirecting at least some of their efforts to the development and training of appropriate learning skills. It is suggested that such training include an emphasis on both primary and support strategies.

The strategies should be focused on creating integrated knowledge structures that would facilitate subsequent transfer (see "Transfer Framework" for a discussion of Gagné & White's 1978 formulations of integrated knowledge structures). The networking and knowledge schema strategies discussed earlier should provide good bases for the creation of integrated knowledge structures.

Finally, the recent work on peer tutoring (cooperative learning) strongly indicates that this can serve as a relatively low-cost option for enhancing skill-to-content transfer.

VI. CONCLUSION

In closing, the framework and research presented in this chapter are rudimentary due to the current nature of the field. However, as instructional psychology matures as a discipline, we can expect to see more formalized models and theories regarding instructional transfer. Hopefully, this research will offer the practitioner explicit and sound advice on how to enhance the appropriate transfer of information. On the other hand, the practitioner will be invaluable as a barometer for how well these models perform when confronted with "real"-world problems and situations. With this chapter, we have attempted to make an initial step toward bridging the gap between researcher and practitioner by organizing and presenting some of the research related to instructional transfer so that a few, reasonable straightforward recommendations can be made regarding the implementation of instructional transfer techniques and strategies in a variety of educational settings.

REFERENCES

Alabiso, F. (1975). Operant control of attention behavior: A treatment for hyperactivity. *Behavior Therapy, 6*, 39–42.

Anderson, J. R. (1982). Acquisition of cognitive skill. *Psychological Review, 89*, 369–406.

Anderson, J. R. (1983). *The architecture of cognition.* Cambridge, MA: Harvard University Press.

Anderson, J. R., & Bower, G. H. (1973). *Human associative memory.* Washington, DC: Winston.

Anderson, R. C., & Biddle, W. B. (1975). On asking people questions about what they are reading. In G. Bower (Ed.), *Psychology of learning and motivation* (Vol. 9). New York: Academic Press.

Andre, T. (1979). Will answering high-level questions while reading facilitate productive learning? *Review of Educational Research, 49*, 280–318.

Ausubel, D. P. (1963). *The psychology of meaningful verbal learning.* New York: Grune & Stratton.

Ausubel, D. P. (1978). In defense of advance organizers: A reply to critics. *Review of Educational Research, 48*, 251–257.

Baker, L., & Brown, A. L. (1986). Metacognitive skills in reading. In D. Pearson (Ed.), *Handbook of reading research.* New York: Longmans, Green.

Bartlett, F. (1958). *Thinking: An experimental and social study.* London: Allen & Unwin.

Bellezza, F. S. (1981). Mnemonic devices: Classification, characteristics, and criteria. *Review of Educational Research, 51*, 247–275.

Berg, K. S., & Stone, G. L. (1978). Modeling and instructional effects as a function of conceptual level. *Canadian Journal of Behavioral Science/Revue Canadienne des Science du Comportement, 10* (2), 152–161.

Bodden, J. L., Osterhouse, R., & Gelso, C. (1972). The value of a study skills inventory for feedback and criterion purposes in an educational skills course. *Journal of Educational Research, 65*, 309–311.

Briggs, R. D., Tosi, D. J., & Morley, R. M. (1971). Study habit modification and its effect on academic performance: A behavioral approach. *Journal of Educational Research, 64*, 347–450.

Brooks, L. W. (1986). *Effects of summarized and expanded text on readers' content and organizational knowledge acquisition.* Presented at the Army Science Conference, West Point Military Academy, New York.

Brooks, L. W., & Dansereau, D. F. (1983). Effects of structural schema training and text organization on expository prose processing. *Journal of Educational Psychology, 75*, 511–520.

Brooks, L. W., & Given, B. (1986). *Cognitive and metacognitive strategies for studying text.* Unpublished manuscript.

Brown, A. L. (1980). Metacognitive development and reading. In R. J. Spiro, B. C. Bruce, & W. F. Brewer (Eds.), *Theoretical issues in reading comprehension.* Hillsdale, NJ: Erlbaum.

Brown, A. L., & Day J. D. (1983). Macrorules for summarizing texts: The development of expertise. *Journal Of Verbal Learning and Verbal Behavior, 22*, 1–14.

Brown, A. L., & Smiley, S. S. (1977). Rating the importance of structural units of prose passages: A problem of metacognitive development. *Child Development, 48*, 1–8.

Brown, A. L., & Smiley, S. S. (1978). The development of strategies for studying texts. *Child Development, 49*, 1076–1088.

Butterfield, E. C., Belmont, J. M., & Peltzman, D. J. (1971). Effects of recall requirements on acquisition strategy. *Journal of Experimental Psychology, 90*, 347–348.

Cermak, L. S. (1972). Rehearsal strategy as a function of recall expectation. *Quarterly Journal of Experimental Psychology, 24,* 378–385.

Chase, W. G., & Simon, H. A. (1973a). The mind's eye in chess. In W. G. Chase (Ed.), *Visual information processing.* New York: Academic Press.

Chase, W. G., & Simon, H. A. (1973b). Perception in chess. *Cognitive Psychology, 4,* 55–81.

Collins, K. W., Dansereau, D. F., Garland, J. C., Holley, C. D., & McDonald, B. A. (1981). Control of affective responses during academic tasks. *Journal of Educational Psychology, 73,* 122–128.

Covington, M. V., Crutchfield, R. S., Davies, L., & Olton, R. M. (1974). *The productive thinking program: A course in learning to think.* Columbus, OH: Merrill.

Dansereau, D. F. (1978). The development of a learning strategy curriculum. In H. F. O'Neil, Jr. (Ed.), *Learning strategies.* New York: Academic Press.

Dansereau, D. F. (1985). Learning strategy research. In J. W. Segal, S. F. Chipman, & R. Glaser (Eds.), *Thinking and learning skills: Vol. 1. Relating instruction to research.* Hillsdale, NJ: Erlbaum, 1985.

Dansereau, D. F. (1986). Cooperative learning strategies. In C. E. Weinstein, E. T. Goetz, & P. A. Alexander (Eds.), *Learning and study strategies.* Orlando, FL: Academic Press.

Dansereau, D. F., Evans, S. H., Wright, A. D., Long, G. L., & Actkinson, T. A. (1974). *Factors related to developing instructional information sequences: Phase I* (AFHRL-TR-63-51 (I)). Lowery Air Force Base, CO: Air Force Human Resources Laboratory, Technical Training Division.

Dansereau, D. F., Long, G., Evans, S. H., & Actkinson, T. R. (1980). Objective ordering of instructional material using multidimensional scaling. *Journal of Structural Learning, 6,* 299–314.

Dansereau, D. F., Long, G. L., McDonald, B. A., & Actkinson, T. R. (1975a). *Learning strategy inventory development and assessment* (AFHRL-TR-75-40). Lowery Air Force Base, CO: Air Force Human Resources Laboratory.

Dansereau, D. F., Long, G. L., McDonald, B. A., Actkinson, T. R., Ellis, A. M., Collins, K. W., Williams, S., & Evans, S. H. (1975b). *Effective learning strategy training program: Development and assessment* (AFHRL-TR-75-41). Lowery Air Force Base, CO: Air Force Human Resources Laboratory.

Dansereau, D. F., McDonald, B. A., Collins, K. W., Garland, J. C., Holley, C. D., Diekhoff, G., & Evans, S. H. (1979). Development and evaluation of a learning strategy system. In H. F. O'Neil, Jr. & C. D. Spielberger (Eds.), *Cognitive and affective learning strategies.* New York: Academic Press.

Dapra, R. A., & Felker, D. B. (1974). *Effects of comprehension and verbatim adjunct questions on problem-solving ability from prose material: Extension of the mathemagenic hypothesis.* Paper presented at the annual convention of the American Psychological Association, New Orleans, LA.

de Groot, A. (1966). Perception and memory versus thought: Some old ideas and recent findings. In B. Kleinmuntz (Ed.), *Problem solving: Research, method, and theory.* New York: Wiley.

DelGiorno, W., Jenkins, J. R., & Bausell, R. B. (1974). Effects of recitation in the acquisition of prose. *Journal of Educational Research, 67,* 293–294.

DiVesta, F. J., Schultz, C. B., & Dangel, I. R. (1973). Passage organization and imposed learning strategies in comprehension and recall of connected discourse. *Memory and Cognition, 1,* 471–476.

Egan, D. E., & Greeno, J. G. (1973). Acquiring cognitive structure by discovery and rule learning. *Journal of Educational Psychology, 64,* 85–97.

Ellis, A. (1963). *Reason and emotion in psychotherapy.* New York: Lyle Stuart.

Frase, L. T. (1973). Integration of written text. *Journal of Educational Psychology, 65,* 252–261.

Frederiksen, N. (1984). Implications of cognitive theory for instruction in problem solving. *Review of Educational Research, 54*, 363–407.

Gagné, R. M. (1976). The learning basis of teaching methods. In N. L. Gage (Ed.), *The psychology of teaching methods. Seventy-fifth Yearbook. National Society for the Study of Education Part I.*. Chicago, IL: Chicago University Press.

Gagné, R. M., & White, R. T. (1978). Memory structures and learning outcomes. *Review of Educational Research, 48*, 187–222.

Gentner, D., & Gentner, D. R. (1983). Flowing waters or teeming crowds: Mental models of electricity. In D. Gentner & A. L. Stevens (Eds.), *Mental models*. Hillsdale, NJ: Erlbaum.

Gick, M. L., & Holyoak, K. J. (1980). Analogical problem solving. *Cognitive Psychology, 12*, 306–355.

Hartley, J., & Davies, L. K. (1976). Preinstructional strategies: The role of pretests, behavioral objectives, overviews, and advance organizers. *Review of Educational Research, 46*, 239–265.

Hayes, J. R. & Simon, H. A. (1974). Understanding written problem instructions. In L. W. Gregg (Ed.), *Knowledge and cognition*. Hillsdale, NJ: Erlbaum.

Holley, C. D., & Dansereau, D. F. (1984). *Spatial learning strategies*. New York: Academic Press.

Holley, C. D., Dansereau, D. F., McDonald, B. A., Garland, J. C., & Collins, K. W. (1979). Evaluation of a hierarchical mapping technique as an aid to prose processing. *Contemporary Educational Psychology, 4*, 227–237.

Holyoak, K. J. (1985). The pragmatics of analogical transfer. In G. H. Bower (Ed.), *The psychology of learning and motivation* (Vol. 19). Orlando: Academic Press.

Hythecker, V. I., Rocklin, T. R., Dansereau, D. F., Lambiotte, J. G., Larson, C. O., & O'Donnell, A. M. (1985). A computer-based learning strategy training module: Development and evaluation. *Journal of Educational Computing Research, 1*, 275–283.

Jacoby, L. L. (1973). Test appropriate strategies in retention of categorized lists. *Journal of Verbal Learning and Verbal Behavior, 12*, 675–685.

Kintsch, W., Kosminsky, E., Streby, W. J., McKoon, G., & Keenan, J. M. (1975). Comprehension and recall of text as a function of content variables. *Journal of Verbal Learning and Verbal Behavior, 14*, 196–214.

Lambiotte, J. G., Dansereau, D. F., Hythecker, V. I., O'Donnell, A. M., Young, M. D., & Rocklin, T. R. (1986). *Technical learning strategies: Acquisition of structural and functional information*. Paper presented at the annual meeting of the Southwestern Psychological Association, Fort Worth, TX.

Larkin, J. H. (1980). Teaching problem solving in physics: The psychological laboratory and the practical classroom. In D. T. Tuma & F. Rief (Eds.), *Problem solving and education: Issues in teaching and research*. Hillsdale, NJ: Erlbaum.

Larson, C. O., Dansereau, D. F., O'Donnell, A. M., Hythecker, V. I., Lambiotte, J. G., & Rocklin, T. R. (1985). Effects of metacognitive and elaborative activity on cooperative learning and transfer. *Contemporary Educational Psychology, 10*, 342–348.

Latane, B., Williams, K., & Harkins, S. (1979). Many hands make light work: Causes and consequences of social loafing. *Journal of Personality and Social Psychology, 37*, 822–832.

Levin, J. R., & Pressley M. (1985). Mnemonic vocabulary instruction: What's fact, what's fiction. In R. F. Dillon (Ed.), *Individual differences in cognition* Vol. 2). New York: Academic Press.

Mansfield, R. S., Busse, T. V., & Krepelka, E. J. (1978). The effectiveness of creativity training. *Review of Educational Research, 48*, 517–536.

Markman, E. M. (1977). Realizing that you don't understand. *Child Development, 48*, 986–992.

Mayer, R. E. (1975). Forward transfer of different reading strategies evoked by testlike events in mathematics text. *Journal of Educational Psychology, 67*, 165–169.

Mayer, R. E. (1976). Some conditions of meaningful learning for computer programing: Advance organizers and subject control of frame order. *Journal of Educational Psychology, 68*, 143-150.

Mayer, R. E. (1978). Advance organizers that compensate for the organizing of text. *Journal of Educational Psychology*, 1978, 70, 880-886.

Mayer, R. E. (1980). Elaboration techniques that increase the meaningfulness of technical text: An experimental test of the learning strategy hypothesis. *Journal of Educational Psychology, 6*, 770-784.

Mayer, R. E., Stiehl, C. C., & Greeno, J. P. (1975). Acquisition of understanding and skill in relation to subjects' preparation and meaningfulness of instruction. *Journal of Educational Psychology, 67*, 331-350.

McConkie, G. W., Rayner, K., & Wilson, J. S. (1973). Experimental manipulation of reading strategies. *Journal of Educational Psychology, 65*, 1-8.

McDonald, B. A., Larson, C. O., Dansereau, D. F., & Spurlin, J. E. (1985). Cooperative dyads: Impact on text learning and transfer. *Contemporary Educational Psychology, 10*, 369-377.

Meichenbaum, D. H., & Goodman, J. (1971). Training impulsive children to talk to themselves: A means of self-control. *Journal of Abnormal Psychology, 77*, 115-126.

Meyer, B. J. F. (1975). *The organization of prose and its effects on memory*. New York: American Elsevier.

Minsky, M. (1975). A framework for representing knowledge. In P. H. Winston (Ed.), *The psychology of computer vision*. New York: McGraw-Hill.

Miyake, N., & Norman, D. A. (1979). To ask a question, one must know enough to know what is not known. *Journal of Verbal Learning and Verbal Behavior, 18*, 357-364.

Newell, A., Simon, H. A., & Shaw, J. D. (1958). Elements of a theory of human problem solving. *Psychological Review, 65*, 151-166.

Norman, D. A. (1973). Memory, knowledge, and the answering of questions. In R. L. Solso (Ed.), *Contemporary issues in cognitive psychology: The Loyola Symposium*. Washington, DC: Winston.

O'Donnell, A. M., Dansereau, D. F., Hythecker, V. I., Larson, C. O., Rocklin, T. R., Lambiotte, J. G., & Young, M. D. (1986). *Effects of various cooperative scenarios on amount and accuracy of text recall: Two's company, three's a crowd*. Paper presented at the American Educational Research Association, San Francisco, CA.

O'Donnell, A. M., Dansereau, D. F., Hythecker, V. I., Larson, C. O., Rocklin, T. R., Lambiotte, J. G., & Young, M. D. (in press). Effects of monitoring on cooperative learning. *Journal of Experimental Education*.

O'Donnell, A. M., Dansereau, D. F., Rocklin, T. R., Lambiotte, J. G., Hythecker, V. I., & Larson, C. O. (1985). Cooperative writing: Direct effects and transfer. *Written Communication, 2*, 307-315.

Paivio, A. (1971). *Imagery and verbal processes*. New York: Holt.

Patterson, C. J., & Mischel, W. (1975). Plans to resist distraction. *Developmental Psychology, 11*, 369-378.

Pellegrino, J. W. (1985). Inductive reasoning ability. In R. J. Sternberg (Ed.), *Human abilities*. New York: Freeman.

Polya, G. (1957). How to solve it. Garden City, NY: Doubleday Anchor.

Pressley, M., & Levin, J. R. (1983). *Cognitive strategy research: Psychological foundations*. Berlin & New York: Springer-Verlag.

Reder, L. M., & Anderson, J. R. (1980). A comparison of texts and their summaries: Memorial consequences. *Journal of Verbal Learning and Verbal Behavior, 19*, 121-134.

Reder, L. M., & Anderson, J. R. (1982). Effects of spacing and embellishments on memory for the main points of a text. *Memory and Cognition, 10*, 97-102.

Rickards, J. P. (1979) Adjunct postquestions in text: A critical review of methods and processes. *Review of Educational Research, 49,* 181–196.

Rickards, J. P., & Denner, P. R. (1978). Inserted questions as aids to reading text. *Instructional Science, 7,* 313–346.

Ritter, K., Kaprove, B. H. Fitch, J. P., & Flavell, J. H. (1973). The development of retrieval strategies in young children. *Cognitive Psychology, 5,* 310–321.

Robinson, F. P. (1946). *Effective study.* New York: Harper.

Royer, J. M. (1979). Theories of the transfer of learning. *Educational Psychologist, 14,* 53–69.

Rubinstein, M. F. (1975). *Patterns of problem solving.* Englewood Cliffs, NJ: Prentice-Hall.

Rubinstein, M. F. (1980). A decade of experience in teaching an introductory problem solving course. In D. T. Tuma & F. Reif (Eds.), *Problem solving and education: Issues in teaching and research.* Hillsdale, NJ: Erlbaum.

Rumelhart, D. E., Lindsay, P. H., & Norman, D. A. (1972). A process model for long-term memory. In E. Tulving & W. Donaldson (Eds.), *Organization of memory.* New York: Academic Press.

Rumelhart, D. E., & Ortony, A. (1977). The representation of knowledge in memory. In R. C. Anderson, R. J. Spiro, & W. E. Montague (Eds.), *Schooling and the acquisition of knowledge.* Hillsdale, NJ: Erlbaum.

Schallert, D. L. (1980). The role of illustrations in reading comprehension. In R. J. Spiro, B. C. Bruce, & W. F. Brewer (Eds.), *Theoretical issues in reading comprehension.* Hillsdale, NJ: Erlbaum.

Schallert, D. L. (1982). The significance of knowledge: A synthesis of research related to schema theory. In W. Otto & S. White (Eds.), *Reading expository material.* New York: Academic Press.

Schank, R., & Abelson, R. P. (1977). *Scripts, plans, goals, and understanding.* Hillsdale, NJ: Erlbaum.

Segal, J. W., Chipman, S. F., & Glaser, R. (1986). *Thinking and learning skills* (Vols. 1 & 2). Hillsdale, NJ: Erlbaum.

Shavelson, R. J., Berliner, D. C., Ravitch, M. M., & Loeding, D. (1974). Effects of position and type of question on learning from prose material: Interaction of treatments with individual differences. *Journal of Educational Psychology, 66,* 40–48.

Simon, H. A. (1978). Information processing theory of human problem solving. In W. K. Estes (Ed.), *Handbook of learning and cognitive processes: Vol. 5: Human information processing.* Hillsdale, NJ: Erlbaum.

Simon, H. A. (1980). Problem solving and education. In D. T. Tuma & F. Reif (Eds.), *Problem solving and education: Issues in teaching and research.* Hillsdale, NJ: Erlbaum.

Spurlin, J. E., Dansereau, D. F., Larson, C. O., & Brooks, L. W. (1984). Cooperative learning strategies in processing descriptive text: Effects of role and activity level of the learner. *Cognition and Instruction, 1,* 451–463.

Thorndyke, P. W. (1977). Cognitive structures in comprehension and memory of narrative discourse. *Cognitive Psychology, 9,* 77–110.

Trollip, S. R. (1979). The evaluation of a complex computer-based flight procedures trainer. *Human Factors, 21,* 47–54.

Tulving, E. (1972). Episodic and semantic memory. In E. Tulving & W. Donaldson (Eds.), *Organization of memory.* New York: Academic Press.

van Dijk, T. A., & Kintsch, W. (1977). Cognitive psychology and discourse. In W. Dressler (Ed.), *Current trends in text linguistics.* Berlin: deGruyter.

Voss, J. F. (1978). Cognition and instruction: Toward a cognitive theory of learning. In A. M. Lesgold, J. W. Pellegrino, S. D. Fokkema, & R. Glaser (Eds.), *Cognitive psychology and instruction.* New York: Plenum Press.

Watts, G. H., & Anderson, R. C. (1971). Effects of three types of inserted questions on learning from prose. *Journal of Educational Psychology, 62,* 387–394.

Whitehill, R. P. (1972). The development of effective learning skills programs. *Journal of Educational Research, 65*, 281–285.
Wickelgren, W. A. (1973). *How to solve problems*. San Francisco, CA: Freeman.
Wolpe, J. (1969). *The practice of behavioral therapy*. New York: Pergamon Press.

CHAPTER 6

The Structural Processes Underlying Transfer of Training

STEPHEN M. CORMIER[1]

This chapter represents an attempt to identify and describe the most fundamental information-processing factors underlying the transfer of learning. Many variables, ranging from training procedures involving task variety (e.g., Hagman, 1980) to subject variables such as ability level (e.g., Campione, Brown, Ferrara, Jones, & Steinberg, 1985) affect the magnitude and direction (positive or negative) of transfer. However, some factors must be more fundamental to the expression of transfer than others.

Three criteria that would seem to be important in making distinctions between variables are the degree of criticality, the likelihood of variation, and the directness of their effect on transfer. Fundamental variables should exert a significant effect on the magnitude and direction of transfer in a wide variety of circumstances. In addition, they should exert this effect directly rather than through the action of an intervening variable.

For example, a runner's ability to run a marathon is affected by stamina, balance, and the temperature during the race. Intuitively, stamina seems more fundamental to a marathoner's running performance than the other two variables. In terms of the above argument, stamina is a highly critical variable in affecting the likelihood of running a marathon. In addition, the degree of stamina is likely to vary, not only for different runners, but also for the same runner on different occasions. Finally, stamina exerts its effect directly on the runner's capacity to run a marathon. On the other hand, the other two variables do not meet all these criteria. Balance is certainly critical to running ability, and it exerts its effect directly but is not likely to vary

---

[1]The views expressed are the author's and not necessarily those of the Army Research Institute, Department of the Army, or Department of Defense.

151

under typical race conditions, either between runners or for the same runner at different times. Similarly, ambient temperature has high criticality and is likely to vary but does not exert its effect on running ability directly.

In the context of transfer of learning, three information-processing factors are considered fundamental to its expression in the sense considered above: (a) the match–mismatch retrieval process, (b) study-phase retrieval, and (c) performance automatization. These three factors are described and their effects on transfer in laboratory and applied settings are analyzed in separate sections of this chapter. A particular aim is to show the diversity of procedural and other methodological variables whose transfer effects can be shown to be mediated by these factors.

I. THE MATCH–MISMATCH RETRIEVAL PROCESS AND TRANSFER

At the turn of the century, Thorndike and Woodworth (1901) proposed one of the first, and most durable, theories of transfer. They suggested that transfer from one task to another would occur only if the two tasks contained identical S–R elements. Recent research on encoding and retrieval processes offers new and more analytic ways of conceptualizing this identical elements view of transfer.

For Task 1 (original task) learning to influence Task 2 (transfer task) acquisition, the trainee must retrieve Task 1 information from memory (consciously or not) while being trained on Task 2. In the absence of this retrieval, transfer should be zero. For this reason, an understanding of the operation of the structural process of retrieval in these circumstances seems essential. Atkinson and Shiffrin (1968) emphasized the distinction between structural processes, which constitute the basic (information-processing) properties of the brain, with control processes, or the voluntary strategies that people can employ in facilitating information processing. One example of this distinction would be the capacity limits of working memory for discrete items as a structural process as opposed to rehearsal or categorization strategies useful in increasing memory performance. In the present context, structural processes are the best place to look for fundamental factors of transfer.

A. CHARACTERISTICS OF THE RETRIEVAL PROCESS

Once an item is encoded and stored in a memorial representation, its later use is dependent on the degree to which it can be accessed in appropriate circumstances. At the most basic level, the Task 1 representation needs to be retrieved when the same stimulus information is presented again in Task 2 so that recognition can occur. Recognition involves a comparison of the memorial representation with the presented stimulus information (cf. Cormier, 1986; Neisser, 1967; Seymour, 1979). A match between the two items on certain critical dimensions results in the recognition of the presented stimulus as familiar, while a mismatch would result in a failure to retrieve the memorial representation and thus a decision that the stimulus is unfamiliar (cf. Sokolov, 1976).

In transfer settings the critical question is to what extent stimulus information in Task 2 can match or retrieve relevant Task 1 information which has been encoded by the trainee. Such a comparison process suggests that the probability of a match will depend upon the way in which Task 1 information is encoded and the nature of the Task 2 retrieval cues. In essence, the information learned on Task 1 needs to be analyzed with respect to the retrieval cues likely to be present in Task 2. One line of research that has demonstrated the importance of cuing relationships has been the analysis of encoding specificity.

The encoding specificity principle states that no cue can be an effective aid to an item's retrieval unless it has been encoded with that item (Tulving, 1976). Thus, retrieval is dependent on reinstatement of the precise way in which the item was encoded. This principle is assumed to hold true for all testing procedures such as free recall, cued recall, or recognition.

For example, Thomson and Tulving (1970) presented to-be-remembered (TBR) words in the company of weak associate cues during acquisition and then tested recall of the TBR word using a novel (extralist) strong-associate cue (Table 1). As one instance, BLACK was a TBR word encoded with the weak associate *train*. A strong associate *white* was then presented to see if it would facilitate the recall of BLACK. It was found that when BLACK had been encoded in the presence of the weak associate *train*, the strong extralist cue *white* was a less effective retrieval cue for BLACK than the original weak associate. In general, research evidence has shown that the relation between encoding and retrieval information is highly predictive of retrieval probability, although the process is not as rigid as implied by the encoding specificity principle (e.g., Rabinowitz, Mandler, & Barsalou, 1979).

Thus, encoding specificity emphasizes both the importance of the encoding context in determining the conditions under which items can be retrieved and the necessity of retrieval cues directly overlapping the information encoded initially. The retrieval cue can be a copy of the TBR item as in recognition, some co-occurring item, or some attribute or dimension of the item. This last point is important because it suggests that it is possible to retrieve an item with partial stimulus information.

Researchers have suggested that a stimulus can be conceptualized as a collection of attributes or features (e.g., E. E. Smith, Shoben, & Rips, 1974; Underwood, 1969). Different contexts can be viewed as biasing different

Table 1
The Recall Probabilities Associated with the Conditions of Input and Output Cues

	Output cue					
	Strong			Weak		
	List					
Input cue	1	2	3	1	2	3
Strong						
Proportion	.840	.840	.833	—	—	.035
SD	.143	.195	.170	—	—	.085
Weak						
Proportion	—	—	.326	.750	.753	.729
SD	—	—	.297	.207	.235	.234

Note. Preexisting strong associative connections between cue and TBR word as in the weak-strong condition have much less effect on recall than consistency of encoding and retrieval conditions as in the weak-weak condition. (From D. M. Thomson and E. Tulving, 1970. Copyright 1970 by the American Psychological Association. Reprinted by permission.)

features of the same stimulus. For example, Barclay, Bransford, Franks, McCarrell, and Nitsch (1974) had subjects learn TBR words presented in different sentences which biased their interpretation, for example, *The PIANO was tuned*, or *The PIANO was lifted*, suggesting the piano as either a musical instrument or a heavy object. Recall was better when retrieval cues suggested features that were relevant to the specific context of the encoded TBR word. Cues which suggested other aspects of the TBR word were less effective.

Flexser and Tulving (1978) among others have also suggested that different stimulus features vary in their redintegrative capacity. Redintegration refers to the capacity of one part of a stimulus complex to reevoke or cue the entire complex. A stimulus feature which can usually reevoke the entire stimulus complex can be considered a cue with high redintegrative capacity, while a feature which has only a low probability of reinstating the stimulus complex can be considered to have low redintegrative capacity. For example, the first letters of words are typically better cues for recalling the word than are interior letters (Nelson, 1979). The concept of redintegration as applied to stimulus features is important for two reasons: first, it provides a basis for the full retrieval of the TBR item using partial information, and second, it helps explain why some features are more effective than others. Variations in the encoding of TBR material will affect the relative salience or importance of the constituent features, and this will in turn affect their redintegrative capacity (cf. Adams, 1971; Horowitz & Manelis, 1972). In slightly different circumstances, stimulus selection can develop. In this case, some part of the total stimulus complex gains control over a response to the exclusion of the remaining parts (Richardson, 1976).

How do the concepts of encoding specificity, redintegration, and selection provide a basis for explaining transfer? Encoding specificity has emphasized that retrieval probability is a joint function of the way in which the material was originally encoded and the cues or information available at the time of retrieval. To the extent that the information stored on the first task is encoded in such a way as to be retrievable with the cues available on the transfer task, then we should see positive transfer given similar responses. However, if the encoding of Task 1 material is idiosyncratic or otherwise incompatible with the retrieval information present in the transfer task, we should see little or no positive transfer.

The experimental literature (e.g., Underwood, 1969) further shows that the stimulus can be conceptualized as a collection of attributes or features that enter into an association with the verbal or motor response component. Certain elements or features of the stimulus carry a disproportionate weight in the formation of such an association. Features which have high redintegrative value or have survived a process of stimulus selection will thus have the greatest effect on transfer (Figure 1). Now we examine several areas of transfer research to see whether these concepts have explanatory power.

B. Cuing Properties of Simulators

1. Fidelity

The use of simulators to teach trainees how to operate aircraft and other equipment has been an area of research based on the identical elements approach. For example, the airplane simulator is supposed to provide the kind of environment that would be experienced by a pilot in an actual airplane. To the extent that the simulator has a high correspondence (more identical elements) with the actual equipment, it can be said to possess high physical fidelity.

The transfer effectiveness of simulators is well established (e.g., Lintern, 1980), and as Gerathewohl (1969) has noted, high-fidelity simulators specifically have demonstrated their value. Unfortunately, high-physical-fidelity simulators are expensive to construct, and the amount is usually directly proportional to the degree of fidelity. As a result of this cost, much effort has gone into determining how much fidelity is needed, in other words, how far a simulator can deviate from the actual equipment and still produce high positive transfer.

A consideration of cuing relationships between tasks can help to clarify

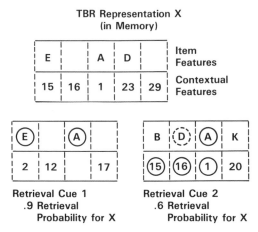

Redintegration

Figure 1. A conceptualization of the way in which feature correspondences between target and cue can affect the likelihood of redintegration. Circled numbers indicate correspondence of feature and its representational weight between cue and target. A broken circle indicates correspondence of feature only. The relative weights of the features are indicated by position, with leftmost and topmost features having the highest weight. The retrieval effectiveness of a cue is determined more by the correspondence of salient features and weights than by the simple number of similar features. (Adapted from Figure 5, A. J. Flexser and E. Tulving, 1978. Copyright 1978 by the American Psychological Association. Reprinted by permission.)

some of the inconsistent research findings on the degree of fidelity required, findings which have proved refractory to analysis in the identical elements approach. Motion has been a cuing dimension found to exert inconsistent effects on performance (e.g., Caro, 1979; Jacobs & Roscoe, 1975). One reason for this inconsistency is that different kinds of motion (e.g., cockpit motion, rough-air simulation, etc.) have different effects (Ince, Williges, & Roscoe, 1975). National Air and Space Administration researchers (Rathert, Creer, & Sadoff, 1961) found a significant correlation between increased motion and pilot performance with an unstable or sluggishly responding aircraft. Ruocco, Vitale, and Benfari (1965) showed that cockpit motion on a simulated carrier-landing task did improve task performance as measured by successful landings, altitude error, and time outside the flight path. Jacobs and Roscoe (1975) found that motion cues are not useful in transfer to aircraft that are easy to fly, however (cf. Nautaupsky, Waag, Meyer, McFadden, & McDowell, 1979).

Gundry (1977) notes that aircraft motion cues can occur either because of pilot control (e.g., changes in direction or altitude) or because of external forces (e.g., turbulence). He has hypothesized that motion cues may be redundant in the case of pilot-initiated changes not only because the pilot is already alerted to the change but also because aircraft are designed to be as stable and easy to control as possible in normal use. In such a case, other stimulus information is enough to cue the appropriate response. Disturbance-induced motion cues, on the other hand, may be more essential to pilot response when other cues (e.g., visual) are inadequate (Perry & Naish, 1964). For example, Ricard and Parrish (1984) showed that cab motion was useful for helicopter pilots on a simulated hover task on disturbance maneuvers but not for pilot-initiated maneuvers. Martin and Waag (1978) found that pilot-maneuver motion did not enhance transfer using a flight simulator.

The motion studies mentioned above support two basic conclusions relevant to the current information-processing approach. First of all, positive transfer was not a rigid function of the degree of identical elements in Tasks 1 and 2 (simulator and flight). Similar levels of positive transfer were found despite variations in the level of correspondence between Tasks 1 and 2. Secondly, some stimulus attributes of the training environment were more important to the retrieval of TBR material than were other attributes. The degree to which a particular stimulus attribute functioned as a retrieval cue for current responding seemed to depend on the nature of the TBR material and the extent to which other retrieval information was available.

The examination of these cuing relationships permits the predictive analysis of transfer effects prior to actual Task 2 training (cf. Kruk, Regan, Beverly, & Longridge, 1983). For example if the sequence of flight tasks necessary to perform restricted-visibility landings has to be recalled by the pilot (in Task 2), then Task 1 training must insure that the sequence can be performed under recall conditions. Task 1 training which provided only recognition training of the task sequence should result in less positive transfer than the recall training.

In other words, knowledge about the Task 2 cues should permit at least some prediction of transfer effects, given training on some Task 1, since the cuing correspondence is then analyzable in principle. Effective training tasks may have surface characteristics quite different from the target task as long as the essential cue-response relationships are preserved. In this view, it is not physical fidelity per se that contributes to high positive transfer; rather, it is the presence of retrieval information in Task 2 which has a high cuing and redintegrative capacity for the essential Task 1 material. Low-fidelity devices should be effective in producing transfer as long as they provide the trainee with the essential cuing relationships between the stimulus attributes of the task environment and the appropriate responses.

Decreases in simulator fidelity seem most easily achieved for tasks that require fixed procedures (e.g., Bernstein & Gonzalez, 1968). For example, Prophet and Boyd (1970) found that a cockpit mock-up made of plywood and photographs was about as effective as instruction in the aircraft itself on tasks such as aircraft pre-start-up, start run-up, and shutdown procedures.

Tasks in which it is difficult to identify the specific cues which control responding may require more physical fidelity in the training situation. Salvendy and Pilitsis (1980) developed training simulators to teach suturing techniques to medical students. Three training methods were used: electromechanical, perceptual, and a combination of both. A standard instruction (lecture) group was used as controls. The electromechanical method taught students how to puncture simulated tissue with the aid of a mechanical device which provided auditory and visual information on the correctness of the technique performed. The perceptual method involved watching filmed performance of both expert surgeons and inexperienced medical students. The trainee was instructed to analyze the student's performance by comparing it to that of the surgeon's. The third experimental method was simply a combination of both procedures.

The results showed that the electromechanical and combined electromechanical-perceptual groups had the highest transfer performance levels and were essentially equivalent. The perceptual-only group's performance was not significantly different from the control group in the number of good sutures, although instructors did rate their performance as somewhat higher. These results suggest that essential cuing information is provided by the actual performance of the suturing technique, which is difficult to impart through alternative (lower fidelity) means.

2. Augmented Feedback

Up to now we have considered the effects of cuing relationships on positive transfer; however, it is possible for (inappropriate) cuing relationships to exist between Tasks 1 and 2 which could lead to zero or negative transfer. One such example would be when relevant Task 1 information has been encoded and retrieved using attributes which are not present on Task 2, for example, augmented feedback. Augmented feedback, or the use of special cues which provide supplementary or augmented information concerning responding, often facilitates Task 1 performance (e.g., Briggs, 1969). However, its effect on Task 2 performance is much more variable and can produce zero or negative transfer (e.g., Bilodeau & Bilodeau, 1961). As Welford (1968) notes, augmented feedback cannot be expected to increase transfer when the subject comes to rely on it for performing the correct response instead of helping the subject to observe and better use inherent task information that will also be available in Task 2.

Eberts and Schneider (1985) studied the effects of different kinds of augmented cues on performance of a second-order tracking task. (In a first-order system, the pointer moves in direct relationship to movements of the joy stick, while in a second-order system, movements of the joy stick produce changes in *acceleration* of the pointer). While a variety of augmented cues enhanced performance while present, only one such cue, presenting the expected parabolic path of the pointer produced by a given joy-stick movement, increased transfer to a task without augmented feedback. The parabolic cue not only guided behavior, as the other cues did, but also clarified and increased the salience of the important cue relationships between joy-stick movement and pointer movement. In other words, the trainee's mental model of the system more closely corresponded to its actual mode of operation. These and the other findings discussed previously highlight the importance of examining and specifying the precise relationship between the retrieval information and the encoded materials present on Tasks 1 and 2.

Although the importance of cuing relationships in determining transfer has been shown through consideration of such phenomena as encoding specificity, we have not specifically discussed ways of manipulating the relationship between cues and TBR material which increase the likelihood of positive transfer. Therefore, we will next consider one line of research which sheds some light on this question.

C. DISTINCTIVENESS OF THE CUING RELATIONSHIP

1. Distinctiveness and Memory

Basic research or encoding and retrieval processes involved in the initial acquisition of material has highlighted the importance of the distinctiveness and differentiation of cue-TBR-item associations from each other. Items differentiated in memory are more likely to be retrieved given appropriate retrieval information than are items not differentiated (cf. Nelson, 1979).

To the extent that a particular stimulus contains features which are unique or infrequent relative to the set of items from which it has to be discriminated, a retrieval cue containing those features will contact that particular item better than the others (cf. Watkins, 1979). Decreased distinctiveness, for example, in the form of acoustic similarity between letters or words impairs discrimination of such items (Nelson & Rowe, 1969), and words with irregular orthographic patterns are retained better than words that are orthographically common (Hunt & Mitchell, 1978).

Stimulus distinctiveness has been demonstrated to play a crucial role in negative transfer situations (cf. Postman, 1976, for a review of many relevant articles). Proactive interference (PI) which produces negative transfer is generally defined as increases in the time or error rate involved in Task 2 acquisition. For example, Deese and Marder (1957) showed that increases in between-list errors were found when a long delay was interposed before final testing after presenting subjects with two lists of words to learn. These errors were presumably due to a decrease in the relative temporal separation between the lists (Runquist & Runquist, 1978).

Proactive interference is often studied in an A-B, A-D procedure in which different (verbal or motor) responses (B and D) are successively learned to the same stimulus (A). The amount of negative transfer is usually assessed by comparing the A-B, A-D group's performance on the A-D list with a control group's performance on a C-D list on an A-B, C-D procedure. Actually, negative transfer is difficult to show if an overall decrement in performance is taken as its definition, since the A-B, A-D group often performs better on the A-D list than a control group with no Task 1 learning (cf. Deese & Hulse, 1967).

The relation between distinctiveness in the encoding of stimuli and PI has also been investigated in short-term retention studies. Perhaps best known are the release from PI studies conducted by Wickens and his associates (e.g., Gardiner, Craik, & Birtwistle, 1972; Wickens, 1972; Wickens, Moody, & Dow, 1981). This paradigm provides a means of analytically determining the perceived degree of distinctiveness between different classes of TBR material. For example, in the Gardiner *et al.* (1972) study, subjects were given a number of short-term memory trials with items from one of several categories. It was consistently found that PI built up rapidly when items were all from the same category. However, a shift between different categories produced a reduction in PI (e.g., garden flowers versus wild flowers). Bird (1977) showed that a shift from semantic to structural processing (e.g., adjectives, verbs) or vice versa produced more release from PI than did shifting from one semantic task to another. Similarly, no release from PI was obtained with two related structural tasks (Bird & Roberts, 1980). In general, category shifts which are meaningful promote the retrieval of the TBR items.

2. Stimulus Predifferentiation

Stimulus predifferentiation (SP) is another methodology which has been used to analyze the effect of distinctiveness of encoding on transfer. In SP studies, individuals are typically either simply preexposed to stimuli used in the training task (e.g., observation training) or are given training emphasizing their distinctiveness (e.g., labeling training). During SP (Task 1) training, the subject learns to differentiate among the task stimuli, and it is this knowledge which has to be transferred to the new task, a typical measure of transfer being the facility with which the Task 2 responses are associated with these stimuli (cf. Ellis, Parente, & Walter, 1974).

Price and Slive (1970) have argued that the principal effect of label relevance is to increase the probability that the representation formed at the time of encoding will be matched by the representation given at the time of retrieval. Nagae (1980) has provided independent evidence that the verbal labels do possess an effective discriminating function at encoding.

Ellis and Muller (1964) studied SP effects using verbal labels for random shapes. Although observation training yielded superior transfer for recognition of simpler 6-point shapes, distinctiveness pretraining was superior for 24-point shapes. A large number of trials were provided, allowing for the observation group to locate distinguishing features without the aid of explicit distinctive labels. Ellis and Schaffer (1974) showed somewhat similar results in that predifferentiation training was more effective with transfer stimuli consisting of complex random shapes and letter matrices than it was with CCC trigrams. We can, thus, see a general effect of task difficulty on predifferentiation effectiveness.

Significant transfer effects have been shown as a result of stimulus predifferentiation in applied tasks as well. Wood and Gerlach (1974) studied the effects of audiovisual pretraining on a continuous perceptual motor task used in flight simulation. The predifferentiation training consisted of the presentation of specific instruments involved in the criterion task of takeoff and controlled climb or descent. Only three states were allowed for each instrument in pretraining, thus permitting the discrete presentation of the relevant stimuli in the flight task. A first measure of transfer was level-off time. Significant increases in performance as a result of stimulus training were found late in transfer task training. A second transfer measure was a combination of two pitch-error scores. On this measure, significant differences between conditions were evident only during the early Task 2 trials.

In summary, increasing the distinctiveness of TBR material significantly increases the probability of positive transfer when multiple, similar items exist which have overlapping attributes and when retrieval cues present in Task 2 are not themselves able to match exclusively the TBR items.

D. SUMMARY

In keeping with its status as a fundamental factor, the retrieval process was shown to exert a significant influence on transfer in a variety of experimental paradigms. The experimental literature on cuing relationships between encoded material and retrieval cues demonstrated the importance of overlaps between items on attributes which were salient and which had high discriminative value relative to other similar items in memory. The application of these concepts to the transfer literature pertaining to simulator training, augmented feedback, SP, and PI provided a unifying and consistent interpretation for a number of transfer effects in these different paradigms. Experimental manipulations which increased the degree of overlap of Task 2 retrieval information with the encoded attributes of TBR material acquired in Task 1 had a positive effect on transfer. The concepts of redintegration and stimulus selection provided an explanation for partial cuing effects which are difficult to account for in the identical elements approach to transfer.

II. AUTOMATIZATION OF PERFORMANCE AND TRANSFER

In this section, we will examine the second proposed fundamental factor affecting transfer: automatized encoding and responding. One of the most common findings in the training literature is that increased practice almost always leads to improved performance, in terms of both quality and speed (e.g., Newell & Rosenbloom, 1981). It has been widely suggested that skilled performance is due in large part to a decrease in the total amount of attentional capacity that must be devoted to a task and to an increase in the efficiency of responding through the removal of unnecessary elements (e.g., Kahneman, 1973).

The mechanisms by which reductions in attentional capacity can be made without reducing performance have not been completely specified; however, there is substantial evidence that as stimuli become increasingly familiar, they are more likely to be recognized before entering working or short-term memory. The processing of highly familiar stimuli is believed to occur in what is termed a preattentional processing stage (e.g., Egeth, 1977; Shiffrin & Schneider, 1977). Such preattentive processing has at most a minimal effect on the available resources of working memory so that the individual can process other information simultaneously without deficit. The available evidence indicates that automatization develops when conditions permit lower level processing regions of the brain to assume control over encoding (and responding) (e.g., Gabriel, Foster, Orona, Saltwick, & Stanton, 1980; Thatcher & John, 1977).

Although the automatization of stimulus processing and responding has the obvious benefit of reducing the processing load on higher brain regions such as the cerebral cortex, it can create a potential problem when stimulus information is confusable or when cue-response requirements change. If the individual is performing only elementary processing operations on a stimulus, for example, reacting to the color of a stimulus rather than to its meaning, changes in the nonattended dimensions will naturally not influence the automatized responding. On the other hand, when a change in cue-response relationships has been detected, the individual not only must perform the correct response but must inhibit the incorrect response. If the automatized response is not under the full control of working memory, however, it may be performed whenever the individual's attention to inhibiting the response diminishes, for example, getting off on the wrong floor when the office location has changed.

Given the accuracy of the above reasoning, there are three implications for transfer performance with automatized stimulus processing and responding. First, there should be a high degree of positive transfer to those stimuli in Task 2 which have become automatized in Task 1. Second, negative transfer should occur to a greater degree when automatized cue-response relationships are changed from Task 1 to Task 2 than for nonautomatized components. Third, the reduction of processing effort should permit increased positive transfer to complex tasks which overutilize the available working memory capacity of the individual.

At this point, we will now concentrate on the specific characteristics of automatized processing as it is acquired and utilized by the subject.

A. Characteristics of Automatized Processing

1. Development of Automatization

Automatized processing seems to develop only under particular conditions. Increasing practice or stimulus familiarity is a necessary but not sufficient condition for automatization to develop. It is critical that there also be consistency of practice or stimulus presentation (Schneider & Fisk, 1982). For example, in visual-search experiments in which the subject must look for particular items (targets) in an array or field of irrelevant stimuli, large increases in performance speed are found when the same targets are used consistently over different trials (e.g., Logan, 1979). The occurrence of parallel search and processing of stimuli by subjects is indicated by the findings that set size functions (i.e., the number of targets and the time it takes to find them) tend toward zero as practice becomes extended. On the other hand, if the targets are changed from trial to trial, then automatized encoding does not seem to develop even after prolonged practice (Kristofferson, 1972).

Fisk and Schneider (1981) showed that both qualitative and quantitative differences existed in stimulus processing in consistent as opposed to variable stimulus-search conditions. Under vigilance conditions, variable-target search was characterized by serial and effortful processing, while consistent target search was parallel and easy in the sense that it did not overly tax the resources of working memory. Stimulus detection sensitivities dropped significantly under consistent-search but not under variable-search conditions with prolonged practice: In addition, related changes in cue utilization can be seen. Such changes in the cues which control responding or stimulus-processing presumably occur in the direction of stimulus attributes which are more useful (e.g., more distinctive and correlated) in identifying the stimulus or directing the response to occur. Kessel and Wickens (1982) showed that monitors of automatic pursuit displays who had prior experience relied upon different perceptual cues in making signal detection responses compared with naive subjects (cf. Fleishman & Rich, 1963). Koonce (1979) showed that motion cues in simulators were more important to experienced pilots' performance, although they did not enhance transfer from the simulator to the aircraft.

2. Task Restructuring

It is important to note that automatization cannot be assumed to be operating simply because the speed and accuracy of performance have increased through practice. Cheng (1985) has argued that much, if not all, of this performance improvement can be attributed to task restructuring, which involves learning more efficient procedures to perform the task. For example, multiplication is more efficient than addition, but the reduction in time to perform equivalent multiplication problems over addition cannot be reasonably attributed to automatization since working memory capacity is fully utilized with both procedures.

In the present view, the key difference between task restructuring and automatization lies in the level of processing which must be employed for task performance. Automatization cannot be operating when task performance places substantial demands on working memory and cortical analysis. Conversely, evidence for low-level processing would implicate automatization over task restructuring. For example, Chechile and Sadowski (1983) assessed the effectiveness of verbal and symbolic cuing on the task of editing flight route-way-point information during flight training. Symbolic cuing consisted of small panel light indicators which directed operators to the appropriate keys. Improvement in accuracy and speed on this divided-attention task was more pronounced with symbolic cuing than with verbal cuing because of reduced cognitive load in processing such information.That is, verbal analysis includes not only detection, recognition, and response but also semantic analyses dependent on cortical processing.

B. Stimulus Specificity of Transfer
   with Automatized Processing

The question arises as to the degree to which automatized training is specific to the stimuli trained in Task 1. Actually, the weight of evidence seems to indicate that the generalizibility of automated training is somewhat narrower than for other types of Task 1 training. Schneider and Fisk (1984) showed high transfer of automatized processing to stimuli in the same class as the original stimuli. Subjects were trained under consistent conditions to detect words from a particular category such as colors. After extended training, subjects were presented with novel words from the same category

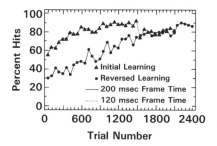

Figure 2. After reversal of automatized targets, hit rates drop to levels well below those seen in novices. In addition, a retardation of learning rate is seen in the reversal condition. Note the large number of trials needed by the reversal group to achieve comparability. (From Shiffrin and Schneider, 1977, Expt. 1. Copyright 1977 by the American Psychological Association. Reprinted by permission.)

and showed high (92%) transfer from the old to the new words (cf. W. O. Shaffer & LaBerge, 1979).

Nevertheless, the similarities between the original and the transfer task must be substantial, at least on those dimensions that have become automatized, for such positive transfer to be demonstrated. Slight changes in the processing conditions during dual task performance on which one or both components have been automatized, for example, typically disrupts such performance initially (Logan, 1979). Eberts and Schneider (1985) had subjects detect a sequence of three discrete movements of a line segment. Although automatic processing developed after consistent training to a particular sequence, when the pattern was spatially rotated, the degree of transfer was no greater than after variable training, which does not produce automatized encoding.

There is contradictory evidence on whether automatized processing can be maintained to one component on the transfer task if other components are different from Task 1. For example, conjunction searches, in which a subject must search for a stimulus with two particular attributes (e.g., a red triangle or a green square) do not seem to be automatized to the same degree as searches for stimuli with a single critical dimension (Treisman & Gelade, 1980). On the other hand, Schneider and Fisk (1984) have shown that automatized processing can occur to task components that have consistent requirements even if there are other task components that are not consistent. In general, there seems to be at least an initial deficit in performance even with small changes in the transfer task (Figure 2).

Interestingly, the transfer deficits to different stimuli become greater when stimulus training is extended in Task 1 (Salthouse & Somberg. 1982). The automatized processing becomes stimulus specific to such an extent that almost any stimulus change results in the disruption of such processing.

The stimulus specificity of automatized processing can also create more subtle deficits in transfer. Eriksen and Eriksen (1974) showed that reaction times were slowed when irrelevant flanking stimuli were present that were similar to the automatized stimuli even though consistent training occurred only with the latter. The subjects could not stop processing the irrelevant stimuli even when instructed to do so. Shiffrin and Schneider (1977) also found that subjects were unable to stop processing consistently trained stimuli under reversal conditions, although they were able to do so with variably trained stimuli. In other words, once stimuli or responses become automatized, it may be difficult (although not necessarily impossible) to inhibit such processing or responding when conditions change.

Friedman (1978) presented subjects with target pictures containing objects which the subject expected or did not expect to be represented. The subjects had to discriminate the pictures from difficult distractor pictures. Automatized encoding did seem to occur with the expected objects, which were apparently processed on the basis of global physical features. On the other hand, unexpected objects elicited more controlled processing; for example, fixations to unexpected objects were roughly twice as long as to the expected objects. The automatized encoding of expected objects decreased transfer performance for the detection of missing expected objects or the replacement of one expected object by another. Friedman noted that two events which constitute the same class to the subject may be indistinguishable in automatic encoding.

These findings suggest that automatization of processing is characterized by a reduction in the amount of information processed about a given stimulus. Presumably, only those attributes which are most highly correlated with the stimulus are processed. However, if other stimuli are presented which share these attributes but differ on others, they may be a failure to note the change because of the more superficial stimulus analysis which the subject is performing. In other words, there is inappropriate transfer from Task 1 training.

C. Dual Task Performance

One implication of automatized stimulus processing is that the reduction of attentional resources devoted to one task makes the simultaneous performance of a second task more feasible. In the most favorable case, a fully automatized task should permit Task 2 training of a second task (not incompatible with the first) without deficits in the simultaneous performance of either of the tasks (Rieck, Ogden, & Anderson, 1980). It should be noted that dual task performance can also be affected by task restructuring (Cheng, 1985), although the effects of restructuring would not necessarily produce identical dual task performance compared with automatization.

There have been several studies showing that after extensive practice, dual task performance can display no appreciable deficit on either task, such as reading and dictation (Spelke, Hirst, & Neisser, 1976), flying an airplane while digit canceling (Colle & De Maio, 1978), and typing while shadowing prose (L. H. Shaffer, 1974). Similar effects have been found in dichotic listening tasks in which subjects wear earphones and different stimuli are simultaneously presented in the different channels. After consistent training, subjects can follow both channels at the same time as long as target stimuli are not simultaneously present (Duncan, 1980). Dual task performance on dichotomous listening tasks will show significant decrements, however, if one of the tasks has not become automatized (e.g., Treisman, 1969).

An important issue is the kind of Task 1 training that should be given to maximize dual task performance. Should Task 1 training be on a single task or should dual practice performance be given as well? To some degree we are dealing with the problem of part–whole training transfer if the two tasks together can be considered as the whole and individually as the part.

Clearly, the trainee must have some level of proficiency on the individual tasks and a number of studies have found that constituent task performance was an important part of dual task performance (e.g., Ackerman, Schneider, & Wickens, 1984; Freedle, Zavala, & Fleishman, 1968). However, the constituent tasks cannot be considered in isolation since their mutual integrality is a critical factor. For example, Kramer, Wickens, and Donchin (1985) analytically examined dual task performance on a pursuit-tracking task/discriminative task involving stimulus intensity or spatial position. Factors which affected the degree of dual task integrality such as intertask redundancy, spatial proximity of the primary and secondary task displays, and the resource demands of the two tasks were manipulated (Figure 3). Task pairs that involved processing different properties of the same stimulus were better performed than task pairs involving different objects.

In addition to the effects of constituent task performance, a number of studies have provided tentative evidence for some additional contribution from dual task time-sharing practice (e.g., Jennings & Chiles, 1977; Rieck, et al., 1980). Hirst, Spelke, Reaves, Charack, and Neisser (1980) have argued for the existence of a separate time-sharing ability which can be trained, but the evidence for this interpretation is rather weak. Instead, time sharing appears to be a set of procedural skills involved in the integration of the two tasks (e.g., Cheng, 1985; Schneider & Fisk, 1982). As would be expected, some of these skills seem quite generalizable (transferable) while others seem more task specific (e.g., Gopher & North, 1977). In the Gopher and North study, using a tracking/choice reaction-time task pair, for example, tracking

**Spatial Position of
Primary and Secondary Task**

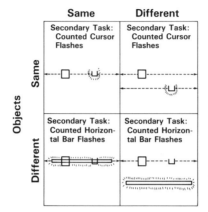

Figure 3. A graphic illustration of the intensity discrimination task used by Kramer *et al.* The primary task was pursuit step tracking of the (square) target along the horizontal axis. In the secondary task, subjects counted cursor flashes (same object) or horizontal bar flashes (different object) along the same axis as the primary task or 2 cm below it. A change in the intensity of the secondary-task stimulus predicted the direction of primary target movement 85% of the time. (From A. F. Kramer *et al.*, 1985. Copyright 1985 by the American Psychological Association. Reprinted by permission.)

performance was increased by both single and dual task training trials while performance on the reaction-time task increased only after dual task training. These results indicate that tracking was dependent to a greater extent on task-specific skills, while the reaction-time task was relatively more affected by time-sharing skills.

D. SUMMARY

Automatized performance can occur after extended consistent practice with particular cues or responses. Qualitative and quantitative differences exist between automatized performance and performance that is not automatized, both in terms of the effect required to process and respond to cues and in the nature of the performance itself. Changes in the utilization of the cues controlling responding have been shown to occur over the course of training in a variety of perceptual motor tasks, for example. Such changes usually occur in the direction of more efficient stimulus processing or motor performance. As a consequence, transfer can be affected by the relationship of the particular cues utilized in Task 1 and in the transfer task. In addition, the more efficient performance on tasks can permit time-sharing activities or the simultaneous performance of two tasks. Automatized performance tends to be highly specific to the elements consistently presented in original training. Thus, there may be little transfer to other elements that differ in some way from those that have become automatized. In addition, it can be difficult to suppress inappropriate automatized performance in transfer environments if the controlling cues are presented.

III. STUDY-PHASE RETRIEVAL AND TRANSFER

In the first section, we examined the situation in which Task 2 retrieval information provided access to the relevant information encoded in Task 1. The TBR information was useful in more or less direct fashion for transfer task performance. However, in different circumstances, the information retrieved from Task 1 can be put to other uses. If it is compared and integrated with information that is under study, then a higher order concept or new relation may emerge under appropriate conditions. This use of retrieved information is usually termed study-phase retrieval, in which information in a second task acts as a retrieval cue for Task 1 information necessary for a higher order integration of both items or sets of material (cf. Jacoby, 1974). It should be noted that this situation falls within the definition of transfer in that Task 1 (or Item 1) learning influences the way in which the transfer task (or item) is learned (cf. Clark, 1978). In this section, we will be examining several kinds of transfer phenomena which involve the integration of information over successive occurrences of related material. First, we will examine some of the variables influencing the integration of textual materials. Following this, there will be an extensive analysis of the way in which stimulus variability in Task 1 training promotes transfer and the connection of these phenomena with the operation of an abstractive process based on the integration of information across successive presentations of TBR material.

A. Textual Integration

One common use of a study-phase retrieval process is in the processing of prose materials as in a textbook. Information from one sentence or passage typically has to be compared to or integrated with information from a prior passage. Often, the comprehension of the second passage is dependent on retrieval of the prior encoded material. Thus, the second passage would need to act as a retrieval cue for that information. The relationship between the two passages can be explicit, as in verbatim repetition or directed reference to the other passage, or it can be implied as with anaphoric reference or ellipsis. (An example of an anaphora would be the word *so* in the sentence They are going to lunch and so are we.)

In general, it is the clarity of the reference which is the key factor in producing comprehension or integration (Carpenter & Just, 1977). For example, Yekovich and Walker (1978) have shown that mere repetition of a word is of little help in integrating sentences when a common conceptual representation has not also been identified. A number of specific variables have been shown to be important in promoting reference clarity, such as the degree of linguistic correspondence between the cuing and TBR information (Yekovich, Walker, & Blackman, 1979) and whether or not related items occur consecutively in the text (Hayes-Roth & Thorndyke, 1979).

It would be expected that the learning of a second passage containing referents to previous material would be facilitated to the extent that such information could be used in comprehending the transfer material. Haberlandt and Bingham (1978) showed that certain inferences are activated by the first sentence in a set of sentences and that subsequent sentences are processed faster if their content is consistent with these inferences.

Royer and Cable (1975) examined the pattern of subjects' learning involving two passages dealing with scientific material (heat and electricity). For the experimental subjects, the initial passage contained either concrete or abstract referents for difficult (abstract) material in the transfer passage. Control subjects received an initial passage unrelated to the transfer material. The subjects in the concrete-abstract condition recalled significantly more of the transfer material than did subjects in the abstract-abstract condition or the control-abstract condition receiving the same second passage. As the authors note, such treatment differences are more likely when the transfer material cannot be easily related to existing knowledge.

Study-phase retrieval may be a necessary but not a sufficient condition for positive transfer to a second passage, since it is the task-specific effects of the study-phase retrieval of encoded information which are important in a particular situation. Campione and Brown (1974) showed that transfer on discrimination problems was affected by the degree to which the training format on different discrimination problems fostered integration of the *relevant* information.

Study-phase retrieval may also play a role in the appearance of interference or negative transfer in cases in which new responses have to be performed to previously acquired stimulus cues. When the stimulus cue is presented in the Task 2 setting, it will induce the study-phase retrieval of the former associated response learned in Task 1. This old response will then compete for processing space with the new response, thereby retarding its acquisition (Gilani & Ceraso, 1982). (It should be noted that negative transfer is not assumed to produce forgetting of the old response per se, cf. Petrich, 1975.)

B. STIMULUS VARIABILITY AND TRANSFER

1. The Effects of Task Variation

One of the most studied training factors has been the relative effectiveness of variation or stability of Task 1 training on Task 2 performance (e.g., Hunt, Parente, & Ellis, 1974). Variety of training conditions in Task 1 often produces increased positive transfer except when Task 2 is highly similar or identical to Task 1. The beneficial effects of variety on transfer have been demonstrated in many different types of tasks such as free-recall learning (Ellis *et al.*, 1974), serial learning (Baker, Santa, & Gentry, 1977), the acquisition of elementary mathematics (Burton, Lemke, & Williams, 1975), and maintenance task training (Hagman, 1980).

There is increasing evidence that an important factor in the positive transfer often induced by task or item variety in training is the operation of an abstractive process linked with study-phase retrieval. The retrieval of relevant information during the performance of the different training tasks would be used for the purpose of comparing and abstracting the existing commonalities or invariant relations which unite them.

Nitsch (1977) examined the extent to which different encoding contexts can contribute to positive transfer in verbal concept learning. Novel verbal concepts (e.g., *minge*, "to gang up on someone") were defined by examples that were derived either from one context or a number of varied contexts. Although Task 1 learning was better in the condition using examples from one context, transfer performance to new examples of the concepts in a different context than previously encountered was better after varied-context training. Additionally, Hiew (1977) reported improved retention and transfer in verbal rule learning following training under variable contextual conditions (cf. S. M. Smith, 1982).

Battig (1978) has argued that increased contextual interference (variability) during learning of TBR material can lead to improved retention or transfer, particularly when subjects are tested under changed conditions. Such interference would make irrelevant contextual information, which cannot be functionally grouped into a common representation, less likely to be retrieved along with the TBR item. Thus, the TBR item becomes abstracted or decontextualized. One way of producing interference between irrelevant contextual attributes would be to increase the variability of an item's contextual presentation; the stable attributes would gain associative strength relative to those attributes constantly being varied (Figure 4).

At this point, we have seen that training variability is a factor with important implications for positive transfer. The extent to which the effects of training variability can be ascribed to the integration and abstraction of the TBR material over its successive presentations will now be considered.

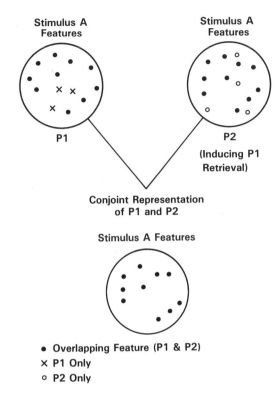

Stimulus A Features

P1

Stimulus A Features

P2
(Inducing P1 Retrieval)

Conjoint Representation of P1 and P2

Stimulus A Features

• Overlapping Feature (P1 & P2)
× P1 Only
○ P2 Only

Figure 4. Stimulus abstraction. Through the correlational analysis of repeated stimulus events, features idiosyncratic to particular occurrences drop out in favor of features correlated across presentations. (From Cormier, 1986. Copyright 1986 by Lawrence Erlbaum Associates. Reprinted by permission.)

2. Concept Formation or Abstraction

In this section we are interested in those transfer studies which examine the way in which subjects integrate information from a number of events to aid abstraction and the formation of simple concepts. Such simple concepts or prototypes are often nonverbal in nature, consisting of geometric or other kinds of figures or patterns which can be varied systematically on particular dimensions.

Posner and Keele (1968) trained subjects to correctly classify four distortions each of four unseen dot pattern prototypes. The subjects were then tested on transfer to patterns consisting of the prototypes they had not previously seen, old previously learned distortions or control patterns which were equated so that they had the same mean variation as the original distortions. In the transfer task, the prototypes were classified into the correct group significantly more often than were any of the equated control patterns.

Posner and Keele (1970) used the same test but with a delay of a week inter-posed between stimulus exemplar presentation and the transfer task. The previously unseen prototypes were "recognized" at least as well as the four presented distortions derived from it. Furthermore, correct classification of the prototype showed no loss over the week, while performance on the original patterns suffered significantly. Thus, extraction of information concerning central tendency takes place during original learning of the distorted (varied) patterns and is not thereafter mediated by them. This result suggests that another representation has been formed which represents the abstracted or prototypical knowledge.

Homa (1978) used figure drawings of ill-defined forms to further in-vestigate this abstractive process. Subjects initially classified 18 different patterns into three categories which contained 3, 6, or 9 members. Follow-ing this task, a transfer test was given in which old exemplars, new ex-emplars, prototype and random patterns were presented for classification. In another experiment, categories were defined in Task 1 by 4, 8, 16, or 32 exemplars, followed by a transfer test which contained unrelated and new patterns based on the categories at each of six distortion levels. In both ex-periments, prior training on numerous different exemplars enhanced transfer compared with training with a few exemplars (Figure 5).

Elio and Anderson (1984) investigated category-learning transfer by manipulating the variability and frequency of category members presented to the subjects in four successive study samples. In the high-variance condi-tion, each sample was representative of the allowable variation in the

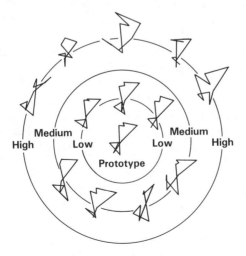

Figure 5. A prototypical form, surrounded by exemplars of varying distortion (low, medium, and high) from the prototype. (From D. Homa, 1978. Copyright 1978 by the American Psychological Association. Reprinted by permission.)

category as a whole and the occurrence frequency of the category members. In the low-variance condition, the initial study sample presented the most frequently occurring members and then gradually introduced the additional exemplars of the remaining study samples without additional instructions. Transfer performance was better when the variance of the category members was introduced gradually, as in the low-variance condition, compared with the high-variance condition. However, if subjects were instructed to be analytic, they showed greater transfer in the high-variance condition. In this connection, Nakamura (1985) showed that prior knowledge influenced similar kinds of classification learning and transfer. Prior knowledge facilitated the learning of separable categories but interfered with learning of nonseparable categories. In the case of separable categories, prior knowledge apparently induced an analytic approach by influencing the storage and reliance on both prototypical and exemplar information (cf. Gilbert, Spring, & Sassenrath, 1977).

Lewis and Anderson (1985) studied the use of schemata in problem solving, in which subjects appear to learn the sets of problem features (schemata) that predict the success of different problem-solving actions (or operations). Interestingly, in studying performance on geometry proofs, evidence was gathered that the same mechanisms produce concept formation and abstraction, in that performance increased the prototypicality of the feature set increased. Brown and Day (1983) examined the ability to use macrorules for paraphrasing expository texts. Experts in college rhetoric outperformed college freshmen in their ability to combine information across paragraphs (cf. Kintsch & van Dyke, 1978).

These studies support the idea that subjects, when sensitive to the occurrence of related or similar TBR material across different presentations, can integrate new material with that already in memory into a common representation. Stimulus variability aids transfer by exerting an effect on this process in two ways: it provides a means by which the subject can distinguish relevant from irrelevant attributes (abstraction) and enhances the probability that additional relevant attributes will be encoded into the functional representation of the TBR item. The integration of the new material with that already in memory would necessitate some form of a study-phase retrieval process.

C. SUMMARY

The integration of information across successive instances or related-information presentation through study-phase retrieval seems to be a critical process in increasing positive transfer to novel tasks and information. The juxtaposition of different events can result in the formation of higher order concepts, as in textual prose comprehension, or can facilitate the abstraction of critical dimensions of task performance and stimulus recognition. This process can be accomplished through the appropriate variation in initial training used to define the critical dimensions. Task 1 variety is most likely to increase positive transfer when it approximates the range of differences found between Task 1 and Task 2.

IV. CHAPTER SUMMARY

It has been argued that many aspects of transfer performance stem from the influence of three fundamental factors of information processing. These factors are (a) the relation of Task 2 retrieval information to the material encoded in Task 1, (b) performance automatization, and (c) study-phase retrieval. These factors are deemed to be fundamental because they have a direct influence on the degree of transfer, are likely to vary in typical training situations, and are likely to have a significant effect on transfer. In addition to describing these factors, this chapter has shown that they can integrate transfer phenomena produced by a variety of methodological procedures and other indirect variables. In this connection, the transfer effects of organizational strategies such as categorization and schema formation were shown to exert their effect through these fundamental processes.

The essential problem for the learner in a transfer task is to retrieve appropriate Task 1 information in accordance with the performance requirements on Task 2. The Task 1 information can contribute to Task 2 performance either directly or through integration with Task 2 material. In the former case, the processes of match–mismatch retrieval and automatization are critical to transfer effects. For positive transfer to occur, the cues present in Task 2 must overlap the attributes of information encoded during Task 1 performance. While most stimulus encodings have multiple attributes, some of these attributes are more likely to be critical to retrieval probability than others. Thus, the correspondence between Task 2 and Task 1 need only be partial for higher transfer to occur as long as the overlapping features have high selection or redintegrative value. These concepts help explain why the identical elements principle of transfer was heuristically useful without being conceptually or empirically accurate in many cases.

Under conditions of consistent, highly practiced S–R relationships, the process of automatization is evoked in which information is processed and responses are controlled at lower levels of the nervous system than were initially required. With automatization, positive transfer is very high along automatized S–R dimensions, but increased levels of negative transfer occur under even moderate changes between Task 1 and 2.

The integration of Tasks 1 and 2 information involves a process of study-phase retrieval in which information in Task 2 results in the retrieval of

Task 1 information so that both are simultaneously present in working memory. In such circumstances, this juxtaposition can result in the creation of new information or the abstraction of items undergoing varied repetition. When the Task 1 and Task 2 information is not combinable, negative transfer can occur.

In addition to describing several fundamental factors underlying transfer phenomena, this chapter seeks to make a larger point by emphasizing the relationship of direct and indirect variables to the expression of transfer. Innumerable variables can affect the details of transfer in any given study in much the same way that a runner's performance in a race can be affected by a multitude of variables.

In such circumstances, it becomes critical to identify the nature of the relationship between performance and the factors being analyzed. For example, the degree of correspondence between Task 1 encodings and Task 2 retrieval cues can be changed through manipulations of stimulus meaningfulness, trainee attention, degree of practice, delays between Task 1 and Task 2 training, and learning strategies, to name a few variables. However, the effect of these variables on transfer is not direct; instead they exert an effect on the match–mismatch retrieval process, which affects the degree of transfer directly.

Although these effects might appear to be confusing at the level of the indirect variable, when the operation of more fundamental processes are considered, the inconsistencies are resolved into an underlying unity of effect.

REFERENCES

Ackerman, P. L., Schneider, W., & Wickens, C. D. (1984). Deciding the existence of a time sharing ability: A combined methodological and theoretical approach. *Human Factors*, *26*, 71–82.

Adams, J. A. (1971). A closed loop theory of motor learning. *Journal of Motor Behavior*, *3*, 111–149.

Atkinson, R. C., & Shiffrin, R. M. (1968). Human memory: A proposed system and its control processes. In K. W. Spence & J. T. Spence (Eds.), *The psychology of learning and motivation* (Vol. 2). New York: Academic Press.

Baker, L., Santa, J. L., & Gentry, J. M. (1977). Consequences of rigid and flexible learning. *Bulletin of the Psychonomic Society*, *9*, 58–60.

Barclay, J. R., Bransford, J. D., Franks, J. J., McCarrell, N. S., & Nitsch, K. (1974). Comprehension and semantic flexibility. *Journal of Verbal Learning and Verbal Behavior*, *13*, 471–481.

Battig, W. F. (1978). The flexibility of human memory. In L. S. Cermak & F. I. M. Craik (Eds.), *Levels of processing and human memory*. Hillsdale, NJ: Erlbaum.

Bernstein, B. R., & Gonzalez, B. K. (1968). *Learning, retention, and transfer* (Vol. 1, Tech. Rep. 68-C-0215-1). Orlando, FL: Naval Training Device Center.

Bilodeau, I. M., & Bilodeau, E. A. (1961). Motor skills learning. *Annual Review of Psychology*, *12*, 243–280.

Bird, C. P. (1977). Proactive inhibition as a function of orienting task characteristics. *Memory and Cognition, 5,* 27–31.

Bird, C. P., & Roberts, R. (1980). An examination of orienting task relationships in a proactive interference paradigm. *Memory and Cognition, 8,* 468–475.

Briggs, G. E. (1969). Transfer of training. In E. A. Bilodeau (Ed.), *Principles of skill acquisition.* New York: Academic Press.

Brown, A. L., & Day, J. D. (1983). Macrorules for summarizing texts: The development of expertise. *Journal of Verbal Learning and Verbal Behavior, 22,* 1–14.

Burton, J. K., Lemke, E. A., & Williams, J. R. (1975). Transfer effects as a function of variety of method and ability level in elementary mathematics. *Journal for Research in Mathematics in Education, 6,* 228–231.

Campione, J. C., & Brown, A. L. (1974). Transfer of training: Effects of successive pretraining of components in a dimension abstracted oddity task. *Journal of Experimental Child Psychology, 18,* 398–411.

Campione, J. C., Brown, A. L., Ferrara, D. A., Jones, R. S., & Steinberg, E. (1985). Breakdowns in flexible use of information: Intelligence related differences on transfer following equivalent learning performance. *Intelligence, 9,* 297–315.

Caro, P. W. (1979). The relationship between flight simulator motion and training requirements. *Human Factors, 21,* 493–501.

Carpenter, P. A., & Just, M. A. (1977). Integrative processes in comprehension. In D. La Berge & S. J. Samuels (Eds.), *Perception and comprehension.* Hillsdale, NJ: Erlbaum.

Chechile, R. A., & Sadowski, D. M. (1983). The effects of cuing in time shared tasks. *Human Factors, 25,* 371–377.

Cheng, P. W. (1985). Restructuring versus automaticity: Alternative accounts of skill acquisition. *Psychological Review, 92,* 414–423.

Clark, H. (1978). Inferences in comprehension. In D. La Berge & S. J. Samuels (Eds.), *Basic processes in reading, perception, and comprehension.* Hillsdale, NJ: Erlbaum.

Colle, H. A., & De Maio, J. (1978, April). *Measurement of attentional capacity load using dual task performance operating curves* (AFHRL-TR-78-5). Brooks Air Force Base, TX: Human Resources Laboratory.

Cormier, S. M. (1986). *Basic processes of learning, cognition, and motivation.* Hillsdale, NJ: Erlbaum.

Deese, J., & Hulse, S. W. (1967). *The psychology of learning.* New York: McGraw-Hill.

Deese, J., & Marder, V. J. (1957). The pattern of errors in delayed recall of serial learning after interpolation. *American Journal of Psychology, 60,* 594–599.

Duncan, J. (1980). The locus of interference in the perception of simultaneous stimuli. *Psychological Review, 87,* 272–300.

Eberts, R., & Schneider, W. (1985). Internalizing the system dynamics for a second order system. *Human Factors, 27,* 371–393.

Egeth, H. (1977). Attention and preattention. In G. H. Bower (Ed.). *The psychology of learning and motivation* (Vol. 11). New York: Academic Press.

Elio, R., & Anderson, J. R. (1984). The effects of information order and learning mode on schema abstraction. *Memory and Cognition, 12,* 20–30.

Ellis, H. C., & Muller, D. G. (1964). Transfer in perceptual learning following stimulus predifferentiation. *Journal of Experimental Psychology, 68,* 388–395.

Ellis, H. C., Parente, F. J., & Walker, C. W. (1974). Coding and varied input versus repetition in human memory. *Journal of Experimental Psychology, 102,* 284–290.

Ellis, H. C., & Shaffer, R. W. (1974). Stimulus encoding and the transfer of stimulus differentiation. *Journal of Verbal Learning and Verbal Behavior, 13,* 393–400.

Eriksen, B. A., & Eriksen, C. W. (1974). Effects of noise letters upon the identification of a target letter in a nonsearch task. *Perception and Psychophysics, 16,* 143–149.

Fisk, A. W., & Schneider, W. (1981). Control and automatic processing during tasks requiring sustained attention: A new approach to vigilance. *Human Factors, 23,* 737–750.

Fleishman, E. A., & Rich, S. (1963). Role of kinesthetic and spatial-visual abilities in perceptual motor learning. *Journal of Experimental Psychology, 66,* 6–12.

Flexser, A. J., & Tulving, E. (1978). Retrieval independence in recognition and recall. *Psychological Review, 85,* 153–171.

Freedle, D. O., Zavala, A., & Fleishman, E. A. (1968). Studies of component-total task relations: Order of components, total task practice, and total task predictability. *Human Factors, 10,* 283–296.

Friedman, A. (1978). Framing pictures: The role of knowledge in automatic encoding and memory for gist. *Journal of Experimental Psychology: General, 108,* 316–355.

Gabriel, M., Foster, K., Orona, E., Saltwick, S. E., & Stanton, M. (1980). Neuronal activity of cingulate cortex, anteroventral thalamus, hippocampal formation and discriminative conditioning. In J. M. Sprague & A. N. Epstein (Eds.), *Progress in psychobiology, and physiological psychology* (Vol. 9) New York: Academic Press.

Gardiner, J. M., Craik, F. I. M., & Birtwistle, J. (1972). Retrieval cues and release from proactive inhibition. *Journal of Verbal Learning and Verbal Behavior, 11,* 778–783.

Gerathewohl, S. J. (1969). *Fidelity of simulation and transfer of training: A review of the problem* (AM 69–24). Federal Aeronautics Administration; Office of Aviation Medicine. Washington, DC.

Gilani, Z. H., & Ceraso, J. (1982). Transfer and temporal organization. *Journal of Verbal Learning and Verbal Behavior, 21,* 437–450.

Gilbert, N., Spring, C., & Sassenrath, J. (1977). Effects of overlearning and similarity on transfer in word recognition. *Perceptual and Motor Skills, 44,* 591–598.

Gopher, D., & North, R. A. (1977). Manipulating the conditions of training in time-sharing performance. *Human Factors, 19,* 583–593.

Gundry, A. J. (1977). Thresholds to roll motion in a flight simulator. *Journal of Aircraft, 14,* 624–630.

Haberlandt, K., & Bingham, G. (1978). Verbs contribute to the coherence of brief narratives: Reading related and unrelated sentence triples. *Journal of Verbal Learning and Verbal Behavior, 17,* 419–425.

Hagman, J. D. (1980). *Effects of training task repetition on retention and transfer of maintenance skill* (RR 1271). Alexandria, VA: Army Research Institute.

Hayes-Roth, B., & Thorndyke, P. W. (1979). Integration of knowledge from text. *Journal of Verbal Learning and Verbal Behavior, 18,* 91–108.

Hiew, C. C. (1977). Sequence effects in rule learning and conceptual generalization. *American Journal of Psychology, 90,* 207–218.

Hirst, W., Spelke, E. S., Reaves, C. C., Charack, G., & Neisser, V. (1980). Dividing attention without alternation or automaticity. *Journal of Experimental Psychology: General, 109,* 98–117.

Homa, D. (1978). Abstraction of ill-defined form. *Journal of Experimental Psychology: Human Learning and Memory, 4,* 407–416.

Horowitz, L. M., & Manelis, C. (1972). Toward a theory of redintegrative memory: Adjective-noun phrases. In G. H. Bower (Ed.) *The psychology of learning and motivation* (Vol. 6). New York: Academic Press.

Hunt, R. R., & Mitchell, D. B. (1978). Specificity in nonsemantic orienting tasks and distinctive memory traces. *Journal of Experimental Psychology: Human Learning and Memory, 4,* 136–145.

Hunt, R. R., Parente, P. J., & Ellis, H. C. (1974). Transfer of coding strategies in free recall with constant and varied input. *Journal of Experimental Psychology, 103,* 619–624.

Ince, F., Williges, R. C., & Roscoe, S. N. (1975). Aircraft simulator motion and the order of merit of flight attitude and steering guidance displays. *Human Factors, 17,* 388–400.

Jacobs, R. S., & Roscoe, S. N. (1975). Simulator cockpit motion and the transfer of initial flight training. *Proceedings of the Human Factors Society 19th Annual Meeting*. Santa Monica, CA: Human Factors Society.

Jacoby, L. L. (1974). The role of mental contiguity in memory: Registration and retrieval effects. *Journal of Verbal Learning and Verbal Behavior, 13*, 483–496.

Jennings, A. E., & Chiles, W. D. (1977). An investigation of time-sharing ability as a factor in complex performance. *Human Factors, 19*, 535–547.

Kahneman, D. (1973). *Attention and effort*. Englewood Cliffs, NJ: Prentice-Hall.

Kessel, C. J., & Wickens, C. D. (1982). The transfer of failure detection skills between monitoring and controlling dynamic systems. *Human Factors, 24*, 49–60.

Kintsch, W., & van Dyk, T. A. (1978). Toward a model of text comprehension and production. *Psychological Review, 85*, 363–394.

Koonce, J. M. (1979). *Effects of ground-based aircraft simulator motion conditions upon prediction of pilot proficiency*. Unpublished doctoral dissertation, University of Illinois, Champaign–Urbana.

Kramer, A. F., Wickens, C. D., & Donchin, E. (1985). Processing of stimulus properties: Evidence for dual task integrality. *Journal of Experimental Psychology: Human Perception and Performance, 11*, 393–408.

Kristofferson, M. W. (1972). Effects of practice on character classification performance. *Canadian Journal of Psychology, 26*, 54–60.

Kruk, R., Regan, D., Beverly, K. I., & Longridge, T. (1983). Flying performance on the advanced simulator for pilot training and laboratory tests of vision. *Human Factors, 25*, 457–466.

Lewis, M. W., & Anderson, J. R. (1985). Discrimination of operator schemata in problem solving: Learning from examples. *Cognitive Psychology, 17*, 26–65.

Lintern, G. (1980). Transfer of landing skill after training with supplementary visual cues. *Human Factors, 22*, 81–88.

Logan, G. D. (1979). On the use of a concurrent memory load to measure attention and automaticity. *Journal of Experimental Psychology: Human Perception and Performance, 5*, 189–207.

Martin, E. L., & Waag, W. L. (1978). *Contribution of platform motion to simulator training effectiveness: Study I Basic Contact* (AFHRL-TR-78-51). Williams Air Force Base, AZ: Air Force Human Resource Laboratory.

Nagae, S. (1980). Nature of discriminating and categorizing functions of verbal labels on recognition memory for shape. *Journal of Experimental Psychology: Human Learning and Memory, 6*, 421–429.

Nakamura, G. V. (1985). Knowledge based classification of ill-defined categories. *Memory and Cognition, 13*, 377–384.

Nautapsky, M., Waag, W. L., Meyer, D. C., McFadden, R. W., & McDowell, E. (1979). *Platform motion contributions to simulator effectiveness: Study III* (AFHRL-TR-79-25). Williams Air Force Base, AZ: Air Force Human Resources Laboratory.

Neisser, U. (1967). *Cognitive psychology*. New York: Appleton.

Nelson, D. L. (1979). Remembering pictures and words: Appearance, significance, and name. In L. S. Cermak & F. I. M. Craik (Eds.), *Levels of processing in human memory*. Hillsdale, NJ: Erlbaum.

Nelson, D. L., & Rowe, F. A. (1969). Information theory and stimulus encoding in paired-associate acquisition: Ordinal position of formal similarity. *Journal of Experimental Psychology, 79*, 342–346.

Newell, A., & Rosenbloom, P. S. (1981). Mechanisms of skill acquisition and the law of practice. In J. R. Anderson (Ed.), *Cognitive skills and their acquisition*. Hillsdale, NJ: Erlbaum.

Nitsch, K. E. (1977). Structuring decontextualized forms of knowledge. Unpublished doctoral dissertation, Vanderbilt University, Nashville, TN.

Perry, D. H., & Naish, J. M. (1964). Flight simulation for research. *Journal of the Royal Aeronautical Society, 68*, 645–662.

Petrich, J. A. (1975). Organization of recall in the retroactive inhibition paradigm. *Journal of Verbal Learning and Verbal Behavior, 12*, 294–301.

Posner, M. I., & Keele, S. W. (1968). On the genesis of abstract ideas. *Journal of Experimental Psychology, 77*, 353–363.

Posner, M. I., & Keele, S. W. (1970). Retention of abstract ideas. *Journal of Experimental Psychology, 83*, 304–308.

Postman, L. (1976). Interference theory revisited. In J. Brown (Ed.), *Recall and recognition*. New York: Wiley.

Price, R. H., & Slive, A. B. (1970). Verbal processes in shape recognition. *Journal of Experimental Psychology, 83*, 373–379.

Prophet, W. W., & Boyd, H. A. (1970). *Device task fidelity and transfer of training: Aircraft cockpit procedures training* (Tech. Rep. No. 70-10). Alexandria, VA: Human Resources Research Laboratory.

Rathert, G. A., Creer, B. Y., & Sadoff, M. (1961). *The use of piloted flight simulators in general research* (Tech. Rep. No. 365). Paris, France: NATO, Advisory Group for Aeronautical Research and Development.

Ricard, G. L., & Parrish, R. V. (1984). Pilot differences and motion cuing effects on simulated helicopter hover. *Human Factors, 26*, 249–256.

Rabinowitz, J. C., Mandler, G., Barsalou, L. W. (1979). Generation-recognition as an auxiliary retrieval strategy. *Journal of Verbal Learning and Verbal Behavior, 18*, 57–72.

Richardson, J. (1976). Component selection in paired associate learning. *American Journal of Psychology, 89*, 3–49.

Rieck, A. M., Ogden, G. D., & Anderson, N. S. (1980). An investigation of varying amounts of component task practice on dual task performance. *Human Factors, 22,* 373–384.

Royer, J. M., & Cable, G. W. (1975). Facilitated learning in connected discourse. *Journal of Educational Psychology, 67*, 116–123.

Runquist, W. N., & Runquist, P. A. (1978). Interference reduction with conceptually similar paired associations. *Journal of Experimental Psychology: Human Learning and Memory, 4*, 370–381.

Ruocco, J. N., Vitale, P. A., & Benfari, R. C. (1965). *Kinetic cueing in simulated carrier approaches* (AD 617689). Port Washington, NY: Naval Training Device Center.

Salthouse, T. A., & Somberg, B. L. (1982). Skilled performance: Effects of adult age and experience on elementary processes. *Journal of Experimental Psychology: General, 111*, 176–207.

Salvendy, G., & Pilitsis, J. (1980). The development and validation of an analytical training program for medical suturing. *Human Factors, 22*, 753–770.

Schneider, W., & Fisk, A. D. (1982). Degree of consistent training: Improvements in search performance and automatic process development. *Perception and Psychophysics, 31*, 160–168.

Schneider, W., & Fisk, A. D. (1984). Automatic category search and its transfer. *Journal of Experimental Psychology: Learning, Memory, and Cognition, 10*, 1–16.

Seymour, P. H. K. (1979). *Human visual cognition*. New York: St. Martins Press.

Shaffer, L. H. (1974). Multiple attention in continuous verbal tasks. In P. M. A. Rabbit & S. Dornic (Eds.), *Attention and performance V*. New York: Academic Press.

Shaffer, W. O., & LaBerge, D. (1979). Automatic semantic processing of unattended words. *Journal of Verbal Learning and Verbal Behavior, 18*, 413–426.

Shiffrin, R. M., & Schneider, W. (1977). Controlled and automatic human information processing: II. Perceptual learning, automatic attending and a general theory. *Psychological Review, 84,* 127–190.

Smith, E. E., Shoben, E. J. & Rips, L. J. (1974). Structure and process in semantic memory: A feature model for semantic decisions. *Phychological Review, 81,* 214–241.

Smith, S. M. (1982). Enhancement of recall using multiple environmental contexts during learning. *Memory and Cognition, 10,* 405–412.

Sokolov, E. N. (1969). The modeling properties of the nervous system. In M. Cole & I. Maltzman (Eds.), *A handbook of contemporary Soviet psychology.* New York: Basic Books.

Spelke, E., Hirst, W., & Neisser, U. (1976). Skills of divided attention. *Cognition, 4,* 215–230.

Thatcher, R., & John, E. (1977). *Foundations of cognitive processes.* Hillsdale, NJ: Erlbaum.

Thomson, D. M., & Tulving, E. (1970). Associative encoding and retrieval: Weak and strong cues. *Journal of Experimental Psychology, 86,* 255–262.

Thorndike, E. L., & Woodworth, R. S. (1901). The influence of improvement in one mental function upon the efficiency of other functions. *Psychological Review, 8,* 247–261.

Treisman, A. M., (1969). Strategies and models of selective attention. *Psychological Review, 76,* 282–299.

Treisman, A. M., & Gelade, G. (1980). A feature-integration theory of attention. *Cognitive Psychology, 12,* 97–136.

Tulving, E. (1976). Ecphoric processes in recall and recognition. In J. Brown (Ed.), *Recall and recognition.* New York: Wiley.

Underwood, B. J. (1969). Attributes of memory. *Psychological Review, 76,* 559–573.

Welford, A. T. (1968). *Fundamentals of skill.* London: Methuen.

Wickens, D. D. (1972). Characteristics of word encoding. In A. W. Melton & E. Martin (Eds.), *Coding processes in human memory.* Washington, DC: Winston.

Wickens, D. D., Moody, M. J., & Dow, R. (1981). The nature and timing of the retrieval process and of interference effects. *Journal of Experimental Psychology: General, 110,* 1–20.

Wood, M. E., & Gerlach, V. S. (1974). *Transfer from audiovisual pretraining to a continuous perceptual motor task* (AFHRL-TR-74-8). Brooks Air Force Base, TX: Human Resources Laboratory.

Yekovich, F. R., & Walker, C. H. (1978). Identifying and using referents in sentence comprehension. *Journal of Verbal Learning and Verbal Behavior, 17,* 265–277.

Yekovich, F. R., Walker, C., & Blackman, H. S. (1979). The rule of presupposed and focal information in integrating sentences. *Journal of Verbal Learning and Verbal Behavior, 18,* 535–548.

CHAPTER 7

Transfer of
Cognitive Skills

WAYNE D. GRAY[1]
JUDITH M. ORASANU

I. INTRODUCTION

The cognitive science revolution (Baars, 1986; Gardner, 1985) has made impressive advances in our understanding of cognitive performance and the acquisition of cognitive skills. Based upon these successes powerful theories are emerging that can predict when and how much transfer will occur. While these theories are diverse, their common denominator is the *problem space hypothesis* (Newell & Simon, 1972), with many of these theories using *production systems* (Brownston, Farrell, Kant, & Martin, 1985) as a tool for theory development and representation.

In this chapter we discuss the transfer of complex cognitive skills, such as text editing, with an emphasis on the relationship between transfer and learning. In this section we introduce our topic by comparing the cognitive science approach to transfer with the older verbal learning tradition. We then provide a short discussion of the central facts of transfer and finish the section by considering a number of cognitive science concepts and methods that are importatnt to the new study of transfer.

A. A BRIEF COMPARISON OF THE VERBAL LEARNING AND THE COGNITIVE SCIENCE APPROACHES TO TRANSFER

To compare the verbal learning and cognitive science approaches to transfer, we must introduce two key concepts: the distinction between general (or nonspecific) and specific transfer (e.g., McGeoch, 1942; Postman, 1971) and the cognitive science distinction between declarative and procedural knowledge (Winograd, 1975).

[1]This chapter represents the views of the authors and does not reflect Army policy.

Specific transfer refers to the identity or similarity of elements in the transfer task to elements in the prior task(s). According to Thorndike (1914; Thorndike & Woodworth, 1901), positive transfer is a function of the number of elements in common between two tasks. General or nonspecific transfer refers to the carry-over of attitudes, methods, or techniques of attack (Garrett, 1941), or what McGeoch (1942) referred to as general principles, modes of attack, or set. Such theories of transfer by generalization (Allport, 1937; Judd, 1908) were proposed as alternatives to Thorndike's identical elements position. However, by the early 1940s, these conflicting theories were viewed as different aspects of the same underlying phenomena, the main difference being one of emphasis (Garrett, 1941; McGeoch, 1942).

It is clear that by the 1950s and 1960s the mainstream of transfer research, the verbal learning tradition, no longer viewed general and specific as competing theories, but rather as separate components. Most theory development focused on specific transfer. Here the common elements approach carried the day. The theoretical controversies concerned the mechanisms by which various common elements facilitated or interfered with the acquisition or retention (Postman & Underwood, 1973) of other common elements.

In contrast, general transfer was most typically viewed as something to control for in experiments on specific transfer (as witnessed by the popularity of the C-D control group in studies of paired-associate transfer or retention, see Postman, 1971). When general transfer was studied directly, it was not to resolve a theoretical dispute, but more commonly to describe basic empirical relationships such as whether experience with the method of practice or class of material yielded greater positive transfer (Postman & Schwartz, 1964).

With the emphasis on empirical description, theoretical discussions of the basis of general transfer remained at the *common something* level. For example, in discussing the general transfer phenomena of learning-to-learn, Postman, Keppel, and Zacks (1968) concluded that it "reflects circumscribed habits and skills determined by the particular conditions of training and capable of varying degrees of generalization to new learning situations." It is in defining this *common something* that the cognitive science distinction between declarative and procedural knowledge (Winograd, 1975) becomes important.

Declarative knowledge is knowledge of facts or static knowledge (e.g., in what year did Neil Armstrong walk on the moon?), whereas procedural knowledge is knowledge of how to process or manipulate information to accomplish a given task (such as required to do multicolumn multiplication). Models of cognitive skill performance (Newell & Simon, 1972) use this procedural/declarative distinction together with the problem space hypothesis (see section I.C) to represent the knowledge involved in tasks such as solving cryptarithmetic puzzles (Newell & Simon, 1972), physics problems (Larkin, McDermott, Simon, & Simon, 1980), and text editing (Card, Moran, &

Newell, 1980). These tasks have been analyzed into elements of procedural knowledge such as goals and subgoals, methods, selection rules, and operators which either incorporate or act upon declarative (or static) knowledge (Card, Moran, & Newell, 1980, 1983). Hence the cognitive approach can identify the common elements "supplied by the behaving person as well as by the situation" (Garrett, 1941, p.96). This emphasis on common elements puts the cognitive science approach squarely in the tradition of Thorndike's approach to transfer, the difference being that cognitive elements are much more abstract than the usual interpretation of Thorndike's dictum as S–R pairs.

While the distinction between procedural and declarative knowledge serves to bring general transfer under the sway of a cognitive common elements approach, it also represents a major difference in the types of knowledge studied by the verbal learners and the cognitive scientists. Verbal learning studies of specific transfer (Postman, 1971) emphasized the acquisition of the declarative knowledge involved in learning lists of words or nonsense syllables. In contrast, the cognitive science studies that we review show an overwhelming tendency to study the transfer of procedural knowledge, specifically that knowledge involved in *goal directed* cognitive skills (for example, text editing, operating a device, solving the eight-square puzzle, and a performing a second-order tracking task).

B. THE SURPRISING SPECIFICITY OF TRANSFER

Commenting upon early research on transfer, Postman (1971) observed that "the repeated failures to find broad transfer effects implied that the habits permitting the efficient performance of a given task were highly specific and unlikely to generalize to new situations" (p. 1032). Such failure of transfer is found in recent studies as well. For example, Simon and Hayes (1976) found that people did not translate a difficult problem into one which was structurally isomorphic but much simpler. Likewise, Perfetto, Bransford, and Franks (1983) have found that people do not transfer declarative knowledge acquired in one condition to a new and seemingly relevant condition, despite evidence that the knowledge can be assessed under different eliciting conditions. Similarly, efforts to enhance intellectual performance by training cognitive skills have met with limited success. The skills simply do not transfer to novel contexts (Bransford, Arbitman-Smith, Stein, & Vye, 1985; Polson & Jeffries, 1985). Cognitive science approaches provide an insight into this surprising specificity of transfer.

The cognitive theorists, whose work we discuss, have focused on two areas of importance to transfer: The problem space per se and the procedures used to solve problems (or move) in that space. Transfer of cognitive skills involves either the use of a familiar problem space to solve a novel problem or the use of well-learned procedures in new applications.

Problem space approaches to transfer emphasize *how* knowledge is used rather than *what* knowledge is used. Declarative knowledge is viewed as quite flexible, with the same bit of declarative knowledge used in many different ways. However, the various procedures in which the same bit of declarative knowledge is embedded can be quite different. Transfer is predicted when the same knowledge is used in the same way across different tasks. No transfer is predicted when the same knowledge is used in different ways (Anderson, 1987).

This emphasis on knowledge use is one of the major differences between cognitive science and older identical elements theory. The cognitive science approach does not view transfer as guaranteed merely because the same knowledge is present in A as is required to perform B. Not only must the knowledge be the same, but how it is used must be the same. The problem space hypothesis provides a way of representing knowledge that by making these distinctions clear provides insight into the surprising specificity of transfer.

C. THE PROBLEM SPACE HYPOTHESIS: A BRIEF INTRODUCTION

The problem space hypothesis (Newell, 1980) states that "the fundamental organizational unit of all human goal-oriented symbolic activity is the problem space"(p. 696). The constraints imposed upon a cognitive architecture by the problem space hypothesis can be easily mimicked by production system models. To understand the problem space hypothesis is to understand why many cognitive scientists use production systems as a tool for theory development as well as a convenient format for representation.

A problem space is a symbolic structure consisting of *states* and *operators*. Each operator takes a state as input and produces a state as output. A *path* is a sequence of operators that thread their way through a sequence of states. A problem in a problem space consists of a set of *initial* states, a set of *goal* states, and a set of *path constraints*. Solving a problem involves finding a path through the space, starting at an initial state, passing only along paths that satisfy the path constraints, and ending at a goal state.

As an example, consider the problem of trying to get from Washington, D.C., to San Francisco. The initial state is the Washington National Airport. Your goal state is the San Francisco Airport. The *states* consist of all airports in the United States. You have three operators: The *direct-flight* operator enables you to ask the ticket agent for a direct flight to some goal city, in this case San Francisco; the *next-flight-west* operator enables you to get on a plane heading west from where you are now; finally, the *next-flight* operator simply books you on the next flight out, regardless of destination. You may apply one of these operators to get to a new state (literally and figuratively). For example, your next state could be airports in Philadelphia, Newark, New York City, Pittsburgh, Boston, Atlanta, Chicago, and so on. (Note that there are no direct flights from Washington National to San Francisco. This is an example of a path constraint.) Once in the next state, you can again apply an operator to reach another state. This process continues until you find yourself in the goal state, that is, the San Francisco Airport.

By the problem space hypothesis, problem solving is synonymous with *searching* the space. The search (that is, solving the problem) begins by applying operators to the current state. Each application of operator to state produces a new state, which is added to the stock of states. The new state is evaluated to determine if it is any closer to the goal state than the existing stock of states. If so, then an operator is applied to this new state; if not then another operator is applied to an old state. To carry out this search process, cognitive scientists postulate a fixed cognitive architecture or mechanism that works for all problem spaces.

Since the problem space hypothesis is a model of human goal-oriented cognition, human resource and capacity limitations impose constraints upon what can take place. The number of previous states which a human can remember affects the probability of revisiting a given state or of learning experience-based, short-cut methods. Speed of retrieval from long-term memory, number of chunks, and information per chunk, all affect the mental representation of the problem space and operations in the problem space.

The cognitive skills involved in activities as diverse as text editing, taking airline travel reservations, playing bridge, installing an electric light fixture, troubleshooting a radar system, programming, and so on, all can be said to occur in some problem space, and all are potentially representable within a production system framework. The strong claim is made that anything found to be true about the transfer of one cognitive skill can be applied to all other cognitive skills. Any exceptions must be capable of being explicitly accounted for within the problem space framework.

D. Tools for Problem Space Theorists: Production Systems

The production systems are special-purpose programming languages that seem especially suited to dealing with information-processing theories of human performance (Neches, Langley, & Klahr, 1987; Newell & Simon, 1972). Production systems allow the full complexity of the human information-processing system to be represented and demand that theoreticians explain how the various mechanisms interact. Complexities such as under what circumstances processing involves short-term versus long-term memory, parallel versus serial processing, or pattern matching versus problem solving must be considered and incorporated into the resulting theory.

Production system models are evaluated by criteria of *sufficiency* and *power*. A model is sufficient if its mechanisms and their interactions mimic human performance in some context. It is powerful if this mimicking extends over a wide range of inputs and contexts, such as programming in LISP, solving geometry problems, or text editing.

Given that production systems may be useful, what exactly are they? At the simplest level of description, a production system consists of two data structures which interact via a simple processing cycle. When modeling human cognition, the two data structures are thought of as *working memory* and *production memory*. The processing cycle consists of a three-stage recognize-act cycle. It *matches* one or more *production rules* (from production memory) with the contents of working memory, decides which of the matched rules to fire (sometimes called *conflict resolution*), and fires (the execution or *act* stage) the selected rule(s). Firing a rule may result in actions in the external world as well as changes to the contents of working memory.

The production rule given below (from, Neches *et al.*, 1987, p.5) is taken from a set of production rules for subtracting two numbers:

FIND DIFFERENCE

IF: you are processing *column*,
and *number1* is in *column* and *row1*,
and *number2* is in *column* and *row2*,
and *row1* is above *row2*,
and *number1* is greater than or equal to *number2*,

THEN: compute the difference of *number1* and *number2*,
and write the result in *column*.

As with all production rules, this rule consists of a *condition-action* pair which will fire or execute based upon the outcome of the three-stage recognize-act cycle. In the match stage, the condition (or IF) side of all rules in production memory is compared with the contents of working memory (this is usually assumed to be a parallel process). In the production system from which the above rule is taken, the words in italics are considered variables. So, not only does the entire subcondition "*number2* is in *column* and *row2*" have to match, but each variable must be *instantiated* with an element from working memory. (Note that not all production rules will have variables.)

After the match stage, the conflict resolution stage selects one or more production rules to fire or apply. How this selection process works depends upon the theory being modeled. For a simple expert system that does not purport to model human cognition, this stage may be eliminated so that all productions that match are fired. Depending upon the theory, the conflict resolution stage may select those productions which match the most recent, the oldest, the strongest, the most important, and so on, information in working memory.

The act stage then executes the production rule(s) selected. Executing our sample production rule modifies the contents of working memory (by adding the result of the computation) and the external environment (by writing the result in the correct column).

Within the production system framework, different parts of this recognize-act cycle may be considered as involving serial or parallel processing. Likewise, different capacity, decay rate, and so on can be assumed for working memory as well as production memory. Since the firing of a production rule results in the modification of working memory, this recognize-act cycle can continue indefinitely. In practice, it continues until a certain prespecified *goal state* (such as solving a subtraction problem) is achieved.

E. PERFORMING IN A PROBLEM SPACE: PREREQUISITES TO
   LEARNING AND TRANSFER

Problem space theories of learning and transfer are firmly rooted in problem space analyses and theories of performance. To understand the problem space approach to transfer, the reader must have some acquaintance with these analyses. To this end, we introduce GOMS (Card *et al.,* 1980, 1983).

GOMS stands for *goals, operators, methods,* and *selection rules.* The *goals* are the goals and subgoals of goal-oriented cognition. Beyond this, "the dynamic function of a goal is to provide a memory point to which the system can return on failure or error and from which information can be obtained about what is desired, what methods are avalable, and what has been already tried" (Card *et al.,* 1980, p. 38). *Operators* are the elementary motor or information-processing acts that a person uses in performing the task. The operators that are selected for study depend upon the level or *grain of analysis* desired. As our interests go from the macro to the micro, the *elementary* operators we choose for our analysis go from a mixture of basic information-processing mechanisms and learned behavior to purely low-level information-processing mechanisms. For example, at a macro level, the elementary operators used to describe the process of preparing this chapter include writing, reading, talking, and listening. In contrast, a micro analysis of proofreading the chapter might examine more elementary memory retrieval and pattern-matching operators.

A *method* is a particular combination of subgoals and operators that can be used to accomplish a goal. There may be several methods available to accomplish any given goal. Which method is chosen depends upon the *selection rules* which provide the *control structure* of cognition. However, the selection of a method cannot be the result of an extended deliberation (Newell, 1980). If so, it would not be a selection rule but would itself be a method that is executed in another problem space.

GOMS is based upon general human information-processing theory (see especially, Card *et al.,* 1983). While it was developed in the context of analyzing text-editing expertise (Card *et al.,* 1980, 1983), it is not specific either to experts or to text editing. For example, it has been extended to analyze the learning (Kay & Black, 1985) and transfer (Singley & Anderson, 1985, in press) of text-editing skills and has begun to be used in other domains (Kieras & Polson, 1985).

F. SUMMARY AND OVERVIEW OF THE CHAPTER

We began this section by comparing the cognitive science and verbal learning approaches to transfer. Interesting enough, both traditions base their transfer theories upon Thorndike's (1914) common elements theory. The verbal learning theories emphasized specific transfer and all but ignored general transfer. From the cognitive science perspective, this lopsided development stemmed from impoverished conceptions of learning and a complete absence of theories of performance. The theories of learning used by the verbal learners could not yield an analytic representation of the cognitive skills involved in such general transfer phenomena as modes of attack or the use of general principles. In contrast, these general transfer phenomena are exactly those aspects of transfer that the cognitive scientists have chosen to emphasize. The relative lack of attention given to specific transfer phenomena does not show some inherent limitation of the cognitive approach. Rather, it reflects a tradition which emphasizes skilled performance over rote learning. Despite these differences, we believe that there is much that the cognitive theorists can learn from the older verbal learning studies (especially in the area of methodology and measurement). Furthermore, the cognitive approach cannot be fully accepted until it provide an account of the specific transfer phenomena favored by the verbal learners.

The problem space is the fundamental architectural assumption of those cognitive scientists whose theories we review in this chapter. In the next section we discuss cognitive theories of between-task transfer. This is followed by a discussion of several theories of learning for which production system models have been created. We discuss research that shows how the ability to represent the interaction of knowledge and learning mechanisms in precise ways explains and predicts *within-task* transfer. Finally, we summarize our conclusions about the utility of this new approach to transfer and where we see it heading.

II. TRANSFER THEMES FROM PROBLEM SPACE APPROACHES

Acquiring cognitive skill on a task involves acquiring knowledge of the states in the task problem space and knowledge of operators for moving from one state to another. Transfer of cognitive skills involves the transfer of knowledge about states and operators to new problems in the same or different problem space. Knowing what, at least, some of the states are in a new problem space is a tremendous aid to solving problems in that space. For example, knowing that a state *x* exists which is closer to the goal state than is the current state (and is therefore a desirable intermediate step) allows the problem solver to set a subgoal of achieving state *x*. Likewise, having operators already organized into methods or procedures for moving between states provides a powerful set of ready-made tools.

Transfer of states and procedures (operators) that occurs totally within a given problem space is usually considered a type of learning and, as such, will be considered in the next section. In this section we consider transfer between problem spaces of varying degrees of dissimilarity.

Two sets of studies from two different laboratories are discussed. The approaches these laboratories take is as remarkable for the similarities as for the differences. Similarities include a strong commitment to the problem space hypothesis and a primary (but not exclusive) use of text-editing skills as the domain of transfer. Differences stem from the emphasis of one laboratory, Moran and associates, on the cognitive engineering of software/hardware design and training, and the other, Anderson *et al.*, on extending a powerful theory of learning, ACT*, to account for transfer. A secondary difference in the two approaches is the emphasis of Anderson *et al.* on casting their theoretical mechanisms in a production system format.

A. A COGNITIVE ENGINEERING APPROACH TO TRANSFER

Learning a new cognitive skill or a new version of an old skill can entail borrowing pieces from somewhat similar problem spaces. Clearly there are cases where this strategy is advantageous (if not 100% positive), as when learning to drive a car with a stick shift after already knowing how to drive an automatic. However, it is interesting to ask whether borrowing a problem space may entail negative as well as positive transfer and, if so, to predict which type of transfer occurs when.

1. Borrowing a Problem Space: Analogical Models

Borrowing from other, already mastered problem spaces may involve the use of analogical models (Douglas & Moran, 1983; Halasz & Moran, 1982). Such borrowing entails mapping the known structure of one complex task onto parts of the new task. By this process, objects, relations, operations, and so on in the known *source* problem space are mapped, or transferred, to corresponding objects, relations, operations, and so on in the unknown *target* system (Douglas & Moran, 1983). For example, an analogical model might involve using what people know about file cabinets to teach someone how a computer file system works.

While analogy works fine for simple situations, it breaks down when elaborated to deal with the complexities of a new system. Continuing the example, how would you add the notion of *password protection* to the filing cabinet model of computer file systems? With such elaborations, the once simple analogical model quickly becomes "a baroque collection of special-purpose models pasted together in a more-or-less integrated and a more-or-less consistent fashion" (Halasz & Moran, 1982, p. 384).

A reliance upon analogical models produces two sorts of problems. First, the user has to decide which model out of his or her "baroque collection of special-purpose models" applies to the situation at hand. Second, an analogical model tends to explain too much. In his file cabinet, one of us has Halasz and Moran, Douglas and Moran, and Moran all filed in his "Moran" folder. Trying to save his notes on each of these papers in a computer file {DSK}<LISPFILES>NOTECARDS>MORAN would have the effect of generating three different versions of the "MORAN" file. The file cabinet analogy, in this case, would mislead the user and interfere with the acquisition of a more accurate model of how a computer file system works. Problems with borrowing from analogical models lead to the conclusion that the best way to teach a novice to reason about a new domain is to create an abstract conceptual model that is tailored for the task at hand (Halasz & Moran, 1982). (This is similar to the conclusion that Pirolli and Anderson, 1985, [see below] reach regarding what type of recursion example to teach novice LISP programmers.)

A problem with this conclusion is that few specialized frameworks exist that a novice can use in learning about a new system. Hence, while the use of analogical models may yield negative transfer when compared to some optimal *tailor-made* model, our intuitions are that analogical models yield positive transfer when compared to using no model (or building a brand-new model from scratch).

Douglas and Moran (1983) developed an analysis technique for generating a taxonomy of analogical misconceptions. The analysis focuses on operators in the GOMS sense. It looks at operators in the two problem spaces (that of the analogical model and that of the to-be-learned model) and marks an operator in Problem Space 1 as similar to an operator in Problem Space 2 if the two operators produce similar effects (postconditions) or have surface features in common. Misconceptions arise when either the preconditions or the postconditions for use of the operator in the new problem space are not yet known. They result in similar operators from the analogical model being substituted for the unknown (or less known) operator from the new problem space. An example from the problem spaces of typewriting and text editing is the use of the space-bar operator. In typewriting, the space bar moves the print element to the next cell or character to the right. For text editing, the space-bar inserts a blank space between the currrent position and next cell or character to the right. This mix-up is a common mistake for novice text editors.

In analyzing the text editing and typewriter problem spaces, Douglas and Moran distinguish between *locative* and *mutative* operators. Locative operators move the pointer around (such as the space bar for typewriting and <control>-H for text editing) while mutative operators change the text. They show that three locative operators for the typewriter are similar to mutative text-editor operators which insert formating characters. In their observations of novice text editors, these three errors, involving an "ontological shift," accounted for 30 out of 75 errors.

The operator-mapping technique shows the utility of the problem space construct for identifying points of negative transfer between two tasks. Douglas and Moran see their technique as a potentially useful design tool. We concur. For example, there are many times in private life, industry, and the military when people already familiar with one version of a piece of equipment, software program, and so on are required to deal with an "improved" version. Applying the operator-mapping technique to these new versions could result in engineering changes or, at least, identification of training needs.

2. Differences between Problem Spaces as a Measure of Transfer

Moran (1983) builds upon his interest in mapping operators between problem spaces to create an analysis framework for use in systems design and as a competence (performance) model of the user. This ETIT analysis consists of (a) an *external task space,* (b) an *internal task space,* and (c) a *mapping* from the external task space to the internal task space. The notion is that a user comes to a system with a task already formulated in terms external to the system. An example of a mapping problem is putting a household budget onto a computer spreadsheet. The budget-keeping task is already well formulated according to the user's (probably idiosyncratic) bookkeeping methods. The problem is to reformulate the task to *fit* the spreadsheet. The system's complexity relative to its target external task space is assessed by examining its mapping rules. The technique can, at least in principle, be used to predict transfer among devices merely by gauging the differences between the mappings for different devices. The degree of overlap predicts the degree of transfer.

Moran has used ETIT to compare a line editor (LINED) with a display editor (DISPED). First, a mapping was done from the external problem space to each editor. These two mappings were then mapped onto each other. Every DISPED rule had a corresponding LINED rule. This suggests easy transfer from LINED to DISPED, but the transfer should not be as effective the other way. There were five LINED rules that had no correspondence in DISPED, and the LINED rules were more highly conditionalized than DISPED.

At this point ETIT is not a finished tool but is a research program based upon the notion that all goal-directed cognitive processes occur in a problem space of one sort or another. With further development, ETIT will be a useful tool for predicting ease of learning and operating new devices. Note that ETIT defines ease of learning and operating in terms of the mapping or number of common elements between how a person currently thinks about a task and the way that task must be performed if a given device is used.

3. Summary

Borrowing pieces of a problem space can be risky but beneficial. Carefully defining an analogy's boundary conditions should help to maximize its benefits, although, when possible, a carefully crafted specialized framework is preferred.

A goal for cognitive engineering is to develop a metric for determining what aspects of one problem space transfer positively or negatively to another problem space. As witnessed by Douglas and Moran (1983) and Moran (1983), useful steps in this direction are being made. (Kieras and Polson's 1985 model is similar in spirit to Moran's; however, due to space limitations we chose to discuss the Moran model as illustrative of this type of cognitive engineering effort.)

B. Production Rules as the Elements of Transfer: ACT* and Its Implications

A prerequisite to the common elements approach to transfer is being able to precisely specify what the common elements are. We believe that it was the ability to describe common elements in terms of S and R features and the corresponding inability to precisely describe cognitive elements that drove the verbal learners to emphasize *specific* transfer and to all but ignore *general* transfer.

The problem space hypothesis provides us with a basic vocabulary to describe the states and operators involved in performing a cognitive skill. Likewise, GOMS (Card *et al.*, 1980; 1983) provides a way to increase our analytic precision by analyzing expertise as operators organized into methods to accomplish certain goals when selected according to certain rules. Yet another step in precisely describing the cognitive elements is provided by the production rule.

Anderson (1987) takes a strong view of production rules as the common elements of transfer for which Thorndike was searching. Of course, production rules are more abstract than the usual interpretation of Thorndike's dictum as S–R pairs. For ACT* (Anderson, 1983, 1987), this abstraction comes in several ways. First, a production rule with variables (see section I.D.) in its conditions functions as a template which can be matched to a family of patterns rather than one specific pattern. Second, the function of many production rules is to generate hierarchical goal structures (to control behavior) rather than to execute a specific behavior. Third, the conditions and actions of many production rules deal with elements of cognition and are likely to affect change in the internal, cognitive environment as in the external one.

Singley and Anderson (in press) propose an explanation of the specificity of transfer that is essentially an extension of Anderson's theory of learning (Anderson, 1982, 1983, 1986, 1987). By their view, the elements of transfer are subsets of the elements of learning, which makes any common elements approach to transfer totally accounted for by learning theory.

We begin this section with a discussion of ACT*'s learning mechanisms. While it is beyond the scope of this chapter to give a detailed exposition of ACT*, we intend to provide just enough information about the theory so that the reader can appreciate ACT*'s account of the specificity of transfer: It is not *what,* but *how,* knowledge is used that is important.

1. A Selective Overview of ACT*

"Knowledge comes in a declarative form, and is used by weak methods to generate solutions, and the knowledge compilation process forms new productions. The key step is the knowledge compilation process, which produces the domain-specific skill" (Anderson, 1987, p. 197). This statement is central to ACT*'s account of transfer. When learning a new domain, general, nonspecific problem-solving procedures (production rules in ACT*'s implementation) are used to interpret declarative knowledge in working memory. Skill acquisition proceeds through the processes of *knowledge compilation* that gradually build up a set of domain-specific productions. These new productions speed performance by the processes of *composition* and *proceduralization*. The composition process speeds performance by collapsing general procedures into a smaller number of more specific procedures. Proceduralization eliminates the need to retrieve repeatedly the same knowledge from declarative memory by directly incorporating that knowledge into new productions.

For ACT*, cognitive skill acquisition is a goal-directed, problem-solving activity. Hierarchical goal structures underlie all of ACT*'s activities. Existing hierarchical goal structures direct performance, learning, and transfer and ensure that any new productions are embedded with new goal structures. These goal structures account "for the ubiquitous hierarchical structure of human behavior, and the focus of attention it produces explains the strong seriality in the overall flow of human cognition" (Anderson, 1983, p. 33). Thus, ACT* can be described as a theory of learning by contiguity, where contiguity is not temporal contiguity, but contiguity in the goal structure of problem solving.

2. Learning by Doing and Other Implications of Knowledge Compilation

The ACT* distinction between declarative and procedural knowledge, how the two are used, and how they are acquired has several implications for transfer.

> Declarative knowledge is flexible and not committed to how it will be used. However, knowledge compilation often derives productions from declarative knowledge that can only be used in certain ways. Often the production sets underlying different uses of the same knowledge can be quite different. (Anderson, 1987, p. 201)

Declarative knowledge is accessible to a large number of general purpose (or weak) problem-solving methods. These methods act upon declarative knowledge in an interpretative mode, which produces performance that is slow and subject to errors. Since all behavior (cognitive and physical) is under the control of procedural memory, skilled performance requires that these slow, interpretative procedures be transformed into domain-specific procedures. This transformation occurs through the knowledge compilation mechanisms of composition and proceduralization.

The way knowledge compilation is carried out has several consequences for learning and transfer. For composition to occur, productions with *contigious goal structures* must be present together in working memory. Since these productions are specific to skilled performance, the best way to ensure that they will occur together in working memory is by practicing the skill itself. In a very real sense, the ACT* system can only learn skills by doing them. The unequivocal prediction is that for cognitive skill acquisition, practice is more important than formal instruction.

The evidence supporting explicit instruction in domain-specific problem-solving strategies is fairly strong. In a recent review of the literature on troubleshooting, Morris and Rouse (1985) conclude that "either troubleshooters should be explicitly instructed in how to approach problems or they should be forced to use their knowledge of the system explicitly in deciding what to do" (p. 527). In ACT* terms, the former provides novice troubleshooters with declarative representations of the appropriate procedures, while the latter forces them to apply general problem-solving methods to their declarative knowledge. In either case, the result is that troubleshooting procedures with contiguous goal structures are likely to be in working memory at the same time and, therefore, available to the knowledge compilation process.

This description of procedural learning has a direct consequence for transfer. Namely, there is no reason to predict transfer between different uses of the same knowledge. Practicing troubleshooting, for example, may strengthen the declarative representation of troubleshooting knowledge while that knowledge is being interpreted by general problem-solving productions; however, this stage passes quickly. Once the knowledge compilation mechanisms start forming new domain-specific productions, then further practice results in increasingly specialized productions. To the extent that the transfer task requires the same procedures, positive transfer will occur. To the extent that it requires different procedures (even those based upon the same declarative knowledge), transfer will be zero. Several studies support this prediction.

Neves and Anderson (1981) found that 10 days of practice giving reasons to justify steps of a worked-out geometry proof had little effect on students' ability to generate a proof. Although the declarative knowledge for the two tasks is the same, there is no overlap in the production rules for generation versus justification of steps.

A similar result was found by McKendree and Anderson (1987) in a study that was concerned primarily with studying knowledge compilation processes. They gave 20 subjects 4 consecutive days of practice in evaluating combinations of four basic LISP functions. Two functions combined items into a list (INSERT and LIST), the other two extracted items from a list (CAR and CDR, but assigned the more mnemonic names of FIRST and REST). Subjects had 150 trials each day for 4 days, and performance improved following a power law function (Newell & Rosenbloom, 1981) in a manner predicted by ACT*.

While these results are interesting, we are more concerned with the transfer data that McKendree and Anderson collected more or less as an aside to the main experiment. After the first and last session, subjects were given a transfer task that required them to generate functions similar to those they had just practiced evaluating. All of the transfer problems involved basic functions or pairs of functions that the subjects had seen immediately before in the evaluation task. Yet, while error rates on the evaluation task decreased dramatically from Day 1 to Day 4 (35% to 15%) the transfer task showed little improvement (29.3% versus 26.6%). Despite becoming significantly better at evaluating functions, subjects are not any better at generating functions than they were on Day 1.

C. TRANSFER OF PRODUCTIONS AMONG TEXT EDITORS: SINGLEY AND ANDERSON

Powerful techniques are required to build theories that predict when and how much transfer will occur. Indeed, theoretical progress on the transfer of cognitive skills has been limited by the absence of techniques precise enough to build a sufficiently detailed empirical data base. The studies reported by Singley and Anderson (1985, in press) are an important step in remedying this deficit. They apply the analytic power of ACT* (Anderson, 1983) and GOMS (Card *et al.*, 1980, 1983) to keystroke data to produce powerful analysis techniques which are applied to study the complex cognitive skill of text editing.

(While the military and industrial literatures contain many studies of the transfer of complex skills, as far as we know, all of these have focused on relatively large-scale measures of transfer. The empirical data base that Singley and Anderson [in press] desire would be based upon the detailed analysis of the cognitive skills required to perform the task [performance model]. The analysis of transfer would examine how the various goals and subgoals, operators, methods, and selection rules transfer from one task to another.)

The domain of text editing was picked because of the existence of independently performed task analyses of the productions involved. The production system-like models that existed (Card *et al.*, 1983; Kieras & Polson, 1985) served to constrain the ACT* production system models (Anderson, 1987). These exploratory studies were to observe and characterize the magnitude and direction of transfer between different text editors, the components of learning and transfer, the grain size that would yield the most interesting data, and any strategic components that were important, such as goal structure.

1. Methods and Macroanalyses

In the experiment reported in both the Singley and Anderson papers (1985, in press), transfer among two-line text editors (UNIX ED, VMS EDT) and a screen editor (UNIX EMACS) was studied. For each editor a subset of commands was chosen. Expert typists, with no prior text-editing experience, edited 3 h a day for 6 days. All groups spent the last 2 days using EMACS. The ED and EDT group spent the first 4 days on ED or EDT respectively. The ED-EDT and EDT-ED groups spent 2 days on one line editor and the next 2 days on the other. The EMACS group spent all 6 days on EMACS. The control group spent 4 days typing at the terminal. Keystroke data were recorded.

Transfer data from the macroanalyses showed near total transfer between the two line editors (Days 3 and 4), moderate transfer from line editors to screen editor (Days 5 and 6), and slight transfer from typing-only to screen editor (Days 5 and 6). All measures of macrotransfer (including reduction in total time, reduction in total keystrokes, reduction in residual errors, and increase in keying rate) concur with these overall statements.

2. GOMS-based Microanalyses

The most interesting data are provided by microanalyses that vary the grain size of transfer. These GOMS-based (Card *et al., 1980, 1983*) analyses consider text editing as a series of largely independent *unit tasks*. (A unit task is a text-editing operation. *Delete character, insert word, replace line* are three examples of unit tasks.) Three subgoals are required to accomplish each unit task: encode the edit from the manuscript (*acquire-unit-task*), move to the line requiring modification (*locate-line*), and modify the test (*modify-text*). This analysis provides the hierarchical goal structure shown in Figure 1.

Singley and Anderson (in press) developed a parsing algorithm to identify each burst and pause in the keystroke data and attribute it to the planning or execution of each unit task as well as its major subgoals: acquire-unit-task, locate-line, and modify-text. First, for each page, the algorithm segments the data into six unit-task episodes, one for each edit on the page. Second, it subdivides each segment into a *locate-line* (LL) or *modify-text* (MT) component. The *LL component* includes time and keystrokes spent moving to the site of the modification and time spent acquiring the unit task from the manuscript. The *MT component* includes the time and keystrokes needed to modify the text. Third, each component, LL or MT, is split into *planning* and *execution* subcomponents which are defined as follows: Execution equals the time from first to last keystroke minus any inter-keystroke pauses of greater than 2 s. Planning equals the sum of all pauses greater than 2 s.

To summarize the microanalyses, the parsing algorithm yielded learning and transfer curves for each of the 12 text-editing operations (unit tasks) that subjects performed. Each curve was further divided into LL and MT components and divided again into planning and execution.

The learning curves for each kind of modification (unit task) had a

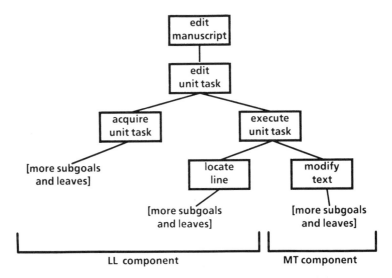

Figure 1. A hierarchical goal structure for text editing. (Adapted with permission from Singley and Anderson, in preparation.)

characteristic shape regardless of editor. For simplicity, Singley and Anderson (in press) discuss the curve yielded by the delete-character unit task. The total time for this edit dropped from 74 s/edit on Day 1 to 25 s/edit on Day 4. However, a finer grain analysis showed that execution time for this edit was constant with all the improvements in seconds per edit due to reductions in planning time.

Next, Singley and Anderson report the results of examining six dependent variables ([planning time, execution time, and number of keystrokes] × [LL and MT]) for each editor. The interesting finding is that EMACS is not uniformly superior to the line editors on all components. Its advantage is primarily due to more efficient MT methods that require fewer keystrokes and less planning time. For the LL component, ED is superior to EMACS (difference in execution time is significant; difference in planning time is not).

Based upon their task analysis (see Figure 1), Singley and Anderson (in press) predict differences in the pattern of transfer among the three editors for the LL versus MT component. For LL all three editors use different methods to locate lines; but, the LL component spans not only locate-line procedures but also acquire-unit-task procedures and the superordinate goal nodes (edit-unit-task and edit-manuscript). Therefore, "traversing the top nodes in the goal tree and encoding the edits are the same regardless of editor" (p. 34); they predict moderate and equal degrees of transfer among the three editors for the LL component.

For MT, the predicted pattern is different. For the line editors the surface features of the MT commands differ, but the underlying conceptual structures are nearly identical. In contrast, for the line editors (ED and EDT) versus the screen editor (EMACS), the MT procedures are completely different. For the MT component they predict nearly total transfer between the line editors but essentially none from the line editors to EMACS.

For line editors, as predicted, they find more transfer for the MT component (102%) than for LL (89%). (Note that by the formula used, greater than 100% transfer occurs when the transfer groups [ED-EDT and EDT-ED) do better on Days 3 and 4 than the groups that do not switch [ED and EDT only].) However, they predicted moderate transfer for the LL component while transfer, in fact, was high. The keystroke data suggests that the LL component is inflated due to the increased use among transfer subjects of a common secondary method for addressing line location, namely, the use of carriage returns rather than line addressing (for example, *10p*) in ED and string searching (for example, *t 'unique*) in EDT.

Transfer from the line editors to EMACS yielded surprising findings. Singley and Anderson found 61% transfer of the LL component from the line editors (LineEd) to EMACS and 35% from the typing control (TypeCon) group (average of 48%). For the MT component, transfer was 62% (LineEd) and 29% (TypeCon) (average of 46%). Hence, contrary to prediction, the LL component is not as large for transfer from line editors to EMACS as from one line editor to another. Also, transfer of the MT component is as large as for the LL component.

While Singley and Anderson (in press) report many of these detailed and interesting analyses, we will focus on one last result: the attempt to determine why there was so much MT component transfer to EMACS from both the line editor (LineEd 62%) and typing control (TypeCon 29%) groups. Candidate hypotheses include: portions of the upper-level goal tree (LineEd only) and subskills for encoding the edit from the manuscript (LineEd and TypeCon).

Singley and Anderson (in press) first look at all 12 editing operations and find no evidence for any general trend. They then decide to focus on those subgoals that show the most and the least transfer to EMACS. Delete-Character shows the most transfer for both groups (LineEd 90%, TypeCon 89%), Delete-String the least (LineEd 28%, TypeCon −98%). Delete-Word shows strong transfer for both groups as well (83% and 74%). DeleteLine shows strong transfer only for LineEd groups (77% and 29%).

Both the LineEd and TypeCon groups learned a deletion operation that can transfer to EMACS: the delete key. This explains why delete char and word is so high whereas delete string is low (there are much easier ways for EMACS to delete a string than using the delete key). This hypothesis predicts that the transfer subjects should use the delete key more often than the EMACS only subjects. Indeed, the transfer groups used the delete key 68% of the time versus 50% for EMACS only. This difference was not significant but is in the right direction.

The delete-line procedure has same goal structure in EMACS as in the line editors, but not for TypeCon. For both EMACS and LineEd the user moves to the line requiring deletion and types the delete line operator (typing .d in ED and d in EDT, and <control>k in EMACS).

3. Summary of Singley and Anderson

The Singley and Anderson experiment represents a milestone in the examination of the components of transfer. Using a problem space–based analysis, GOMS, they took apart a complex cognitive skill, text editing, and were able to examine the various components to determine the locus of transfer effects.

As they point out, the number of methods for performing any one edit makes quantitative predictions very difficult. For example, the LineEd and TypeCon groups were able to "fixate" on using the delete key rather than learning more efficient EMACS-specific methods for deleting characters and words. Analyses at a bigger grain size completely missed this phenomenon.

A next step in understanding the transfer between text editors would be to derive an ACT*-based production system simulation. Such an analysis would demonstrate the power of the ACT* theory to account for detailed transfer data. This extremely time-consuming endeavor would be justified by the increased understanding in the transfer of complex cognitive skills.

III. LEARNING-AS-TRANSFER

> It is not possible at present to formulate a theory of transfer which will incorporate all of the [known facts of transfer] in a thoroughly systematic manner. . . . When such a system is constructed, it will take into account . . . the necessary transfer from trial to trial during practice . . . and the other ways in which transfer pervades a majority of the phenomena of learning. (McGeoch, 1942, p. 438)

The issue of learning-as-transfer is important in structuring any program of instruction that teaches a complex skill. For example, programming or operating a device involve skills that are so complex that we do not expect students to master them at one sitting. In fact, for many such skills we do not expect to teach students all they need to know. Rather, the best we can do is to teach them a critical subset of skills that will enable them to tackle and solve new problems as they arise. Unfortunately, we still do not have a learning theory that will enable us to design an optimal program of instruction. We are, however, beginning to get answers to the question of what is learned in one exercise (or session) that can be transferred to the next.

In this section we discuss four different approaches to learning within a problem space context. For each we will sketch its theoretical assumptions and present some empirical evidence that addresses the relation between learning and transfer.

A. BUILDING A PROBLEM SPACE: MENTAL MODELS

Section I.C. emphasized a novice's search in a problem space in which only the initial state, goal state, and set of operators was known. In a reasonably complex problem space, such as for troubleshooting a radar system, many problems each with a different initial state and a different goal state will be encountered. With much experience the problem solver (no longer a novice) acquires knowledge about many states in the problem space and how to reach a given state x from state y by the application of various sequences of operators. (In GOMS/ACT* terminology, states along the path between x and y are treated as *subgoals* to be achieved by applying various combinations of operators. Alternative paths to state x are composed of different combinations of states and operators. These paths become compiled into *methods,* and so on). Depending upon the problem space chosen to represent the task, as well as other factors, at some point the problem solver becomes able to describe probable paths between two states for which a known path does not exist. At this point, the problem solver has a *mental model* of the problem space.

In our view, the difference between mental models and analogical models (discussed in section II.A.1) is one of emphasis, not essence. Research on both is concerned with defining the types of conceptual knowledge used to accomplish a task. Research on analogy tends to emphasize how conceptual models of *Task a* are used in learning or performing *Task b*. Research on mental models tends to emphasize either the existence and importance of such conceptual knowledge in perfoming *Task a* (Gentner & Stevens, 1983) or how such knowledge is acquired when it does not already exist (Kieras & Bovair, 1984; White & Fredericksen, 1986). Both can be described in terms of the problem space hypothesis.

Research on the effectiveness of mental models for aiding learning and transfer is just beginning. Kieras and Bovair (1984) taught their subjects a Star Trek–like model of a "phaser-bank" device. The explanation was in terms of physical principles which do not exist, that carried out tasks which are nonexistent. However, subjects who were taught this mental model were able to learn procedures faster, retain them better, and execute them faster than subjects not taught the mental model. In a very different task, Eberts and Schneider (1985) compared performance of subjects on a second-order tracking task. Two groups were given *augmentation cues* while learning the task; a third group received no cues. For the augmentation groups, one group was given a standard augmentation cue which Eberts and Schneider believed was not conducive to developing a mental model, while the other group was given a cue that was hypothesized to lead to the development of accurate mental models. In the absence of augmentation cues, the three groups did not differ in either performance or speed of learning (over 5 days). However, in a series of transfer tasks, the mental model group was consistently superior. (This manipulation is reminiscent of one used by Judd, 1908, with similar results. In that experiment two groups of boys practiced hitting targets underwater, first under 12 in. and then under 4 in. Prior to the first task, one group was taught the principle of refraction; the other was not. Performance on the first task did not differ; however, performance on the second task consistently favored the refraction group.)

Teaching a problem solver a mental model is a type of learning-as-transfer. Mental models contain declarative knowledge about the states and combinations of methods required to solve problems in the task problem space. After learning a mental model, the problem solver should be able to apply his, hers, or its general problem-solving strategies to the declarative representation of the mental model to determine what path through the problem space leads to the goal state. The problem-solving behavior of a novice who has been taught a mental model should have much in common with an expert's behavior. (For example, while performance should be slower and subject to errors due to working memory failures, more expertlike forward, as opposed to backward, search may be shown.)

B. PRODUCTION SYSTEMS FOR COGNITIVE ENGINEERING: KIERAS AND POLSON

In a series of studies, Kieras and Polson modeled the procedures involved in operating different devices as sets of production rules (Kieras & Bovair, 1986; Kieras & Polson, 1985; Polson & Kieras, 1984, 1985). Each production rule was translated into an English sentence, and the entire procedure was taught to novices as declarative knowledge. Despite the declarative representation, they found that the number of new productions predicts how fast a new procedure will be learned, while the number of productions that two procedures have in common predicts the amount of positive transfer from one to the other.

The Kieras and Polson production system is the "most elementary form of production system in that there are no conflict resolution rules, and very simple kinds of pattern matching are used in evaluating conditions" (Polson & Kieras, 1985, p.207). Likewise, they make no attempt to represent fundamental cognitive processes such as memory retrieval or reading comprehension. This limitation greatly simplifies the production system without adversely affecting its utility for cognitive engineering of man-machine interfaces.

Their system assumes that each production takes the same amount of time to learn or execute. It predicts that the time to learn a new procedure depends upon the number of new productions in its description. From this prediction, a simple common elements theory of transfer is derived: The more procedures that two tasks have in common, the greater the transfer. (Note that this theory cannot predict negative transfer.)

1. The Experiments

Kieras and Polson have tested their production system in a series of three experiments (Kieras & Bovair, 1986; Polson & Kieras, 1984, 1985). The results are consistent across tasks (text editing, Polson & Kieras, 1985; operating a computer, Polson & Kieras, 1984; and operating a simple device, Kieras & Bovair, 1986) and across minor variations in procedures. For the sake of simplicity, we focus here on Kieras and Bovair (1986).

Kieras and Bovair (1986) required their subjects to learn 10 procedures for operating a device. For each procedure a GOMS-based analysis was performed and translated into a set of from 6 to 8 production rules. Instructions were prepared for each procedure by translating each production rule into a sentence. The 10 procedures were taught in one of three fixed training orders with substantial variation in the number of new rules in each procedure and in each serial position. (For example, assume that Procedure A involves learning 8 rules, of which 3 are in common with Procedure B and none are in common with procedures C or D. In order B A C, A has 5 new rules, 3 old rules (for 8 total). In order C D A B, A has 8 new rules.) For each procedure, total training time equals study time plus test time until the procedure was performed correctly three times in a row.

For each procedure, total training time varied as a function of what procedures (with what production rules) were learned before it. "The number of new rules alone accounts for 69% of the variance and is a better predictor of training time on a single procedure than the subjects' individual means" (p. 518). In addition, the reading times for instructional steps varied greatly depending upon whether the step was new or identical. This difference appeared on the first reading, implying that subjects immediately recognized new rules versus known rules and changed their study times accordingly.

In similar experiments, Polson and Kieras (1984, 1985) found that the number of new productions accounted for 61% and 83%, respectively, of the variance of learning time with approximately 30 s required to learn a new production (Polson & Kieras, 1985).

2. Summary: Kieras and Polson

These results show that production rules can provide a precise characterization of what is to be learned (Kieras & Polson, 1985). Such a production rule analysis could be used to derive an instructional sequence, for example, that is uniformly challenging but never overwhelming to the student. However, the connection between Kieras and Polson's use of production rules and that of other researchers is not as direct as it may at first seem. For most researchers, production rules, typically are used to describe well-learned skills. For Kieras and Bovair, 1986, the earliest stage of skill acquisition involves the translation of an "instruction sentence into a declarative representation of a production rule." Next, this declarative representation is interpreted by a general procedure for following instructions and, eventually, the procedural form of these rules is created by processes such as those postulated by Anderson (1983; see section II.B.1. above).

Kieras and Polson's research shows the utility that a relatively simple (from the psychological viewpoint) but powerful (because of the production system framework) model can have for cognitive engineering. The model is simple because it provides an essentially static representation of novice knowledge structures and does not represent fundamental cognitive processes. It assumes the operation of general procedures for operating upon declarative knowledge but postulates no mechanisms for acquiring greater levels of expertise. However, the seriousness of this limitation depends upon exactly how the model is used. Kieras and Polson are primarily interested in how such a simple model of novice memory structures interacts with a formalism they have developed (Kieras & Polson, 1985) to describe devices. Given this finely focused interest, their model seems adequate. In fact, we predict that the Kieras and Polson approach is the forerunner to a series of production rule models for cognitive engineering, each of limited scope, but each yielding useful prescriptions for real-world problems.

C. CHUNK THEORY MEETS THE PROBLEM SPACE: NEWELL AND ASSOCIATES

Newell and Rosenbloom (1981) set upon the task of trying to explain the "ubiquitous law of practice" and, in the process, postulate a powerful learning mechanism that has direct implications for within- and between-task transfer.

Skilled performance shows continual improvement with practice. This observation holds true for cigar making (3 million trials), choice–reaction-time tasks (40,000 trials), recall from long-term memory (approximately 5,000 trials), keystroke editing (approximately 1,000 trials), geometry proof justification (over 100 trials), the game of solitaire (500 trials), and many others. Newell and Rosenbloom considered many functions that might fit this phenomenon and concluded that the more general form of the power law is the best. That is, plotting trials against time on log–log paper yields a straight line that follows the general form of the power law:

$$T = A + B(N + E)^{-a}$$

where T = time

B = performance time of first trial

a = slope

A = the asymptote of learning as trial number N increases indefinitely

E = the number of trials of learning that occurred prior to the first trial measured (that is, prior experience).

Satisfied with the power law description, they went on to consider various ways in which such a function could arise and finally proposed the chunking hypothesis: "A human acquires and organizes knowledge of the environment by forming and storing expressions, called chunks, which are structured collections of the chunks existing at the time of learning" (p. 41). To this they add three assumptions:

1. Performance assumption: The performance program of the system is coded in terms of high-level chunks, with the time to process a chunk being less than the time to process its constituent chunks.
2. Task structure assumption: The probability of occurrence of an environmental pattern decreases as pattern size increases.
3. Learning assumption: Chunks are learned at a constant time rate on average from the relevant patterns of stimuli and responses that occur in the specifc environments experienced. (p. 42)

With chunking as the only learning mechanism, Newell and associates develop two production system architectures, XAPS and Soar, which have interesting implications for the relation between learning and transfer. Of the two, we focus our discussion on Soar, which Newell and associates are developing as a general architecture of cognition.

1. Soar

Soar (Laird, Rosenbloom, & Newell, 1984) is a production system which treats chunking as a general learning mechanism and combines it with a general problem space problem solver. Chunking is a data-driven recorder of goal-based experience. The chunks formed represent the processing involved in achieving a subgoal in a problem-solving task. The next time the same subgoal is encountered (or generated by the problem-solving mechanism), the chunk is used in place of the rather complex problem-solving processes that were originally required.

Soar has "a reflective problem-solving architecture that has a uniform representation and can create goals to reason about any aspect of its problem-solving behavior" (p. 188). Implementing the relatively simple, but powerful chunking hypothesis within an architecture based upon the even more powerful problem space hypothesis expands the role of chunking.

1. Chunking can be applied to a general problem-solver to speed up its performance.
2. Chunking can improve *all* aspects of a problem-solver's behavior.

3. *Significant transfer of chunked knowledge is possible via the implicit generalization of chunks* [italics added].
4. Chunking can perform strategy acquisition, leading to qualitatively new behavior. (p. 188)

In Soar, both problem solving and routine cognitive processes are formulated as heuristic search in problem spaces. Soar can automatically generate subgoals for problems in any aspect of its problem-solving process. This ability is referred to as universal subgoaling and is an innovation of the Soar production system. Chunking acts on this subgoaling process by replacing the problem-solving activity with a production that can be used the next time the subgoal is encountered.

As chunking of search control knowledge continues, performance is improved by a continual reduction in the amount of search. Eventually, enough search control knowledge may be chunked so that no search is required, and what started out as a problem-solving activity ends up as an efficient algorithm for a task.

2. Transfer Implications of Soar

Based on the architecture of Soar and how chunking is implemented within it, several transfer issues emerge. (This is an excellent example of the constraints upon a transfer theory which emerge from a well-specified learning theory.)

> If a given task shares subgoals with another task, a chunk learned for one task can apply to the other, yielding *across-task* transfer of learning. *Within-trial* transfer of learning can occur when a subgoal arises more than once during a single attempt on a task. Generality is possible because a chunk only contains conditions for the aspects that were accessed in the subgoal. This is an *implicit generalization,* by which many aspects of the context—the irrelevant ones—are automatically ignored by the chunk. (Laird *et al.,* 1984)

Laird *et al.* (1984) tested the implications of Soar with chunking in a series of simulations. They first evaluated the effect of the chunking construct in learning to solve the eight-puzzle problem. (The eight-puzzle is the familiar child's toy in which eight plastic squares with numbers on them are in a 3×3 space frame. The goal is to change the initial configuration of plastic squares into a goal configuration by moving one square at a time into the one empty square in the frame.) Because this is a computer simulation, Laird *et al.* were able to compare how long Soar took to solve the eight-puzzle problem with chunking (Soar-with) and without (Soar-without.) Soar-without required 10 *evaluate-operator* subgoal searches. Soar-with required only 5. This dramatic reduction in search shows *within-trial transfer.*

They then gave Soar an across-trial transfer task. In this task Soar first solved a new eight-puzzle problem in which the initial and final states were different from the original and no intermediate states were the same. Chunking was turned on (soar-with) for this puzzle. After Soar had solved this, chunking was turned off, and Soar was then given the original puzzle (soar-without). (Note that since Soar is a computer simulation, it was relatively easy for Laird *et al.* to induce complete amnesia for the original task.) Performance on the original problem in this across-trial task was much better than Soar's performance in the above-reported within-trial task. Transfer occurred because in solving the original puzzle in the across-trial task, subgoals were generated that were identical in all of the relevant ways to subgoals in the new puzzle. As predicted, Soar showed *implicit generalization* when the only thing in common between the two puzzles were some of the subgoals created by Soar's problem-solving processes.

In further simulations with tick tack toe, Soar exhibited overgeneralization resulting in negative transfer. The next step in the Soar project is "to investigate how a problem solver can recover from over-general knowledge, and then carry out problem-solving activities so that new chunks can be learned that will override the over-general chunks" (p. 191).

Soar is an interesting example of the use of computer simulations in theory development. Only in a computer simulation could within- versus between-trial transfer be neatly turned on or off to examine the effect of one in isolation from the other. For theory development, this control over the theoretical mechanisms allows the theorists to study how much each postulated mechanism contributes and how it interacts with other mechanisms. Likewise, the overgeneralization shown by Soar in solving ticktacktoe problems is an example of a simulation leading to the identification of a too powerful mechanism and the recognition that the theory has to be extended to explicitly model discrimination-type processes.

D. THE IMPORTANCE OF A GOOD EXAMPLE: ACT*

The ACT* theory predicts that what students learn from solving a problem, and how they try to solve subsequent problems, are very much influenced by the examples provided. For ACT*, powerful learning mechanisms "summarize solutions to these initial problems into new problem-solving operators which can apply to future problems" (Pirolli & Anderson, 1985, p. 242). As these new problem-solving operators are built, students rely less upon analogy and more upon these domain-specific operators. It is easy to see how the generality of the new problem-solving operators should be greatly influenced by the example used. This is the topic studied by Pirolli and Anderson (1985).

Using an interactive combination of protocol analysis and computer simulations, Pirolli and Anderson took protocols from students trying to solve *recursion* problems in LISP and then created a simulation of each student. The simulation was initialized with a set of productions assumed to represent the student's prior knowledge of LISP. To this initial set was added the student's solution to the first problem. The simulation was run, allowing ACT*'s knowledge compilation process to add new production rules to the model. Note that after production rules simulating the student's solution of the first problem were added to the initial set of production rules, the only way additional productions were added was by ACT*'s knowledge compilation processes. Thus the results of the compilation process represent predictions of the way the next problem will be solved. Both ACT* and the student are then given the second problem and so on. ACT*'s model of knowledge compilation is validated to the extent that each student actually solves his or her second problem the way that ACT* does. The results of this study support ACT*'s predictions. In general, ACT* predicted the approach that each student used to attack each problem. Where the student had a difficulty solving a new recursion problem, so did ACT*.

Of more direct relevance to transfer is the effect that different types of examples had on the students' and ACT*'s success at solving later problems. First, Pirolli and Anderson note that the analogical mapping that students were performing was "never a mindless symbol-for-symbol mapping. Rather, it involved the subjects' knowledge of LISP and a representation of the meaning of what was mapped" (1985, p. 258). Second, the particular example provided did affect the way the students tried to solve later problems, as well as their success.

A contrast between two students, SS and AD, is particularly revealing. SS was provided with the recursion example used in a well-known LISP textbook. AD was provided with a description, or template, of recursive functions that was derived from the expert model. The textbook example was of a particular type of recursion. SS was able to solve resursive problems of this type but required help to solve different problems (such help was not available in the textbook). In contrast, AD's example provided her with a general strategy for coding a large class of recursive functions.

Pirolli and Anderson report an experiment which supports their empirical analysis. Two groups of subjects were provided with instruction on recursion and then required to write four training problems. The *process* group was given the standard textbook description (which emphasized how the process of recursion worked), while the *structure* group was provided with instruction that emphasized the structure of recursion problems. The structure group took 57.4 min to write correctly four training problems, while the process group took 85.3 min (a savings of 33%), but the groups did not differ in the time or correctness of writing 16 transfer problems. Pirolli and Anderson suggest that to deal with the four training problems, both groups had to acquire the same set of productions; however, the structure group "got to this state in a more efficient manner because they had learned a general strategy for structuring their code very early on in the training phase" (p. 271).

The Pirolli and Anderson study supports ACT*'s knowledge compilation process. By knowledge compilation, general or weak problem-solving methods acting upon declarative knowledge are transformed into more powerful domain-specific methods. Furthermore, by knowing something about the student's instructional history, ACT* is able to predict what domain-specific methods will be formed and which problems they will solve.

IV. SUMMARY

A fast summary of this chapter is that the common elements theory of transfer is alive and well but looks very different than it used to. What has been gained and what has been lost in the translation from verbal learning to problem space theories of transfer? At this point we believe that much has been gained and that the only losses are short term.

Among the most important gains is a concern with the procedural knowledge involved in performing complex cognitive tasks. While the approach is still too new to judge, there is significant progress in understanding how skills as complex as text editing, LISP programming, operating a device, and solving the eight-puzzle are transferred from one set of tasks to another. This gain should not be underestimated. The verbal learning approach never attempted an analysis of skills at such a level of complexity and, indeed, it is hard even to imagine how the verbal learning analyses could be applied.

Another gain is the recognition that common elements include such purely cognitive constructs as goals and subgoals, operators, methods, and selection rules. An example of the importance to transfer of knowing the goal structure of a domain can be attested to by anyone who has learned two text-editing programs. As Singley and Anderson (1985, in press) point out, the goal structure of different text-editing programs is largely identical, as are the individual goals and subgoals (for example, moving text, inserting text, altering text, and formating paragraphs). These abstract goals and goal structures are readily transferred to any new text editor. Singley and Anderson (1985, in press) and Moran (Douglas & Moran, 1983; Halasz & Moran, 1982; Moran, 1983) have used such abstract cognitive constructs to predict transfer among a number of text-editing systems.

By including cognitive constructs as among the common elements that can be transferred, the cognitive approach has eliminated the old verbal learning distinction between specific and general transfer. The entire task, including aspects of the stimulus and response as well as more general or cognitive aspects, can be described or analyzed under a unified system.

The adoption of the production rule as the unit of transfer provides a quasi-standard way of describing what the common elements are. A greater contribution is their use in constructing computer models of cognitive processes, that then can be evaluated by the standard of how well they mimic the human data. Although some people harbor an almost Luddite suspicion of such efforts, it is difficult to see how else all the elements of a complex theory can be shown to work in the manner proposed. Furthermore, such models provide a way for theorists to study the emergent behavior of their systems. For example, a test of the Soar theory/production system (Laird *et al.*, 1984) showed that while it did very well with one type of task, with a different task it produced rampant overgeneralizations.

An important gain is the notion that problem spaces can be transferred, either borrowed whole or built out of pieces of other problem spaces. In solving a completely new problem, borrowing a familiar problem space immediately gives one access to all of the states and operators of that familiar space. This is sometimes an absolute advantage as in those cases where the new problem is an isomorph of one already known (Simon & Hayes, 1976). However, it can be a disadvantage and potential source of negative transfer when some states and operators from the borrowed problem space are completely irrelevant to the task at hand.

Another gain is in the arena of within-task transfer. The greater precision of the problem space–based learning theories such as ACT*, and Soar make it clear that many within-task transfer phenomena are actually examples of learning-as-transfer and thereby completely explained by learning theory. Thus, what was thought to be a manifestation of a higher order phenomenon, within-task transfer, is shown to be an example of a lower order phenomenon, learning.

Given all of these gains, what has been lost? We see only short-term losses. For the short-term, the field has abandoned paradigms, such as paired-associate learning, for which a wealth of empirical data exists. Eventually such paradigms will have to be subjected to a rigorous cognitive task analysis so that performance models can be created (and perhaps modeled in a production system). Such models will make two important contributions. First, they would provide an impressive demonstration of the power and generality of the cognitive science approach. Second, they would allow the existing empirical data on transfer to be interpreted in such a way as to have direct relevance to the learning and transfer of more complex cognitive skills.

A. THE ROLE OF SIMPLIFIED THEORIES FOR COGNITIVE ENGINEERING

In their many studies, Kieras, Polson, and Moran assume a static representation of cognitive skills. This contradicts what we know about how skills change with learning (see especially Pirolli & Anderson, 1985; Laird *et al.*, 1984). It is interesting that the two research labs which make this static representation assumption are also the two with the greatest interest in real-world applications. This is not a coincidence. Theories of learning and transfer are in an interesting intermediate state. While they can explain more data than ever before, they are not powerful enough to account for all of the interactions of the cognitive apparatus. By this view, the assumption of a static representation is a simplifying assumption that makes it possible to build useful, if limited, systems for cognitive engineering. These limited systems are more than adequate as long as their boundary conditions are well noted. Learning theories will help the cognitive engineers define what these boundary conditions are. However, in the long run, truely powerful theories and applications depend upon knowing what a person's current knowledge representation is (this issue is clearest in the field of intelligent tutoring systems; see Gray, Mutter, Swartz, & Psotka, 1986; Sleeman & Brown, 1982). "Determining the representation a subject is using is one of the hardest problems we face and it is unclear whether the study of representation will lead the study of transfer or vice versa" (Singley & Anderson, in press).

B. THEORIES *ET AL.*

Writing this chapter has convinced us totally of the symbiotic relationship between theories of learning and transfer. The theoretical and practical goal of understanding the conditions of transfer of cognitive skills cannot go on in a vacuum. Before we can possibly understand what is transferred, we must understand skilled performance and how it is acquired. This remains true whether we eventually define transfer in terms of a simple common elements model or whether we decide that the entire problem space apparatus is involved in significant (and no doubt convoluted) ways.

REFERENCES

Allport, G. W. (1937). *Personality: A psychological interpretation.* New York: Holt.
Anderson, J. R. (1982). Acquisition of cognitive skill. *Psychological Review, 4,* 369–406.
Anderson, J. R. (1983). *The architecture of cognition.* Cambridge, MA: Harvard University Press.
Anderson, J. R. (1987). Skill acquisition: Compilation of weak-method problem-solutions. *Psychological Review 94,* 192–210.
Anderson, J. R. (1986). Knowledge compilation: The general learning mechanism. In Michalski, R. S., Carbonell, J. G., & Michell, T. M. (Eds.), *Machine learning II.* Los Altos, CA: Morgan Kaufman Publishers, Inc.
Baars, B. J. (1986). *The cognitive revolution in psychology.* New York: Guilford Press.
Bransford, J. D., Arbitman-Smith, R., Stein, B. S., & Vye, N. J. (1985). Improving thinking and learning skills: An analysis of three approaches. In J. W. Segal, S. F. Chipman, & R. Glaser (Eds.), *Thinking and learning skills: Vol. 1. Relating instruction to research.* Hillsdale, NJ: Erlbaum.

Brownston, L., Farrell, R., Kant, E., & Martin, N. (1985). *Programming expert systems in OPS5: An introduction to rule-based programming.* Reading, MA: Addison-Wesley.

Card, S. K., Moran, T. P., & Newell, A. (1980). Computer text-editing: An information-processing analysis of a routine cognitive skill. *Cognitive Psychology, 12,* 32–74.

Card, S. K., Moran, T. P., & Newell, A. (1983). *The psychology of human-computer interaction.* Hillsdale, NJ: Erlbaum.

Douglas, S. A., & Moran, T. P. (1983). Learning operator semantics by analogy. In *Proceedings of the National Conference on Artificial Intelligence* (pp. 100–103). Washington, DC.

Eberts, R., & Schneider, W. (1985). Internalizing the system dynamics for a second-order system. *Human Factors, 27,* 371–393.

Gardner, H. (1985). *The mind's new science: A history of the cognitive revolution.* New York: Basic Books.

Garrett, H. E. (1941). *Great experiments in psychology* (2nd ed.). New York: Appleton.

Gentner, D., & Stevens, A. L. (Eds.). (1983). *Mental models.* Hillsdale, NJ: Erlbaum.

Gray, W. D., Mutter, S. A., Swartz, M. L., & Psotka, J. (1986). Novice to expert: Implications for AI systems. In *Proceedings of the Army Science Conference.* West Point, NY.

Halasz, F., & Moran, T. P. (1982). Analogy considered harmful. In *Proceedings CHI'83 Human Factors in Computer Systems* (pp. 212–216). ACM, New York.

Judd, C. H. (1908). The relation of special training to general intelligence. *Educational Review, 36,* 28–42.

Kay, D. S., & Black, J. B. (1985). The evolution of knowledge representations with increasing expertise in using systems. In *Proceedings of the Seventh Annual Conference of the Cognitive Science Society* (pp. 140–149). Irvine, CA.

Kieras, D. E. & Bovair, S. (1984). The role of a mental model in learning to operate a device. *Cognitive Science, 8,* 255–273.

Kieras, D. E., & Bovair, S. (1986). The acquisition of procedures from text: A production-system anaylsis of transfer of training *J. of Memory and Language, 25,* 507–524.

Kieras, D., & Polson, P. G. (1985). An approach to the formal analysis of user complexity. *International Journal of Man-Machine Studies, 22,* 365–394.

Laird, J. E., Rosenbloom, P. S., & Newell, A. (1984). Towards chunking as a general learning mechanism. In *Proceedings of the National Conference on Artificial Intelligence* (pp. 188–192). Los Altos, CA: W. Kaufman, Inc.

Larkin, J. H., McDermott, J., Simon, D. P., & Simon, H. A. (1980). Expert and novice performance in solving physics problems. *Science, 208,* 1335–1342.

McGeoch, J. A. (1942). *The psycology of human learning.* New York: Longmans, Green.

McKendree, J., & Anderson, J. R. (1987). Effect of practice on knowledge and use of basic LISP. In J. M. Carroll (Ed.), *Interfacing thought: Cognitive aspects of human-computer interaction.* Cambridge, MA: Bradford Books/MIT Press.

Moran, T. P. (1983). Getting into a system: External–internal task mapping analysis. In *Proceedings CHI'83 Human Factors in Computing Systems* (pp. 45–49). New York: ACM.

Morris, N. M., & Rouse, W. B. (1985). Review and evaluation of empirical research in trouble-shooting. *Human Factors, 27,* 503–530.

Neches, R., Langley, P., & Klahr, D. (1987). Learning, development, and production systems. In D. Klahr, P. Langley, & R. Neches (Eds.), *Production system models of learning and development.* Cambridge, MA: MIT Press.

Neves, D. M., & Anderson, J. R. (1981). Knowledge compilation: Mechanisms for the automatization of cognitive skills. In J. R. Anderson (Ed.), *Cognitive skills and their acquisition.* Hillsdale, NJ: Erlbaum.

Newell, A. (1980). Reasoning, problem-solving, and decision processes: The problem space as a fundamental category. In R. Nickerson, (Ed.), *Attention and performance VIII.* Hillsdale, NJ: Erlbaum.

Newell, A., & Rosenbloom, P. (1981). Mechanisms of skill acquisition and the law of practice. In J. R. Anderson, (Ed.), *Cognitive skills and their acquisition*. Hillsdale, NJ: Erlbaum.

Newell, A., & Simon, H. A. (1972). *Human problem-solving*. Englewood Cliffs, NJ: Prentice-Hall.

Perfetto, G. A., Bransford, J. D., & Franks, J. J. (1983). Constraints on access in a problem-solving context. *Memory and Cognition, 11,* 24–31.

Pirolli, P. L., & Anderson, J. R. (1985). The role of learning from examples in the acquisition of recursive programming skill. *Canadian Journal of Psychology, 39,* 240–272.

Polson, P. G., & Jeffries, R. (1985). Analysis—Instruction in general problem-solving skills: An analysis of four approaches. In J. W. Segal, S. F. Chipman, & R. Glaser (Eds.), *Thinking and learning skills: Vol. 1. Relating instruction to research*. Hillsdale, NJ: Erlbaum.

Polson, P. G., & Kieras, D. E. (1984). A formal description of users' knowledge of how to operate a device and user complexity. *Behavior Research Methods, Instruments, & Computers, 16,* 249–255.

Polson, P. G., & Kieras, D. E. (1985). An approach to the formal analysis of user complexity. *International Journal of Man-Machine Studies, 22,* 365–394.

Postman, L. (1971). Transfer, interference and forgetting. In J. W. Kling & L. A. Riggs (Eds.), *Woodworth and Schlosberg's experimental psychology*. New York: Holt.

Postman, L., Keppel, G., & Zacks, R. (1968). Studies of learning to learn: VII. The effects of practice on response integration. *Journal of Verbal Learning and Verbal Behavior, 7,* 776–784.

Postman, L., & Schwartz, M. (1964). Studies of learning to learn: I. Transfer as a function of method of practice and class of verbal materials. *Journal of Verbal Learning and Verbal Behavior, 3,* 37–49.

Postman, L., & Underwood, B. J. (1973). Critical issues in interference theory. *Memory and Cognition, 1,* 19–40.

Simon, H. A., & Hayes, J. R. (1976). The understanding process: Problem isomorphs. *Cognitive Psychology, 8,* 165–190.

Singley, M. K., & Anderson, J. R. (1985). The transfer of text-editing skill. *Journal of Man-Machine Studies, 22,* 403–423.

Singley, M. K., & Anderson, J. R. (in press). *A key-stroke analysis of learning and transfer in text-editing. Human-Computer Interaction*.

Sleeman, D., & Brown, J. S.(Eds.). (1982). *Intelligent tutoring systems*. New York: Academic Press.

Thorndike, E. L. (1914). *The psychology of learning*. New York: Teachers College.

Thorndike, E. L., & Woodworth, R. S. (1901). The influence of improvement in one mental function upon the efficiency of other functions. *Psychological Review, 8,* 247–261, 384–395, 553–564.

White, B. Y., & Frederiksen, J. R. (1986). Intelligent tutoring systems based upon qualitative model evolutions. In *Proceedings of AAAI-86: The National Conference on Artificial Intelligence* (vol. 1, pp. 313–319) Philadelphia, PA.

Winograd, T. W. (1975). Frame representations and the declarative-procedural controversy. In D. G. Bobrow & A. M. Collins (Eds.), *Representation and understanding: Studies in cognitive science*. New York: Academic Press.

CHAPTER 8

The Design of Industrial and Flight Simulators

E. Scott Baudhuin

The major objective of virtually any sophisticated "full-scope" industrial or military simulator training device is to provide the highest degree of transfer possible to its operational system counterpart. Commercial interest in system optimization and military concern for operational readiness have stimulated interest in the concept of transfer of training. In the case of commercial interests, this may include everything from the nuclear power facility, to the petrochemical plant, to the oil refinery, all searching for an optimal operating scenario with the highest production at the lowest cost. In the sense used by training operators, optimization means more effective and "efficient" training, thereby optimizing plant operations. In the case of the military, there is always the concern for being "ready" for any eventuality, which in turn means being able to run the operational platforms (airplanes, ships, tanks, etc.) in the safest, and most cost-efficient manner. In short, the degree of transfer from the simulator to the system often equates to dollars saved in the operation of the real system and in materials and lives saved.

The primary objective of this chapter is to provide an overview of the role of transfer of training concepts in the design and development of commercial and military simulator training devices. To achieve this objective it is necessary to

Focus on the issue of transfer of training relative to simulator training devices:

TRANSFER OF LEARNING

Define the specific simulator applications related to military and commercial concerns
Provide the reader with particular cases of transfer of training research related to selected commercial and military simulator systems

I. TRANSFER OF TRAINING:
A GENERAL PERSPECTIVE

In the context of simulator use, training transfer simply means producing people who are able to perform their job more efficiently and effectively. Spears (1983) provides a preliminary basis for understanding transfer of training in the present context by suggesting the idea of functionally equivalent learned responses (response generalizations) as the key to transfer of training. For example, Spears writes:

> A stimulus generated on a cathode ray tube (CRT) in a training device, and a mentally rehearsed response to it, *can* be functionally equivalent to, respectively, an instrument reading and a resulting actual control input in operational equipment. Equivalence requires only an understanding of what is involved to complete indicated actions. (pp. 17–18)

Spears suggests that often training designers favor physical similarity in a training device to the real system to produce transfer, for example, rather than the idea of a generalized "functional equivalence" of the training device to the real system. Spears views the idea of "functional equivalence" as a better way of defining "transfer of training," particularly for complex human behaviors such as one sees in the operation of nuclear control rooms or in flying a state-of-the-art aircraft.

A. A GENERIC DEFINITION OF TRANSFER

"Functional equivalence" makes it possible to sketch a generic definition of transfer of training as it relates to simulator training devices. There are several conditions which lead to transfer of training. First, meanings must be attached to the training stimuli in the context of goal-oriented activities. Second, the trainee must develop and associate a set of responses appropriate to the training context. Finally, there must be a generalization of the trainees' learning task derived from the simulator trainer stimuli and his associated responses to other Task situations.

It is important to emphasize that the content of the training environment plays an important role in establishing the context of goal-oriented behavior. As we shall see, the degree to which the training environment or device must be physically similar to the operational equipment to optimize transfer is very much an open question. Device designers believe, however, that a highly realistic training environment is required for the training stimuli to acquire meaning, where the trainee does not have to work hard at visualizing the connection between the training stimuli and goal-oriented behavior. In any event, the trainee must have a clear idea of the training objectives so that there is no misunderstanding about the goal-oriented behavior which must be present in the training situation.

The second condition, the development and utilization of an appropriate set of contextual responses, requires appropriately structured training experiences for the development of these response sets. This complicated process has been examined in some detail by Stark (1976) in the context of aircraft simulation. This condition requires the simulator training device, its associated "scenario developments," and the curriculum attached to the simulator to carefully incorporate the interrelationships between tasks and functions that the operational system performs.

Provided the first two conditions have been met to an appropriate degree, then Condition 3, the generalization of meanings and response sets from the simulator training system to operational systems should follow, producing transfer of training.

B. THE SIMULATOR DESIGN PROCESS

How do simulator manufacturers address these issues as they develop complex simulator training devices for military and industrial applications? As we have already indicated, training designers are very likely to subscribe to the idea that transfer of training is directly related to the degree to which the simulator replicates the actual system. To achieve a high degree of "similarity" or "equivalence" between the simulator and the operational systems, two major areas of concern are evidenced in the design and development process: (a) systems analysis which includes both functional analysis and engineering analysis and (b) functional task and skills analysis. In short, the normal simulator development cycle includes a comprehensive front-end analysis with detailed systems analysis and functional task and skills analysis leading to a meaningful set of task modules which are designed into training scenarios for the simulator in order to satisfy the transfer criteria discussed above.

Figure 1 depicts a very general model of deployment for a typical simulator development. The model is presented to illustrate some of the normal inputs, throughputs, and outputs relevant to the development of a high-fidelity simulator for a military or industrial application. The conduct of this process is based on the specified systems analysis and functional task data. It is important to emphasize that training devices and/or operational systems are sometimes developed without careful attention to the FEA activities and all of the inputs to the front-end analysis (FEA) depicted in Figure 1. The result of an inadequate FEA is usually an ill-defined training, or operational, system and a likelihood of low transfer.

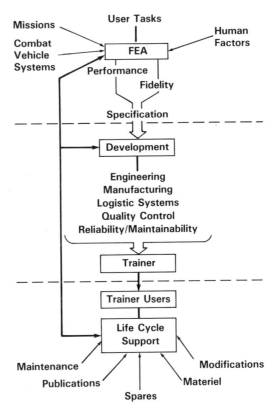

Figure 1. A very general model of deployment for a typical simulator development, illustrating some of the normal inputs, throughputs, and outputs.

Based on this model, the items critical to the FEA and simulator development process include a comprehensive analysis of task data and human-factor concerns relative to the operational systems which will be used for the training and the instructor control system (sometimes referred to as the instructor operator station, or IOS) (see Lenzychi & Finley, 1980). The IOS is designed so that the instructor can administer defined training stimuli or scenarios to the trainee.

The specific steps in the FEA methodology often used for the determination of simulator fidelity issues are illustrated in Figure 2. These steps are usually taken in gathering and analyzing task data for the system which will be simulated. The basic approach to the FEA consists of two major phases: a task identification and description phase and a task/training analysis phase.

Regardless of the system selected for simulation and the information available to the device designer, the first step in the FEA identifies and

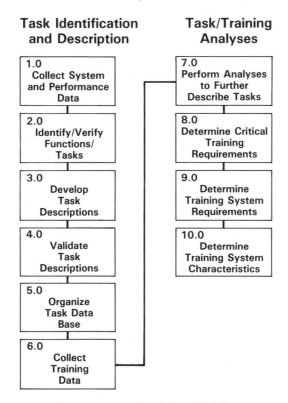

Figure 2. Front-end analysis methodology.

describes those tasks that have been designated for human operators to perform in the operational environment. This kind of information comes not only from the development of the task listing but also from the analysis of operational system missions and the engineering data available for the system. This is one of the most important steps in the whole process because the data obtained in this step will provide the baseline for a valid functionally derived and effective training program. At this point, it is also important to develop a baseline of job description information which is sufficient relative to each individual job being analyzed as well as providing the developer with data on "when," "where," and "how" each job (operator position) interacts with other jobs in each subsystem. To achieve this objective, task descriptions are first developed and validated as indicated in Blocks 1.0–4.0 of Figure 2. After the task descriptions have been validated, individual and interactive tasks are arranged by operator position for the subsequent task analysis (Block 5.0).

The collection of training data in Block 6.0 is an ongoing activity which can be done concurrently and/or in parallel with the previous steps. This information will impact the final determination of the simulator characteristics. These data usually consist of information relative to the training site, the training population, and functional characteristics of the program.

Following the task description validation, the next stop is to prepare and implement an analysis to further describe the tasks (Block 7.0). Here the training analysts and designers select evaluation criteria, rating scales, data collection forms; identify subject matter experts (SMEs); and conduct interviews. Close coordination between the simulator buyer or sponsor and the simulator manufacturer is necessary here to identify SMEs and sites for the interviews.

Since the major product of the FEA methodology is to determine simulator trainer requirements and characteristics, in Block 8.0 system operator tasks requiring training are defined. Additionally, each task is assigned a criticality with respect to the overall operational system requirements. This exercise will allow the training analyst to assign priorities to training tasks, thereby eliminating tasks which are noncritical to overall system operation.

In Block 9.0 the tasks selected for training are analyzed against the requirement for critical training requirements to decide which tasks actually require a simulator trainer. Basically, this activity is accomplished through a series of screening processes utilizing task practice, performance, and skill requirements as the criteria for analysis.

The last step in the FEA process is to determine the characteristics of the trainer that are needed to promote the training process for the final set of selected tasks. Here the analysis focuses on the physical and instructional characteristics of the simulator training system. Physical characteristics refer to the specific "knobs and dials" which must be simulated in each of the operational systems so that skills required in the real world are covered in the simulator training mode. For example, the fidelity requirements for controls, the number of controls required, the degree of fidelity required of environmental factors, and the host of other parameters associated with the real world must be clearly defined. Instructional characteristics refer to the features of the trainer that enhance the acquisition of learning for the trainee.

To better understand the training and simulator requirements, it is also necessary to obtain data with respect to the various missions performed by the system being simulated. Finally, data relative to each of the subsystems with the operational pieces must undergo an engineering analysis with respect to the issues such as simulation/stimulation, points of stimulation, and the requirements for the computer models or algorithms that will have to be developed in order to make the simulator act like the real equipment. All of these inputs from the model are analyzed during the FEA and lead to a determination of training performance and fidelity requirements. The final result of the level in this model would be a specification for the simulator. Often this development activity is performed by the customer or organization buying the simulator.

C. DESIGN FIDELITY

One of the major issues one sees in the literature and in simulator specifications is the degree of fidelity or the physical and functional similarity of the simulator to the operational equipment. For example, simulator designers of an antisubmarine warfare simulator are required to address, among many things, such issues as the degree of realism and number of targets that will be simulated and available to the trainee. In the case of the industrial simulators such as those designed for a power plant control room, this concern is translated into designing simulator training systems which must be a virtual replica of the operational system, all the way down to the last bolt or screw on the control room panels (Figure 3). Additionally, industrial specifications may call for the manufacturer to include upwards of a thousand different simulation models for various malfunctions which may potentially occur in the real plant.

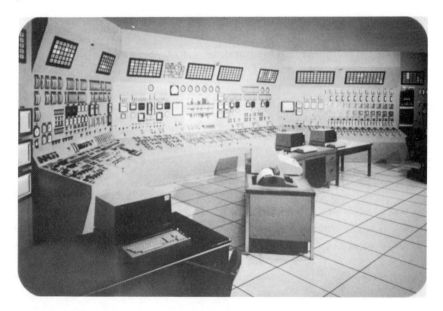

Figure 3. Fossil-fueled power plant simulator faithfully representing a 1,300 MWe coal-fired generating station. (Reprinted by permission of The Singer Company, Link Simulation Systems Division.)

Laughery, Ditzian, and Houtman (1982) suggest, however, that transfer of training must concern itself with the "simulator's ability to *substitute* for operational equipment training in the training curriculum (p. 215, emphasis added). Furthermore, as Morris and Thomas (1976) point out, from the training point of view, it may be more important for the simulator to be functionally equivalent to the plant than to be an exact replica of the plant. The discussion which follows examines the various attempts to determine whether "substitution" really requires a one-to-one correspondence in order for transfer of training to occur.

It must be pointed out that aside from the general research conducted in aviation and with flight simulators, little transfer research has been done. Much of the aviation research which immediately follows has served to develop the transfer models which are reviewed here. The research indicates an awareness of the important role that human information-processing capabilities and/or limitations should play in the development of simulators designed to replicate complex operational systems such as a high-performance military aircraft. Finally, as the factors contributing to simulator cost (computer simulation models and hardware) become more critical to the buyer, we shall see that functional versus physical fidelity issues receive more attention in transfer studies.

In the next section, we examine some specific instances of research and applications relative to military simulators.

II. MILITARY AVIATION APPLICATIONS

Applications of simulation to military training problems and the attention to research in military transfer of training have been extensive. While most of the applications in the military are either directly or indirectly related to aircraft simulators, military devices cover the entire spectrum from water-based to ground-based vehicles or platforms.

The amount of transfer a simulator can deliver is critically important since much of the training capability resident in flight simulators is something which could not be replicated in the real aircraft. The history of aviation has been replete with examples of human errors in system design and operation leading to disaster, which highlight human information-processing limitations. The United Airlines incident at O'Hare field in Chicago is a case in point: Following this disaster, simulator manufacturers were asked to include scenarios and computer models to simulate malfunctions like the engine detaching itself from the wing, as it did in Chicago. Thus, there are instances where it is assumed that effective simulator training includes training for "unusual" performance situations not likely to be encountered during flight operations.

A. MEASUREMENT MODELS

What research models have the military typically used to determine transfer of training? Virtually all of the military interest in transfer of training as it relates to simulator systems, as well as that for industrial applications, has been based on the assumption that positive transfer will result from simulator training. As Su (1984) suggests:

(1) When stimuli are varied and responses are identical, positive transfer is obtained.
(2) When stimuli are identical and responses are varied, negative transfer is obtained. (p. 15)

A majority of the military research on transfer of training has been based on the research paradigm indicated below.

	Simulator training	Real-system training
Experimental group	x	x
Control group		x

Here, the experimental group receives training in the simulator and, during a second session, training on the real system. The control group receives only training on the real system. The dependent measures can be either a measure of time-to-train reduction achieved as a function of the simulator training or an initial trial performance measure for trainees on the real system after training on the simulator.

Micheli (1972) defines a "time-savings" performance measure, used in many military transfer of training studies, as the percentage of transfer determined by improvement in performance on the real system. Thus,

$$\text{percentage transfer} = (c - e)100/c$$

where c = performance or time to reach criterion for the control group on the real system

e = performance or time to reach criterion for the experimental group on the real system.

Roscoe (1971) suggests that measures of training transfer are more meaningful, particularly in determining cost effectiveness, if the time spent on the simulator training system is also factored into the formula. To tap this dimension, a cumulative transfer effectiveness ratio was developed to express savings in time or errors to reach criterion on the operational system as a function of time in training on the simulator:

$$\text{TER} = (c - e)/t_e$$

where c = time or errors required to reach criterion (on a transfer task) on the real system by control group

e = time or errors required to reach criterion (on a transfer task) on the real system by experimental group

t_e = time the experimental group spent training on simulator.

When performance measures are taken for experimental and control groups, there are some obvious "confounds" or "artifacts" because control-group data may not be available, or the simulated task is more difficult than the real task. One of the selling points for simulator training devices has, after all, been that through extensive math modeling, simulator tasks can be made as complex as desired. In short, a simulator task many include virtually all potential malfunctions with respect to a given operational system and might therefore not ever be replicable in the real world for the sake of comparability in transfer of training research. In the case of the nuclear control room trainers we shall discuss in the next section, many of the simulator tasks are often much more complex than an operator many ever experience in the operational control room.

Mudd (1968) points out that transfer of training research is not appropriate in cases where the operational equipment is still under development. This condition applies, not only to military systems, but also to industrial simulators. Many nuclear control room simulators, for example, are developed in parallel or preceding the completion of the nuclear plant. In either case, Mudd argues that if the operational system is so complicated or, in the case of high-performance military aircraft, so dangerous, then transfer research which measures an uninitiated control group on a first-shot basis would be out of the question. Mudd also suggests that being able to "generalize" from transfer studies is next to impossible in such circumstances.

B. SIMULATOR FIDELITY: FLIGHT VISUAL SYSTEMS

The literature on military training device effectiveness is too extensive and varied to examine in full. Therefore, we will focus on the effect of variations in the fidelity of simulator visual systems and displays on transfer in order to illustrate the issues described in previous sections. An issue of major concern with respect to the visual system for a flight simulator is the kind of visual system necessary to satisfy the training requirements. There are basically three types of image simulation which currently exist, each with various advantages and disadvantages relative to this training problem. Two techniques use standard film as the image media, while a third approach utilizes computer-generated images for the visual system.

With standard films it is only possible to have a predetermined number of scenarios which may be filmed in actual flying situations. Given the nature of this general training problem, namely, scenarios where all types of potential hazards can be realistically created, there may be a serious potential for accidents during the filming of a scenario. If the general training requirements indicate that there is not a need for a great number of actual flying scenarios, then this approach may be sufficient.

The second filming approach makes use of model boards which use a miniaturized version of an actual flight scene. The model board approach appears to have technical difficulties since there is no effective way of incorporating moving models or special effects. The model board approach is frequently used in military helicopter trainers to provide a realistic nap-of-the-earth flying scenario where the limited field of view and lens distortions are less critical.

The third possible approach is the use of a computer-generated image (CGI) system where all the necessary visual information can be generated and stored digitally. The obvious advantage of this kind of approach is that it allows for other traffic participants to move in and out of the scene at will and with an independently generated landscape. This approach also allows for all other kinds of factors to be generated, for example, environmental conditions such as day or night, weather, characteristics of the roadway, and so on. New scenarios can be generated quickly and cost effectively. Given the variable number of objects and/or factors which can be developed with such a system and still provide a full 180° angle of vision, the CGI system seems most attractive from an overall cost perspective.

One of the major disadvantages, however, is that CGI systems sacrifice a degree of realism. Individual objects in a CGI system are made up of polygons. The number of polygons that can be processed in real time by an image generator is limited, so tradeoffs are made and the realism of simulated images must also be compromised. One way this problem is minimized is by storing the various objects necessary for any flying scenario at different levels of detail so that those obects that are further away from the pilot's eyes will require less detail and, therefore, fewer polygons. Recent advances in graphics technology have made great strides in enhancing the realism provided by polygon-based image system (cf. Thallman & Thallman, 1985). Whether this tradeoff between the realism of film-derived images and the relative abstractness in the CGI systems approach to image generation is unacceptable remains as a basic human-factor and/or transfer of training research issue.

Rockway and Nullmeyer (1984) studied the effectiveness of the C-130 weapon system trainer (WST) visual system designed to train visually oriented tactical airlift operational tasks. A number of experiments were conducted with personnel from aircrew populations being trained for initial qualification, mission qualification, and continuation training. Most of the experiments compared in-flight performance between those who had received the WST training (simulator training) to the performance of those who had not. Instructors were used to rate performance. The results showed positive transfer as a result of the WST. Thus, compromises in "absolute visual fidelity" were not inconsistent with positive transfer (cf. Semple, Hennessy, Sanders, Cross, & Beith, 1981).

Hughes, Brooks, Graham, Sheen, and Dickens (1982) and Hughes, Graham, Sheen, and Dickens (1983) presented transfer of training findings from an operational exercise designed to assess survival skills under a red-flag combat exercise approximating actual combat conditions. Mission-ready A-10 pilots, who were given simulator training system experience in ground attack skills under simulated threat conditions were found to survive a higher percentage of sorties flown in the subsequent red-flag combat exercise than did a comparable group of pilots who had not received the simulator training. The simulator had a visual system consisting of a wide-field-of-view, 6-arc minute, monochrome computer-generated display system. The authors conclude that, while visual systems continue to be an issue of concern to simulator designers, the ability of this simulator training system to realistically reproduce the critical events in an interactive threat situation such as that found in the typical red-flag combat exercise seems to cast some doubt on previous assertions about the necessity for high physical fidelity.

Holman (1980) examined the overall training effectiveness of the CH-47 helicopter simulators by using a two-part research methodology. The first part utilized a classical two-group transfer of training paradigm with aviators participating in transition training to the CH-47. The second part examined the training benefits attributed to the simulator for aviators who were already operational with the CH-47 helicopter. While the general findings showed that the CH-47 flight simulator is an effective simulator training device, the results did suggest that the simulator may not be adequate for hovering maneuvers, where extensive visual referencing is required at low altitudes.

Wightman, Westra, and Lintern (1985) studied the effect of simulator training on carrier landing. They manipulated the fidelity levels of two visual system factors, field of view and scene detail, in training 72 student pilots on the approach tasks of circling, straight-in, and a segmented combination. Although increased positive transfer was demonstrated for the simulator-trained groups, no effect was found between narrow and wide visual field or high- and low-detail scene conditions. Interestingly, students given 20 trials, as opposed to 40 or 60 trials, on the simulator did no better than controls on transfer performance, indicating that limited simulator practice may produce no real benefit for trainees in some situations. Level of scene detail did effect transfer performance in a study of dive bombing by Lintern, Thomley, Nelson, and Roscoe (1984), however. In short, the requirements for visual fidelity appear to be very much related to the training tasks and the environment surrounding such tasks.

The issue of simulator fidelity can also be viewed in the context of the cost effectiveness of both motion and visual fidelity (cf. Orlansky & String, 1980). In either of these cases, the computer models required to drive these elements are a significant factor in the overall cost of the simulator. Doerfel and Distelmaier (1981) argue that since a simulator is not an "exact" replica of the aircraft, but rather a training or educational device, studies are required to determine approaches needed to achieve educational or training objectives (subjective fidelity). What studies have been done have suggested that subjective fidelity can help to achieve more cost-effective results than if designers only considered the objective fidelity requirements of the simulator.

Nevertheless, there must be limits to the degree to which simulator fidelity can be lowered and still maintain the integrity of the training system. Coward and Rupp (1981) argue that the requirements for flying an aircraft include continuous interpretation of the visual environment from outside and inside the cockpit in order to maintain checks on the status of the aircraft and its location in space. When the flight scenario includes tracking and evaluating the performance and/or status of opposing aircraft such as in a combat situation, the environment is significantly more complex. The successful pilot, in this instance, depends a great deal on the out-of-cockpit visual cues, and such training must therefore take place entirely in the aircraft. Such training provides experience in a high-stress environment which may never be able to be replicated in the simulator training system. Visual cues are critical in certain kinds of flight operations, and the visual cues offered in state-of-the-art computer-generated imagery for simulator training systems may not suffice.

In summary, the transfer studies we have reviewed show that positive transfer can be achieved under varying degrees of fidelity of visual cues in the simulator. It is also clear that much additional multifactor research is needed on transfer of training to sort out effects and to remove some of the artifacts and confounds seen in much of the research. With the increasing emphasis on making simulators a cost-effective alternative to hands-on operational training, the studies of transfer which can isolate the effects of major simulator cost drivers such as visual and motion cues will become more important. In the section which follows, examples of commercial and industrial simulator applications will be reviewed. The focus will be on the development and design process that exists in these areas.

III. INDUSTRIAL APPLICATIONS

The primary objectives for many of the industrial or commercial simulators on the market today are to enhance operational productivity and to increase safety on the job. Clearly, transfer of training drives both of these goals. However, commercial or industrial simulators are, by definition, purchased by "for-profit" organizations. For this reason, the research interests in the industrial community are more closely aligned with identifying ways of using simulators for optimization studies rather than for training purposes, for example, running operating scenarios to determine which combinations of materials under specific test conditions will be most efficient in the production process. Another interest seen in many research labs on the commercial side of the simulation business is the identification of technical solutions to a simulator problem, such as finding an answer to the problem of creating a realistic motion base to simulate acceleration and deceleration in a ground-based vehicle. In neither of these instances, however, do the research objectives focus on measuring transfer of training.

A. THE DAIMLER-BENZ SIMULATOR

Drosdol and Panik (1985) discuss the Mercedes Benz driving simulator's capabilities in aiding the creation of new vehicle enhancements for the Daimler-Benz Company. It must be emphasized that the original Daimler-Benz driving simulator was designed purely as a research and development tool for the company. The basic components of this simulator include an actual Mercedes Benz vehicle which can be mounted on a motion platform, a large projection dome, a motion system with 6 df, a projection system for providing the visuals to the vehicle driver, a digital computer system, and vehicular-modeling software. The actual vehicle is interfaced with the computer system and motion platform to provide realistic simulations of actual driving operations.

If this simulator were eventually selected to serve as a training vehicle, however, it is clear that a number of technical issues would need to be addressed with respect to transfer of training. Once the necessary level of training fidelity is determined through FEA, for example, then the two major technical problems which must be addressed are: (a) the motion system and its ability to simulate particular vehicle motions and (b) the visual system used for simulating the driver's view as he performs driving operations.

The *motion systems* currently available allow for movement in all 6 df: longitudinal, lateral, vertical, heading, pitch, and roll. For flight simulator systems, the actual simulations of the motions for various aircraft can be very realistic. However, for a vehicle motion system such as that needed to realistically simulate vehicle *acceleration*, there are some limitations. Current motion ranges are too small to properly simulate larger scale translational accelerations of longer duration. For example, at a constant acceleration of 0.25 g, the maximum longitude displacement of 2.13 m in current motion systems would be reached in just 1.3 s. To give the driver a realistic simulation for vehicle accelerations of longer duration, current motion-base technology must use inclination simulation. The vehicle (simulator cabin) can be inclined along with the image system to simulate an acceleration of 2.5 m/s/s. However, the rotation must be performed slowly enough not to be noticed by the driver. There may be some other ways of simulating this long-term acceleration such as those used in some flight simulator systems where gravity forces are applied to the seat in the cockpit.

The *visual system* necessary for a driving simulator raises several possible issues and approaches. First it is assumed that a typical vehicle operator will be presented with massive amounts of visual information at various speeds during an actual driving incident. Second, the driver may need even more than the 180° angle of vision afforded in current visual systems; there certainly would be times when the driver must assess information at angles greater than 180° on either side of the vehicle and to the rear of the vehicle. The rear visual could be projected through the rear view mirror and/or window. However, the views on the sides that require greater than 180° may present some technical difficulties which must be addressed. Current experiences seem to indicate that some distortion may occur at angles approaching or greater than 180°.

The Daimler-Benz driving simulator displays an overriding concern for a simulator that is very close to full fidelity in most respects. The problems associated with rapid acceleration and deceleration were largely overcome through innovative engineering design. The CGI visual system represents one area where absolute fidelity was compromised. Since the mission of this simulator was for research and development, developers and end users appear to accept the visual compromise as a limitation of the present technology. However, it seems obvious that one of the variables that is almost never a part of the definition of "full fidelity" is that of the "psychological" environment and the fact that drivers know that they are in a simulator which is controlled by a computer.

While the psychomotor demands of driving a car may not be quite as cumbersome as those found in a high-performance military aircraft, there are still elements which cannot be simulated. There also seems to be an additional phenomenon occurring in many simulators, including the Daimler-Benz device, which is not replicated in the real vehicle: simulator sickness. In many instances the vehicle operator (driver) or aircraft pilot has experienced simulator "sickness," which appears to be due to distortions in the perceptual cues produced by the simulator's visual and motion systems (cf. Long, Ambler, & Guedry, 1975; Puig, 1970).

B. Power Plant Control Room Simulators

The Nuclear Regulatory Commission's (NRC's) requirement that all nuclear power facilities must have a full-scope simulator training device for initial and refresher training for all control room operator personnel has led industry to design simulators which, for all practical purposes, are exact replicas of the actual control rooms they simulate. The NRC responded to the Three Mile Island (TMI) accident by developing both the requirement for a simulator training device and for human-factor design reviews of existing and future nuclear control rooms.

Years of analysis following the incident have suggested that the best solution to the TMI incident may be to change the design of the system. Furthermore, some have suggested that additional operator training would not be necessary if design changes were made in the control room systems that would allow the operator to "make decisions rather than solve problems" (Bailey, 1982, p. 127). Similar views are expressed by Fischetti (1985), who suggests that simulators do provide trainees with practice in various required skills but do not train individuals to handle the *stresses* of being in the operational environment. It is interesting to note that operators involved in the TMI incident said in later investigations that they had never previously had such events happen either in the plant or in simulators. In short, based on the TMI incident, specification developers for the nuclear power plant simulators believe very strongly in the full-fidelity plant-specific approach.

The response to the TMI incident has, in fact, spawned a major part of the simulator industry. Typically, the NRC guidelines and regulations require the nuclear power industry to place a "request for proposal" (RFP) before industry. The typical RFPs for nuclear simulators offer a prime example of the common elements design philosophy. The RFPs call for a "plant-specific" replica of the actual control room for which the simulator will be used. The plant-specific concept implies that in order for transfer of training to occur, the simulator must precisely duplicate all of the knobs, dials, switches, and so forth of each particular control room.

While the NRC now urges a generic approach whenever possible in the design review for existing nuclear control rooms as well as for the design of the new control rooms, industry for the most part has continued to design very dissimilar control rooms depending on the contractor, thereby creating the need for a plant-specific simulator. This concept also implies that the transfer of training is basically limited to one "bridge." In theory, one only gets one "transfer" per simulator, and that transfer is for one specific "destination" only.

Collins (1975) supports this philosophy when he describes the "utility" of using simulators for nuclear power plant training. The NRC allows that if the simulator is a high-fidelity device with characteristics *very similar to the actual plant*, then the simulator may be used for requalification programs where the plant operator is required to manipulate controls and so forth. It must be emphasized that the NRC only allows this condition when the simulator closely copies the nuclear facility for which requalification is being tested. The NRC believes that individuals who have been trained on simulators have a better grasp of the variety of potential normal and abnormal operating conditions which may occur in the designated plant. In short, the simulator must reproduce the operating characteristics of the actual plant, and all of the instrumentation and control must be "very similar" to the actual plant. The model for establishing the level of fidelity is not specified by Collins. Transfer of training is indeed implied but appears not to be verified here.

Very little research specifically related to transfer of training with these types of simulators has been conducted, perhaps due to the relative "newness" of the nuclear control room simulator business. Hollnagel (1982) discusses the development of a methodology for systematic observation of operator personnel performing in a nuclear training simulator. The model is based on subject matter expertise from an experienced instructor, and observations are done in accordance with the structure of a model developed from numerous studies of operator performance, in the real world and in simulators. What this model does not do, however, is consider transfer of training from the simulator to the real world. Essentially, this model is a training-effectiveness protocol which allows the researcher to make predictions about *performance on the simulator*, not necessarily about *performance in the real control room*. Laughery *et al.* (1982) illustrate the difference between transfer research and the evaluation of simulator performance:

> No matter what the measurement validity of the device, and no matter what the training simulator tasks, if the student group using the simulator emerges from it better able to perform actual equipment tasks, transfer of training occurred. . . . Validity refers to the device's utility in *performance prediction*, and transfer of training refers to the device's utility towards *facilitating learning*. . . . A simulator's ability to make valid performance predictions related to its utility in accessing terminal performance . . . and its transfer of training utility relates to the simulator's ability to substitute for operational equipment training in the training curriculum. (p. 215)

Bereznai (1981) describes a hardware and software system designed to allow instructors to objectively evaluate the performance of nuclear control room operator personnel on a training simulator. Predetermined criteria including discrete process parameters, procedures, or a combination of these, along with absolute and relative timing information. The evaluation system appears to provide the instructor with readily accessible information relative to trainee performance on the predetermined criteria, although this model may be only a precursor to determining actual training transfer.

C. SUMMARY

The concern for transfer of training with industrial applications of simulator technology seems to have produced relatively little actual transfer research. The major training issue seems to be the ability to use a simulator to measure *simulator* performance rather than training *transfer*. Much of the literature reviewed here concerns itself more with how much simulator fidelity is needed to validly measure the trainee's performance. As we have seen, training psychologists and theorists try to distinguish between performance evaluation and improving "performance," where performance is, by definition, on the actual equipment or system. A more critical issue worthy of further examination may be determining the criticality of the operator tasks in a real system and then designing both the simulator and the curriculum to provide practice on these tasks. It may in fact be true, as Micheli (1972) observed, that transfer effectiveness is more a function of how the trainer is being utilized than a function of the simulator's fidelity.

Carefully designed training curriculua to support simulators, appropriate selections of "scenarios," and allocation of tasks to be trained via simulators, thereby allowing trainees to practice things that are most critical to the successful operation of the "real bus," may be more important than the exact replication of the operational system in the simulator. On the other hand, if exact replication is the rule, then what is suggested here still holds: It remains important to fully exploit the capabilities of a full-fidelity simulator through judicious planning of curriculum and simulation exercises so that valid performance evaluations and improvements in performance are the rule rather than the exception.

IV. TRANSFER OF TRAINING AND SIMULATOR TRAINING DEVICES: WHAT HAS BEEN LEARNED

Over fifty years ago, Edward Link, working under rather primitive conditions by today's standards, developed the world's first simulator training device. The history of simulation, while not the subject of this chapter, has certainly been an experience closely tied to the advancements in technology alluded to in the present treatment of the transfer of training and simulation subject matter. Obviously, much of what has been reviewed here is entirely consistent with the conclusion that simulators do produce transfer of training, that simulator training devices are an effective way of achieving operator and maintenance training for operational systems where training on the system itself may be either too dangerous or too expensive, and that simulators can be used for a variety of training applications ranging all the way from what Link envisioned in flight training; to nuclear control room operator training; to driving ships, submarines, and tanks.

We have also seen that the design of simulators, according to what many of the learning psychologists and learning theorists have suggested, is often based on the orientation that the simulator must very nearly replicate in every detail the system that it is designed to simulate. This design philosophy has played a major role in many of the commercial and military simulators we have seen since the "blue box" first came off Link's production line. Much of the research reviewed in both the industrial and military aviation domains has suggested that the issue of common elements or full fidelity has not been supported by much of the transfer of training research. Numerous studies in the area of military flight simulation have suggested in fact that full visual and motion fidelity may not contribute in any greater measure to training transfer than less fully replicated simulator training systems.

We have also seen that the models driving transfer of training research may have some bearing on the generalizability of the results. It has become very clear that training transfer studies can be subject to major misinterpretations, for example, attributing transfer to a simulator when, in fact, serious confounds existed in the conduct of the research. We have also seen that transfer is often difficult to measure in some instances where training subjects have had no prior experience on the system being simulated. In some instances, the first-shot measure is virtually impossible because the operational platform is a high-performance jet aircraft and uninitiated trainees would simply not be allowed to serve as "controls." Finally, there are many instances where the simulator is far more complicated than the real system, for example, because of the need to train personnel to respond to malfunctions or tactical maneuvers that they may never encounter while operating the real vehicle.

In short, simulator training systems do produce transfer of training. They have been accepted in most instances as cost-effective alternatives to other means of training with real systems. The degree of fidelity often called for in simulator specifications needs to be evaluated carefully with respect to transfer of training paradigms. As technologies continue to advance, even more cost-effective simulation will be developed.

REFERENCES

Bailey, R. W. (1982). *Human performance engineering: A guide for systems designers.* Englewood Cliffs, NJ: Prentice-Hall.

Bereznai, G. T. (1981). Instructor facility tools to evaluate trainee performance on Candu simulators. In *Proceedings of the 1981 Summer Computer Simulation Conference.* Toronto, Ontario, Canada.

Collins, P. F. (1975). Reactor operator training programs utilizing nuclear power-plant simulators. *Nuclear Safety, 16*(4), 482–488.

Coward, R. E., & Rupp, A. M. (1981). *Simulator for air-to-air combat versus real world: visual cue analysis for simulated air-to-air combat training final report* (AFHRL-TR-81-20). Brooks Air Force Base, TX: Air Force Human Resources Laboratory.

Doerfel, G., & Distelmaier, R. (1981). Cost efficiency versus objective fidelity in flight simulation. In *Deutsche Gesellschaft Fuer Luft—und Raumfahrt, Sumposium Papers*. Cologne, West Germany.

Drosdol, J., & Panik, F. (1985). The Daimler-Benz driving simulator: A tool for vehicle development. *SAE Technical Papers Series*. Detroit, MI: International Congress & Exposition.

Fischetti, M. A., & Truxal, C. (1985). Simulating "the right stuff." *IEEE Spectrum, 22*, 38–47.

Hollnagel, E. (1982, May). Analysis of simulator training. In *Proceedings of the International Conference on Training for Nuclear Power Plant Operation*. Roskilde, Denmark.

Holman, G. L. (1980, January). *Training effectiveness of the CH-47 flight simulators* (ARI-RR-1209). Alexandria, VA: U. S. Army Research Institute for the Social and Behavioral Sciences.

Hughes, R., Brooks, R., Graham, D., Sheen, R., & Dickens, T. (1982). Tactical ground attack: On the transfer of training from flight simulator to operational red flag range exercise. In *Human Factors Society Conference Proceedings*. Seattle, WA.

Hughes, R., Graham, D., Sheen, R., & Dickens, T. (1983). Tactical ground attack: On the transfer of training from flight simulator to operational red flag range exercise. In *International Conference on Simulators - Conference Paper*. London, England: IEEE.

Laughery, K. R., Ditzian, J. L., & Houtman, G. M. (1982). Differences between transfer effectiveness and student performance evaluations on simulators: Theory and practice of evaluation. In *Interservice Industry Training Equipment Conference Proceedings*. Washington; DC: I/ITEC.

Lenzycki, H. P., & Finley, D. L. (1980, May). *How to determine training device requirements and characteristics: A handbook for training developers* (Research Product 80-25). Alexandria, VA: U.S. Army Research Institute for the Behavioral and Social Sciences.

Lintern, G., Thomley, K. E., Nelson, B. E., & Roscoe, S. N. (1984). *Content variety and augmentation of simulated visual scenes for teaching air-to-ground attack* (81-C-0105-3). Orlando, FL: Naval Training Equipment Center.

Long, G. M., Ambler, R. K., & Guedry, F. E. (1975). Relationship between perceptual style and reactivity to motion. *Journal of Applied Psychology, 60*, 599–605.

Marcus, A. J., & Curran, L. E. (1985, January). *Use of flight simulators in measuring and improving training effectiveness* (Report No. CNA-PP-432). Alexandria, VA: Center for Naval Analysis.

Micheli, G. S. (1972). *Analysis of the transfer of training, substitution and fidelity of simulation of training equipment* (TAEG Report No. 2). Orlando, FL: Naval Training Equipment Center.

Morris, R., & Thomas, J. (1976). Simulation in training, Parts 1, 2, 3. *Industrial Training International, 11*, 66–69, 161–163, 202–204.

Mudd, S. (1968). Assessment of the fidelity of dynamic flight simulators. *Human Factors, 10*(4), 351–358.

Orlansky, J., String, J. (1980). Cost-effectiveness of flight simulators for military training. *AGARD Conference Proceedings, AGARD-CP-268*. Arlington, VA: Institute for Defense Analysis.

Rockway, M. R., & Nullmeyer, R. T. (1984). Training effectiveness evaluation of the C-130 weapon system trainer wide-angle visual system. In *Annual Mini-Symposium on Aerospace Science and Technology Conference Proceedings*. Wright-Patterson Air Force Base AIAA.

Roscoe, S. N. (1971). Incremental transfer effectiveness. *Human Factors, 13*(6), 561–567.

Semple, C. A., Hennessy, R. T., Sanders, M. S., Cross, B. K., & Beith, B. H. (1981). *Aircrew training devices: Fidelity features* (AO94665). Brooks Air Force Base, Air Force Human Resource Laboratory.

Spears, W. D. (1983, November). *Processes of skill performance: A foundation for the design and use of training equipment* (NAVTRAEQUIPCEN 78-CO113-4). Orlando, FL: Naval Training Equipment Center.

Stark, E. A. (1976, April). Motion perception and terrain visual cues in air combat simulations. In *American Institute of Aeronautics and Astronautics Simulation Conference Proceedings*. New York: AIAA.

Su, Y. D. (1984, April). *A review of the literature on training simulators: transfer of training and simulator fidelity* (Tech. Rep. 84-1). Arlington, VA: Office of Naval Research.

Thallman, N. M., & Thallman, D. (1985). *Computer animation*. New York: Springer-Verlag.

Wightman, D. C., Westra, D. P., & Lintern, G. (1985). *Simulator design features for helicopter landing on small ships* (A169514). Orlando, FL: Naval Training Systems Center.

CHAPTER 9

Measuring Transfer in Military Settings

JOHN A. BOLDOVICI[1]

I. INTRODUCTION

Of the many ways to estimate the effectiveness of training devices, the most convincing by far is the transfer of training experiment. Transfer refers to the effects of practicing one task (Task A) on learning or performing another task (Task B). Transfer can be:

Positive: Practicing Task A improves learning or performing Task B.
Negative: Practicing Task A interferes with learning or performing Task B.
Neutral: Practicing Task A has no effect on learning or performing Task B.

Transfer experiments for weapon system training devices frequently take the following general form: Two groups of subjects receive different kinds of training on Task A. One group, for example, practices Task A using a training device or simulator. The other group practices Task A using a weapon system and service-practice ammunition. Both groups then practice or are tested on Task B using the weapon system. (Tasks A and B may in cases such as this be identical for the weapon system group.) The scores of the two groups on Task B are compared in terms of amount, quality, or cost of learning or performing Task B.

A frequent finding in experiments designed along the lines outlined above is that no statistically significant differences in proficiency can be ascribed to using the device or the weapon system in training (Deason, Robinson, & Terrell, 1982; Powers, McCluskey, Haggard, Boycan, & Steinheiser, 1975). The findings of no difference are then used to support suggestions that

---

[1]The views expressed are the author's and not necessarily those of the Army Research Institute, Department of the Army, or Department of Defense.

TRANSFER OF LEARNING

devices and weapon systems are equally effective as training media (Orlansky, 1985; Wickham, 1983). Findings of no difference can, of course, result from causes other than the absence of differences. Examining some of the causes constitutes much of what follows in this chapter.

Even if one could confidently ascribe findings of no difference to the absence of differences, the inductive leap to declarations of equal effectiveness would remain considerable. No single transfer of training experiment addresses all aspects of effectiveness, and because research may be consistently biased in favor of Type I or Type II error, meta-analyses and other weight-of-evidence approaches do not solve the problem. Repeated evaluations of training devices with small numbers of subjects, for example, would be consistently biased toward finding no proficiency differences due to using devices and weapon systems in training (Type II error).

A. RATIONALE

The results of device evaluations in which Type I or Type II error occurs may be misleading to persons unfamiliar with causes and effects of Type I and Type II error. Such results also may be dangerous if decision makers use them to justify increased reliance on devices and simulators while decreasing the use of weapon systems for training. If decisions to rely on devices and decrease weapon system use in training are based on invalid inferences from research results, then soldiers may never learn the skills necessary to do their jobs. Undesirable effects on proficiency and readiness may ensue.

Given the consequences of decisions about media for military training, examinations seem warranted of the adequacy of the research and reporting upon which estimates of device effectiveness are based.

B. PURPOSE

The purpose of this chapter is to raise questions about the design of research and the interpretation of results that are used to support contentions that weapon systems and training devices are equally effective as media for weapon system training. In the course of doing so, I shall:

Discuss a few sources of error in tank-gunnery and other research on transfer from training devices to weapon systems.

Present competing hypotheses for equal-effectiveness explanations of finding no proficiency differences due to weapon system and device use in training.

Describe ways to avoid some of the errors in designing device evaluations and interpreting their results.

Suggest topics to be addressed in device evaluation reports.

II. SOURCES OF ERROR IN TRANSFER EXPERIMENTS

Sources of error in transfer experiments with military training devices include:

Small numbers of soldiers or crews are used in the comparison.
Subjects in the compared groups are not matched or randomly assigned.
Groups are treated differently in respects other than those under investigation.
Weapon system error masks training effects.
Amount of practice is insufficient to affect proficiency.
Ceiling or floor effects mask differences between groups.
Measurement of Task B performance is unreliable.
Inappropriate analyses are used to estimate transfer.

A. SMALL NUMBERS OF SOLDIERS OR CREWS ARE USED IN THE COMPARISON

One way to find no significant difference between the effects of device and weapon systems training is to use small numbers of subjects. For any given difference in Task B performance by the compared groups, the probability that the difference will be statistically significant declines with decreasing numbers of subjects (all other things being equal). This is not to suggest that large numbers of subjects be used strictly for increasing the probability of finding between-group differences but that power tests be done to estimate sample sizes. Decisions about probability levels and numbers of subjects can then be made in light of costs, practicality, and other considerations.

Small numbers of subjects are sometimes used in military transfer experiments because the desire for representative samples overrides requirements for reliable measurement: Researchers often draw subjects from the Military Occupational Speciality (MOS) for which the device is intended, without benefit of power tests or other indicators of sample-size adequacy. If the number of soldiers available in the MOS of interest is insufficient to reveal between-group proficiency differences, then consideration should be given to using subjects from another MOS or from outside the military. The disadvantages associated with unrepresentativeness of such samples would be no greater than those associated with generalizing to an entire MOS from results of a small sample, and these disadvantages could be offset by the benefits of increased measurement reliability and avoiding Type II error. The issue of generalizability is in any event an empirical matter; it is not automatically resolved by using soldiers whose MOS matches the MOS for which the device is intended.

B. SUBJECTS IN THE COMPARED GROUPS ARE NOT
MATCHED OR RANDOMLY ASSIGNED

If subjects or crews are not assigned randomly to device and weapon system groups or matched between groups, then one group may perform Task B better than the other group for reasons other than whether the device or weapon system was used for learning Task A. Soldiers were, for example, assigned to groups by company in an evaluation of a tank-gunnery training device: the Unit Conduct-of-Fire Trainer (UCOFT) (Kuma & McConville, 1982). Assignment by company was done to maintain unit integrity throughout the evaluation, even though existing gunnery scores showed one company to be superior to the other before training on Task A began. Whether performance differences on Task B were due to entry-level proficiency or to kinds of training (UCOFT versus alternatives) was not ascertained. Maintaining unit integrity may (or may not) be desirable in training or in combat but seldom is desirable in device evaluations.

Lest these criticisms be construed as broadsides against my colleagues in training device research, please note that I was an advisor to Kuma and McConville for planning the study cited above. Logistics and command decisions simply precluded random assignment. This also was the case in a recent evaluation of a videodisk gunnery simulator (Boldovici, Kraemer, & Lampton, 1986).

Random assignment does not, of course, guarantee the absence of preexperimental proficiency differences between groups. The effect of random assignment should therefore be tested, if possible, by comparing the groups' scores on a test of Task B proficiency before training on Task A begins. Holman (1979) did that in a comparison of the Chinook helicopter and the CH-47 simulator as media for sustaining flight proficiency. The device and weapon system groups differed significantly on pretraining test (pretest) scores, but the difference was controlled neither statistically nor by reforming the groups by matching on pretest scores. The extent to which the results (no difference in Task B proficiency) were influenced by pretraining proficiency differences could not therefore be determined.

C. GROUPS ARE TREATED DIFFERENTLY IN RESPECTS
OTHER THAN THOSE UNDER INVESTIGATION

Objective comparisons of training programs require that the compared groups be treated identically in every respect except those under investigation. The only difference between the treatment of groups in comparisons of device and weapon system training, for example, should be that one uses the device in training, and the other the weapon.

The results of evaluations of tank-gunnery training devices have been confounded because the compared groups were treated differently with respect to:

Degree of command emphasis
Test conditions
Amount of training

1. Degree of Command Emphasis

Command emphasis was reported by Kuma and McConville (1982) to have been greater for the baseline group than for the UCOFT group:

> Because of the extended length of time to train each company on the UCOFT, the commanders of the UCOFT companies were unable to visit each crew being trained. On the other hand, the commander of the baseline company was physically present for virtually all of the baseline training program. He personally ran most of the training. (p. C-9)

The extent to which the results of this evaluation were affected by differences in command emphasis cannot be determined.

2. Test Conditions

One group should not be required to perform Task B under conditions that favor hitting targets (damp ground and no wind) while the other group fires under conditions that favor missing (wind, dust, and resulting obscurity), as was the case in the Powers *et al.* (1975) live-fire study and in the UCOFT Operational Test. Kuma and McConville (1982) reported, "Dust completely obscured the target after the first tank fired. This condition became increasingly worse throughout the post-training BFD [battlefield diagnostic] test. The baseline group fired each BFD test first" (p. C-10).

3. Amount of Training

Of the many variables that promote learning and transfer, one of the most potent is amount of practice. Barring ceiling effects (discussed later), a negative transfer paradigm, and irrelevant training, proficiency will be greater with more practice than with less. A finding of no difference in Task B proficiency after one group practices Task A using a device, and another using the weapon system, is therefore not necessarily a blow for the cause of simulation: One group may have practiced Task A more than the other group did. If so, then finding no difference simply suggests that, given two media of unequal effectiveness, more practice with the less effective medium can yield proficiency levels that are comparable to those achieved with less practice with the more effective medium. When no difference is found between the proficiency of a device group that practiced more than a weapon system group, fundamental questions remain: How would the proficiency of the device and weapon system groups compare if both had the same amount of practice? Was it the device or the amount of practice that produced no difference in proficiency?

Weapon system and device groups sometimes are trained to criterion on Task A in device evaluations. If the two groups do not require identical numbers of trials or identical amounts of time to reach criterion on Task A, then the comparison of the device and the weapon system as training media is confounded by amount of practice or training. Confounding also happens when the number of trials or the amount of time to reach criterion is used as a dependent measure in comparisons of weapon systems and training devices. The confounding is however reversible. The data can be reanalyzed to determine the effects of amount of practice on proficiency. That was done in a comparison of media for tank-gunnery training. Rose, Wheaton, Leonard, Fingerman, and Boycan (1976) trained groups using a subcaliber and a laser device to various criteria on Task A, performed analyses of amounts and kinds of practice, and concluded, "Performance during transfer was unaffected by the type of device on which training occurred. The reported effects were related to amount rather than kind of training" (p. 25).

D. Weapon System Error Masks Training Effects

Research by Fingerman and Wheaton (1978) indicated that with correct sight pictures, tank crews missed targets 2 times in 10. The effect of weapon system error is to lower the maximum possible scores for the compared groups and to underestimate percentage transfer when certain formulas are used. Assume, for example, that a T (transfer or device) group and a C (conventional or control) group each fired 100 rounds on Task B. Assume also that the T group got 80 hits and the C group 70. Assume finally that the following formula is used to estimate transfer:

$$\text{Percentage transfer} = \frac{T - C}{\text{Max} - C} \times 100.$$

If 100 is used as the maximum possible score, the computation is:

$$\text{Percentage transfer} = \frac{80 - 70}{30} \times 100$$

$$= 33.$$

If the 100 maximum possible score is corrected for 20% misses due to weapon system error, however, the maximum possible score becomes 80, and the computation is:

$$\text{Percentage transfer} = \frac{80 - 70}{10} \times 100$$

$$= 100.$$

Device buyers should be wary of bottom lines that are easy to read. Whether a device were reported to yield 33% or 100% transfer might have opposite effects on purchase decisions.

Notice also that small proficiency increments due to training may be masked by weapon system error. In sustainment or refresher training with highly qualified tank crews, for example, only small proficiency increases would be expected. Such increases may be masked if their magnitude is less than that of the weapon system's error.

E. AMOUNT OF PRACTICE IS INSUFFICIENT TO
   AFFECT PROFICIENCY

The effectiveness of the UCOFT as a sustainment (proficiency-maintaining) medium was examined during an operational test (Kuma & McConville, 1982). All tank crews in each group had passed a live-fire qualification test before the experiment began. Plans called for making available the UCOFT to each tank crew in the test group and alternative media to each tank crew in the comparison group for about 2.5 h during each of 3 months. Had test conditions permitted objective comparison of the two groups' performance, the most likely outcome would have been no difference, because 2.5 h practice per month is unlikely to have significant effects on the performance of fully qualified crews. Notice also that when sustainment rather than initial learning is at issue, comparisons of a device and its parent weapon system leave a fundamental question unanswered: How does the device compare, as a sustainment medium, to no training? Answering this question requires a no-training control group. The reasoning here is that one should want to know how the device compares with a no-cost alternative (no training) rather than with a high-cost alternative (tanks), whose infeasibility for widespread use as a sustainment medium is already known.

F. CEILING OR FLOOR EFFECTS MASK
   DIFFERENCES BETWEEN GROUPS

Ceiling effects occur when both groups score high in performing Task B. Little variance and therefore no statistically significant differences in Task B performance can be observed. This can happen because training on Task A was extremely effective, because all subjects were proficient on Task B before training on Task A began, or for any reason that made performance of Task B easy. In evaluations of maintenance trainers, for example, both groups of subjects typically use technical manuals or other step-by-step procedures documents while performing Task B. The result often is that training effects are overpowered by the effects of using the manuals, and both groups score at or near the maximum on the Task B test. Although scoring at or near the maximum may be desirable from a training standpoint, doing so is not desirable in evaluations of training. Ceiling effects mask proficiency differences between device and weapon system groups, either of which may have been superior had Task B been more difficult.

Floor effects are the opposite of ceiling effects. They also seem less common. (I can think of no army training research in which they occurred.) Floor effects might happen, however, if both groups scored low on Task B. No variance and therefore no differences in Task B performance would be observed between groups who used the device and the weapon system for practicing Task A. This could happen if the amount, relevance, or both, of Task A training were insufficient to affect Task B proficiency. Floor effects, like ceiling effects, would mask the merits of device and weapon system training, either of which could be superior had more practice on Task A been given.

G. MEASUREMENT OF TASK B PERFORMANCE IS UNRELIABLE

Reliability refers to the dependability or consistency with which a test yields scores that distinguish between superior and inferior performances (Gagné, 1954). Test reliability may be examined by measuring the extent to which scores on half the items predict scores on the other half, as was done by Powers *et al.* (1975) in examining the contribution of live fire to tank-gunnery proficiency. Reliability also may be examined by correlating scores obtained from repeated administrations of the test. Reliability is important in Task B testing because without it measurement cannot be valid (Popham, 1981). Reliability also is important because it affects the power of statistical tests: Power is the probability of detecting true differences between groups; that is, of correctly rejecting the null hypothesis. Power decreases with decreased measurement reliability, because of increased error variance.

Whether analyses separate from those used to estimate the reliability of mean differences are necessary for examining the reliability of Task B measurement is moot. If significant differences in Task B performance are found as the result of practice with the device and practice with the weapon system or no practice, then one might assume that Task B measurement must have been reliable or that treatment effects were strong enough to overcome the effect of unreliable measurement. In either case, measurement reliability becomes unimportant. A question arises, however, when no differences are found: To what extent were the findings of no difference the result of unreliable measurement? Discussions of the effects of reliability, error variance, power, and intervention strength in device evaluation reports for the military would, I believe, lead to explanations other than equal effectiveness for finding no differences. Reminders along the following lines seem warranted: A finding of no statistically significant difference between the performance of groups trained with weapon systems and groups trained with devices does not mean that no differences exist. It means that if differences existed, they were not sufficiently reliable to meet the criteria for statistical significance. An unreliable difference is just as likely to result from unreliable measurement and other error sources as from the absence of an actual difference, and even more likely in cases of poorly controlled field experiments. Justifying recommendations to substitute devices for weapon systems in training on grounds of finding no proficiency differences is therefore unwarranted. Such recommendations may be justifiable on grounds of safety, cost, or both; but questions of effectiveness always remain open.

Researchers seldom report the reliability of Task B measurement in evaluations of army training devices. Powers et al. (1975) were exceptions. They reported that measuring live-fire performance in their experiment was no more accurate than "random guessing" (p. 26). Authors of other tank-gunnery device evaluations (e.g., Deason et al., 1982; Kuma & McConville, 1982; Racine et al., 1977) did not address the issue of measurement reliability.

H. Inappropriate Analyses Are Used to Estimate Transfer

Researchers use various analyses to estimate transfer. Racine et al. (1977), for example, used chi-square tests with tank-gunnery data. Bessemer (1978) noted however that the data could not be aggregated in a contingency table. The chi-square analyses therefore seem inappropriate.

Kuma and McConville (1982) reported correlation coefficients between training and test scores. Mudge (1939) and Gagne (1954), however, cautioned against using correlation for estimating transfer. High positive correlations between Task A and Task B scores do not establish the causal link necessary for demonstrating transfer. They simply suggest that similar skills or abilities were used in performing Tasks A and B.

1. Transfer Formulas

Transfer formulas also are sometimes misused. They often are used to summarize the results of training device evaluations. Percentage transfer is computed using a T (transfer) or an E (experimental) group score, and a C

(control or conventional) group score. The T or E group learns Task A using the device. The C group uses an alternative to the device; the weapon system, for example. Mean scores for the compared groups are variously combined in one or more of four kinds of formulas.

One kind of transfer formula references the score of the T group against the score of the C group. An example for cases in which a higher score means better performance than a lower score is percentage transfer = $(T - C/C)$ (100). The distribution of percentage transfer computed with this formula is asymmetric, ranging from plus infinity to minus 100. The formula is therefore more suitable for negative than for positive transfer (Murdock, 1957).

A second kind of formula references the T group's score to the maximum possible gain. An example for cases in which a higher score means better performance than a lower score is percentage transfer = $(C - T/C - \text{Max})$ (100). The distribution of percentage transfer is here again asymmetric but this time ranges from plus 100 to minus infinity.

A third kind of formula was proposed by Murdock (1957), who noted the problems with the other two kinds. In response to a personal communication from Harriet Foster, who wrote a review of transfer formulas with Gagné and Crowley (Gagné, Foster, & Crowley, 1948), Murdock sought

> a measure of transfer independent of the raw score units in the sense that the standard deviation is independent of raw score units. . . . a transfer formula . . . such that positive and negative transfer were symmetrical, and . . . [with identical] absolute value of the upper and lower limits (preferably, of course, 100%) (p. 322).

Murdock's solution was (when higher scores mean better performance) percentage transfer = $(T - C/T + C)$ (100).

The formulas mentioned thus far yield estimates of relative amounts of transfer. The formulas for those estimates can be expanded or otherwise changed to reflect the cost (in number of trials, amount of training, or dollars) of the T and C groups' attaining given levels of proficiency with the weapon system. Doing so yields the fourth kind of formula: efficiency or cost effectiveness. Dividing percentage transfer into or by dollars, for example, yields price per percentage transfer or percentage transfer per dollar. Such metrics are attractive because they seem analogous to unit prices and provide bottom lines that are easy to read. They also provide means for extrapolating prices and savings from one or several studies to larger samples; an MOS, for example, or an entire military service. Efficiency or cost-effectiveness metrics may be analogous to, but are by no means identical to, unit pricing in supermarkets. They are analogous in that price in both cases may be divided by the amount of what you buy. They are not identical, however, because ounces, pounds, and other weights and measures used by supermarkets are absolute: A pound is a pound irrespective of what is measured. This is not the case with amount of transfer, which is relative: It is unlikely that 20% transfer to Weapon System A will be the same as 20% transfer to Weapon System B, or for that matter to Weapon System A measured at another time.

Lawrence described several transfer efficiency measures in 1954. Provenmire and Roscoe more recently (1971) introduced the transfer effectiveness ratio (TER), with later variations by Roscoe (1971a, 1971b) in response to personal communications from Beverly Williges, Isaac Harper, and others. The TER takes into account the amount of training (number of trials or amount of time) for the T and C groups to reach given levels of proficiency. The ratio provides estimates of the savings, in trials or time, to be realized by using a training device before learning to operate a weapon system. It is computed by dividing the number of simulator trials or amount of time for the T group into the difference between the numbers of weapon system trials or amount of time for the C and T groups; for example, (WS trials for C) − (WS trials for T)/(Sim. trials for T).

> A ratio of 1.0 indicates that the training device is as efficient as the actual device (weapon system); a ratio greater than 1.0 indicates that the training device is more efficient; and a ratio of less than 1.0 indicates that the training device is less efficient (Holman, 1979, p. 17).

A TER of 1.0 results from any combination of weapon system and simulator trials or time for T that equals the weapon system trials or time for C. Assume, for example, that a C group required 20 trials with the weapon system to reach criterion. If, to reach that same criterion, one T group using Device A required 18 simulator and 2 weapon system trials, or another T group using Device B required 2 simulator and 18 weapon system trials, a TER of 1.0 would result. Device A and Device B would be rated identically efficient to the weapon system. Device A and Device B also would be equally efficient by definition. This seems counterintuitive, inasmuch as the number of weapon system trials required after practice with Device B was nine times the number required after practice with Device A.

The first three kinds of formulas mentioned above were designed to achieve comparability among the amounts of transfer observed in different experiments (Gagné et al., 1948; Murdock, 1957). The fourth kind was designed to achieve comparability, not only with respect to amount of transfer, but also in terms of efficency. Comparability may be useful for basic research purposes. In research with weapon systems, however, the benefits of comparability are less clear. Results might be aggregated across studies and extrapolated to estimate overall savings and other general effects of simulation. But doing so may not be a good idea. The disadvantages of using transfer formulas should in any event be weighed against the advantage of comparability.

One problem with transfer formulas is as implied earlier: Their use invites "spurious quantitative reasoning" (Gagné et al., 1948, p. 98). The numerator in each of the four kinds of formulas discussed above is the mean difference between the experimental and control groups' scores. If that difference is unreliable, then using it as a numerator in computing percentage transfer or efficiency seems unwarranted. The numerator in such cases should be zero. Researchers sometimes overlook that issue when reporting efficiency or percentage transfer. The reliabilities of the mean differences used as numerators in nearly 100 TERs for the Chinook flight simulator, for example, were not reported. How to interpret such results is equivocal, as is the justification for using them in extrapolations of savings and other device effects.

The use of difference scores in transfer formulas presents additional problems: Difference scores do not reflect where trainees began or where they finished, and they compound the unreliability of the two scores from which they are derived. Comparisons of gains for device and conventionally trained groups also provide no indication of how much, if any, of the gain was ascribable to training.

Comparing the measures provided by transfer formulas with the raw scores from which they are derived, Gagné et al. (1948) noted, "The utilization of raw score values to express transfer is a procedure which has a number of advantages, chief among which is precision of meaning" (p. 98). Precision of meaning is, I believe, considerably more important than comparability. Sacrificing one for the other is, however, unnecessary. Researchers who use transfer and efficiency formulas are free to perform conventional analyses of raw scores as well. The reasons for not doing so are unclear.

III. REDUCING SOURCES OF ERROR

Many of the sources of error discussed in this chapter are the result of practical constraints; large numbers of subjects may not be available, for example, and logistics often preclude random assignment. The authors of the reports cited earlier probably had to make concessions in experimental design based on the availability of manpower and other resources. The point made by Horst, Tallmadge, and Wood (1975) is nevertheless well taken: Practical constraints may prevent evaluators from doing controlled experiments, "but many of the problems in current evaluation practices could be avoided with little or no increase in cost or effort" (p. 2).

The first two sources of error discussed earlier can be avoided by issuing and enforcing command directives: The choice between using small or large numbers of soldiers in a device evaluation usually is a matter of the priority placed by unit commanders on evaluation relative to other things soldiers could be doing; and the benefits of randomly assigning subjects or crews (or

Table 1

Schedule for a Transfer Experiment

	Weeks						
	1, 2, 3, 4		5, 6, 7, 8			9, 10, 11, 12	
Device group	Test Task B	Train Task A	Test Task B	Train Task A	Test Task B	Train Task A	Test Task B
Convent'l group	Test Task B	Train Task A	Test Task B	Train Task A	Test Task B	Train Task A	Test Task B
Control group	Test Task B		Test Task B		Test Task B		Test Task B

higher echelon units) to the compared groups should in nearly all cases override maintaining unit integrity in device evaluations. Differing command emphasis for the compared groups also can be avoided by directive.

Other sources of error can be avoided by using an experimental design in which each of the compared groups is tested on Task B before and after various amounts of training on Task A, as shown in Table 1. (The amount of training can be adjusted proportionally for conventional courses that are longer or shorter than 12 weeks.) Although amount of training in this example is given as training time, it also could be expressed as number of trials. In tank gunnery, for example, one might use number of target appearances, that is, opportunities to hit targets. The object in either case is for the device and conventional groups to get an amount of training that is equal to the amount usually given in conventional training and for all groups to be tested after one third, two thirds, and all the usual amount of training. The control group receives no training but is tested at the same times as the other groups. Groups can, of course, be added if more than one device is to be compared to conventional and no training.

The design outlined in Table 1 makes amount of training an investigated effect and thus separates it from the effects of training media. Each group receives various amounts of training, so a hedge is provided against ceiling and floor effects. Because the design permits establishing causal relations between learning Task A and relearning or performing Task B, one need not use correlation or other inappropriate analyses for estimating transfer.

Using the design in Table 1 does not guarantee realiability in measuring Task B performance. It does, however, permit examining the reliability of Task B measurement, because repeated measures of each subject's Task B performance are obtained.[2] If a provision is added to the design for alternating or randomizing the order of testing subjects, then systematic effects of differences in test conditions for the compared groups also can be avoided. Such effects can be avoided by using alternatives to service firing that avoid problems associated with the weapon system's error exceeding training effects. The alternatives will be addressed later.

Repeated-measures analysis of variance can be used on the scores obtained from the design on Table 1. The problems associated with difference scores and relative measures, which characterize transfer and efficiency formulas, are thus avoided. The results of such analyses will show whether statistically significant differences occurred as the result of kinds of training independent of amounts, amounts of training independent of kinds, and kinds and amounts of training in interaction. Simple effects tests also can be performed to determine between which amounts of training, and between which kinds of training, differences did and did not occur. The control group's test scores provide estimates of amounts of proficiency due to taking tests without training; and the initial Task B scores can be used to re-form groups that are found to differ before training begins.

The methods for reducing error discussed thus far can easily be implemented in the short term. Two problems remain, however, that require long-term solutions: estimating proficiency on unsafe tasks and developing reliable Task B tests.

A. Estimating Proficiency on Unsafe Tasks

A problem arises in transfer designs such as outlined in Table 1, where untrained persons serve as a control group. The problem is, of course, that safety considerations rule out service-fire testing of untrained persons. This problem has no fully satisfactory solution. This does not mean that proficiency assessment for unsafe tasks should be abandoned. It means, rather, that part-task knowledge and skill tests should be used.

Nearly all unsafe tasks have component skills and knowledge that not only can be safely tested but also provide strong indications about the extent to which the unsafe tasks have been mastered. These facts provide the rationale for "synthetic performance testing" (Osborn & Ford, 1976). Component skills in tank gunnery, for example, can be tested using dry or subcaliber firing and sight-picture photography. Mastering component skills and knowledge may not be sufficient for proficiency in operating the

---

[2]The points raised by Poulton (1982) seem relevant to choosing between within-subjects and independent-groups designs. Advantages of the within-subjects designs include smaller numbers of subjects and increased opportunities for examining test reliability. These advantages and the benefits of using a no-training control group should be considered in weighing Poulton's objections to within-subjects designs.

weapon system, but strong logical cases can be made for their necessity. Tank gunners, for example, would be hard pressed to hit targets without first being able to distinguish between correct and incorrect sight pictures. Part-task knowledge and skill tests are defensible in light of psychometric, as well as safety, considerations. Dry firing, subcaliber firing, and sight-picture photography in tank gunnery, for example, can be used for testing that is more reliable and therefore potentially more valid than service firing. The reason for this involves relations among test length, reliability, and validity, which I shall now summarize.

B. DEVELOPING RELIABLE TASK B TESTS

Test reliability increases with the number of test items and with standardized administration. Service-fire tests for tank gunnery are too short and unstandardized to be reliable. The qualification test for M1 (Abrams) crews in the United States, for example, consists of only 10 target engagements (or items) and is fired on several different ranges. The shortness of service-fire tests derives from the high price of 105mm ammunition (about $400 per round), fuel, and other requirements for live firing. The lack of standardization results from variations in terrain and attendant safety considerations among the places where service firing is done. Even without these constraints, the use of service-fire tests in device evaluations seems contraindicated: Preliminary analyses have been done on 60 soldiers' scores on a 15-round service-fire test and the same 60 soldiers' scores on a 15-"round" dry-fire test (Boldovici et al., 1986). The targets were the same in both tests, and all shots were photographed (remote video for service fire, and through-sight 35mm for dry fire). Split half reliability, as estimated by Cronbach's alpha, was about .60 for service fire and .90 for dry fire.

The alternatives to service firing are device-mediated testing and dry or subcaliber firing of weapon systems. Verbal (not necessarily written) testing also should be considered. These alternatives to service firing have many advantages. Their low cost permits designing longer tests that will be more reliable and potentially more valid than service-fire tests. The alternatives also are safer than service-fire testing. Adverse effects on standardization due to terrain variations are therefore reduced, and the use of no-training control groups and of pretests with novices becomes feasible.

The alternatives also seem better suited than service firing for measuring specific training effects; they curtail or eliminate the effects of round-to-round dispersion and of vibration and heat (e.g., "tube droop") on main-gun accuracy. Permanent records of lay error also are more easily generated with devices, dry fire, and subcaliber fire than with service fire.

Alternatives to service fire have two characteristics whose effects need to be determined. One charcteristic is that devices can be programmed to provide test takers no indication about whether the targets were hit or missed. The same characteristic inheres in dry-fire testing. Learning effects due to test taking may therefore be smaller with dry fire and appropriately programmed devices than with subcaliber fire. Whether those effects will be smaller or larger with service fire is uncertain, given the imperfect relation between hitting targets and aiming.

Measurement sensitivity is the second characteristic of alternatives to live-fire testing that warrants investigation. Accuracy in tank gunnery, for example, has traditionally been scored hit or miss with no gradations in between. The statistical limits thus placed on variance and reliability may mask between-group differences in accuracy. Permanent records of lay error, numerical for devices and photographic for dry fire, permit accuracy measurement that is more sensitive and therefore potentially more reliable and valid than hit–miss scoring.

Reliability in testing does not, of course, guarantee validity. The criterion problem notwithstanding, alternatives to service-fire testing do have characteristics that threaten validity. One suspects, for example, that master gunners would do less well on a device-mediated test than would persons who had mastered the device without service-fire experience. This suspicion is supported by the research of Weitz and Adler (1973) and by conversations with master gunners, who need familiarization training before they can score high on tests with tank-gunnery devices. Dry-fire and subcaliber tests, which are conducted using tanks, eliminate differences between training and testing media but permit getting hits in ways that might not be possible using service fire. Ascertaining the range to the target, for example, is unnecessary in dry and subcaliber firing. Dry fire also permits ambushing moving targets, that is, laying the gun in front of the target and firing when the target crosses the aiming reticle, rather than tracking the target as is necessary for using automatic lead in service firing. The alternatives also seem less likely than service firing to cause flinching and other responses that are incompatible with hitting targets (D. F. Haggard, personal communication, August 1986).

Improvements undoubtedly are needed in device-mediated, dry-fire, and subcaliber tests. Given the need for measurement and the high costs and other disadvantages of service-fire testing, however, there seems little choice but to act on Gagné's (1954) advice: "The concepts of reliability and validity are well known to psychologists. They appear to be applicable without change or reservation to the measurement of performance by means of a training device" (p. 99).

IV. REPORTING

Hawkridge, Campeau, and Trickett (1970) present excellent guidance for writing evaluation reports. Some issues related to the spirit of evaluation reporting, however, warrant elaboration. The issues involve valid inference, parsimony, balance, and precision.

A. VALID INFERENCE

Practical constraints and other factors undoubtedly cause compromises in experimental designs. Neither the constraints nor the designs, however, justify invalid inference. If, for example, practical constraints prevent using a no-training or an irrelevant-training control group, research may be conducted in which the effects of device and weapon system training are compared. Such research may provide little or no basis for causal inference, however. Attribution of "training effectiveness" to either treatment may therefore be unwarranted. The same is true for intervention (pre–post) designs that do not use a no-training control group.

B. PARSIMONY

Parsimony in evaluation reporting suggests considering all reasonable-appearing causes of obtained results. What, for example, are the suspected effects of variables other than device or weapon system use that may have produced unreliable mean differences? Given the suspected causes and effects, which causes can be discounted? Of the causes remaining, which seem most likely to have produced the effect? An equal-time (or space) criterion might serve as a rule of thumb, and main findings should perhaps be redefined. Consider, for example, evaluations that show no difference between a device and a weapon system in their effects on proficiency, and in which measurement of live-fire performance is no better than random guessing (e.g., Powers *et al.*, 1975). Should the main finding be that no differences were found or that the research produced results that were no better than guessing?

The equal-time criterion is important in written reports. It is also important in oral reports such as briefings. Written reports provide permanent records of their authors' thinking—thinking that can be analyzed in retrospect and at leisure by better or worse thinkers. Written reports are, in effect, stationary targets. Not so with briefings. They move quickly, and their analysis in retrospect and at leisure is difficult because of their agility. Time pressures may force briefers to focus on main findings while giving short shrift to causes and effects of error. The recommendation here is nevertheless as it was for written reporting: Give at least equal time to possible causes of evaluation results other than experimental manipulations, and consider redefining main findings.

C. BALANCE

The demand for efficiency measures, cost-effectiveness estimates, and other bottom lines that are easy to read seems unlikely to diminish. Evaluators should therefore consider supplementing efficiency estimates with conventional analyses of raw scores. The significance of mean proficiency differences between groups who use devices and weapon systems in training should be reported, as should the significance of differences between those groups and a no-training control group.

As for cost effectiveness, Fischoff's (1977) advice seems appropriate: When opposing points of view can be identified, at least two cost-effectiveness analyses should be performed, one by each of the opposing camps. Such a practice would reveal differences, not only between cost estimates, but perhaps more importantly between evaluators' thinking about factors that influence cost and effectiveness.

Balance in device evaluation reporting also suggests acknowledging that transfer and efficiency estimates do not tell the whole story. Other factors include effect size, numbers of persons affected by proposed substitutions, generalization, retention, safety during initial transfer trials, and possible crutch effects. Safety issues and crutch effects seem unduly neglected.

One advantage of simulators and other training devices is that they allow practice that would be unsafe with weapon systems. A disadvantage is that "dissimilarities between the [device and the tank] in position, appearance, and function of controls and indicators, and in task coverage, may create safety hazards during initial trials on the tank after practice using the [device]" (Kuma & McConville, 1982, p. F-4). Many training devices, especially those in prototype or other early stages, have characteristics that promote unsafe learning. The absence of turret rings in tank-gunnery devices, for example, may be at odds with learning not to balance oneself by grasping turret rings in tanks. (Doing so could result in losing fingers.) The absence of negative consequences for improperly loading or standing behind the main gun in a new tactical trainer also may promote unsafe behavior in tanks. And the use of "canned" fire commands in a new gunnery device, coupled with a scoring system that places a premium on speed, may promote learning to fire before the command to do so is given. Transferring this behavior to a tank might injure the loader. Safety problems during initial trials with the weapon system can be reduced by warning trainees about potential hazards. A better solution might be for teams of subject-matter experts and behavioral scientists to analyze what will be or is being learned with new devices and to recommend changes for improved safety during initial trials with the weapon systems. Solutions, however, require acknowledging that problems exist. Current army regulations require that training devices be inspected and certified safe to operate. No requirement exists, however, for identifying unsafe habits that might be promoted by device-mediated practice.

Crutch effects are closely related to safety during initial transfer trials:

> Performance during training can usually be improved through effective presentation of "knowledge of results," for example, through informing the learner regarding the correctness of the way he is operating the trainer. In some situations, however, such information may be used as a crutch, and may result in reducing the trainer's effectiveness in preparing the learner for the operational situation, where immediate "knowledge of results" information may not be available (Bilodeau, 1952, p. iii).

To the extent that soldiers learn to rely on stimuli that are present in simulators and absent in situ, performance breakdowns can be expected. Hughes, Paulsen, Brooks, and Jones (1978), for example, reported performance decrements on withdrawal of a predictor beam used for teaching a weapons-delivery task. One wonders whether similar decrements will occur during identifying vehicles in combat. In training for combat-vehicle identification by viewing slides and filmstrips, are soldiers learning to rely on stimulus characteristics (brightness, hue, detail, angle of regard) that may be different from those that will be encountered in combat? Similar concerns seem warranted for many of the characteristics of tank-gunnery training devices; kill indicators, for example, that change a tank's color when it is hit; color coding of threat priorities; and printed and auditory commendations for hitting targets. A trend seems to have developed in which admonitions to provide feedback and motivation are used to justify bell-and-whistle features in training devices. The analogy with increasing the marketability of baby food by adding sugar is hard to resist. Decisions to pay for such features should be tempered by considering that motivation is only important if it affects learning or performance and that conditions exist under which "feedback" may (a) retard or have no effect on acquisition and (b) facilitate acquisition while retarding or having no effect on transfer.

Some of the problems associated with crutch effects in weapon system training can be solved by selective improvements in device "fidelity," that is, by eliminating from devices those stimuli that seem likely to facilitate acquisition and to retard transfer. Others can be solved by designing instruction to counteract crutch effects. Analyses in either event are needed to identify differences between what is learned with devices and what is necessary for operating weapon systems and to identify potentially undesirable effects of those differences.

D. PRECISION

One way to improve evaluation reporting is through precision in describing what we did. The precision-imprecision continuum is anchored at one end by statements such as "counted the number of hits over 10 blocks of 5 trials each" and at the other end by "evaluated a training device." Between these extremes are other variously imprecise abstractions such as "evaluated practice effects," "measured accuracy," and "measured effectiveness." The abstractions are sometimes useful; in writing about the results of several evaluations in a review article, for example. But in a report about a particular experiment, the abstractions are at best distracting and at worst misleading. They are distracting because careful readers are forced to translate words like "accuracy" and "effectiveness" into the operations that were actually performed. The abstractions are misleading because less careful readers may not go through any translation process at all: The "effectiveness" of devices becomes incorporated as a fact with little or no understanding of what caused what. Bob Glaser's comment at a 1985 North Atlantic Treaty Organization symposium on transfer is well taken (I paraphrase): Having measured the incidence of measles, we should resist the urge to write reports about health.

V. RECOMMENDATIONS

Eliminating all sources of error in device evaluations probably is impossible. Experimental designs such as the one outlined in Table 1 would, however, reduce the sources of error discussed earlier and might thereby increase our confidence in evaluation results. Confidence in evaluations of devices as media for weapon system training also might increase if evaluators would:

1. Use the sources of error discussed in this chapter as a partial checklist for designing experiments and for interpreting their results. I emphasize the word "partial" because the sources of error discussed here are only the common ones that I have observed in evaluations of tank gunnery and other training devices. Campbell (1957) and Horst et al. (1975) have presented more comprehensive treatments of causes and effects of error than mine.

2. Be circumspect in interpreting the results of transfer experiments for use by the military. Treat findings of no difference in proficiency after practice with weapon systems and devices with caution, and acknowledge that such findings frequently result from factors other than those under investigation. My recommendation is to assume, regardless of evaluation results, that diferences in training media and programs do produce differences in kinds or amounts of psychomotor skills. Failure to find such differences is more likely due to unreliable measurement and other error sources than to the absence of differences. Assuming otherwise requires the additional assumption that the research was adequate in terms of sampling and measurement.

3. Shift the research emphasis from questions about the inherent superiority of devices and weapon systems to questions such as How much and what kinds of transfer are produced by various amounts and kinds of practice? Identify the conditions under which transfer is and is not affected.
4. Document, in language understandable by laymen, various explanations of obtained results. Authors might, for example:
   a. Report the separate and interactive effects of amounts and kinds of training and the reliabilities of observed differences.
   b. Report the reliability of the tests used to estimate Task B proficiency and mention the effects of reliability on validity and power.
   c. Perform power tests, when no differences among groups' Task B proficiency are observed, and answer the question Given the number of subjects used in this experiment and the variance among their scores, what was the probability of detecting proficiency differences that may have existed among the groups?
   d. Remind readers of limits on the generalizability of reported results imposed by the use of tests that may be neither comprehensive nor exhaustive of the Task B item domain and that may not have addressed aspects of behavior upon which operation of weapon systems depends: safety considerations, for example, and long-term retention, and generalization to conditions other than those under which Task B testing took place.
   e. Explain, with respect to weapon system and device-mediated training, that findings of no difference and declarations of equal effectiveness are two separate matters.

ACKNOWLEDGMENTS

I thank Bill Osborn and Steve Sabat for the time they have spent listening to and shaping the thoughts in this chapter.

REFERENCES

Bessemer, D. W. (1978). *Observations on the TCATA evaluation of .50 caliber subcaliber devices for tank gunnery training* [Review of Caliber .50 subcaliber training devices for 105mm main gun tanks]. Unpublished manuscript. U.S. Army Research Institute, Fort Knox.

Bilodeau, E. A. (1952). *A further study of the effects of target size and goal attainment upon the development of response accuracy.* San Antonio, TX: US Air Force Human Resources Research Center.

Boldovici, J. A., Kraemer, R. E., & Lampton, D. R. (1986). [Evaluation of a videodisk gunnery trainer]. Unpublished raw data.

Campbell, D. T. (1957). Factors relevant to the validity of experiments in social settings. *Psychological Bulletin, 54,* 297–312.

Deason, P., Robinson, M., & Terrell, G. (1982). *Guns over Boise, Snake River shoot-out phase.* White Sands Missile Range, NM: US Army TRADOC Systems Analysis Activity.

Fingerman, P. W., & Wheaton, G. R. (1978). *A preliminary investigation of weapon-system dispersion and crew marksmanship* (Tech. Rep. No. 78-B5). Alexandria, VA: U.S. Army Research Institute.

Fischoff, B. (1977). *The art of cost-benefit analysis.* McLean, VA: Decisions and Designs, Inc.

Gagné, R. M. (1954). Training devices and simulators: Some research issues. *American Psychologist, 9,* 95-107.

Gagné, R. M., Foster, H., & Crowley, M. E. (1948). The measurement of transfer of training. *) sychological Bulletin, 45,* 97-130.

Hawkridge, D. G., Campeau, P. L., & Trickett, P. K. (1970). *Preparing evaluation reports: A guide for authors* (Monograph No. 6). Washington, DC: American Institutes for Research.

Holman, G. L. (1979). *Training effectiveness of the CH-47 flight simulator* (Research Report No. 1209). Alexandria, VA: U.S. Army Research Institute.

Horst, D. P., Talmadge, G. K., & Wood, C. T. (1975). *A practical guide to measuring project impact on student achievement* (Contract No. DEC-0-73-6662). Washington, DC: U.S. Department of Health, Education, and Welfare.

Hughes, R. G., Paulsen, J., Brooks, R., & Jones, W. (1978). Visual cue manipulation in a simulated air-to-surface weapons delivery task. *Proceedings of the Eleventh NTEC-Industry Conference.* Orlando, FL: Naval Training Equipment Center.

Kuma, D., & McConville, L. (1982). *Independent evaluation report for M1/M60 series Unit Conduct of Fire Training (UCOFT)* (TRADOC ACN 39373). Fort Knox, KY: U.S. Army Armor Center.

Lawrence, D. H. (1954). The evaluation of training and transfer programs in terms of efficiency measures. *Journal of Psychology, 38,* 367-382.

Mudge, E. L. (1939). Transfer of training in chemistry. *Johns Hopkins University Studies in Education,* No. 6.

Murdock, B. B. (1957). Transfer designs and formulas. *Psychological Bulletin, 54,* 313-326.

Orlansky, J. (1985). *The cost-effectiveness of military training.* Brussels: Paper presented at the NATO Symposium on the Military Value and Cost-effectiveness of Training.

Osborn, W. C., & Ford, J. P. (1976) *Research on methods of synthetic performance testing* (FR-CDL-76-1). Alexandria, VA: Human Resources Research Organization.

Popham, W. J. (1981). *Modern educational measurement.* Englewood Cliffs, NJ: Prentice-Hall.

Poulton, E. C. (1982). Influential companions: Effects of one strategy on another in within-subjects designs of cognitive psychology. *Psychological Bulletin, 91,* 678-690.

Powers, T. R., McCluskey, M. R., Haggard, D. F., Boycan, G. G., & Steinheiser, F., Jr. (1975). *Determination of the contribution of live firing to weapons proficiency* (FR-CDC-75-1). Alexandria, VA: Human Resources Research Organization.

Provenmire, H. K., & Roscoe, S. N. (1971). An evaluation of ground-based flight trainers in routine primary flight training. *Human Factors, 13*(2), 109-116.

Racine, A. E., Humphrey, F. T., Harper, M. V., Booher, C. F., Smith, J. L., Jr., & Lutgert, D. A. (1977). *Caliber .50 subcaliber training devices for 105 mm main gun tanks* (Test Rep. No. FM 376). Fort Hood, TX: TRADOC Combined Arms Test Activity.

Roscoe, S. N. (1971a). Incremental transfer effectiveness. *Human Factors, 13,* 561-567.

Roscoe, S. N. (1971b). A little more on incremental transfer effectiveness. *Human Factors, 14,* 363-364.

Rose, A. M., Wheaton, G. R., Leonard, R. L., Jr., Fingerman, P. W., & Boycan, G. G. (1976). *Evaluation of two tank gunnery trainers* (Research Memorandum 76-19). Alexandria, VA: U.S. Army Research Institute.

Weitz, J., & Adler, S. (1973). The optimal use of simulation. *Journal of Applied Psychology, 58,* 219-224.

Wickham, J. A. (1983). Go the extra mile. *Soldiers, 38*(10), 6-10.

CHAPTER 10

Methodological Approaches For Simulator Evaluations

ANDREW ROSE
ROBERT EVANS
GEORGE WHEATON

I. INTRODUCTION

The armed forces of the United States rely on training devices and simulators as indispensable components of training. The design of training devices should, in theory, be based on detailed and precise information about the training requirements to be met, physical and functional characteristics needed to satisfy requirements, intended use of the device, and its effectiveness and cost. In practice, however, unavoidable logistic demands during training device acquisition make empirical tests of effectiveness difficult to conduct. As a necessary consequence, appraisals of a particular design, or competing design alternatives, are primarily analytic.

Formal analytic procedures, however, are inadequate or nonexistent. The bases on which device design decisions are made have not been clearly articulated, nor is it clear what kinds of data or levels of data specificity are needed to support such decisions. There is a need, therefore, for analytic procedures, applicable during both early and later stages of device acquisition, that permit prediction of the potential effectiveness of device designs.

In this chapter, four topics within the area of training device effectiveness are discussed. First, prescribed and actual evaluations of training system effectiveness are discussed. Second, the practical and theoretical problems characterizing these evaluations are addressed. Third, alternatives to transfer of training as criteria for training system effectiveness are presented. Fourth,

TRANSFER OF LEARNING

an emerging model for training system evaluations, the Device Effectiveness Forecast Technique (DEFT), is described.

II. PAST APPROACHES TO EVALUATING THE EFFECTIVENESS OF MILITARY SIMULATORS

A. THE LIFE CYCLE SYSTEM MANAGEMENT MODEL

To support the acquisition of cost-effective training devices, the U.S. Army has formalized a four-phase process linked to the Life Cycle System Management Model (LCSMM) of the parent materiel system (Carroll *et al.*, 1980; CORADCOM, 1980; Kane, 1981; Kinton, Inc., 1980). Kane and Holman (1982) provide an idealized description of the four phases of training device acquistion and the corresponding materiel development cycles.

During the first phase, Evaluation of Alternative System Concepts (EASC), several key decisions are made that will ultimately influence the design of training devices in important ways. Based on results of an initial training development study, for example, a training need statement is prepared that describes requirements for device-mediated training. Alternative training concepts are then considered in the course of selecting a best technical approach to meeting documented needs. These preliminary decisions about a device and its design are reflected in a concept formulation package and outline acquisition plan.

During the second phase, Demonstration and Validation (DVAL), the outline acquisition plan is updated and used to acquire an advanced development prototype, or breadboard training device. It is during this second phase that the breadboard is used to support a variety of empirical investigations. The results of these investigations constitute the update training development study, in which alternative training concepts are assessed and compared. The results serve to define the training device requirement and a final acquisition plan.

In the third phase, Full-Scale Engineering Development (FSED), the acquisition plan is implemented to obtain an engineering development prototype, or "brassboard" training device. At this stage in the acquisition process, training device design has been finalized. Production runs are imminent. Assuming that the brassboard device successfully passes various field test evaluations, the fourth or production phase of acquisition will begin.

The training device acquisition process has been briefly reviewed in order to make an important point. As described above, in each successive phase of acquisition, training device design decisions presumably are based on more detailed and precise information about training requirements to be met, physical and functional characteristics of a device needed to satisfy those requirements, use of a device, and its effectiveness and cost. Clearly, the intent of the formal acquisition process is to ensure that initially vague training concepts are translated into equipment that effectively and economically trains personnel. The appeal of a highly structured acquisition process is that many phases and steps are conceptually coherent, systematically raising design issues and then empirically resolving them.

B. Practical and Theoretical Problems

In practice, unavoidable logistic demands in the LCSMM and the training device acquisition process make it impossible to implement the model in its idealized form. As a consequence, the design of training devices continues to be fraught with difficulty. Constraints, for example, in the acquisition schedule imposed by development of the parent system often preclude empirical evaluations during the design and development process. If such an evaluation is conducted, it is usually too late in the acquisition process for the results to influence device design. Evaluations of a particular design or competing alternatives, therefore, are primarily judgmental. For several reasons, however, judgmental procedures are of questionable utility. There are few reliable and valid analytic tools. There is little research which would support their applications. In addition, there is not uniform agreement on what to base device design decisions. Nor is there agreement as to the kinds and levels of data needed to support such decisions.

C. Analytic Procedures

To date, only a handful of analytic methods and models have been developed that attempt to evaluate or predict the effectiveness of training devices. The objectives of these methods are to predict the performance of trainees, training time, training resource requirements, and transfer of training. Predictions are based on information about a training device and related system characteristics. There have been several recent reviews of these methods (e.g., Goldberg, 1986; Harris & Ford, 1983; Knerr, Nadler, & Dowell, 1984; Tufano & Evans, 1982). In a synthesis of these reviews, Goldberg (1986) identified six approaches to predicting training effectiveness:

Training Development Decision Support System (TDDSS)
HARDMAN Training Resources Requirements Analysis (TRRA)
Job Skills Education Program (JSEP) for Computer-based Instruction
Comparison-based prediction (CBP)
The Training Device Effectiveness (TRAINVICE) model

The Device Effectiveness Forecasting Technique (DEFT) model

The Training Development Decision Support System (Hawley & Fredrickson, 1983) is an automated model, designed to help determine what to train, where to train, and how to train. Based on Instructional Systems Development (ISD) methods, TDDSS can be used to help resolve design decisions, evaluate alternative training programs, and provide cost-benefit assessments. The software guides an analyst through three major analyses:

A function analysis, in which SMEs review job and task analysis data to generate a task list and to provide criticality estimates for each task

A task analysis, in which SMEs generate a task hierarchy and specify the skill requirements for each task

A learning requirement analysis, in which SMEs generate information regarding media selection and training delivery alternatives.

Algorithms convert these data and judgments into aggregate "effectiveness" estimates for each training program alternative. Further analyses provide information concerning resources required for each alternative, the costs associated with each, the "trainability" of the tasks, relative cost-benefits, and a final summary alternative selection. Thus, the overall TDDSS output is a recommendation of that training program which addresses the most critical training requirements and is within cost limits.

The TRRA component of HARDMAN (Dynamics Research Corporation, 1980) is used to estimate costs and resource requirements for training systems. It is essentially a comparison-based method, wherein "predecessor," "reference," and "baseline" systems are identified and training resource requirements are extrapolated. Training programs that are most closely related to the proposed system are identified, and the additional training requirements not present in the existing systems are identified and analyzed. Outputs are cost and effectiveness estimates for new or proposed training systems or devices, based on combining data from systems in use with judgments on the cost and effectiveness of the new components.

Training effectiveness analyses for computer-based instruction in JSEP (Kraft & Farr, 1984) are still undergoing development. The purpose of these analyses is to "obtain the optimum mix of site locations, hardware, software, and personnel to produce the highest achievement in a given period of time at selected Army posts in the Continental United States" (Goldberg, 1986, pp. 4-6).

Several procedures have been defined, including a classification system (used to define operational and functional constraints, define training configurations, and determine site-specific advantages and disadvantages for each design alternative), a cost analysis, and a training effectiveness analysis. The latter procedure is not specified beyond an outline of general required steps, leading to a data base for comparing alternative systems.

Comparison-based prediction (Klein Associates, 1985) is a technique that uses structured SMEs' opinions and data obtained from "similar" devices and systems. Inferences regarding the effectiveness of a device are made from the effectiveness of another similar device, while making adjustments for important differences. There are several potentially useful features of CBP. For example, it can be used without extensive data from the proposed devices; thus, it can be applied in the early stages of the development cycle. Also, predictions are derived from operational experiences: effectiveness of existing systems forms the basis for new system effectiveness estimates. However, there are several potential disadvantages. For example, much depends upon the availability of analogous systems and valid data on their training effectiveness.

First conceptualized by Wheaton, Fingerman, Rose, and Leonard (1976) and modified by several others subsequently (for reviews, see Tufano & Evans, 1982; Knerr *et al.,* 1984), TRAINVICE was an attempt to model transfer of training. Starting with descriptions of the training device and the parent equipment (e.g., an M1 tank), the various components of TRAIN-VICE estimate task commonality between a training device and parent equipment, learning deficit between training and operational tasks, physical and functional fidelity of the training device compared to the parent equipment, and the use of accepted training techniques and principles. The primary output of a TRAINVICE analysis is a "figure of merit," which is an estimate of the expected transfer of training between the training device and the parent equipment.

The Device Effectiveness Forecasting Technique (Rose & Wheaton, 1984a, 1984b) expands the conceptualization of training device/system effectiveness beyond transfer of training. This approach and its rationale are discussed later in this chapter.

The various reviews cited above provide extensive discussions of these methods. These will not be repeated here; rather, we discuss some critical issues that have arisen in the development of these models.

D. ISSUES IN THE DEVELOPMENT OF MODELS TO PREDICT DEVICE EFFECTIVENESS

The development of a predictive model to evaluate training devices may eventually eliminate, or at least minimize, costly empirical evaluations. In addition, such a model could be implemented early in the development cycle to assist training device planners in considering and assessing design changes. Such changes presently seem to be a function of cost considerations rather than effectiveness criteria. While this strategy may be acceptable, engineers and users should be cognizant of the training implications of such design changes.

Before evaluation models such as those cited earlier can be used effectively, a variety of issues must be resolved. Wheaton, Fingerman, Rose, and Leonard (1976) discussed many of these issues previously; however, 10 years later, many of the same concerns remain unresolved. The issues of major concern include: (a) input data—characteristics and requirements; (b) reliability—of single components and of a linear combination of components; and (c) validity—predictive. content, and construct.

1. Input Data

To accomplish an efficient and complete evaluation of a training device at any stage in its development, detailed information is required. Wheaton, Fingerman, Rose, and Leonard (1976) provided a discussion of the kinds and quality of data required to apply an effectiveness model. The kinds of data include: (a) the training objectives; (b) task analysis results for both the parent and training equipment; and (c) trainee characteristics. Currently, means for collecting these data and for making these data available to device designers and evaluators are inadequate.

2. Reliability

The development of a model to evaluate the effectiveness of a training device can be related to constructing a test. Therefore, many of the same psychometric principles apply. As in any test, a device effectiveness model will have systematic and random measurement error:

Scoring. A device evaluation model may be unreliable because a component value or an overall index depends heavily on the person applying it. This problem can be lessened when specific, objective criteria are provided for assigning values to components of a model.

Content. Unreliable measurement with a model, or individual components thereof, may stem from poor sampling of the content under consideration. In the case of a component, such as "functional characteristics analysis," the model designer may not have completely defined the dimension. The parameters included may represent an extremely small sample of the possible considerations.

This leads to another problem: Most of the models discussed earlier combine the values of each of the components into a single figure of merit. While the reliability of individual components can be determined rather easily, the linear combination of these measures is another matter. Each component essentially represents a measure from different domains. The reliability of samples of items from the same domain depends entirely on the average correlation among the samples, but this does not hold for samples of items from different domains. According to Nunnally (1967) the actual reliability of a linear combination would be determined by correlating alternative forms of the linear combination. When this is not possible, however, procedures exist to determine the reliability for linear combinations. This is an issue not previously discussed in relation to the evaluation models, but it probably should be examined in the future.

3. Validity

Simply stated, validity refers to the extent to which a model serves its purpose for a particular training device or several devices. According to Cronbach (1971), the generally accepted types of validity are:

Criterion-related (predictive) validity, which compares test scores, in this case values obtained from an evaluation model, or predictions made from them, with an external variable or criterion considered to provide a direct measure of the characteristics in question (e.g., transfer of training).

Content validity, which is evaluated by showing how well the content of the test, or in this context, the components of a model, sample the class of situations, or subject matter about which conclusions are drawn (i.e., training devices).

Construct validity, evaluated by investigating what the psychological qualities of a test measure; here, the concern is with the constructs or domains that each of the components of a model measures, as well as the construct that an aggregation of these components assesses. Construct validity is established by determining the degree to which certain explanatory concepts or constructs account for performance of a model as a whole.

III. CHARACTERIZING SIMULATOR EFFECTIVENESS

What is meant when a claim is made that a device or simulator is "effective?" Traditionally, effectiveness is expressed in terms of transfer of training. The rationale for transfer as *the* criterion is straightforward: Device 1 is more effective than Device 2 if, after completing training on each device, trainees who used Device 1 perform better (i.e., initial transfer) or achieve proficiency faster (i.e., rate of skill acquisition) on the operational task than trainees who used Device 2. As discussed below, although transfer is an important measure of effectiveness, it is not the only one. There are other measures of effectiveness that should be considered as well.

A. TRANSFER OF TRAINING

There are two important criticisms of a "transfer" rationale for device evaluation. First, some form of operational performance must be measured. This calls for an elaborate specification of "criterion performance," including such considerations as allowable individual trainee variation, control for measurement error, and alternative performance measures. Obviously, the more complex the operational task, the more difficult such specifications are to elaborate.

The second major criticism of the transfer rationale is that it is too restrictive: It ignores the time, cost, and effort associated with the actual accomplishment of training. To use an extreme example, suppose two devices demonstrate the same amount of transfer; however, trainees must spend 10 times longer practicing on Device 1 than on Device 2. Clearly, these devices are not equally effective except in the most general (transfer) sense.

Another way of stating this criticism is to argue that a training device could and should be viewed as part of the larger training program in which it is embedded. A device is effective if it reduces the total time, cost, and effort needed to bring trainees to operational readiness on parent equipment. This more global view is in contrast to the narrower transfer rationale, where device effectiveness is stated solely in terms of proficiency levels observed on parent equipment.

B. Other Effectiveness Criteria

If device evaluators were told that two devices produced equal transfer scores (or that it was impossible to measure operational performance), what else would they want to know about the devices? They might want to know what a trainee learns (or is supposed to learn) on each training device and its relevance to the operational task. In the example above, perhaps the extra time associated with Device 1 results from training more knowledge and skills than is possible with Device 2. Perhaps the extra time was spent training irrelevant knowledge and skills, a distinction that could have significant consequences for effectiveness. The evaluators also might want to know if what is taught is done so efficiently. Similarly, they might inquire about the efficiency with which the device prepares a trainee for the operational task. Both of these efficiency concepts would entail an examination of the device's instructional features. One can think of other kinds of information that the evaluators also would like to have. Each of these is considered below as a potential component of a criterion measure of device effectiveness.

1. Acquisition of Skills and Knowledge

During the training device acquisition process, device evaluators may face two problems: First, it is infeasible or impossible to obtain training or transfer data. Second, empirical transfer of training evaluations are conducted, but the alternative devices do not differ on transfer values. In the former case, evaluators would have to develop a surrogate measure or an estimate of "potential" transfer. In the latter case, they would have to develop different measures or estimates of effectiveness. In both cases, the evaluators could expand their appraisal to look at the *content* of training—*what* is taught and how *efficiently* it is taught.

The "what" of training, when viewed as a surrogate measure of transfer, is typically a measure of overlap between the training objectives and the operational performance objectives. An index, based on such overlap, would represent the amount of required knowledge and skills a trainee has learned (or conversely, still must learn when a trainee progresses to the parent equipment).

An assessment of the content and relevance of a training device is, or should be, part of the characterization of effectiveness. Content specification, in terms of a device-mediated learning objective, is obviously critical to a device designer/developer. It also is important to a training program evaluator in that it could serve as a surrogate measure when an empirical assessment of transfer is infeasible or impossible.

2. Acquisition Efficiency

Suppose two devices produce the same "amount" of transfer and both teach the same content. However, a trainee on one device takes 10 times as long to reach proficiency (i.e., to acquire the content) as does a trainee on another device. Clearly, when everything else is equal, the device that promoted more rapid learning is the more "effective" one. The concept here is "efficiency": How well (rapidly, cheaply) does a device train required content? The "efficiency" of training typically is measured by the rate of acquisition of training objectives. The resulting index would represent time, cost, or effort required to reach proficiency on a training device.

Some aspects of the evaluation of device efficiency include an examination of its instructional features and pattern of use. Care must be taken, however, when examining instructional features, for "more" does not necessarily imply "better." The effectiveness of a given feature will vary as a function of the training content.

3. Transfer Efficiency

Suppose two devices train the same content and do so with equal efficiency. They will not necessarily produce the same amount of transfer. This gives rise to another potential component of device effectiveness; namely, the efficiency with which a trainee is prepared for acquiring the skills and knowledge that still must be learned on the parent equipment. Instructional features can be incorporated in a device that enhance knowledge and skill acquisition of the training objectives independently of enhancing acquisition on the parent equipment.

Another fairly subtle point is that some features that enhance transfer may not necessarily enhance knowledge or skill acquisition. Suppose a training device had a feature that permitted simulation of environmental conditions such as those found in an operational situation (e.g., noise, heat, darkness). This feature would undoubtedly enhance transfer to these situations. Its use, however, would surely slow down the rate of skill acquisition or learning while on the device.

Transfer efficiency, therefore, seems to be another distinct component of device effectiveness, in addition to those previously discussed (i.e., transfer, training content, and training efficiency).

4. User Acceptance

Most other concepts that have been considered as potential measures of device effectiveness fall into the category of "user acceptance." This usually has two parts; instructor acceptance and trainee acceptance. A device presumably will not be effective if instructors and trainees will not or cannot use it.

C. Effectiveness as a Multidimensional Concept

Although these notions of device effectiveness have been treated separately, we do not mean to imply that they are alternative criteria. Rather, they should be viewed as useful and complementary components of an effectiveness criterion that is inherently multidimensional. In order to support the evaluation of a training device, empirical assessments of each component should be obtained whenever possible. While it may be highly desirable to determine how much transfer of training is associated with a given device, such a determination may not be feasible or conclusive.

How can the evaluation of a training device proceed when the various components of effectiveness cannot be assessed empirically, which is the situation typically confronting designers and developers of major training devices? The answer lies in identifying surrogates for the components of device effectiveness discussed above and then using analytic procedures to generate estimates of the various surrogates. For example, it might be possible to use amount of overlap in the content of training and operational (i.e., parent equipment) performance objectives as an estimate of potential transfer of training. Similarly, analyses of the content of training and performance objectives, coupled with an appraisal of instructional features, might provide estimates of acquisition or transfer efficiency.

IV. A METHOD FOR TRAINING SYSTEM EVALUATION

The Device Effectiveness Forecast Technique (Rose & Wheaton, 1984a, 1984b) is a series of interactive, menu-driven computer programs that guide an analyst through the evaluation of a training device–based system. There are several computer programs in all that support the building and maintenance of data files and the conduct of analyses. Each is written in COBOL and designed for use on an IBM PC.

The Device Effectiveness Forecast Technique converts information about various facets of a training system into forecasts of device effectiveness. A DEFT evaluation can be conducted at three different levels of analysis, ranging from micro to macro detail. The level that is chosen depends upon the kind and amount of information available and upon the degree of diagnosis desired. If analysts, for example, have very detailed information about a training system (e.g., descriptions of subtasks, displays, controls, instructional features, data on the trainee population) and want an in-depth evaluation, they would choose the microlevel, or DEFT III. Operating at the "subtask" level, DEFT III involves analyses of individual displays and controls contained in both the training and parent equipment. If analysts have somewhat less detailed information—for example, consisting of general task descriptions—and want a less diagnostic evaluation, DEFT II would be chosen. Operating at the "task" level, DEFT II requires somewhat more global judgments than does DEFT III. Finally, if analysts have only general information about the components of a training system and are interested only in a global evaluation, they might choose the least detailed version, DEFT I. Operating at the "training system" level, DEFT I does not involve the specification of tasks, subtasks, or controls in either the training or parent equipment.

Regardless of the level of DEFT chosen for an evaluation, four major analyses are conducted. The first is an analysis of the *training problem* in order to define skill and knowledge deficiencies that trainees have relative to criterion performance on the training device. As part of the same analysis, the difficulty trainees would have in overcoming identified deficits is estimated. Second, the quality of training provided by the training device is examined. During the *acquisition efficiency* analysis, the instructional features and training principles that have been incorporated in the device to help trainees overcome their deficits are determined. The training problem and training efficiency analyses constitute the acquisition component of DEFT.

The third and fourth analyses are analogues of the first two. In the third, an assessment of the *transfer problem* is undertaken to determine the deficiency in operational criterion performance that remains subsequent to trainee practice on the device, satisfying the device proficiency criterion, and "graduating." The difficulty in overcoming these residual deficits also is determined. The fourth analysis is *transfer efficiency*. It indicates how well use of the training device will promote transfer of the learning that has occurred to the parent or actual equipment. The transfer component of DEFT comprises the transfer problem and transfer efficiency analyses.

DEFT I

(1) Performance Deficit
(2) Learning Difficulty
(3) Quality of Training Acquisition
(4) Residual Deficit
(5) Residual Learning Difficulty
(6) Physical Similarity
(7) Functional Similarity
(8) Quality of Training Transfer
(9) Evaluation Summary

Enter Option Number

Figure 1. DEFT main menu.

Once a particular level of evaluation is selected, it is carried out for all four analyses. In general, an analyst provides a number of judgments or estimates in response to a variety of rating scales. These scales force consideration of different kinds of data about the training system and its parent equipment. Figure 1 shows the DEFT main menu, which is identical for all three levels. The first two analyses, Performance Deficit and Learning Difficulty, define the training problem, first by asking the "amount" of the deficit, then by asking how difficult this deficit is to overcome. Figures 2–4 illustrate the Performance Deficit analysis and how the analysis is implemented for each level of DEFT. As can be seen, DEFT I (Figure 2) asks for a global judgment of the entire training objective; DEFT II (Figure 3) asks for judgments for each task; and DEFT III (Figure 4) further segments the training objective into subtasks. In addition, DEFT III extends the definition of the deficit, making the judgmental criteria more explicit.

The third analysis listed in the main menu (Figure 1), Quality of Training-Acquisition, is the acquisition efficiency portion of DEFT. Based on an extensive review of the literature, principles and techniques of good training have been synthesized into a relatively small number of guidelines. Depending on the level of DEFT selected, the analyst rates the degree to which the training system incorporates these training guidelines: for DEFT I, a single rating is made; for DEFT II, four ratings are made for each task; for DEFT III, eleven ratings are made for each task or subtask.

The fourth through seventh analyses shown in the main menu (Figure 1) make up the transfer problem component. The analyses include Residual Deficit, Residual Learning Difficulty, Physical Similarity, and Functional Similarity. The first two parallel Analyses 1 and 2 (Performance Deficit and

Examine the statement of the training objective(s). Considering what you know about the typical trainee's background, work experience, and prior training, what proportion of the skills and knowledges required in order to meet the training objective(s) will the trainee still have to learn in order to reach criterion proficiency in the training device?

Enter a number from 0 to 100 using the following scale:

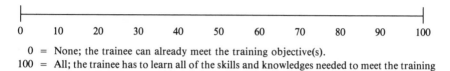

0	10	20	30	40	50	60	70	80	90	100

  0 = None; the trainee can already meet the training objective(s).
100 = All; the trainee has to learn all of the skills and knowledges needed to meet the training objective(s).

Figure 2. Performance deficit analysis for DEFT I.

Examine the statement of the training objective(s) for the task named below. Considering what you know about the typical trainee's background, work experience, and prior training, what proportion of the skills and knowledges required in order to meet the training objective(s) will the trainee still have to learn in order to reach criterion proficiency in the training device?

Enter a number from 0 to 100 using the following scale:

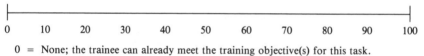

0	10	20	30	40	50	60	70	80	90	100

  0 = None; the trainee can already meet the training objective(s) for this task.
100 = All; the trainee has to learn all of the skills and knowledges needed to meet the training objective(s) for this task.

Figure 3. Performance deficit analysis for DEFT II.

Learning Difficulty); however, the focus here is on the deficits remaining, given that the training objectives have been accomplished. In addition to these remaining deficits, additional deficits may have been created by the particular training device used. Conceptually similar to notions of negative transfer (see Rose & Wheaton, 1984a, for a discussion), additional deficits arise when displays and controls that are physically similar in the training device and operational equipment have different functions in the two situations. In lay terms, trainees must "unlearn" these functions and learn new ones; this unlearning would not have been necessary if the displays and controls were either functionally similar or physically dissimilar. Thus, the Physical and Functional Similarity analyses are included to determine if

Examine descriptions of the subtasks (tasks) that comprise the training objective(s). Considering what you know about the typical trainee's background, work experience, and prior training, rate the typical trainee's current level of proficiency on each subtask (task).

Enter a number from 0 to 4 using the following definitions:

Rating	Definition
0	No experience, training, or familiarity with this subtask (task). Cannot perform this subtask (task).
1	Has only limited knowledge about this subtask (task). Cannot be expected to perform the subtask (task). Has had orientation only.
2	Has received a complete briefing on the subtask (task). Can perform the subtask (task) only if assisted in every step. Requires much more training and experience. Has had familiarization training only.
3	Understands the subtask (task) to be performed. Can perform the subtask (task) in the trainer. Needs more practice under supervision. Has had procedural training.
4	Has a complete understanding of the subtask (task). Can do the subtask (task) completely and accurately without supervision. Has received skill training.

Figure 4. Performance deficit analysis for DEFT III.

there are any additional deficits; a device is "penalized" if its physical similarity (i.e., to the parent equipment) score exceeds its functional similarity score.

The eighth and final analysis (Figure 1), Quality of Training-Transfer, parallels the Quality of Training-Acquisition analysis. Again, principles and techniques of good training have been synthesized; here, the focus is on those principles and techniques associated with promoting transfer (e.g., stimulus variety, representation of operational situation, etc.). Analysts rate the device (as a whole for DEFT I, for each task for DEFT II, and for each subtask for DEFT III) on one or more guidelines for "good transfer."

Within each major analysis, the number and kind of ratings required vary as a function of how available detailed data are and how diagnostic an analyst wants to be. DEFT I requires 8 ratings based on general information about the device and parent equipment. DEFT II entails 13 ratings for each training or operational task under consideration. DEFT III requires 35 different ratings, many for each training or operational subtask. Ratings are entered on a computer keyboard. The sequence in which ratings are completed is determined by the DEFT menus.

At the end of the evaluation exercise, an analyst receives numerical

Table 1

Evaluation Summary

Training Problem	22.50
Acquisition-Efficiency	0.80
Acquisition	28.13
Transfer Problem	27.50
Transfer-Efficiency	0.47
Transfer	58.51
Total Effectiveness	86.64

estimates of device effectiveness and diagnostic information on potential strengths and weaknesses of the device. Table 1 shows an example of an Evaluation Summary screen that may be requested and printed out. Armed with this output, an analyst can go back into the DEFT analyses, make different assumptions about the training system, enter revised ratings on selected scales, and again call for the Evaluation Summary to determine the effect these "what if" changes had on estimates of device effectiveness.

To summarize, this evaluation approach has two major components: first, analyses of the path between inputs and the intermediate outcomes of proficiency on the training device; and second, analyses of the path between the intermediate outcome and the terminal objective. The first, or "acquisition," component is conceived as an estimate of trainee deficits and a determination of the time/cost (efficiency) of training in order to overcome these performance deficits and reach some stated criterion level of proficiency on the training device. The second, or "transfer," component is conceived as an estimation of the remaining trainee deficit that must be overcome in order to demonstrate a criterion level of proficiency on the parent equipment. It is important to keep in mind that the "total" effectiveness of a device involves assessing both of the components.

DEFT was constructed to address many of the limitations of existing analytic methods discussed in section II. Thus, for example, Rose and Martin (1984) conducted a series of analytic assessments to address various aspects of the scalar properties of DEFT. This included Monte Carlo simulations to assess the interpretation of DEFT output, sensitivity of DEFT parameters, comparison of outputs, stability, as well as an examination of interrater agreement. This latter assessment involved collecting ratings from several analysts who applied DEFT to three actual training devices. The devices evaluated were the MK60 gunnery trainer, a burst-on-target trainer, and a maintenance procedure simulator for the E-3A aircraft navigation computer system.

These assessments demonstrated that DEFT outputs could be meaningfully interpreted, were sensitive to variations in training system variables, and were stable across the range of expected input values, given a set of reasonable assumptions regarding expected distributions of these inputs. Similarly, given explicit statements of these assumptions, results indicated a high degree of consistency among raters for all devices for all levels of DEFT. For example, across all three devices evaluated at DEFT Level 1, the average disagreement between raters was approximately 9 points (on a 100-point scale). For the eight individual scales, the average disagreement was between 5.0 and 11.6 points.

Regarding other limitations, DEFT explicitly incorporates variables affecting learning as well as transfer. Extradevice variables such as student capabilities are included, although DEFT does not contain a "resource requirement" component (e.g., a model to estimate training time, student throughput rates, etc.) or a cost model. DEFT is efficient to apply once the data sets have been entered. The computer programs do much of the bookkeeping and all of the calculations. And, although DEFT III is conducted at a micro (i.e., subtask) level, DEFT I and II operate at more global levels, requiring much less effort for the analyst. Finally, the assumptions, algorithms, and rationales for judgments are clearly specified. DEFT still has certain limitations, the most important of which is the lack of empirical validation. However, plans are currently being implemented for further applications that also will involve empirical validation studies. The Naval Training Systems Center is presently implementing a series of research efforts on the DEFT methodology consisting of two concurrent parts. The first will be an a priori investigation of the mathematical sensitivity and distributional properties of DEFT. The second will resemble traditional psychometric validation.

The planned validation also will compare model predictions and empirically obtained transfer of training data. Efforts are presently being made to locate a variety of training devices and simulators that have recently been (or will soon be) empirically evaluated. For each device, judgmental data will be collected for each of the DEFT variables. In this manner, an index of effectiveness can be generated, and all indexes can be compared to the same set of empirical data. This procedure also will permit a refinement of the model. For example, if particular components of the model prove to be sufficiently valid, these variables and procedures can be combined to produce a final version. The collection of a wide spectrum of judgmental data also will facilitate the needed reliability and validity studies. An initial milestone is to turn over a usable version of a model so that widespread, economical data collection can ultimately lead to a final product. While not expected to be perfect, an evaluation approach which systematically assesses a device, backed up by guidance on its interpretation, seems a possibility in the foreseeable future.

ACKNOWLEDGMENTS

Much of the content of sections III and IV stems from a research effort conducted by the American Institutes for Research (AIR) for the U.S. Army Research Institute for the Behavioral and Social Sciences on the TRAINVICE and DEFT evaluation methodologies (Rose & Martin, 1984; Rose & Wheaton, 1984a, 1984b; Wheaton, Fingerman, Rose, & Leonard, 1976; Wheaton, Rose, Fingerman, Korotkin, & Holding, 1976; Wheaton, Rose, Fingerman, Leonard, & Boycan, 1976).

REFERENCES

Carroll, R. B., Rhode, A. S., Skinner, B. B., Mulline, J. L., Friedman, F. L., & Franco, M. M. (1980). *Manpower, personnel, and training requirements for materiel systems acquisition* (Draft). Alexandria, VA: U.S. Army Research Institute for the Behavorial and Social Sciences.

CORADCOM. (1980). *Training acquisition handbook*. Fort Monmouth, NJ: U.S. Army Communications Research and Development Command.

Cronbach, L. J. (1971). Test validation. In R. Thorndike (Ed.), *Educational measurement* (2nd ed.). Washington, DC: American Council on Education.

Dynamics Research Corporation. (1985). HARDMAN methodology handbook (Vol. 1–4, DRC Report No. E-5684). Andover, MA: Author.

Goldberg, I. (1986). *A review of models of cost and training analysis* (CTEA). Washington, DC: Consortium of Washington, DC Universities.

Harris, J. H., & Ford, P. (1983). *Applications of transfer forecast methods to armor training devices* (FR-TD(VA)-83-3). Alexandria, VA: Human Resources Research Organization.

Hawley, J. K., & Frederickson, E. W. (1983). The Training Development Decision Support System: An aid to the design of cost-effective training programs. *Proceedings of the Human Factors Society, 27th Annual Meeting* (pp. 397–401).

Kane, J. J. (1981). *Personnel and training subsystem integration in an armor system* (Research Report No. 1303). Alexandria, VA: U.S. Army Research Institute for the Behavioral and Social Sciences.

Kane, J. J., & Holman, G. L. (1982). *Training device development: Training effectiveness in the army system acquisition process*. McLean, VA: Science Applications Incorporated.

Kinton, Inc. (1980). *Sources of information on integrated personnel and training planning: A handbook for TRADOC system managers (TSM)*. (MESTA 80-1). Alexandria, VA: Author.

Klein Associates. (1985). *Comparison-based prediction of cost and effectiveness of training devices: A guidebook*. Alexandria, VA: U.S. Army Research Institute for the Behavorial and Social Sciences.

Kraft, B. P., & Farr, B. J. (1984). *Job skills education program: Predictive cost and training effectiveness analysis*. Alexandria, VA: U.S. Army Research Institute for the Behavioral and Social Sciences.

Knerr, C. M., Nadler, L., & Dowell, S. (1984). *Training transfer and effectiveness models*. Alexandria, VA: Human Resources Research Organization.

Nunnally, J. C. (1967). *Psychometric theory*. New York: McGraw-Hill.

Rose, A. M., & Martin, A. M. (1984). *Forecasting device effectiveness: III. Analytic assessment of DEFT*. Washington, DC: The American Institutes for Research.

Rose, A. M., & Wheaton, G. R. (1984a). *Forecasting device effectiveness: I. Issues* (Tech. Rep.). Washington, DC: The American Institutes for Research.

Rose, A. M., & Wheaton, G. R. (1984b). *Forecasting device effectiveness: II. Procedures* (Tech. Rep.). Washington, DC: The American Institutes for Research.

Tufano, D. R., & Evans, R. A. (1982). *The prediction of training device effectiveness: A review of army models* (Tech. rep.). Alexandria, VA: U.S. Army Research Institute for the Behavioral and Social Sciences.

Wheaton, G. R., Fingerman, P. W., Rose, A. M., & Leonard, R. (1976). *Evaluation of the effectiveness of training devices: Elaboration and application of the predictive model* (Research Memorandum 76-26). Alexandria, VA: U.S. Army Research Institute for the Behavioral and Social Sciences.

Wheaton, G. R., Rose, A. M., Fingerman, P. W., Korotkin, A. L., & Holding, D. H. (1976). *Evaluation of the effectiveness of training devices: Literature review and preliminary model.* (Research Memorandum 76-6). Alexandria, VA: U.S. Army Research Institute for the Behavioral and Social Sciences.

Wheaton, G. R., Rose, A. M., Fingerman, P. W., Leonard, R., & Boycan, G. (1976). *Evaluation of the effectiveness of training devices: Validation of the predictive model* (Tech. Rep. TR-76-12). Alexandria, VA: U.S. Army Research Institute for the Behavioral and Social Sciences.

Index